Eighth Edition

Sentence Skills
A Workbook for Writers
Form A

D0073710

Eighth Edition

Sentence Skills
A Workbook for Writers
Form A

John Langan
Atlantic Cape Community College

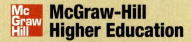

**McGraw-Hill
Higher Education**

Boston   Burr Ridge, IL   Dubuque, IA   New York   San Francisco   St. Louis
Bangkok   Bogotá   Caracas   Kuala Lumpur   Lisbon   London   Madrid   Mexico City
Milan   Montreal   New Delhi   Santiago   Seoul   Singapore   Sydney   Taipei   Toronto

McGraw-Hill
Higher Education

A Division of The McGraw-Hill Companies

Published by McGraw-Hill, an imprint of The McGraw-Hill Companies, Inc., 1221 Avenue of the Americas, New York, NY 10020. Copyright © 2008. All rights reserved. No part of this publication may be reproduced or distributed in any form or by any means, or stored in a database or retrieval system, without the prior written consent of The McGraw-Hill Companies, Inc., including, but not limited to, in any network or other electronic storage or transmission, or broadcast for distance learning.

This book is printed on acid-free paper.

1 2 3 4 5 6 7 8 9 0 DOC/DOC 0 9 8 7

ISBN: 978-0-07-312374-5
MHID: 0-07-312374-9 (Student's Edition)
ISBN: 978-0-07-312375-2
MHID: 0-07-312375-7 (Instructor's Edition)

Editor in Chief: *Emily Barrosse*
Sponsoring Editor: *John Kindler*
Marketing Manager: *Tamara Wederbrand*
Developmental Editor: *Alyson Watts*
Editorial coordinator: *Jesse Hassenger*
Production Editor: *Anne Fuzellier*
Production Service: *The Left Coast Group, Inc.*
Manuscript Editor: *Joan Pendleton*
Art Director: *Jeanne M. Schreiber*

Design Manager: *Preston Thomas*
Text Designer: *Maureen McCutcheon*
Cover Designer: *Preston Thomas*
Art Editor: *Robin Mouat*
Photo Research: *Emily Tietz*
Supplements Producer: *Louis Swaim*
Production Supervisor: *Richard DeVitto*
Composition: *11/13 Times by Aptara-India*
Printing: *45# Pub Matte Plus, R. R. Donnelley & Sons*

Cover: Illustration by Tom White

Credits: The credits section for this book appears on page 577 and is considered an extension of the copyright page.

Library of Congress Cataloging-in-Publication Data

Langan, John
  Sentence skills : a workbook for writers : form A / John Langan. —8th ed.
     p. cm.
"Annotated Instructor's Edition."
Includes bibliographical references and index.
ISBN-13: 978-0-07-312374-5 (pbk. : alk. paper)
ISBN-10: 0-07-312374-9 (pbk. : alk. paper)
ISBN-13: 978-0-07-312375-2 (pbk. : alk. paper)
ISBN-10: 0-07-312375-7 (pbk. : alk. paper)
1. English language—Sentences—Problems, exercises, etc. 2. English language—Grammar—Problems, exercises, etc. I. Title.
PE1441.L352 2007
808'.0427— dc22   2007021189

The Internet addresses listed in the text were accurate at the time of publication. The inclusion of a Web site does not indicate an endorsement by the authors or McGraw-Hill, and McGraw-Hill does not guarantee the accuracy of the information presented at these sites.

www.mhhe.com

Praise for *Sentence Skills*

"Accessibility, simplification of complex content, and relevance to student experiences and daily lives . . . it's a great text."
—E. Ferol Benavides, Anne Arundel Community College

"I can say without reservation that I am impressed with this text, and I would certainly recommend it to colleagues."
—Milton Bentley, Central Georgia Technical College

"The major strengths of this book are its readability, its accuracy, and its completeness. It may be the best of its type."
—Dennis Tettelbach, Georgia Perimeter College

"The book is well organized, concise, and comprehensive. Sentence Skills *is not just for this one course. It is a great reference book. I encourage my students to keep it and refer back to it when any question about basic concepts in English arises."*
—Stephanie Bechtel Gooding, University of Maryland, University College-Europe

"An excellent text for developmental writers because of its clear, concise explanations of sentence skills, multiple opportunities for interactive practice exercises with guided feedback, and mastery testing."
—Debbie Naquin, Northern Virginia Community College

"The mastery tests are one of the real strengths of Sentence Skills, Form A. *My students always feel a sense of accomplishment when they are successful on these small tests. They are at an accessible level for my students, allowing them to apply the skills covered in the text."*
—Daniel Lanelle, Georgia Highlands College

"The Langan books truly provide the clearest explanations of grammar rules."
—Lisa Moreno, Los Angeles Trade Technical College

About the Author

John Langan has taught and authored books on writing and reading skills for over thirty years. Before teaching, he earned advanced degrees in writing at Rutgers University and in reading at Rowan University. John now lives with his wife, Judith Nadell, near Philadelphia. In addition to his wife and Philly sports teams, his passions include reading and turning nonreaders on to the pleasure and power of books. Through Townsend Press, his educational publishing company, he has developed the nonprofit "Townsend Library"—a collection of more than seventy new and classic stories with wide appeal to readers of all ages.

Contents

PART 2   Sentence Skills   64

PART 3   Reinforcement of the Skills   452

APPENDIXES   514

Key Features of the Book

Sentence Skills will help students learn to write effectively. It is an all-in-one text that includes a basic rhetoric and gives full attention to grammar, punctuation, mechanics, and usage.

The book contains eight distinctive features to aid instructors and their students:

1. **Coverage of basic writing skills is exceptionally thorough.**

   The book pays special attention to fragments, run-ons, verbs, and other areas where students have serious problems. At the same time, a glance at the table of contents shows that the book treats skills (such as dictionary use and spelling improvement) not found in most other texts. In addition, parts of the book are devoted to the basics of effective writing, to practice in editing and proofreading, and to achieving variety in sentences.

2. **The book has a clear and flexible format.**

   It is organized in three easy-to-use parts. Part One is a guide to the goals of effective writing followed by a series of activities to help students practice and master those goals. Part Two is a comprehensive treatment of the rules of grammar, mechanics, punctuation, and usage needed for clear writing. Part Three provides a series of combined mastery, editing, and proofreading tests to reinforce the sentence skills presented in Part Two.

   Since parts, sections, and chapters are self-contained, instructors can move easily from, for instance, a rhetorical principle in Part One to a grammar rule in Part Two to a combined mastery test in Part Three.

3. **Opening chapters deal with the writer's attitude, writing as a process, and the importance of specific details in writing.**

   In its opening pages, the book helps students recognize and deal with their attitude toward writing—an important part of learning to write well. In the pages that follow, students are encouraged to see writing as a multistage process that moves from prewriting to proofreading. Later, a series of activities helps students understand the nature of specific details and how to generate and use those details. As writing teachers well know, learning to write concretely is a key step for students to master in becoming effective writers.

4. **Practice activities are numerous.**

   Most skills are reinforced by practice activities, review tests, and mastery tests, as well as tests in the *Instructor's Manual.* For many of the skills in the book, there are over one hundred practice sentences.

5. **Practice materials are varied and lively.**

   In many basic writing texts, exercises are monotonous and dry, causing students to lose interest in the skills presented. In *Sentence Skills,* many exercises involve students in various ways. An inductive opening activity allows students to see what they already know about a given skill. Within chapters, students may be asked to underline answers, add words, generate their own sentences, or edit passages. And the lively and engaging practice materials in the book both maintain interest and help students appreciate the value of vigorous details in writing.

6. **Active learning strategies appear throughout.**

   Key chapters of the book feature *collaborative* and *reflective activities* which help make students active participants in their learning. Using group discussion, team writing, and student-generated examples, these activities lend energy to the classroom and strengthen students' mastery of essential writing skills.

7. **Terminology is kept to a minimum.**

   In general, rules are explained using words students already know. A clause is a *word group;* a coordinating conjunction is a *joining word;* a nonrestrictive element is an *interrupter.* At the same time, traditional grammatical terms are mentioned briefly for students who learned them somewhere in the past and are comfortable seeing them again.

8. **Self-teaching is encouraged.**

   Students may check their answers to the introductory activities and the practice activities in Part One by referring to the answers in Appendix F. In this way, they are given the responsibility for teaching themselves. At the same time, to ensure that the answer key is used as a learning tool only answers are *not* given for the review tests in Part Two or for any of the reinforcement tests in Part Three. These answers appear in the *Annotated Instructor's Edition* and the *Instructor's Manual;* they can be copied and handed out to students at the discretion of the instructor.

9. **Diagnostic and achievement tests are provided.**

   These tests appear in Appendixes D and E of the book. Each test may be given in two parts, the second of which provides instructors with a particularly detailed picture of a student's skill level.

Changes in the Eighth Edition

Here are the major changes to this new edition of *Sentence Skills, Form A:*

- Part One has been revised so that writing guidelines are now integrated with writing activities. Included with an introduction to the four goals of effective writing are a number of practice materials to ensure that students understand those goals. Revised chapters explain the writing process and provide expanded paragraph-writing assignments.

- Part Two has been restructured so that all mastery tests now appear at the end of each chapter. This change makes each chapter inclusive, allowing instructors and students to transition easily from the practice activities for a skill to its tests—without the need to flip through the book.

- Mastery tests have been expanded in four key chapters, with "Fragments," "Run-Ons," "Commas," and "Subject-Verb Agreement" now including five mastery tests. Also, more mastery tests have been added so that *all* chapters in Part Two include tests for each skill. And all the mastery tests now feature a revised, instructor-friendly design which includes space for a student's name, date, and score.

- Part Three has been expanded with "real-world" tests that require students to apply their understanding of sentence skills to documents they are likely to encounter outside the classroom. Part of the "Combined Editing Tests" section of the book, these tests feature a job application form, two cover letters, and two resumés. By addressing sentence skills in a format and context that has direct relevance to students, these tests underscore the importance of each lesson in the book.

- Finally, practice materials have been freshened throughout, with dozens of items added to ensure that content is relevant to today's students.

- A new four-color design adds visual appeal for students while highlighting key material for them and helping them make connections and find the information they need.

- More than twenty visuals—including photographs, cartoons, and artwork—have been added throughout the text to enhance the book's content and give today's visually oriented students even more help making a connection between thinking and writing. In addition, each of the book's three parts now opens with a two-page spread that includes an introduction to the part, as well as a full-page photograph and accompanying caption designed to prompt critical thinking and writing.

Helpful Learning Aids Accompany the Book

Supplements for Instructors

- Access to a toll-free support line dedicated to Langan Series customers and potential customers: 800-MCGRAWH (800-624-7294). E-mail inquiries may be sent to **langan@mcgraw-hill.com**.

- An *Annotated Instructor's Edition* (ISBN 0-07-238133-7) consists of the student text complete with answers to all activities and tests. Throughout the text, marginal Teaching Tips and ESL Tips offer suggestions for various approaches, classroom activities, discussions, and assignments.

- An *Online Learning Center* (**www.mhhe.com/langan**) offers a host of instructional aids and additional resources for instructors, including a comprehensive computerized test bank, the downloadable *Instructor's Manual and Test Bank,* online resources for writing instructors, and more.

- *PageOut!* helps instructors create graphically pleasing and professional Web pages for their courses, in addition to providing classroom management, collaborative learning, and content management tools. PageOut! is **FREE** to adopters of McGraw-Hill textbooks and learning materials. Learn more at **www.mhhe.com/pageout**.

- *The McGraw-Hill Virtual Workbook*
  Donna Matsumoto, Leward Community College
  Powered by Quia, this online workbook offers interactive activities and exercises that reinforce the skills students learn in Part Two of *Sentence Skills*. It is supported by a powerful array of Web-based instructor's tools, including an automated online gradebook.

- *The Classroom Performance System* (**CPS by eInstruction**) is an easy-to-use wireless response system that allows instructors to conduct quizzes and polls in class and provide students with immediate feedback. McGraw-Hill provides a database of questions compatible with *Sentence Skills, Form A*. To download the database, go to the *Sentence Skills, Form A* Online Learning Center (OLC) at **www.mhhe.com/langan**. For further details on CPS, go to **www.mhhe.com/einstruction**.

- **Partners in Teaching** is an online community of composition and basic writing instructors. Two associated listservs, Teaching Composition and Teaching Basic Writing, address issues of pedagogy in theory and in practice. Their goal is to bring together senior members of the college composition community with newer members—junior faculty and teaching assistants—as well as adjuncts. Each month, major figures in the fields of composition and basic writing take turns leading discussions on issues of importance to people in the profession.

We enthusiastically invite you to submit your own ideas for topics and potential contributions to these listservs. Please check out Teaching Composition at **www.mhhe.com/tcomp** and Teaching Basic Writing at **www.mhhe.com/tbw** and join the discussion.

Supplements for Students

- An *Online Learning Center* (**www.mhhe.com/langan**) offers a host of instructional aids and additional resources for students, including self-correcting exercises, writing activities for additional practice, a PowerPoint grammar tutorial, guides to doing research on the Internet and avoiding plagiarism, useful Web links, and more.

- *The McGraw-Hill Virtual Workbook*
  Donna Matsumoto, Leward Community College
  Powered by Quia, this online workbook offers interactive activities and exercises that reinforce the skills students learn in Part Two of *Sentence Skills*.

- *The New McGraw-Hill Exercise Book* (**ISBN 0-07-326032-0**)
  Santi Buscemi, Middlesex College
  This workbook features numerous additional sentence- and paragraph-level editing exercises, as well as research-, documentation-, and writing-related exercises that can be used for any composition course.

- *The McGraw-Hill Exercise Book for Multilingual Writers*
  (**ISBN 0-07-326030-4**)
  Maggie Sokolik, UC Berkeley
  This workbook features numerous sentence-level and paragraph-level editing exercises tailored specifically for multilingual students.

- *A Writer's Journal* (**ISBN 0-07-326031-2**)
  Lynee Gaillet, Georgia State University
  This elegant journal for students includes quotes on writing from famous authors, as well as advice and tips on writing and the writing process.

- *The McGraw-Hill Student Planner* (**ISBN 0-07-322205-4**)
  This practical spiral-bound date book and planner for students is organized around the academic year, offering them a handy tool to structure and plan their work. It includes a brief almanac at the back with important facts from a variety of disciplines.

- **Dictionary and Vocabulary Resources**
  - *Random House Webster's College Dictionary* (**0-07-240011-0**): This authoritative dictionary includes over 160,000 entries and 175,000 definitions. The most commonly used definitions are always listed first, so students can find what they need quickly.

- *The Merriam-Webster Dictionary* **(0-07-310057-9):** Based on the best-selling *Merriam-Webster's Collegiate Dictionary,* it contains over 70,000 definitions.
- *The Merriam-Webster's Thesaurus* **(0-07-310067-6):** This handy paperback thesaurus contains over 157,000 synonyms, antonyms, related and contrasted words, and idioms.
- *Merriam-Webster's Vocabulary Builder* **(0-07-310069-2):** Introduces 3,000 words, and includes quizzes to test progress.
- *Merriam-Webster's Notebook Dictionary* **(0-07-299091-0):** This popular dictionary provides an extremely concise reference to the words that form the core of the English vocabulary, and is conveniently designed for three-ring binders; it provides words and information at students' fingertips.
- *Merriam-Webster's Notebook Thesaurus* **(0-07-310068-4):** Designed for three-ring binders and helps students search for words they might need today. It provides concise, clear guidance for over 157,000 word choices.
- *Merriam-Webster's Collegiate Dictionary and Thesaurus, Electronic Edition* **(0-07-310070-6):** Available on CD-ROM, this online dictionary contains thousands of new words and meanings from all areas of human endeavor, including electronic technology, the sciences, and popular culture.

Contact your local McGraw-Hill representative or consult McGraw-Hill's Web site at **www.mhhe.com/english** for more information on the supplements that accompany *Sentence Skills, Form A 8th Edition.* You may also send an e-mail to **langan@mcgraw-hill.com**.

Acknowledgments

Reviewers who have contributed to this edition through their helpful comments include

Lindy Atoms, *Sierra College*

David Rask Behling, *Waldorf College*

E. Ferol Benavides, *Anne Arundel Community College*

Milton Bentley, *Central Georgia Technical College*

Daniel Lanelle, *Georgia Highlands College*

Stephanie Bechtel Gooding, *University of Maryland University College-Europe*

Valere Hull, *Oklahoma State University*

Jaque Lyman, *Anne Arundel Community College*

Lisa Moreno, *Los Angeles Trade Technical College*

Debbie Naquin, *Northern Virginia Community College*

Dennis Tettelbach, *University of Maryland University College*

Dennielle True, *Manatee Community College*

Maria Villar-Smith, *Miami Dade College*

Arnold Wood Jr., *Florida Community College at Jacksonville*

I owe thanks as well for the support provided by John Kindler and Alyson Watts at McGraw-Hill. My gratitude also goes to Paul Langan, who has helped this book become even more student-friendly than it was before.

Joyce Stern, Assistant Professor at Nassau Community College, contributed the ESL Tips to the *Annotated Instructor's Edition* of *Sentence Skills, Form A*. Professor Stern is also Assistant to the Chair in the department of Reading and Basic Education. An educator for over thirty years, she holds an advanced degree in TESOL from Hunter College, as well as a New York State Teaching Certificate in TESOL. She is currently coordinating the design, implementation, and recruitment of learning communities for both ESL and developmental students at Nassau Community College and has been recognized by the college's Center for Students with Disabilities for her dedication to student learning.

Donna T. Matsumoto, Assistant Professor of English and the Writing Discipline Coordinator at Leeward Community College in Hawaii (Pearl City), wrote the Teaching Tips for the *Annotated Instructor's Edition* of *Sentence Skills, Form A*. Professor Matsumoto has taught writing, women's studies, and American studies for a number of years throughout the University of Hawaii system, at Hawaii Pacific University, and in community schools for adults. She received a 2005 WebCT Exemplary Course Project award for her online writing course and is the author of McGraw-Hill's *The Virtual Workbook,* an online workbook featuring interactive activities and exercises.

John Langan

Eighth Edition

Sentence Skills
A Workbook for Writers
Form A

1

Effective Writing

Introduction

Part One is a guide to the goals of effective writing and includes a series of activities to help you practice and master these goals. Begin with the introductory chapter, which makes clear the reasons for learning sentence skills. Then move on to Chapter 2, which presents all the essentials you need to know to become an effective writer. You will be introduced to the four goals of effective writing and will work through a series of activities designed to strengthen your understanding of these goals. Finally, walk through the steps of the writing process—from prewriting to proofreading—in Chapter 3. Examples and activities are provided to illustrate each step, and after completing the activities, you'll be ready to take on the paragraph writing assignments at the end of the chapter.

At the same time that you are writing papers, start working through the sentence skills in Parts Two and Three of the book. Practicing the sentence skills in the context of actual writing assignments is the surest way to master the rules of grammar, mechanics, punctuation, and usage.

Good written communication skills are a vital requirement for almost any career today. Look at the photo above and think of all the ways effective writing skills must be essential to these employees. Now think about your ideal job and imagine your day-to-day tasks. How will having effective writing skills help you on the job?

1

Learning Sentence Skills

Why Learn Sentence Skills?

Why should someone planning a career as a nurse have to learn sentence skills? Why should an accounting major have to pass a competency test in grammar as part of a college education? Why should a potential physical therapist or graphic artist or computer programmer have to spend hours on the rules of English? Perhaps you are asking questions like these after finding yourself in a class with this book. On the other hand, perhaps you *know* you need to strengthen basic writing skills, even though you may be unclear about the specific ways the skills will be of use to you. Whatever your views, you should understand why sentence skills—all the rules that make up standard English—are so important.

Clear Communication

Standard English, or "language by the book," is needed to communicate your thoughts to others with a minimal amount of distortion and misinterpretation. Knowing the traditional rules of grammar, punctuation, and usage will help you write clear sentences when communicating with others. You may have heard of the party game in which one person whispers a message to the next person; the message is passed, in turn, along a line of several other people. By the time the last person in line is asked to give the message aloud, it is usually so garbled and inaccurate that it barely resembles the original. Written communication in some form of English other than standard English carries the same potential for disaster.

To see how important standard English is to written communication, examine the pairs of sentences in the box on the following pages and answer the questions in each case.

1. Which sentence indicates that there might be a plot against Ted?

    a. We should leave Ted. These fumes might be poisonous.

    b. We should leave, Ted. These fumes might be poisonous.

2. Which sentence encourages self-mutilation?

    a. Leave your paper and hand in the dissecting kit.

    b. Leave your paper, and hand in the dissecting kit.

3. Which sentence indicates that the writer has a weak grasp of geography?

    a. As a child, I lived in Lake Worth, which is close to Palm Beach and Alaska.

    b. As a child, I lived in Lake Worth, which is close to Palm Beach, and Alaska.

4. In which sentence does the dog warden seem dangerous?

    a. Foaming at the mouth, the dog warden picked up the stray.

    b. Foaming at the mouth, the stray was picked up by the dog warden.

5. Which announcer was probably fired from the job?

    a. Outside the Academy Awards theater, the announcer called the guests names as they arrived.

    b. Outside the Academy Awards theater, the announcer called the guests' names as they arrived.

6. Below are the opening lines of two students' exam essays. Which student seems likely to earn a higher grade?

    a. Defense mechanisms is the way people hides their inner feelings and deals with stress. There is several types that we use to be protecting our true feelings.

    b. Defense mechanisms are the methods people use to cope with stress. Using a defense mechanism allows a person to hide his or her real desires and goals.

7. The following lines are taken from two English papers. Which student seems likely to earn a higher grade?

    a. A big problem on this campus is apathy, students don't participate in college activities. Such as clubs, student government, and plays.

    b. The most pressing problem on campus is the disgraceful state of the student lounge area. The floor is dirty, the chairs are torn, and the ceiling leaks.

continued

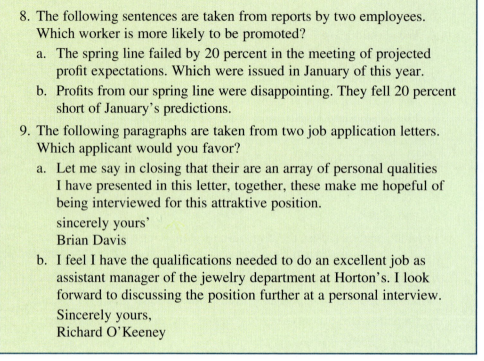

8. The following sentences are taken from reports by two employees. Which worker is more likely to be promoted?

   a. The spring line failed by 20 percent in the meeting of projected profit expectations. Which were issued in January of this year.

   b. Profits from our spring line were disappointing. They fell 20 percent short of January's predictions.

9. The following paragraphs are taken from two job application letters. Which applicant would you favor?

   a. Let me say in closing that their are an array of personal qualities I have presented in this letter, together, these make me hopeful of being interviewed for this attraktive position.

      sincerely yours'
      Brian Davis

   b. I feel I have the qualifications needed to do an excellent job as assistant manager of the jewelry department at Horton's. I look forward to discussing the position further at a personal interview.

      Sincerely yours,
      Richard O'Keeney

In each case, the first choice (*a*) contains sentence-skills mistakes. These mistakes include missing or misplaced commas and misspellings. As a result of such mistakes, clear communication cannot occur—and misunderstandings, lower grades, and missed job opportunities are probable results. The point, then, is that all the rules that make up standard written English should be a priority if you want your writing to be clear and effective.

Success in College

Standard English is essential if you want to succeed in college. Any report, paper, review, essay exam, or assignment you are responsible for should be written in the best standard English you can produce. If you don't do this, it won't matter how fine your ideas are or how hard you worked—most likely, you will receive a lower grade than you would otherwise deserve. In addition, because standard English requires you to express your thoughts in precise, clear sentences, training yourself to follow the rules can help you think more logically. The basic logic you learn to practice at the sentence level will help as you work to produce well-reasoned papers in all your subjects.

Success at Work

Knowing standard English will also help you achieve success on the job. Studies have found repeatedly that skillful communication, more than any other factor, is the key to job satisfaction and steady progress in a career. A solid understanding of standard English is a basic part of this vital ability to communicate. Moreover, most experts agree that we are now living in an "age of information"—a time when people who use language skillfully have a great advantage over those who do not. Fewer of us will be working in factories or at other types of manual labor. Many more of us will be working with information in various forms—accumulating it, processing it, analyzing it. No matter what kind of job you are preparing yourself for, technical or not, you will need to know standard English to keep pace with this new age. Otherwise, you are likely to be left behind, limited to low-paying jobs that offer few challenges or financial rewards.

"Oh, good heavens. We already know EVERYTHING about you. The resume is just to see if you can write a complete sentence."

Success in Everyday Life

Standard English will help you succeed not just at school and work but in everyday life as well. It will help you feel more comfortable, for example, in writing letters to friends and relatives. It will enable you to write effective notes to your children's schools. It will help you get action when you write a letter of complaint to a company about a product. It will allow you to write letters inquiring about bills—hospital, medical, utility, or legal—or about any kind of service. To put it simply, in our daily lives, those who can use and write standard English have more power than those who cannot.

Your Attitude about Writing

Your attitude toward writing is an important part of learning to write well. To get a sense of just how you feel about writing, read the following statements. Put a check beside those statements with which you agree. (This activity is not a test, so try to be as honest as possible.)

_____ 1. A good writer should be able to sit down and write a paper straight through without stopping.

_____ 2. Writing is a skill that anyone can learn with practice.

_____ 3. I'll never be good at writing, because I make too many mistakes in spelling, grammar, and punctuation.

_____ 4. Because I dislike writing, I always start a paper at the last possible minute.

_____ 5. I've always done poorly in English, and I don't expect that to change.

Now read the following comments about these five statements. The comments will help you see if your attitude is hurting or helping your efforts to become a better writer.

1. **A good writer should be able to sit down and write a paper straight through without stopping.**

    The statement is *false*. Writing is, in fact, a process. It is done not in one easy step but in a series of steps, and seldom at one sitting. If you cannot do a paper all at once, you are like most of the other people on the planet. It is harmful to carry around the false idea that writing should be an easy matter.

2. **Writing is a skill that anyone can learn with practice.**

    This statement is *absolutely true*. Writing is a skill, like driving or cooking, that you can master with hard work. If you want to learn to write, you can. It is as simple as that. If you believe this, you are ready to learn how to become a competent writer.

    Some people hold the false belief that writing is a natural gift which some have and others do not. Because of this belief, they never make a truly honest effort to learn to write—and so they never learn.

3. **I'll never be good at writing, because I make too many mistakes in spelling, grammar, and punctuation.**

    The first concern in good writing should be *content*—what you have to say. Your ideas and feelings are what matter most. You should not worry about spelling, grammar, and punctuation while working on content.

    Unfortunately, some people are so self-conscious about making mistakes that they do not focus on what they want to say. They need to realize that a paper is best done in stages and that the rules can and should wait until a later stage in the writing process. Through review and practice, you will eventually learn how to follow the rules with confidence.

4. **Because I dislike writing, I always start a paper at the last minute.**

    This practice is all too common. You feel you are *going to* do poorly, and then your behavior ensures that you *will* do poorly! Your attitude is so negative that you defeat yourself—not even allowing enough time to really try.

    Again, what you need to realize is that writing is a process. Because it is done in steps, you don't have to get it right all at once. Just get started well in advance. If you allow yourself enough time, you'll find a way to make a paper come together.

5. **I've done poorly in English in the past, and I don't expect that to change now.**

   How you may have performed in the *past* does not control how you can perform in the *present*. Even if you did poorly in English in high school, it is in your power to make this one of your best subjects in college. If you believe writing can be learned, and if you work hard at it, you *will* become a better writer.

In brief, your attitude is crucial. If you believe you are a poor writer and always will be, chances are you will not improve. If you realize you can become a better writer, chances are you will improve. Depending on how you allow yourself to think, you can be your own best friend or your own worst enemy.

How This Book Is Organized

- A good way to get a quick sense of any book is to turn to the table of contents. By referring to the Contents pages, you will see that the book is organized into three basic parts. What are they?

  Part One: Effective Writing

  Part Two: Sentence Skills

  Part Three: Reinforcement of the Skills

- In Part One, the final section of Chapter 3 includes activities in the *writing process*.

- Part Two deals with sentence skills. The first section is "Sentences." How many sections (skills areas) are covered in all? Count them. *five*

- Part Three reinforces the skills presented in Part Two. What are the three kinds of reinforcement activities in Part Three?

  Combined Mastery Tests

  Editing and Proofreading Tests

  Combined Editing Tests

- A helpful charts in the book includes (*fill in the missing words*) the *checklist of sentence skills* on the inside back cover.

- Finally, the six appendixes at the end of the book are: *(A) How a Computer Can Help, (B) Parts of Speech, (C) ESL Pointers, (D) Sentence-Skills Diagnostic Test, (E) Sentence-Skills Achievement Test, (F) Answers to Introductory Activities and Practice Exercises.*

How to Use This Book

Here is a way to use *Sentence Skills*. First, read and work through Part One, Effective Writing—a guide to the goals of effective writing followed by a series of activities to help you practice and master these goals. Your instructor may direct you to certain activities, depending on your needs.

Second, take the diagnostic test on pages 533–551. By analyzing which sections of the test give you trouble, you will discover which skills you need to concentrate on. When you turn to an individual skill in Part Two, begin by reading and thinking about the introductory activity. Often, you will be pleasantly surprised to find that you know more about this area of English than you thought you did. After all, you have probably been speaking English with fluency and ease for many years; you have an instinctive knowledge of how the language works. This knowledge gives you a solid base for refining your skills.

Your third step is to work on the skills in Part Two by reading the explanations and completing the practices. You can check your answers to each practice activity in this part by turning to the answer key at the back of the book (Appendix F). Try to figure out *why* you got the answers wrong—you want to uncover any weak spots in your understanding.

Your next step is to use the review tests and mastery tests at the end of each chapter in Part Two to evaluate your understanding of a skill in its entirety. Your instructor may also ask you to take the other reinforcement tests in Part Three of the book. To help ensure that you take the time needed to learn each skill thoroughly, the answers to these tests are *not* in the answer key.

The emphasis in this book is on writing clear, error-free sentences. And the heart of the book is the practice material that helps reinforce the sentence skills you learn. A great deal of effort has been taken to make the practices lively and engaging and to avoid the dull, repetitive skills work that has given grammar books such a bad reputation. This text will help you stay interested as you work on the rules of English that you need to learn. The rest is a matter of your personal determination and hard work. If you decide—and only you can decide—that effective writing is important to your school and career goals and that you want to learn the basic skills needed to write clearly and effectively, this book will help you reach those goals.

A Brief Guide to Effective Writing

2

This chapter and Chapter 3 will show you how to write effective paragraphs. The following questions will be answered in turn:

1. What is a paragraph?
2. What are the goals of effective writing?
3. How do you reach the goals of effective writing?

What Is a Paragraph?

A *paragraph* is a series of sentences about one main idea, or *point*. A paragraph typically starts with a point, and the rest of the paragraph provides specific details to support and develop that point.

Consider the following paragraph, written by a student named Gary Callahan.

www.mhhe.com/langan

Returning to School

Starting college at age twenty-nine was difficult. For one thing, I did not have much support from my parents and friends. My father asked, "Didn't you get dumped on enough in high school? Why go back for more?" My mother worried about where the money would come from. My friends seemed threatened. "Hey, there's the college man," they would say when they saw me. Another reason that starting college was hard was that I had bad memories of school. I had spent years of my life sitting in classrooms

---

continued

completely bored, watching clocks tick ever so slowly toward the final bell. When I was not bored, I was afraid of being embarrassed. Once a teacher called on me and then said, "Ah, forget it, Callahan," when he realized I did not know the answer. Finally, I soon learned that college would give me little time with my family. After work every day, I have just an hour and ten minutes to eat and spend time with my wife and daughter before going off to class. When I get back, my daughter is in bed, and my wife and I have only a little time together. Then the weekends go by quickly, with all the homework I have to do. But I am going to persist because I believe a better life awaits me with a college degree.

The preceding paragraph, like many effective paragraphs, starts by stating a main idea, or point. A *point* is a general idea that contains an opinion. In this case, the point is that starting college at age twenty-nine was not easy.

In our everyday lives, we constantly make points about all kinds of matters. We express all kinds of opinions: "That was a terrible movie." "My psychology instructor is the best teacher I have ever had." "My sister is a generous person." "Eating at that restaurant was a mistake." "That team should win the playoff game." "Waitressing is the worst job I ever had." "Our state should allow the death penalty." "Cigarette smoking should be banned everywhere." In *talking* to people, we don't always give the reasons for our opinions. But in *writing,* we *must* provide reasons to support our ideas. Only by supplying solid evidence for any point that we make can we communicate effectively with readers.

An effective paragraph, then, must not only make a point but support it with *specific evidence*—reasons, examples, and other details. Such specifics help prove to readers that the point is reasonable. Even if readers do not agree with the writer, at least they have in front of them the evidence on which the writer has based his or her opinion. Readers are like juries; they want to see the evidence so that they can make their own judgments.

Take a moment now to examine the evidence that Gary has provided to back up his point about starting college at twenty-nine. Complete the following outline of Gary's paragraph by summarizing in a few words his reasons and the details that develop them. The first reason and its supporting details are summarized for you as an example.

POINT: Starting college at age twenty-nine was difficult.

REASON 1: *Little support from parents and friends*

DETAILS THAT DEVELOP REASON 1: *Father asked why I wanted to be dumped on again, mother worried about tuition money, friends seemed threatened*

REASON 2: _____

DETAILS THAT DEVELOP REASON 2: _____

REASON 3: _____

DETAILS THAT DEVELOP REASON 3: _____

_____

_____

As the outline makes clear, Gary provides three reasons to support his point about starting college at twenty-nine: (1) he had little support from his friends or parents, (2) he had bad memories of school, and (3) college left him little time with his family. Gary also provides vivid details to back up each of his three reasons. His reasons and descriptive details enable readers to see why he feels that starting college at twenty-nine was difficult.

To write an effective paragraph, then, aim to do what Gary has done: begin by making a point, and then go on to support that point with specific evidence. Finally, like Gary, end your paper with a sentence that rounds off the paragraph and provides a sense of completion.

If you were to write a paragraph about why you are in college, what point would you begin your paper with and what three reasons would you provide to support that point?

The Goals of Effective Writing

Now that you have considered an effective student paragraph, it is time to look at four goals of effective writing.

Goal 1: Make a Point

It is often best to state your point in the first sentence of your paper, just as Gary does in his paragraph about returning to school. The sentence that expresses the main idea, or point, of a paragraph is called the *topic sentence.* Your paper will be unified if you make sure that all the details support the point in your topic sentence. Activities on pages 15–18 will help you learn how to write a topic sentence.

Goal 2: Support the Point

To support your point, you need to provide specific reasons, examples, and other details that explain and develop it. The more precise and particular your supporting details are, the better your readers can "see," "hear," and "feel" them. Activities on pages 18–33 will help you learn how to be specific in your writing.

Goal 3: Organize the Support

You will find it helpful to learn two common ways of organizing support in a paragraph—*listing order* and *time order.* You should also learn the signal words, known as *transitions,* that increase the effectiveness of each method. Activities on pages 33–40 will give you practice in the use of listing order and time order, as well as transitions, to organize the supporting details of a paragraph.

Goal 4: Write Error-Free Sentences

If you use correct spelling and follow the rules of grammar, punctuation, and usage, your sentences will be clear and well written. But by no means must you have all that information in your head. Even the best of writers need to use reference materials to be sure their writing is correct. So when you write your papers, keep a good dictionary and grammar handbook (you can use Part Two of this book) nearby.

In general, however, save them for after you've gotten your ideas firmly down in writing. You'll see in the next part of this guide that Gary made a number of sentence errors as he worked on his paragraph. But he simply ignored them until he got to a later draft of his paper, when there would be time enough to make the needed corrections.

Activities in the Goals of Effective Writing

The following series of activities will strengthen your understanding of the four goals of effective writing and how to reach those goals. The practice will also help you prepare for the demands of your college classes.

Your instructor may ask you to do the entire series of activities or may select those activities most suited to your particular needs.

www.mhhe.com/langan

Activities in Goal 1: Make a Point

Effective writing advances a point, or main idea, in a general statement known as the *topic sentence.* Other sentences in the paragraph provide specific support for the topic sentence.

The activities in this section will give you practice in the following:

- Identifying the Point
- Understanding the Topic Sentence
- Identifying Topics, Topic Sentences, and Support

Identifying the Point

Each group of sentences below could be written as a short paragraph. Circle the letter of the topic sentence in each case. To find the topic sentence, ask yourself, "Which is a general statement supported by the specific details in the other three statements?"

Begin by trying the example below. First circle the letter of the sentence you think expresses the main idea. Then read the explanation.

Activity

1

EXAMPLE

    a. Newspapers are a good source of local, national, and world news.

    b. The cartoons and crossword puzzles in newspapers are entertaining.

    (c.) Newspapers have a lot to offer.

    d. Newspapers often include coupons worth far more than the cost of the paper.

> **EXPLANATION**   Sentence *a* explains one important benefit of newspapers. Sentences *b* and *d* provide other specific advantages of newspapers. In sentence *c,* however, no one specific benefit is explained. Instead, the words "a lot to offer" refer only generally to such benefits. Therefore sentence *c* is the topic sentence; it expresses the main idea. The other sentences support that idea by providing examples.

1. a. Even when Food City is crowded, there are only two cash registers open.
    b. The frozen foods are often partially thawed.
    c. I will never shop at Food City again.
    d. The market is usually out of sale items within a few hours.

2. a. Buy only clothes that will match what's already in your closet.
    b. To be sure you're getting the best price, shop in a number of stores before buying.
    c. Avoid trendy clothes; buy basic pieces that never go out of style.
    d. By following a few simple rules, you can have nice clothes without spending a fortune.

3. a. Once my son said a vase jumped off the shelf by itself.
    b. When my son breaks something, he always has an excuse.
    c. He claimed that my three-month-old daughter climbed out of her crib and knocked a glass over.
    d. Another time, he said an earthquake must have caused a mirror to crack.

4. a. Mars should be the first planet explored by astronauts.
    b. Astronauts could mine Mars for aluminum, magnesium, and iron.
    c. The huge volcano on Mars would be fascinating to study.
    d. Since Mars is close to Earth, we might want to have colonies there one day.

5. a. Instead of talking on the telephone, we send text-messages.
    b. People rarely talk to one another these days.
    c. Rather than talking with family members, we sit silently in front of our TV sets all evening.
    d. In cars, we ignore our traveling companions to listen to the radio.

Understanding the Topic Sentence

As already explained, most paragraphs center on a main idea, which is often expressed in a topic sentence. An effective topic sentence does two things. First, it presents the topic of the paragraph. Second, it expresses the writer's attitude or opinion or idea about the topic. For example, look at the following topic sentence:

> *Professional athletes are overpaid.*

In the topic sentence, the topic is *professional athletes;* the writer's idea about the topic is that professional athletes *are overpaid.*

For each topic sentence below, underline the topic and double-underline the point of view that the writer takes toward the topic.

EXAMPLES

Living in a small town has many advantages.

Talking on a cell phone while driving should be banned in every state.

1. The apartments on Walnut Avenue are a fire hazard.

2. Losing my job turned out to have benefits.

3. Blues is the most interesting form of American music.

4. Our neighbor's backyard is a dangerous place.

5. Paula and Jeff are a stingy couple.

6. Snakes do not deserve their bad reputation.

7. Pollution causes many problems in American cities.

8. New fathers should receive "paternity leave."

9. People with low self-esteem often need to criticize others.

10. Learning to write effectively is largely a matter of practice.

Identifying Topics, Topic Sentences, and Support

The following activity will sharpen your sense of the differences between topics, topic sentences, and supporting sentences.

Each group of items below includes one topic, one main idea (expressed in a topic sentence), and two supporting details for that idea. In the space provided, label each item with one of the following:

> *T* — **topic**
> *MI* — **main idea**
> *SD* — **supporting details**

1. _____ a. The weather in the summer is often hot and sticky.

   _____ b. Summer can be an unpleasant time of year.

   _____ c. Summer.

   _____ d. Bug bites, poison ivy, and allergies are a big part of summertime.

2. _____ a. The new Ultimate sports car is bound to be very popular.

   _____ b. The company has promised to provide any repairs needed during the first three years at no charge.

   _____ c. Because it gets thirty miles per gallon of gas, it offers real savings on fuel costs.

   _____ d. The new Ultimate sports car.

3. _____ a. Decorating an apartment doesn't need to be expensive.

   _____ b. A few plants add a touch of color without costing a lot of money.

   _____ c. Inexpensive braided rugs can be bought to match nearly any furniture.

   _____ d. Decorating an apartment.

4. _____ a. Long practice sessions and busy game schedules take too much time away from schoolwork.

   _____ b. High school sports.

   _____ c. The competition between schools may become so intense that, depending on the outcome of one game, athletes are either adored or scorned.

   _____ d. High school sports put too much pressure on young athletes.

5. _____ a. After mapping out the best route to your destination, phone ahead for motel reservations.

   _____ b. A long car trip.

   _____ c. Following a few guidelines before a long car trip can help you avoid potential problems.

   _____ d. Have your car's engine tuned as well, and have the tires, brakes, and exhaust system inspected.

Activities in Goal 2: Support the Point

www.mhhe.com/langan

Effective writing gives support—reasons, facts, examples, and other evidence—for each main point. While main points are general (see page 15), support is *specific;* it provides the details that explain the main point.

To write well, you must know the difference between general and specific ideas. It is helpful to realize that you use general and specific ideas all the time in your everyday life. For example, in choosing a DVD to rent, you may think, "Which should I rent, an action movie, a comedy, or a romance?" In such a case, *DVD* is the general idea, and *action movie, comedy,* and *romance* are the specific ideas.

Or you may decide to begin an exercise program. In that case, you might consider walking, jumping rope, or lifting weights. In this case, *exercise* is the general idea, and *walking, jumping rope,* and *lifting weights* are the specific ideas.

Or if you are talking to a friend about a date that didn't work out well, you may say, "The dinner was terrible, the car broke down, and we had little to say to each other." In this case, the general idea is *the date didn't work out well,* and the specific ideas are the three reasons you named.

The activities in this section will give you practice in the following:

- Understanding General and Specific Ideas
- Recognizing Specific Details
- Providing Specific Details
- Selecting Details That Fit
- Providing Details That Fit
- Providing Details in a Paragraph

Understanding General and Specific Ideas

Each group of words consists of one general idea and four specific ideas. The general idea includes all the specific ideas. Underline the general idea in each group.

Activity

4

EXAMPLE

   jeep   van   truck   <u>vehicle</u>   sedan

1. salty   bitter   flavor   sweet   sour

2. jewelry   necklace   ring   earrings   bracelet

3. dime   nickel   coin   quarter   half-dollar

4. fax machine   copier   computer   calculator   office machine

5. theft   murder   rape   crime   holdup

6. cracker   snack   carrot stick   cookie   popcorn

7. mascara   cosmetic   foundation   lipstick   eyeshadow

8. yes   no   I don't know   answer   maybe

9. yard work   mowing   planting   trimming hedges   feeding plants

10. job interviews   weddings   car accidents   being fired   stressful times

Activity

5

In each item below, one idea is general and the others are specific. The general idea includes the specific ones. In the spaces provided, write in two more specific ideas that are covered by the general idea.

EXAMPLE

General: exercises
Specific: chin-ups, lunges, _____*sit-ups*_____ , _____*push-ups*_____

1. *General:* pizza toppings
   Specific: sausage, mushrooms, _____ , _____

2. *General:* furniture
   Specific: rocking chair,
   coffee table, _____ , _____

3. *General:* magazines
   Specific: Reader's Digest,
   Newsweek, _____ , _____

4. *General:* birds
   Specific: eagle, pigeon, _____ , _____

5. *General:* types of music
   Specific: jazz, classical, _____ , _____

6. *General:* cold symptoms
   Specific: aching muscles,
   watery eyes, _____ , _____

7. *General:* children's games
   Specific: hopscotch, dodgeball, _____ , _____

8. *General:* transportation
   Specific: plane, motorcycle, _____ , _____

9. *General:* city problems
   Specific: overcrowding,
   pollution, _____ , _____

10. *General:* types of TV shows
    Specific: cartoons,
    situation comedies, _____ , _____

Read each group of specific ideas below. Then circle the letter of the general idea that tells what the specific ideas have in common. Note that the general idea should not be too broad or too narrow. Begin by trying the example item, and then read the explanation that follows.

EXAMPLE

> *Specific ideas:* peeling potatoes, washing dishes, cracking eggs, cleaning out refrigerator
>
> The general idea is
>
> a. household jobs.
> b. kitchen tasks.
> c. steps in making dinner.

EXPLANATION It is true that the specific ideas are all household jobs, but they have in common something even more specific—they are all tasks done in the kitchen. Therefore answer *a* is too broad, and the correct answer is *b*. Answer *c* is too narrow because it doesn't cover all the specific ideas. While two of them could be steps in making a dinner ("peeling potatoes" and "cracking eggs"), two have nothing to do with making dinner.

---

1. *Specific ideas:* crowded office, rude co-workers, demanding boss, unreasonable deadlines
   The general idea is
   a. problems.
   b. work problems.
   c. problems with work schedules.

2. *Specific ideas:* trout, whales, salmon, frogs
   The general idea is
   a. animals.
   b. fish.
   c. animals living in water.

3. *Specific ideas:* "Go to bed," "Pick up that trash," "Run twenty laps," "Type this letter."
   The general idea is
   a. remarks.
   b. orders.
   c. the boss's orders.

4. *Specific ideas:* "I had no time to study," "The questions were unfair," "I had a headache," "The instructor didn't give us enough time."

The general idea is

a. statements.
b. excuses for being late.
c. excuses for not doing well on a test.

5. *Specific ideas:* driving with expired license plates, driving over the speed limit, parking without putting money in the meter, driving without a license

The general idea is

a. ways to cause a traffic accident.
b. traffic problems.
c. ways to get a ticket.

Activity

7

In the following items, the specific ideas are given but the general ideas are unstated. Fill in the blanks with the unstated general ideas.

EXAMPLE

General idea:	*car problems*
Specific ideas:	flat tire dented bumper
	cracked windshield dirty oil filter

1. *General idea:* _____
   Specific ideas: nephew   grandmother
                       aunt   cousin

2. *General idea:* _____
   Specific ideas: camping   hiking
                       fishing   hunting

3. *General idea:* _____
   Specific ideas: broom   sponge
                       mop   glass cleaner

4. *General idea:* _____
   Specific ideas: fleas in carpeting   loud barking
                       tangled fur   veterinary bills

5. *General idea:* _____
   Specific ideas: diabetes   cancer
                       appendicitis   broken leg

Recognizing Specific Details

Specific details are examples, reasons, particulars, and facts. Such details are needed to support and explain a topic sentence effectively. They provide the evidence needed for us to understand, as well as to feel and experience, a writer's point.

Below is a topic sentence followed by two sets of supporting sentences. Put a check mark next to the set that provides sharp, specific details.

Topic sentence: Ticket sales for a recent U2 concert proved that the rock band is still very popular.

_____ a. Fans came from everywhere to buy tickets to the concert. People wanted good seats and were willing to endure a great deal of various kinds of discomfort as they waited in line for many hours. Some people actually waited for days, sleeping at night in uncomfortable circumstances. Good tickets were sold out extremely quickly.

_____ b. The first person in the long ticket line spent three days standing in the hot sun and three nights sleeping on the concrete without even a pillow. The man behind her waited equally long in his wheelchair. The ticket window opened at 10:00 A.M, and the tickets for the good seats—those in front of the stage—were sold out an hour later.

EXPLANATION The second set (*b*) provides specific details. Instead of a vague statement about fans who were "willing to endure a great deal of various kinds of discomforts," we get vivid details we can see and picture clearly: "three days standing in the hot sun," "three nights sleeping on the concrete without even a pillow," "The man behind her waited equally long in his wheelchair."

Instead of a vague statement that tickets were "sold out extremely quickly," we get exact and vivid details: "The ticket window opened at 10:00 A.M., and the tickets for the good seats—those in front of the stage— were sold out an hour later."

Specific details are often like a movie script. They provide us with such clear pictures that we could make a film of them if we wanted to. You would know just how to film the information given in the second set of sentences. You would show the fans in line under a hot sun and, later, sleeping on the concrete. The first person in line would be shown sleeping without a pillow under her head. You would show tickets finally going on sale, and after an hour you could show the ticket seller explaining that all the seats in front of the stage were sold out.

continued

> In contrast, the writer of the first set of sentences (*a*) fails to provide the specific information needed. If you were asked to make a film based on set *a*, you would have to figure out on your own just what particulars to show.
>
> When you are working to provide specific supporting information in a paper, it might help to ask yourself, "Could someone easily film this information?" If the answer is yes, your supporting details are specific enough for your readers to visualize.

Activity 8

Each topic sentence below is followed by two sets of supporting details. Write *S* (for *specific*) in the space next to the set that provides specific support for the point. Write *G* (for *general*) next to the set that offers only vague, general support.

> **HINT** Which set of supporting details could you more readily use in a film?

1. *Topic sentence:* The West Side shopping mall is an unpleasant place.

   _____ a. The floors are covered with cigarette butts, dirty paper plates, and spilled food. The stores are so crowded I had to wait twenty minutes just to get a dressing room to try on a shirt.

   _____ b. It's very dirty, and not enough places are provided for trash. The stores are not equipped to handle the large number of shoppers that often show up.

2. *Topic sentence:* Our golden retriever is a wonderful pet for children.

   _____ a. He is gentle, patient, eager to please, and affectionate. Capable of following orders, he is also ready to think for himself and find solutions to a problem. He senses children's moods and goes along with their wishes.

   _____ b. He doesn't bite, even when children pull his tail. After learning to catch a ball, he will bring it back again and again, seemingly always ready to play. If the children don't want to play anymore, he will just sit by their side, gazing at them with his faithful eyes.

3. *Topic sentence:* My two-year-old daughter's fearlessness is a constant source of danger to her.

   _____ a. She doesn't realize that certain activities are dangerous. Even when I warn her, she will go ahead and do something that could hurt her. I have to constantly be on the lookout for dangerous situations and try to protect her from them.

_____ b. For instance, she loves going to the swimming pool. That's great. But she will jump into water that is way over her head. She likes animals and will run to pet any dog that wanders by, no matter how unfriendly.

4. *Topic sentence:* People's views of scientists are often more fiction than fact.

_____ a. Scientists are portrayed in movies as crazy guys with long hair, thick glasses, and shabby clothes. Incapable of remembering the time of day, these imaginary scientists skip meals and prefer the company of laboratory animals to that of their own children. In reality, scientists get hungry at mealtime, love their children, and go to work in suits.

_____ b. People don't know exactly what scientists do and fantasize a lot about their work. Instead of thinking of scientists as real people who do a particular type of work, people think of them as weird, antisocial geniuses whom one could spot a mile away. In reality, most scientists look and act much like their neighbors.

5. *Topic sentence:* Early theories of child raising were very different from today's theories.

_____ a. The first books on child raising came out hundreds of years ago. The advice they contained was based almost entirely on superstitions and other untrue beliefs. Some of the advice was harmless, but some could lead to long-term effects. They told parents to do things to their children that seem to us to make no sense at all.

_____ b. One early book, for example, advised mothers not to breast-feed their babies right after feeling anger because the anger would go into the milk and injure the child. Another told parents to begin toilet training their children at the age of three weeks and to tie their babies' arms down for several months to prevent thumb sucking.

At several points in each of the following paragraphs, you are given a choice of two sets of supporting details. Write *S* (for *specific*) in the space next to the set that provides specific support for the point. Write *G* (for *general*) next to the set that offers only vague, general support.

Activity

9

Paragraph 1
My daughter is as shy as I am, and it breaks my heart to see her dealing with the same problems I had to deal with in my childhood because of my shyness. I feel very sad for her when I see the problems she has making friends.

_____ a. It takes her a long time to begin to do the things other children do to make friends, and her feelings get hurt very easily over one thing and another. She is not at all comfortable about making connections with her classmates at school.

_____ b. She usually spends Christmas vacation alone because by that time of year she doesn't have friends yet. Only when her birthday comes in the summer is she confident enough to invite school friends to her party. Once she sends out the invitations, she almost sleeps by the telephone, waiting for the children to respond. If they say they can't come, her eyes fill with tears.

I recognize very well her signs of shyness, which make her look smaller and more fragile than she really is.

_____ c. When she has to talk to someone she doesn't know well, she speaks in a whisper and stares sideways. Pressing her hands together, she lifts her shoulders as though she wished she could hide her head between them.

_____ d. When she is forced to talk to anyone other than her family and her closest friends, the sound of her voice and the position of her head change. Even her posture changes in a way that makes it look as if she's trying to make her body disappear.

It is hard for me to watch her passing unnoticed at school.

_____ e. She never gets chosen for a special job or privilege, even though she tries her best, practicing in privacy at home. She just doesn't measure up. Worst of all, even her teacher seems to forget her existence much of the time.

_____ f. Although she rehearses in our basement, she never gets chosen for a good part in a play. Her voice is never loud or clear enough. Worst of all, her teacher doesn't call on her in class for days at a time.

Paragraph 2

It is said that the dog is man's best friend, but I strongly believe that the honor belongs to my computer. A computer won't fetch a stick for me, but it can help me entertain myself in many ways.

_____ a. If I am bored, tired, or out of ideas, the computer allows me to explore things that interest me such as anything relating to the world of professional sports.

_____   b. The other day, I used my computer to visit the National Football League's Web site. I was then able to get injury updates for players on my favorite team, the Philadelphia Eagles.

While the dog is a faithful friend, it does not allow me to be a more responsible person the way my computer does.

_____   c. I use my computer to pay all my bills automatically over the Internet. I also use it to balance my checkbook and keep track of my expenses. Now I always know how much money is in my account at the end of the month.

_____   d. The computer helps me be responsible with financial matters because it records my transactions. With the computer I have access to more information, which allows me to make good decisions with my money.

A dog might help me meet strangers I see in the park, but the computer helps me meet people who share my interests.

_____   e. With my computer, I can go online and find people with every type of hobby or interest. Thousands of online chat rooms and discussion groups are available featuring people from all over the country—and the world. The computer can even allow me to develop meaningful personal relationships with others.

_____   f. Two months ago, I discovered a Web site for people in my community who enjoy hiking. I'm planning to meet a group next Saturday for a day hike. And earlier this year, I met my wonderful fiancée, Shelly, through a computer dating service.

Providing Specific Details

Each of the following sentences contains a general word or words, set off in *italic* type. Substitute sharp, specific words in each case.

EXAMPLE

After the parade, the city street was littered with *garbage*.

After the parade, the city street was littered with multicolored confetti, dirty popcorn, and lifeless balloons.

Activity

10

1. If I had enough money, I'd visit *several places*.

   _____

   _____

2. It took her *a long time* to get home.

   _____

   _____

3. Ron is often stared at because of his *unusual hair color and hairstyle.*

   _____

   _____

4. After you pass *two buildings,* you'll see my house on the left.

   _____

   _____

5. Nia's purse is crammed with *lots of stuff.*

   _____

   _____

6. I bought *some junk food* for the long car trip.

   _____

   _____

7. The floor in the front of my car is covered with *things.*

   _____

   _____

8. When his mother said no to his request for a toy, the child *reacted strongly.*

   _____

   _____

9. Devan gave his girlfriend a *surprise present* for Valentine's Day.

   _____

   _____

10. My cat can *do a wonderful trick.*

    _____

    _____

Selecting Details That Fit

The details in your paper must all clearly relate to and support your opening point. If a detail does not support your point, leave it out. Otherwise, your paper will lack unity. For example, see if you can circle the letter of the two sentences that do *not* support the topic sentence below.

> *Topic sentence:* Mario is a very talented person.
> (a.) Mario is always courteous to his professors.
> b. He has created beautiful paintings in his art course.
> c. Mario is the lead singer in a local band.
> d. He won an award in a photography contest.
> (e.) He is hoping to become a professional photographer.

> **EXPLANATION** Being courteous may be a virtue, but it is not a talent, so sentence *a* does not support the topic sentence. Also, Mario's desire to become a professional photographer tells us nothing about his talent; thus sentence *e* does not support the topic sentence either. The other three statements all clearly back up the topic sentence. Each in some way supports the idea that Mario is talented—in art, as a singer, or as a photographer.

In each group below, circle the two items that do *not* support the topic sentence.

Activity

11

1. *Topic sentence:* Carla seems attracted only to men who are unavailable.
   a. She once fell in love with a man serving a life sentence in prison.
   b. Her parents worry about her inability to connect with a nice single man.
   c. She wants to get married and have kids before she is thirty.
   d. Her current boyfriend is married.
   e. Recently she had a huge crush on a movie star.

2. *Topic sentence:* Some dog owners have little consideration for other people.
   a. Obedience lessons can be a good experience for both the dog and the owner.
   b. Some dog owners let their dogs leave droppings on the sidewalk or in other people's yards.
   c. They leave the dog home alone for hours, barking and howling and waking the neighbors.
   d. Some people keep very large dogs in small apartments.
   e. Even when small children are playing nearby, they let their bad-tempered dogs run loose.

3. *Topic sentence:* Dr. Eliot is a very poor teacher.

   a. He cancels class frequently with no explanation.

   b. When a student asks a question that he can't answer, he becomes irritated with the student.

   c. He got his Ph.D at a university in another country.

   d. He's taught at the college for many years and is on a number of faculty committees.

   e. He puts off grading papers until the end of the semester and then returns them all at once.

4. *Topic sentence:* Some doctors seem to think it is all right to keep patients waiting.

   a. Pharmaceutical sales representatives sometimes must wait hours to see a doctor.

   b. The doctors stand in the hallway chatting with nurses and secretaries even when they have a waiting room full of patients.

   c. Patients sometimes travel long distances to consult with a particular doctor.

   d. When a patient calls before an appointment to see if the doctor is on time, the answer is often yes even when the doctor is two hours behind schedule.

   e. Some doctors schedule appointments in a way that ensures long lines, to make it appear that they are especially skillful.

5. *Topic sentence:* Several factors were responsible for the staggering loss of lives when the *Titanic* sank.

   a. Over 1,500 people died in the *Titanic* disaster; only 711 survived.

   b. Despite warnings about the presence of icebergs, the captain allowed the *Titanic* to continue at high speed.

   c. If the ship had hit the iceberg head on, its watertight compartments might have kept it from sinking; however, it hit on the side, resulting in a long, jagged gash through which water poured in.

   d. The *Titanic*, equipped with the very best communication systems available in 1912, sent out SOS messages.

   e. When the captain gave orders to abandon the *Titanic,* many passengers refused because they believed the ship was unsinkable, so many lifeboats were only partly filled.

Providing Details That Fit

Each topic sentence below is followed by one supporting detail. Add a second detail in each case. Make sure your detail supports the topic sentence.

1. *Topic sentence:* There are good reasons why the video store is losing so many customers.
   a. The store stocks only one copy of every movie, even the most popular titles.
   b. _____

2. *Topic sentence:* The little boy did some dangerous stunts on his bicycle.
   a. He rode down a flight of steps at top speed.
   b. _____

3. *Topic sentence:* Craig has awful table manners.
   a. He stuffs his mouth with food and then begins a conversation.
   b. _____

4. *Topic sentence:* There are many advantages to living in the city.
   a. One can meet many new people with interesting backgrounds.
   b. _____

5. *Topic sentence:* All high school students should have summer jobs.
   a. Summer jobs help teens learn to handle a budget.
   b. _____

Add two supporting details for each of the topic sentences below.

1. *Topic sentence:* The managers of this apartment building don't care about their tenants.
   a. Mrs. Harris has been asking them to fix her leaky faucet for two months.
   b. _____
   c. _____

2. *Topic sentence:* None of the shirts for sale were satisfactory.
   a. Some were attractive but too expensive.
   b. _____
   c. _____

3. *Topic sentence:* After being married for forty years, Mr. and Mrs. Lambert have grown similar in odd ways.
    a. They both love to have a cup of warm apple juice just before bed.
    b. _____
    c. _____

4. *Topic sentence:* It is a special time for me when my brother is in town.
    a. We always go bowling together and then stop for pizza.
    b. _____
    c. _____

5. *Topic sentence:* Our neighbor's daughter is very spoiled.
    a. When anyone else in the family has a birthday, she gets several presents too.
    b. _____
    c. _____

Providing Details in a Paragraph

Activity

14

The following paragraph needs specific details to back up its three supporting points. In the spaces provided, write two or three sentences of convincing details for each supporting point.

A Disappointing Concert

Although I had looked forward to seeing my favorite musical group in concert, the experience was disappointing. For one thing, our seats were terrible, in two ways. _____

_____

_____

_____

_____

In addition, the crowd made it hard to enjoy the music. _____

_____

_____

_____

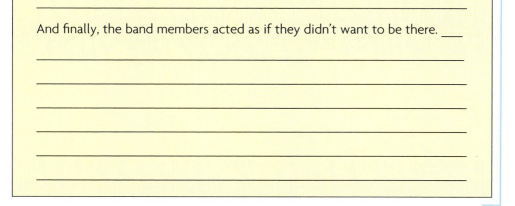

And finally, the band members acted as if they didn't want to be there. ___

Activities in Goal 3: Organize the Support

Effective writing includes clearly organized support. In a paragraph, details are often arranged in a *listing order* or *time order* so readers can make sense of them. In addition, *transitions* or signal words help make the support easy to read and understand.

The activities in this section will give you practice in the following:

- Understanding Listing and Time Order
- Understanding Transitions
- Using Transitions
- Organizing Details in a Paragraph

Understanding Listing and Time Order

Listing Order The writer can organize supporting evidence in a paper by providing a list of two or more reasons, examples, or details. Often the most important or interesting item is saved for last because the reader is most likely to remember the last thing read.

Transition words that indicate listing order include the following:

one	**second**	**also**	**next**	**last of all**
for one thing	**third**	**another**	**moreover**	**finally**
first of all	**next**	**in addition**	**furthermore**	

The paragraph about starting college on page 11 uses a listing order: it lists three reasons why starting college at twenty-nine is not easy, and each of those three reasons is introduced by one of the transitions in the box on page 33. In the spaces below, write in the three transitions:

_____ *For one thing* _____   _____ *Another* _____   _____ *Finally* _____

The first reason in the paragraph about starting college is introduced with *for one thing,* the second reason by *another,* and the third reason by *finally.*

Time Order When a writer uses time order, supporting details are presented in the order in which they occurred. *First* this happened; *next* this; *after* that, this; and so on. Many paragraphs, especially paragraphs that tell a story or give a series of directions, are organized in time order.

Transition words that show time relationships include the following:

first	**before**	**after**	**when**	**then**
next	**during**	**now**	**while**	**until**
as	**soon**	**later**	**often**	**finally**

Read the paragraph below, which is organized in time order. See if you can underline the six transition words that show the time relationships.

> Della had a sad experience while driving home last night. She traveled along the dark, winding road that led toward her home. She was only two miles from her house when she noticed a glimmer of light in the road. The next thing she knew, she heard a sickening thud and realized she had struck an animal. The light, she realized, had been its eyes reflected in her car's headlights. Della stopped the car and ran back to see what she had hit. It was a handsome cocker spaniel, with blond fur and long ears. As she bent over the still form, she realized there was nothing to be done. The dog was dead. Della searched the dog for a collar and tags. There was nothing. Before leaving, she walked to several nearby houses, asking if anyone knew who owned the dog. No one did. Finally Della gave up and drove on. She was sad to leave someone's pet lying there alone.

The main point of the paragraph is stated in its first sentence: "Della had a sad experience while driving home last night." The support for this point is all the details of Della's experience. Those details are presented in the order in which they occurred. The time relationships are highlighted by these transitions: *while, when, next, as, before,* and *finally.*

Understanding Transitions

Transitions are words and phrases that indicate relationships between ideas. They are like signposts that guide travelers, showing them how to move smoothly from one spot to the next. Be sure to take advantage of transitions. They will help organize and connect your ideas, and they will help your readers follow the direction of your thoughts.

To see how transitions help, write a check beside the item in each pair that is easier to read and understand.

Pair A

_____ One way to stay in shape is to eat low-calorie, low-fat foods. A good strategy is to walk or jog at least twenty minutes four times a week.

_____ One way to stay in shape is to eat low-calorie, low-fat foods. Another good strategy is to walk or jog at least twenty minutes four times a week.

Pair B

_____ I begin each study session by going to a quiet place and setting out my textbook, pen, and notebook. I check my assignment book to see what I have to read.

_____ I begin each study session by going to a quiet place and setting out my textbook, pen, and notebook. Then I check my assignment book to see what I have to read.

EXPLANATION   In each pair, the second item is easier to read and understand. In pair A, the listing word *another* makes it clear that the writer is going on to a second way to stay in shape. In pair B, the time word *then* makes the relationship between the sentences clear. The writer first sets out the textbook and a pen and notebook and *then* checks an assignment book to see what to do.

Using Transitions

As already stated, transitions are signal words that help readers follow the direction of the writer's thought. To see the value of transitions, look at the two versions of the short paragraph below. Check the version that is easier to read and understand.

_____ a. Where will you get the material for your writing assignments? There are several good sources. Your own experience is a major resource. For an assignment about childhood, for instance, you can draw on your own numerous memories of childhood. Other people's experience is extremely useful. You may have heard people you know or even people on TV or radio talking about their childhood. Or you can interview people with a specific writing assignment in mind. Books and magazines are a good source of material for assignments. Many experts, for example, have written about various aspects of childhood.

_____ b. Where will you get the material for your writing assignments? There are several good sources. First of all, your own experience is a major resource. For an assignment about childhood, for instance, you can draw on your own numerous memories of childhood. In addition, other people's experiences are extremely useful. You may have heard people you know or even people on TV or radio talking about their childhood. Or you can interview people with a specific writing assignment in mind. Finally, books and magazines are a good source of material for assignments. Many experts, for example, have written about various aspects of childhood.

> **EXPLANATION**   You no doubt chose the second version, *b*. The listing transitions—*first of all, in addition,* and *finally*—make it clear when the author is introducing a new supporting point. The reader of paragraph *b* is better able to follow the author's line of thinking and to note that three main sources of material for assignments are being listed: your own experience, other people's experience, and books and magazines.

Activity

15

The following paragraphs use listing order or time order. In each case, fill in the blanks with appropriate transitions from the box above the paragraph. Use each transition once.

1. | **after   now   first   soon   while** |

My husband has developed an involving hobby, in which I, unfortunately, am unable to share. He _____ enrolled in ground flight instruction classes at the local community college. The lessons were all about air safety regulations and procedures. _____ passing a difficult exam, he decided to take flying lessons at the city airport. Every Monday he would wake at six o'clock in the morning and drive happily to the airport, eager to see his instructor. _____ he was taking lessons, he started to buy airplane magazines and talk about them constantly. "Look at that Cessna 150," he would say. "Isn't she a beauty?" _____, after many lessons, he he is flying by himself. _____ he will be able to carry passengers. That is my biggest nightmare. I know he will want me to fly with him, but I am not a lover of heights. I can't understand why someone would leave the safety of the ground to be in the sky, defenseless as a kite.

2. | **finally   for one thing   second** |

The karate class I took last week convinced me that martial arts may never be my strong point. _____, there is the issue of balance. The instructor asked everyone in class to stand on one foot to practice kicking. Each time I tired, I wobbled and had to spread my arms out wide to avoid falling. I even stumbled into Mr. Kim, my instructor, who glared at me. _____, there was the issue of flexibility. Mr. Kim asked us to stretch and touch our toes. Everyone did this without a problem—except me. I could barely reach my knees before pain raced up and down my back. _____, there was my lack of coordination. When everyone started practicing blocks, I got confused. I couldn't figure out where to move my arms and legs. By the time I got the first move right, the whole group had finished three more. By the end of my first lesson, I was completely lost.

3. | **later   soon   when   then** |

At the age of thirty-one I finally had the opportunity to see snow for the first time in my life. It was in New York City on a cloudy afternoon in November. My daughter and I had gone to the American Museum of Natural History. _____ we left the museum, snow was falling gently. I thought that it was so beautiful! It made me remember movies I had seen countless times in my native Brazil. We decided to find a taxi. _____ we were crossing Central Park, snuggled in the cozy cab, watching the snow cover trees, bushes, branches, and grass. We were amazed to see the landscape quickly change from fall to winter. _____ we arrived in front of our hotel, and I still remember stepping on the crisp snow and laughing like a child who is touched by magic. _____ that day, I heard on the radio that another snowstorm was coming. I was naive enough to wait for thunder and the other sounds of a rainstorm. I did not know yet that snow, even a snowstorm, is silent and soft.

4. | **last of all   another   first of all   in addition** |

Public school students who expect to attend school from September to June, and then have a long summer vacation, may be in for a big surprise before long. For a number of reasons, many schools are switching to a year-round calendar. _____, many educators point out that the traditional school calendar was established years ago when young people had to be available during the summer months to work on farms, but this necessity has long since passed. _____ reason is that a longer school year accommodates individual learning rates more effectively. That is, fast learners can go into more depth about a subject that interests them, while those who learn at a slower pace have more time to master the essential material. _____, many communities have gone to year-round school to relieve overcrowding, since students can be put on different schedules throughout the year. _____, and perhaps most important, educators feel that year-round schools eliminate the loss of learning that many students experience over a long summer break.

Organizing Details in a Paragraph

The supporting details in a paragraph must be organized in a meaningful way. The two most common methods of organizing details are listing order and time order. The activities that follow will give you practice in both methods of organization.

Use *listing order* to arrange the scrambled list of sentences below. Number each supporting sentence 1, 2, 3,... so that you go from the least important item to what is presented as the most important item.

Activity

16

Note that transitions will help by making clear the relationships between some of the sentences.

Topic sentence: I am no longer a big fan of professional sports, for a number of reasons.

_____ Basketball and hockey continue well into the baseball season, and football doesn't have its Super Bowl until the middle of winter, when basketball should be at center stage.

_____ In addition, I detest the high fives, taunting, and trash talk that so many professional athletes now indulge in during games.

_____ Second, I am bothered by the length of professional sports seasons.

_____ Also, professional athletes have no loyalty to a team or city as they greedily sell their abilities to the highest bidder.

_____ For one thing, greed is the engine running professional sports.

_____ There are numerous news stories of professional athletes in trouble with the law because of drugs, guns, fights, traffic accidents, or domestic violence.

_____ After a good year, athletes making millions become unhappy if they aren't rewarded with a new contract calling for even more millions.

_____ But the main reason I've become disenchanted with professional sports is the disgusting behavior of so many of its performers.

Use *time order* to arrange the scrambled sentences below. Number the supporting sentences in the order in which they occur in time (1, 2, 3,...).

Activity

17

Note that transitions will help by making clear the relationships between sentences.

Topic sentence: If you are a smoker, the following steps should help you quit.

_____ Before your "quit day" arrives, have a medical checkup to make sure it will be all right for you to begin an exercise program.

_____ You should then write down on a card your decision to quit and the date of your "quit day."

_____ When your "quit day" arrives, stop smoking and start your exercise program.

_____ Finally, remind yourself repeatedly how good you will feel when you can confidently tell yourself and others that you are a nonsmoker.

_____ Place the card in a location where you will be sure to see it every day.

_____ When you begin this exercise program, be sure to drink plenty of water every day and to follow a sensible diet.

_____ After making a definite decision to stop smoking, select a specific "quit day."

_____ Eventually, your exercise program should include activities strenuous enough to strengthen your lung capacity and your overall stamina.

Activities in Goal 4: Write Error-Free Sentences

Effective writing is free of errors that distract or confuse readers. Whether you are writing a paragraph, letter, job application, or resume, you must learn to write clear, error-free sentences. The activities in Part Two of this book will help you do just that.

www.mhhe.com/langan

The Writing Process

3

Steps in the Writing Process

Even professional writers do not sit down and write a paper automatically, in one draft. Instead, they have to work on it a step at a time. Writing a paper is a process that can be divided into the following steps:

- *Step 1:* Getting Started through Prewriting
- *Step 2:* Preparing a Scratch Outline
- *Step 3*: Writing the First Draft
- *Step 4:* Revising
- *Step 5:* Editing and Proofreading

These steps are described on the following pages.

Step 1: Getting Started through Prewriting

What you need to learn first are strategies for working on a paper. These strategies will help you do the thinking needed to figure out both the point you want to make and the support you have for that point.

There are several *prewriting strategies*—strategies you use before writing the first draft of your paper:

- Freewriting
- Questioning
- Clustering
- Making a list

Freewriting

www.mhhe.com/langan

Freewriting is just sitting down and writing whatever comes into your mind about a topic. Do this for ten minutes or so. Write without stopping and without worrying at all about spelling, grammar, or the like. Simply get down on paper all the information about the topic that occurs to you.

Here is the freewriting Gary did on his problems with returning to school. Gary had been given the assignment "Write about a problem you are facing at the present time." Gary felt right away that he could write about his college situation. He began prewriting as a way to explore and generate details on his topic.

EXAMPLE OF FREEWRITING

One thing I want to write about is going back to school. At age twenty-nine. A lot to deal with. I sometimes wonder if Im nuts to try to do this or just stupid. I had to deal with my folks when I decided. My dad hated school. He knew when to quit, I'll say that for him. But he doesn't understand Im different. I have a right to my own life. And I want to better myself. He teases me alot. Says things like didnt you get dumped on enough in high school, why go back for more. My mom doesnt understand either. Just keeps worring about where the money was coming from. Then my friends. They make fun of me. Also my wife has to do more of the heavy house stuff because I'm out so much. Getting back to my friends, they say dumb things to get my goat. Like calling me the college man or saying ooh, we'd better watch our grammer. Sometimes I think my dads right, school was no fun for me. Spent years just sitting in class waiting for final bell so I could escape. Teachers didnt help me or take an intrest, some of them made me feel like a real loser. Now things are different and I like most of my teachers. I can talk to the teacher after class or to ask questions if I'm confused. But I really need more time to spend with family, I hardly see them any more. What I am doing is hard all round for them and me.

Look at the photo above and freewrite for several minutes about an electronic device you could not live without.

Notice that there are problems with spelling, grammar, and punctuation in Gary's freewriting. Gary is not worried about such matters, nor should he be. He is just concentrating on getting ideas and details down on paper. He knows that it is best to focus on one thing at a time. At this stage, he just wants to write out thoughts as they come to him, to do some thinking on paper.

You should take the same approach when freewriting: explore your topic without worrying at all about being "correct." At this early stage of the writing process, focus all your attention on figuring out what you want to say.

Questioning

Questioning means that you think about your topic by writing down a series of questions and answers about it. Your questions can start with words like *what, when, where, why,* and *how.*

Here are some questions that Gary might have asked while developing his paper, as well as some answers to those questions.

www.mhhe.com/langan

EXAMPLE OF QUESTIONING

Why do I have a problem with returning to school?	My parents and friends don't support me.
How do they not support me?	Dad asks why I want to be dumped on more. Mom is upset because college costs lots of money. Friends tease me about being a college man.
When do they not support me?	When I go to my parents' home for Friday night visits, when my friends see me walking toward them.
Where do I have this problem?	At home, where I barely see my wife and daughter before having to go to class, and where I have to let my wife do house things on weekends while I'm studying.
Why else do I have this problem?	High school was bad experience.
What details back up the idea that high school was bad experience?	Sat in class bored, couldn't wait to get out, teachers didn't help me. One embarrassed me when I didn't know the answer.

Clustering

Clustering is another prewriting strategy that can be used to generate material for a paper. It is helpful for people who like to do their thinking in a visual way.

In *clustering,* you begin by stating your subject in a few words in the center of a blank sheet of paper. Then as ideas come to you, put them in ovals, boxes, or circles around the subject, and draw lines to connect them to the subject. Put minor ideas or details in smaller boxes or circles, and also use connecting lines to show how they relate.

Keep in mind that there is no right or wrong way of clustering. It is a way to think on paper about how various ideas and details relate to one another. Below is an example of clustering that Gary might have done to develop his idea.

EXAMPLE OF CLUSTERING

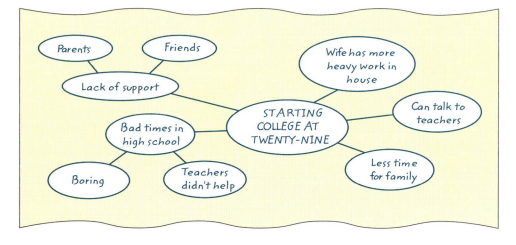

Making a List

In *making a list*—a prewriting strategy also known as *listing, list making,* and *brainstorming*—you make a list of ideas and details that could go into your paper. Simply pile these items up, one after another, without worrying about putting them in any special order. Try to accumulate as many details as you can think of.

After Gary did his freewriting about returning to school, he made up the list of details shown below.

EXAMPLE OF LISTING

parents give me hard time when they see me

Dad hated school

Dad quit school after eighth grade

Dad says I was dumped on enough in high school

Dad asks why I want to go back for more

Mom also doesnt understand

continued

keeps asking how Ill pay for it

friends give me a hard time too

friends call me college man

say they have to watch their grammar

my wife has more heavy work around the house

also high school had been no fun for me

just sat in class after class

couldnt wait for final bell to ring

wanted to escape

teachers didnt help me

teachers didnt take an interest in me

one called on me, then told me to forget it

I felt like a real loser

I didnt want to go back to his class

now I'm more sure of myself

OK not to know an answer

talk to teachers after class

job plus schoolwork take all my time

get home late, then rush through dinner

then spend evening studying

even have to do homework on weekends

One detail led to another as Gary expanded his list. Slowly but surely, more supporting material emerged that he could use in developing his paper. By the time he had finished his list, he was ready to plan an outline of his paragraph and to write his first draft.

Notice that in making a list, as in freewriting, details are included that will not actually end up in the final paragraph. Gary decided later not to develop the idea that his wife now has more heavy work to do in the house. And he realized that several of his details were about why school is easier in college ("now I'm more sure of myself," "OK not to know an answer," and "talk to instructors after class"); such details were not relevant to his point.

It is natural for a number of such extra or unrelated details to appear as part of the prewriting process. The goal of prewriting is to get a lot of information down on paper. You can then add to, shape, and subtract from your raw material as you take your paper through the series of writing drafts.

Important Points about Prewriting Strategies

Some writers may use only one of the prewriting strategies described here. Others may use bits and pieces of all four strategies. Any one strategy can lead to another. Freewriting may lead to questioning or clustering, which may then lead to a list. Or a writer may start with a list and then use freewriting or questioning to develop items on the list. During this early stage of the writing process, as you do your thinking on paper, anything goes. You should not expect a straight-line progression from the beginning to the end of your paper. Instead, there probably will be a continual moving back and forth as you work to discover your point and decide just how you will develop it.

Keep in mind that prewriting can also help you choose from among several topics. Gary might not have been so sure about which problem to write about. Then he could have made a list of possible topics—areas in his life in which he has had problems. After selecting two or three topics from the list, he could have done some prewriting on each to see which seemed most promising. After finding a likely topic, Gary would have continued with his prewriting activities until he had a solid main point and plenty of support.

Finally, remember that you are not ready to begin writing a paper until you know your main point and many of the details to support it. Don't rush through prewriting. It's better to spend more time on this stage than to waste time writing a paragraph for which you have no solid point and not enough interesting support.

Step 2: Preparing a Scratch Outline

A *scratch outline* is a brief plan for a paragraph. It shows at a glance the point of the paragraph and the main support for that point. It is the logical backbone on which the paper is built.

This rough outline often follows freewriting, questioning, clustering, or listing—or all four. Or it may gradually emerge in the midst of these strategies. In fact, trying to outline is a good way to see if you need to do more prewriting. If a solid outline does not emerge, then you know you need to do more prewriting to clarify your main point or its support. Once you have a workable outline, you may realize, for instance, that you want to do more listing to develop one of the supporting details in the outline.

In Gary's case, as he was working on his list of details, he suddenly discovered what the plan of his paragraph could be. He went back to the list, crossed out items that he now realized did not fit, and added the following comments.

EXAMPLE OF LIST WITH COMMENTS

Starting college at twenty-nine isn't easy—three reasons

parents give me hard time when they see me

Dad hated school

Dad quit school after eighth grade

Dad says I was dumped on enough in high school

Dad asks why I want to go back for more

Mom also doesnt understand

keeps asking how Ill pay for it

friends give me a hard time too

friends call me college man

say they have to watch their grammar

~~my wife has more heavy work around the house~~

also high school had been no fun for me

just sat in class after class

couldnt wait for final bell to ring

wanted to escape

teachers didnt help me

teachers didnt take an interest in me

one called on me, then told me to forget it

I felt like a real loser

I didnt want to go back to his class

~~now I'm more sure of myself~~

~~OK not to know an answer~~

~~talk to teachers after class~~

job and schoolwork take all my time

get home late, then rush through dinner

then spend evening studying

even have to do homework on weekends

Parents and friends
don't support me

Bad memories
of school

Not enough time
with family

Under the list, Gary was now able to prepare his scratch outline.

EXAMPLE OF SCRATCH OUTLINE

> *Starting college at age twenty-nine isn't easy.*
> 1. *Little support from parents or friends*
> 2. *Bad memories of school*
> 3. *Not enough time to spend with family*

After all his preliminary writing, Gary sat back, pleased. He knew he had a promising paper—one with a clear point and solid support. Gary was now ready to write the first draft of his paper, using his outline as a guide.

Step 3: Writing the First Draft

When you write your first draft, be prepared to put in additional thoughts and details that didn't emerge in your prewriting. And don't worry if you hit a snag. Just leave a blank space or add a comment such as "Do later" and press on to finish the paper. Also, don't worry yet about grammar, punctuation, or spelling. You don't want to take time correcting words or sentences that you may decide to remove later. Instead, make it your goal to develop the content of your paper with plenty of specific details.

Here is Gary's first draft.

> *First Draft*
>
> *Last fall, I finaly realized that I was stuck in a dead-end job. I wasnt making enough money and I was bored to tears. I figured I had to get some new skills which meant going back to school. Beginning college at age twenty-nine turned out to be much tougher than I thought it would be. My father didnt understand, he hated school. That's why he quit after eighth grade. He would ask, Didnt you get dumped on enough in high school? Then wondered why I wanted to go back for more of the same thing. My mother was*

continued

> worried about where the money were coming from and said so. When my friends saw me coming down the st. They would make fun of me with remarks like Hey theres the college man. They may have a point. School never was much fun for me. I spent years just siting in class waiting for the bell to ring. So I could escape. The teachers werent much help to me. One time, a teacher called on me then told me to forget it. I felt like a real loser and didnt want to go back to his class. College takes time away from my family. ADD MORE DETAILS LATER. All this makes it very hard for me.

After Gary finished the draft, he was able to put it aside until the next day. You will benefit as well if you can allow some time between finishing a draft and starting to revise.

Step 4: Revising

Revising is as much a stage in the writing process as prewriting, outlining, and writing a first draft. *Revising* means rewriting a paper, building on what has been done, to make it stronger. One writer has said about revision, "It's like cleaning house—getting rid of all the junk and putting things in the right order." It is not just "straightening up"; instead, you must be ready to roll up your sleeves and do whatever is needed to create an effective paper. Too many students think that the first draft *is* the paper. They start to become writers when they realize that revising a rough draft three or four times is often at the heart of the writing process.

Here are some quick hints that can help make revision easier:

- Ideally, set your first draft aside for a while. A few hours are fine, but a day or two is best. You can then come back with a fresh, more objective point of view.

- Work from typed or printed text. You'll be able to see the paper more impartially in this way than if you were just looking at your own familiar handwriting.

- Read your draft aloud. Hearing how your writing sounds will help you pick up problems with meaning as well as style.

- As you do all these things, add your thoughts and changes above the lines or in the margins of your paper. Your written comments can serve as a guide when you work on the next draft.

Here is Gary's second draft.

Second Draft

Starting college at age twenty-nine turned out to be really tough. I did not have much support from my parents and friends. My father hated school, so he asked, Didnt you get dumped on enough in high school? Why go back for more? My mother asking about where the money were coming from. Friends would be making fun of me. Hey theres the college man they would say as soon as they saw me. Another factor was what happened to me in high school. I spent years just siting in class waiting for the bell to ring. I was really bored. Also the teachers liked to embaras me. One teacher called on me and then said forget it. He must of relized I didnt know the answer. I felt like a real loser and didnt want to go back in his class for weeks. Finally I've learned that college takes time away from my family. I have to go to work every day. I have a little over one hour to eat dinner and spend time with my wife and daughter. Then I have to go off to class and when I get back my daughter is in bed asleep. My wife and I have only a little time together. On weekends I have lots of homework to do, so the time goes by like a shot. College is hard for me, but I am going to stay there so I can have a better life.

Notice the improvements made in the second draft:

- Gary started by clearly stating the point of his paragraph. He remembered the first goal in effective writing: *Make a point.*

- To keep the focus on his own difficulties, he omitted the detail about his father quitting school. He remembered that the first goal in effective writing is also to *stick to one point,* so the paper will have unity.

- He added more details so that he would have enough support for his reasons why college was hard. He remembered the second goal in effective writing: *Support the point.*

- He inserted transitions to set off the second reason ("Another factor") and third reason ("Finally") why starting college at twenty-nine was difficult for him. He remembered the third goal in effective writing: *Organize the support.*

Gary then went on to revise the second draft. Since he was doing the paper on a computer, he was able to print it out quickly. He double-spaced the lines, allowing room for revisions, which he added in longhand during his third draft. (Note that if you are not using a computer, you may want to do each draft on one side of a page, so that you see your entire paper at one time.) Shown below are some of the changes that Gary made in longhand as he worked on his third draft.

Part of Third Draft

was difficult.   For one thing
Starting college at age twenty-nine ~~turned out to be really tough~~. I did

not have much support from my parents and friends. My father ~~hated~~

~~school, so he~~ asked, Didnt you get dumped on enough in high school? Why

woried
go back for more? My mother ~~asking~~ about where the money were coming

make
from. Friends would ~~be making~~ fun of me. Hey theres the college man they

reason that starting college was hard
would say as soon as they saw me. Another ~~factor~~ was what happened to

final
me in high school. I spent years just siting in class waiting for the bell to

ring. I was really bored. Also the teachers liked to embaras me. . . .

After writing these and other changes, Gary typed them into his computer file and printed out the almost-final draft of his paper. He knew he had come to the fourth goal in effective writing: *aim for error-free sentences.*

Step 5: Editing and Proofreading

The next-to-last major stage in the writing process is *editing*—checking a paper for mistakes in grammar, punctuation, usage, and spelling. Students often find it hard to edit a paper carefully. They have put so much work into their writing, or so little, that it's almost painful for them to look at the paper one more time. You may simply have to *will* yourself to carry out this important closing step in the writing process. Remember that eliminating sentence-skills mistakes will improve an average paper and help ensure a strong grade on a good paper. Further, as you get into the habit of checking your papers, you will also get into the habit of using sentence skills consistently. They are an integral part of clear, effective writing. The checklist of sentence skills on the inside back cover of the book will serve as a guide while you are editing your paper.

Here are hints that can help you edit the next-to-final draft of a paper for sentence-skills mistakes.

EDITING HINTS

1. Have at hand two essential tools: a good dictionary (see page 388) and a grammar handbook (you can use Part Two of this book).

2. Use a sheet of paper to cover your essay so that you expose only one sentence at a time. Look for errors in grammar, spelling, and typing. It may help to read each sentence out loud. If the sentence does not read clearly and smoothly, chances are something is wrong.

3. Pay special attention to the kinds of errors you tend to make. For example, if you tend to write run-ons or fragments, be especially on the lookout for these errors.

4. Try to work on a typewritten or word-processed draft, where you'll be able to see your writing more objectively than you can on a handwritten page; use a pen with colored ink so that your corrections will stand out.

Shown below are some of the corrections in spelling, grammar, and punctuation that Gary made when editing his paper.

Part of Gary's Edited Draft

Starting college at age twenty-nine was difficult. For one thing I did not have much support from my parents and friends. My father asked, "Didn't you get dumped on enough in high school? Why go back for more?" My mother ~~woried~~ *worried* about where the money ~~were~~ *was* coming from. Friends would make fun of me. "Hey, there's the college man" they would say as soon as they saw me. . . .

All that remained for Gary to do was to enter in his corrections, print out the final draft of the paper, and proofread it (see the next page for hints on proofreading) for any typos or other careless errors. He was then ready to hand the paper in to his instructor.

Proofreading, the final stage in the writing process, means checking a paper carefully for errors in spelling, grammar, punctuation, and so on. You are ready for this stage when you are satisfied with your choice of supporting details, the order in which they are presented, and the way they and your topic sentence are worded. You will already have attempted to correct all grammar, spelling, and punctuation errors.

At this point in his work, Gary used his dictionary to do final checks on his spelling. He used a grammar handbook (such as the one in Part Two of this text) to be sure about grammar, punctuation, and usage. Gary also read through his paper carefully, looking for typing errors, omitted words, and any other errors he may have missed before. Proofreading is often hard to do—again, students have spent so much time with their work, or so little, that they want to avoid it. But if it is done carefully, this important final step will ensure that your paper looks as good as possible.

PROOFREADING HINTS

1. One helpful trick at this stage is to read your paper out loud. You will probably hear awkward wordings and become aware of spots where the punctuation needs to be improved. Make the changes needed for your sentences to read smoothly and clearly.

2. Another helpful technique is to take a sheet of paper and cover your paragraph so that you expose just one line at a time and check it carefully.

3. A third strategy is to read your paper backward, from the last sentence to the first. This helps keep you from getting caught up in the flow of the paper and missing small mistakes—which is easy to do, since you're so familiar with what you mean to say.

Activities in the Writing Process

These activities will give you practice in some of the prewriting strategies you can use to generate material for a paper. Try to do two or more of these prewriting activities.

Activity

1

Freewriting

On a sheet of paper, freewrite for several minutes about the best or most disappointing friend you ever had. Don't worry about grammar, punctuation, or spelling. Try to write, without stopping, about whatever comes into your head concerning your best or most disappointing friend.

Questioning

On another sheet of paper, answer the following questions about the friend you've started to write about.

1. When did this friendship take place?
2. Where did it take place?
3. What is one reason you liked or were disappointed in this friend? Give one quality, action, comment, etc. Also, give some details to illustrate this quality.
4. What is another reason that you liked or were disappointed in your friend? What are some details that support the second reason?
5. Can you think of a third thing about your friend that you liked or were disappointed in? What are some details that support the third reason?

Activity

2

Clustering

In the center of a blank sheet of paper, write and circle the words *best friend* or *most disappointing friend.* Then, around the circle, add reasons and details about the friend. Use a series of boxes, circles, or other shapes, along with connecting lines, to set off the reasons and details. In other words, try to think about and explore your topic in a very visual way.

Activity

3

Making a List

On separate paper, make a list of details about the friend. Don't worry about putting them in a certain order. Just get down as many details about the friend as occur to you. The list can include specific reasons you liked or were disappointed in the person and specific details supporting those reasons.

Activity

4

Scratch Outline

On the basis of your prewriting, prepare a scratch outline made up of your main idea and the three main reasons you liked or were disappointed in your friend. Use the form below:

Activity

5

_____ was my best *or* most disappointing friend.

*Reason 1:*_____

*Reason 2:*_____

*Reason 3:*_____

Activity 6

First Draft

Now write a first draft of your paper. Begin with your topic sentence, stating that a certain friend was the best or most disappointing one you ever had. Then state the first reason to support your main idea, followed by specific details supporting that reason. Next, state the second reason, again, followed by specific details supporting that reason. Finally, state the third reason, followed by support.

Don't worry about grammar, punctuation, or spelling. Just concentrate on getting down on paper the details about your friend.

Activity 7

Revising the Draft

Ideally, you will have a chance to put your paper aside for a while before writing the second draft. In your second draft, try to do all of the following:

1. Add transition words such as *first of all, another,* and *finally* to introduce each of the three reasons you liked or were disappointed in the friend you're writing about.

2. Omit any details that do not truly support your topic sentence.

3. Add more details as needed, making sure you have plenty of support for each of your three reasons.

4. Check to see that your details are vivid and specific. Can you make a supporting detail more concrete? Are there any persuasive, colorful specifics you can add?

5. Try to eliminate wordiness (see page 441) and clichés (see page 438).

6. In general, improve the flow of your writing.

7. Be sure to include a final sentence that rounds off the paper, bringing it to a close.

Activity 8

Editing and Proofreading

When you have your almost-final draft of the paper, proofread it as follows:

1. Using your dictionary, check any words that you think might be misspelled. Or use a spell-check program on your computer.

2. Using Part Two of this book, check your paper for mistakes in grammar, punctuation, and usage.

3. Read the paper aloud, listening for awkward or unclear spots. Make the changes needed for the paragraph to read smoothly and clearly. Even better, see if you can get another person to read the draft aloud to you. The spots that this person has trouble reading are spots where you may have to do some rewriting.

4. Take a sheet of paper and cover your writing so that you expose and carefully check one line at a time. Or read your writing backward, from the end of the paragraph to the beginning. Look for typing errors, omitted words, and other remaining errors.

Don't fail to edit and proofread carefully. You may be tired of working on your paper at this point, but you want to give the extra effort needed to make it as good as possible. A final push can mean the difference between a higher and a lower grade.

Ten Writing Assignments

Your instructor may ask you to do one or more of the following paragraph writing assignments. Be sure to check the rules for paper format on page 285.

Writing Assignment

A Vivid Memory of Your Mother or Father   1

Think of a particularly clear memory you have of your mother or father. It might be a happy memory that warms your heart. Or it could be humorous, frightening, or enraging. The important thing is that it is a sharp, specific recollection that produces a strong emotional response in you. Then write a paragraph about your memory.

Your goal will be to let the reader see exactly what happened and understand what you felt. To accomplish this, you must provide very specific details. Remember that your reader will have no prior knowledge of your mother or father. You are responsible for painting a "word picture" that will let your reader see your parent the way you saw him or her.

Before you begin writing the paragraph itself, do some prewriting. You might jot down answers to the kind of questions a curious reader would have about your memory. Here are a few such questions: Where did this event take place? When? Who was present? How old was your parent when this occurred? How old were you? What did your parent look like? What did he or she say? How did he or she say it? Why is this memory so vivid for you? The answers to questions like these will provide the kind of concrete detail that will make your paragraph come alive. Begin your paragraph with a summary statement, such as these:

One of my family's most amusing experiences took place when I found my father sleepwalking in the kitchen.

Seeing my mother trip on the sidewalk was the beginning of a difficult morning for me.

Your paragraph will probably be organized in time order, describing the events that occurred from beginning to end. You can help your reader understand the sequence of events if you use time transitions such as *first, next, then, later,* and *finally.*

If you prefer, write instead about a memory of another relative.

Writing Assignment

2 | A Disagreeable Characteristic

Even the most saintly person has one or more unpleasant traits. Write a paragraph about a particularly disagreeable characteristic of someone you know. Your topic sentence will be a general statement about that person and the quality you've chosen to write about. For example, if you decide to write about your own extreme impatience, your topic sentence might be the following.

> When I let my impatience get out of hand, I often damage my relationships with others.

A paragraph with this topic sentence might list two or three experiences supporting that main idea. Here are two other examples of topic sentences for this paper:

> Our neighbor Mr. Nagle is a cruel person.
>
> While my minister is basically a kind man, he much prefers hearing his own voice to anyone else's.

Writing Assignment

3 | A Special Goal

We all have goals, long-term and short-term. Write a paragraph about one of your important goals. It might be something you hope to achieve over the next few months or the next few years.

Perhaps you plan to overcome a bad habit or get a better job. Begin your paragraph with a topic sentence that clearly states the goal and when you expect to reach it, such as "I hope to have quit smoking by the end of this year" or "After I graduate, I hope to get a nursing job at a local hospital." Then go on to list and explain two or three reasons you wish to reach the goal. To generate some reasons, make a list, and then choose the three you feel are the strongest. Save the most important reason for last.

In Praise of Something

We all are fans of something that we feel greatly enriches our life, such as a pet, basketball, or chocolate. Write a paragraph in which your supporting details show the benefits or virtues of something you adore. For instance, you could write about the advantages of having a dog around the house. Use whatever prewriting strategy you choose to help you come up with more benefits or virtues than you need. Then choose two or three you feel you can explain in colorful detail.

One benefit you might list, for instance, is that a dog makes one feel loved. You could illustrate this benefit by describing an experience such as the following:

> A week ago, I spilled hot coffee on a customer's lap. He was not amused. After the customer left—without leaving a tip, of course—the manager walked past me and said quietly, "Strike one!" When I got home that day and collapsed on a chair, my friend Goldie, a cocker spaniel, hopped onto my lap and licked my face with his broad, warm tongue. I could feel the knot in my stomach loosening.

Here's a sample scratch outline for this assignment.

Topic sentence: Having a dog around the house is one of life's rich pleasures.

(1) A dog is entertaining.

(2) A dog brings out the best in a person.

(3) A dog makes a person feel loved.

A Popular Saying

It seems there are sayings to cover every type of experience, from our sleeping habits ("Early to bed, early to rise, makes a man healthy, wealthy, and wise") to our expectations ("Hope for the best but expect the worst"). Write a paragraph in which you demonstrate through an experience you have had that a particular saying is either true or false.

Begin your paragraph with a clear statement supporting or opposing the saying, such as "When I painted my house last summer, I learned the truth of the saying 'Haste makes waste'" or "When it comes to escaping a fire, the saying 'Haste makes waste' doesn't apply." Then go on to describe your experience in vivid detail. To help your reader follow the sequence of events involved, use a few time transitions (*before, then, during, now,* and so on). Below are some other popular sayings you might wish to consider using in your paper—or use some other popular saying.

> Here today, gone tomorrow.
>
> If you don't help yourself, nobody will.
>
> A penny saved is a penny earned.
>
> The early bird catches the worm.
>
> Curiosity killed the cat.
>
> You get what you pay for.
>
> A rolling stone gathers no moss.
>
> Don't count your chickens before they're hatched.
>
> An ounce of prevention is worth a pound of cure.
>
> A journey of a thousand miles must begin with a single step.
>
> Whatever can go wrong will go wrong.
>
> Don't judge someone until you've walked a mile in his shoes.

Writing Assignment

6 Writing on the Job

Imagine that at the place where you work, one employee has just quit, creating a new job opening. Since you have been working there for a while, your boss has asked you to write a description of the position. That description, a detailed definition of the job, will be sent to employment agencies. These agencies will be responsible for interviewing candidates. Choose any position you know about, and write a paragraph defining it. First state the purpose of the job, and then list its duties and responsibilities. Finally, describe the qualifications for the position. Below is a sample topic sentence for this assignment.

> Purchasing-department secretary is a position in which someone provides a variety of services to the purchasing-department managers.

In a paragraph with the topic sentence above, the writer would go on to list and explain the various services the secretary must provide.

Looking Back

Occasionally we call someone a "Monday-morning quarterback." By this we mean that it's easy to say what should have been done after an event (or game) is over. But while we're in the midst of our daily lives, it's hard to know which is the right decision to make or what is the right course of action. We've all looked back and thought, "I wish I'd done . . ." or "I wish I'd said . . ."

Think back to a year or two ago. What is the best advice someone could have given you then? Freewrite for ten minutes or so about how your life might have changed if you have been given that advice. Then write a paragraph that begins with a topic sentence something like this: "I wish someone had told me a year ago to cut back a little on my work hours while I was in school."

An Embarrassing Moment

8

In a paragraph, tell about a time you felt ashamed or embarrassed. Provide details that show clearly what happened. Explain what you and the other people involved said and did. Also explain how you felt and why you were so uncomfortable.

For example, you might begin with a sentence like this:

I was deeply ashamed when I was caught cheating on a spelling test in fifth grade.

The paragraph could continue by telling how the writer cheated and how he was caught; how the teacher and other students looked, spoke, and acted; what the writer did when he was caught; and what emotions and thoughts the writer experienced throughout the incident.

Below are some other topic sentence possibilities. Develop one of them or a variation on one of them. Feel free as well to come up with and write about an entirely different idea.

- My first real date was the occasion of an embarrassing moment in my life.
- To this day, I wince when I think of an incident that happened to me at a family party.
- An event that occurred in high school makes my cheeks glow hot and red even today.

Writing Assignment

9 | A Personal Treasure

Imagine your apartment or house is burning down. After making sure all the people in your building are safe, you realize you have time to rescue *just one* of your possessions. What would it be? In a paragraph, discuss the item and why it has such importance to you. Be sure you provide supporting details that explain why you value this object. Here are some possible topic sentences for this paragraph:

- If I could save just one of my possessions, it would be my journal.
- My grandmother's wedding ring is the most important object I own.
- Nothing is more valuable to me than my giant photo album.

Writing Assignment

10 | Reaching a Goal

Write a paragraph telling of something you wanted very badly, but were afraid you would not be able to attain. Describe the struggles you had to overcome to get to your goal. How did you finally reach it? Include some details that communicate how strongly you wanted the goal and how difficult it was to reach. In thinking about a topic for this paper, you may wish to consider the following common goals:

a certain job

enough money for college

a passing grade

quitting smoking or drugs

overcoming an illness

Once you have decided on the goal you wish to write about, use it to write a topic sentence such as any of the following:

- After several false starts, I finally quite smoking.
- After gradually changing my attitude about school, I have begun to get good grades.
- Following a careful budget, I was finally able to afford to . . .

2

Sentence Skills

Introduction

Part Two explains the basic skills needed to write clear, error-free sentences. While the skills are presented within five traditional categories (sentences; verbs, pronouns, and agreement; modifiers and parallelism; punctuation and mechanics; word use), each section is self-contained so that you can go directly to the skills you need to work on. Note, however, that you may find it helpful to cover Chapter 4, "Subjects and Verbs," before turning to other skills. Typically, the main features of a skill are presented on the first pages of a section; secondary points are developed later. Numerous activities are provided so that you can practice skills enough to make them habits. The activities are varied and range from underlining answers to writing complete sentences involving the skill in question. One or more review tests at the end of each section offer additional practice activities. Mastery tests conclude each chapter, allowing you to immediately test your understanding of each skill.

Look at the photo above and imagine you have been asked to write a paper about your plans after graduation. Where do you see yourself? What would you like to accomplish? Using any of the prewriting techniques (freewriting, questioning, clustering, making a list), spend time prewriting for a paper on this topic.

Subjects and Verbs

Introductory Activity

Understanding subjects and verbs is a big step toward mastering many sentence skills. As a speaker of English, you already have an instinctive feel **for these basic building blocks of English sentences.** See if you can insert an appropriate word in each space below. The answer will be a subject.

1. The _____ will soon be over.

2. _____ cannot be trusted.

3. A strange _____ appeared in my backyard.

4. _____ is one of my favorite activities.

Now insert an appropriate word in the following spaces. Each answer will be a verb.

5. The prisoner _____ at the judge.

6. My sister _____ much harder than I do.

7. The players _____ in the locker room.

8. Rob and Marilyn _____ with the teacher.

Finally, insert appropriate words in the following spaces. Each answer will be a subject in the first space and a verb in the second.

9. The _____ almost _____ out of the tree.

10. Many _____ today _____ sex and violence.

11. The _____ carefully _____ the patient.

12. A _____ quickly _____ the ball.

The basic building blocks of English sentences are subjects and verbs. Understanding them is an important first step toward mastering a number of sentence skills.

Every sentence has a subject and a verb. Who or what the sentence speaks about is called the *subject;* what the sentence says about the subject is called the *verb.* In the following sentences, the subject is underlined once and the verb twice:

1. People gossip.

2. The truck belched fumes.

3. He waved at me.

4. Alaska contains the largest wilderness area in the United States.

5. That woman is a millionaire.

6. The pants feel itchy.

A Simple Way to Find a Subject

To find a subject, ask *who* or *what* the sentence is about. As shown below, your answer is the subject.

Who is the first sentence about? People

What is the second sentence about? The truck

Who is the third sentence about? He

What is the fourth sentence about? Alaska

Who is the fifth sentence about? That woman

What is the sixth sentence about? The pants

It helps to remember that the subject of a sentence is always a *noun* (any person, place, or thing) or a pronoun. A *pronoun* is simply a word like *he, she, it, you,* or *they* used in place of a noun. In the preceding sentences, the subjects are persons (*People, He, woman*), a place (*Alaska*), and things (*truck, pants*). And note that one pronoun (*He*) is used as a subject.

A Simple Way to Find a Verb

To find a verb, ask what the sentence *says* about the subject. As shown below, your answer is the verb.

What does the first sentence *say about* people? They gossip.

What does the second sentence *say about* the truck? It belched (fumes).

What does the third sentence *say about* him? He waved (at me).

What does the fourth sentence *say about* Alaska? It contains (the largest wilderness area in the United States).

What does the fifth sentence *say about* that woman? She is (a millionaire).

What does the sixth sentence *say about* the pants? They feel (itchy).

A second way to find the verb is to put *I, you, he, she, it,* or *they* in front of the word you think is a verb. If the result makes sense, you have a verb. For example, you could put *they* in front of *gossip* in the first sentence above, with the result, *they gossip,* making sense. Therefore, you know that *gossip* is a verb. You could use the same test with the other verbs as well.

Finally, it helps to remember that most verbs show action. In "People gossip," the action is gossiping. In "The truck belched fumes," the action is belching. In "He waved at me," the action is waving. In "Alaska contains the largest wilderness area in the United States," the action is containing.

Certain other verbs, known as *linking verbs,* do not show action. They do, however, give information about the subject of the sentence. In "That woman is a millionaire," the linking verb *is* tells us that the woman is a millionaire. In "The pants feel itchy," the linking verb *feel* gives us the information that the pants are itchy.

Practice

1

In each of the following sentences, draw one line under the subject and two lines under the verb.

To find the subject, ask *who* or *what* the sentence is about. Then, to find the verb, ask what the sentence *says about* the subject.

1. I ate an entire pizza by myself.

2. Alligators swim in that lake.

3. April failed the test.

4. The television movie ended suddenly.

5. Keiko borrowed change for the pay telephone.

6. The children stared in wide-eyed wonderment at the Thanksgiving Day floats.

7. An old newspaper tumbled down the dirty street.

8. Lola starts every morning with a series of yoga exercises.

9. My part-time job limits my study time.

10. The windstorm blew over the storage shed in the backyard.

Practice 2

Follow the directions given for Practice 1. Note that all of the verbs here are linking verbs.

1. My sister is a terrible speller.

2. Potato chips are Ramon's favorite snack.

3. The defendant appeared very nervous on the witness stand.

4. Art became a father at the age of twenty.

5. The ride going somewhere always seems longer than the ride coming back.

6. That apartment building was an abandoned factory two years ago.

7. My first two weeks on the sales job were the worst of my life.

8. The plastic banana split and Styrofoam birthday cake in the bakery window look like real desserts.

9. Jane always feels energized after a cup of coffee.

10. Rooms with white walls seem larger than those with dark-colored walls.

Practice 3

Follow the directions given for Practice 1.

1. That clock runs about five minutes fast.

2. The new player on the team is much too sure of himself.

3. Late-afternoon shoppers filled the aisles of the supermarket.

4. Garbage trucks rumbled down my street on their way to the dump.

5. The children drew pictures on the steamed window.

6. The picture fell suddenly to the floor.

7. Chipmunks live in the woodpile behind my house.

8. Our loud uncle monopolized the conversation at the dinner table.

9. The tomatoes were soft to the touch.

10. The insurance company canceled my policy because of a speeding ticket.

www.mhhe.com/langan

More about Subjects and Verbs

Distinguishing Subjects from Prepositional Phrases

The subject of a sentence never appears within a prepositional phrase. A *prepositional phrase* is simply a group of words beginning with a preposition and ending with the answer to the question *what, when,* or *where.* Here is a list of common prepositions.

Common Prepositions				
about	before	by	inside	over
above	behind	during	into	through
across	below	except	of	to
among	beneath	for	off	toward
around	beside	from	on	under
at	between	in	onto	with

When you are looking for the subject of a sentence, it is helpful to cross out prepositional phrases.

~~In the middle of the night,~~ we heard footsteps ~~on the roof~~.

The magazines ~~on the table~~ belong ~~in the garage~~.

~~Before the opening kickoff,~~ a brass band marched ~~onto the field~~.

The hardware store ~~across the street~~ went ~~out of business~~.

~~In spite of our advice,~~ Sally quit her job ~~at Burger King~~.

Practice

4

Cross out prepositional phrases. Then draw a single line under subjects and a double line under verbs.

1. For that course, you need three different books.

2. The key to the front door slipped from my hand into a puddle.

3. The checkout lines at the supermarket moved very slowly.

4. With his son, Jamal walked to the playground.

5. No quarrel between good friends lasts for a very long time.

6. In one weekend, Martha planted a large vegetable garden in her backyard.

7. Either of my brothers is a reliable worker.

8. The drawer of the bureau sticks on rainy days.

9. During the movie, several people walked out in protest.

10. At a single sitting, my brother reads five or more comic books.

Verbs of More Than One Word

Many verbs consist of more than one word. Here, for example, are some of the many forms of the verb *help:*

Some Forms of the Verb *Help*

helps	should have been helping	will have helped
helping	can help	would have been helped
is helping	would have been helping	has been helped
was helping	will be helping	had been helped
may help	had been helping	must have helped
should help	helped	having helped
will help	have helped	should have been helped
does help	has helped	had helped

Below are sentences that contain verbs of more than one word:

Yolanda is working overtime this week.

Another book has been written about the Kennedy family.

We should have stopped for gas at the last station.

The game has just been canceled.

> ### TIPS
>
> 1. Words like *not, just, never, only,* and *always* are not part of the verb, although they may appear within the verb.
>
>   Yolanda is not working overtime next week.
>
>   The boys should just not have stayed out so late.
>
>   The game has always been played regardless of the weather.
>
> 2. No verb preceded by *to* is ever the verb of a sentence.
>
>   Sue wants to go with us.
>
>   The newly married couple decided to rent a house for a year.
>
>   The store needs extra people to help out at Christmas.
>
> 3. No *-ing* word by itself is ever the verb of a sentence. (It may be part of the verb, but it must have a helping verb in front of it.)
>
>   We planning the trip for months. (This is not a sentence, because the verb is not complete.)
>
>   We were planning the trip for months. (This is a complete sentence.)

Practice 5

Draw a single line under subjects and a double line under verbs. Be sure to include all parts of the verb.

1. He has been sleeping all day.

2. The wood foundations of the shed were attacked by termites.

3. I have not washed my car for several months.

4. The instructor had not warned us about the quiz.

5. The bus will be leaving shortly.

6. You should not try to pet that temperamental hamster.

7. They have just been married by a justice of the peace.

8. He could make a living with his wood carvings.

9. Kim has decided to ask her boss for a raise.

10. The employees should have warned us about the wet floor.

Compound Subjects and Verbs

A sentence may have more than one verb:

> The dancer stumbled and fell.

> Lola washed her hair, blew it dry, and parted it in the middle.

A sentence may have more than one subject:

> Cats and dogs are sometimes the best of friends.

> The striking workers and their bosses could not come to an agreement.

A sentence may have several subjects and several verbs:

> Holly and I read the book and reported on it to the class.

> Pete, Nick, and Eric caught the fish in the morning, cleaned them in the afternoon, and ate them that night.

Draw a single line under subjects and a double line under verbs. Be sure to mark *all* the subjects and verbs.

Practice

6

1. The hypnotist locked his assistant in a box and sawed her in half.

2. Trina began her paper at 7:30 and finished it at midnight.

3. On the shipping pier, the Nissans, Toyotas, and Hondas glittered in the sun.

4. Tony added the column of figures three times and got three different totals.

5. The car sputtered, stalled, and then started again.

6. Whiteflies, mites, and aphids infected my houseplants.

7. Ruth disconnected the computers and carried them to her car.

8. We walked over to the corner deli and bought extra cheese for the party.

9. At the new shopping mall, Tony and Lola looked in windows for two hours and then bought one pair of socks.

10. My aunt and uncle married in their twenties, divorced in their thirties, and then remarried in their forties.

Review Test   1

Draw one line under the subjects and two lines under the verbs. As necessary, cross out prepositional phrases to help find subjects. Underline all the parts of a verb. And remember that you may find more than one subject and verb in a sentence.

1. I had not heard about the cancellation of the class.

2. James should have gotten an estimate from the plumber.

3. The family played badminton and volleyball at the picnic.

4. A solution to the problem popped suddenly into my head.

5. My roommate and I will need to study all night for the test.

6. Chang has not been eating in the cafeteria this semester.

7. The white moon hung above the castle like a grinning skull.

8. Len and Marie drove all night and arrived at their vacation cottage early Saturday morning.

9. The game has been postponed because of bad weather and will be rescheduled for later in the season.

10. The sun reflected sharply off the lake and forced me to wear sunglasses.

Review Test   2

Follow the directions given for Review Test 1.

1. The doctors were speaking gently to the parents of the little girl.

2. A rumor has been spreading about the possible closing of the plant.

3. Diesel trucks with heavy exhaust fumes should be banned from the road.

4. The dental assistant should have warned me about the pain.

5. With their fingers, the children started to draw pictures on the steamed window.

6. Three buildings down the street from my house have been demolished.

7. Rats, squirrels, and bats lived in the attic of the abandoned house.

8. Jack and Bob will be anchoring the long-distance team in the track meet.

9. Reluctantly, I crawled from my bed and stumbled to the bathroom.

10. Tiddlywinks, pickup sticks, and hearts were our favorite childhood games.

SCORE
Number Correct

_____ x 10

_____ %

NAME: _____

DATE: _____

Subjects and Verbs

Draw one line under subjects and two lines under verbs. Cross out prepositional phrases as necessary to help find subjects. (Be sure to underline all the parts of a verb. Also, remember that you may find more than one subject and one verb in a sentence.)

1. My son pours chocolate milk on his cereal.

2. A solution to the problem popped suddenly into my head.

3. The salad and potatoes fed only half the guests.

4. That man on the corner may ask you for a quarter.

5. The fallen power line jumped and sparked on the street.

6. Lola likes to walk barefoot across the campus.

7. Nick and Fran sang together and banged on the piano.

8. The flashing lights of the police car appeared unexpectedly in my rearview mirror.

9. Juan often plays CDs but almost never watches television.

10. We sat by a large rock, munched peanuts, and talked for hours.

NAME: _____

DATE: _____

Subjects and Verbs

Draw one line under subjects and two lines under verbs. Cross out prepositional phrases as necessary to help find subjects. (Be sure to underline all the parts of a verb. Also, remember that you may find more than one subject and one verb in a sentence.)

1. I may hitchhike to the Mardi Gras this year.

2. Those tulips make my eyes itch.

3. Layla will be studying all day for the test.

4. Strange behavior in our house is the norm at all hours.

5. The prices of jewelry items in that specialty store have been reduced.

6. Jamon and Yvonne refuse to drive their car at-night.

7. I walked out to the garage last night and ran into a rug on the clothesline.

8. The rising tide will start to wash away that sand castle.

9. Jessica buys clothing impulsively, sends off for lots of mail order items, and in general quickly spends her money.

10. The girls paddled their canoe across the lake and visited some boys at the camp on the other side.

NAME: _____

DATE: _____

Subjects and Verbs   MASTERY TEST 3

Draw one line under subjects and two lines under verbs. Cross out prepositional phrases as necessary to help find subjects. (Be sure to underline all the parts of a verb. Also, remember that you may find more than one subject and one verb in a sentence.)

1. Lola believes in extrasensory perception.

2. The drawer of the bureau sticks on rainy days.

3. The little boy squirmed impatiently in his father's arms.

4. The window fan made a clanking sound and kept them awake at night.

5. The shrubs are starting to grow too close to the side of the house.

6. Three members of the basketball team have been suspended from school.

7. Jerry began to study seriously before final exams.

8. The newspaper boy shouted out the headlines and soon sold all his papers.

9. They won a lifetime supply of dish detergent on the game show but do not have any room for it in their house.

10. The shattered glass, cracked foundations, and fallen signs throughout the city resulted from earthquake tremors.

NAME: _____

DATE: _____

Subjects and Verbs

Draw one line under subjects and two lines under verbs. Cross out prepositional phrases as necessary to help find subjects. (Be sure to underline all the parts of a verb. Also, remember that you may find more than one subject and one verb in a sentence.)

1. The nail under the rug barely missed my toe.

2. I have studied over eight hours for my biology test.

3. Tony and Lola just bought matching sweatshirts.

4. The game has been postponed because of bad weather.

5. Our families played badminton and volleyball at the picnic.

6. Behind all that mud you will see my daughter's face.

7. The beginning of that movie should not be missed.

8. Fred began to exercise seriously after his heart attack.

9. Hakim has been thinking about the job offer but has not made a decision yet.

10. The people on the tour bus dozed, read magazines, talked to each other, or snapped pictures.

Fragments

Introductory Activity

Every sentence must have a subject and a verb and must express a complete thought. A word group that lacks a subject or a verb and that does not express a complete thought is a *fragment*.

   Listed below are a number of fragments and sentences. See if you can complete the statement that explains each fragment.

1. Teapots.   *Fragment*

    Teapots whistled.   *Sentence*

    "Teapots" is a fragment because, while it has a subject (*Teapots*), it lacks

    a _____ (*whistled*) and so does not express a complete thought.

2. Instructs.   *Fragment*

    Quincy instructs.   *Sentence*

    "Instructs" is a fragment because, while it has a verb (*Instructs*), it lacks

    a _____ (*Quincy*) and does not express a complete thought.

3. Discussing homework in class.   *Fragment*

    Ellie was discussing homework in class.   *Sentence*

    "Discussing homework in class" is a fragment because it lacks a

    _____ (*Ellie*) and also part of the _____ (*was*). As a result,

    it does not express a complete thought.

continued

4. When my mother began lecturing me.   *Fragment*

When my mother began lecturing me, I rolled my eyes.   *Sentence*

"When my mother began lecturing me" is a fragment because we want to know *what happened when* the mother began lecturing. The word group does not follow through and express a complete _____.

Answers are on page 559.

What Fragments Are

Every sentence must have a subject and a verb and must express a complete thought. A word group that lacks a subject or a verb and does not express a complete thought is a *fragment*. Following are the most common types of fragments that people write:

1. Dependent-word fragments
2. *-ing* and *to* fragments
3. Added-detail fragments
4. Missing-subject fragments

Once you understand the specific kind or kinds of fragments that you might write, you should be able to eliminate them from your writing. The following pages explain all four types of fragments.

Dependent-Word Fragments

Some word groups that begin with a dependent word are fragments. Here is a list of common dependent words:

Common Dependent Words	
after	unless
although, though	until
as	what, whatever
because	when, whenever
before	where, wherever
even though	whether
how	which, whichever
if, even if	while
in order that	who
since	whose
that, so that	

Whenever you start a sentence with one of these dependent words, you must be careful that a dependent-word fragment does not result. The word group beginning with the dependent word *after* in the selection below is a fragment.

> After I stopped drinking coffee. I began sleeping better at night.

A *dependent statement*—one starting with a dependent word like *after*—cannot stand alone. It depends on another statement to complete the thought. "After I stopped drinking coffee" is a dependent statement. It leaves us hanging. We expect in the same sentence to find out *what happened after* the writer stopped drinking coffee. When a writer does not follow through and complete a thought, a fragment results. To correct the fragment, follow through and complete the thought:

> After I stopped drinking coffee, I began sleeping better at night.

Remember, then, that *dependent statements by themselves* are fragments. They must be attached to a statement that makes sense standing alone.* Here are two other examples of dependent-word fragments.

> Brian sat nervously in the dental clinic. While waiting to have his wisdom tooth pulled.

> Maria decided to throw away the boxes. That had accumulated for years in the basement.

"While waiting to have his wisdom tooth pulled" is a fragment; it does not make sense standing by itself. We want to know in the same statement *what Brian did* while waiting to have his tooth pulled. The writer must complete the thought. Likewise, "That had accumulated for years in the basement" is not in itself a complete thought. We want to know in the same statement what *that* refers to.

How to | Correct Dependent-Word Fragments

In most cases, you can correct a dependent-word fragment by attaching it to the sentence that comes after it or to the sentence that comes before it:

> After I stopped drinking coffee, I began sleeping better at night. (The fragment has been attached to the sentence that comes after it.)

> Brian sat nervously in the dental clinic while waiting to have his wisdom tooth pulled. (The fragment has been attached to the sentence that comes before it.)

continued

---

*Some instructors refer to a dependent-word fragment as a *dependent clause*. A *clause* is simply a group of words having a subject and a verb. A clause may be *independent* (expressing a complete thought and able to stand alone) or *dependent* (not expressing a complete thought and not able to stand alone). A dependent clause by itself is a fragment. It can be corrected simply by adding an independent clause.

Maria decided to throw away the boxes that had accumulated for years in the basement. (The fragment has been attached to the sentence that comes before it.)

Another way of correcting a dependent-word fragment is to eliminate the dependent word and make a new sentence:

I stopped drinking coffee.

He was waiting to have his wisdom tooth pulled.

They had accumulated for years in the basement.

Do not use the second method of correction too frequently, however, for it may cut down on interest and variety in your writing style.

TIPS

1. Use a comma if a dependent-word group comes at the *beginning* of a sentence (see also page 357):

After I stopped drinking coffee, I began sleeping better at night.

However, do not generally use a comma if the dependent-word group comes at the end of a sentence:

Brian sat nervously in the dental clinic while waiting to have his wisdom tooth pulled.

Maria decided to throw away the boxes that had accumulated for years in the basement.

2. Sometimes the dependent words *who, that, which,* or *where* appear not at the very start but *near* the start of a word group. A fragment often results.

Today I visited Hilda Cooper. A friend who is in the hospital.

"A friend who is in the hospital" is not in itself a complete thought. We want to know in the same statement *who* the friend is. The fragment can be corrected by attaching it to the sentence that comes before it:

Today I visited Hilda Cooper, a friend who is in the hospital.

(Here a comma is used to set off "a friend who is in the hospital," which is extra material placed at the end of the sentence.)

Practice

1

Turn each of the dependent-word groups into a sentence by adding a complete thought. Put a comma after the dependent-word group if a dependent word starts the sentence.

SECTION 1: SENTENCES

EXAMPLES

After I got out of high school

After I got out of high school, I spent a year traveling.

The watch that I got fixed

The watch that I got fixed has just stopped working again.

1. After I finished work on Friday

2. Because the class was canceled

3. When my car stalled on the highway

4. The supermarket that I went to

5. Before I left the house

Underline the dependent-word fragment (or fragments) in each item. Then correct each fragment by attaching it to the sentence that comes before or the sentence that comes after—whichever sounds more natural. Put a comma after the dependent-word group if it starts the sentence.

Practice

2

1. Although the air conditioner was working. I still felt warm in the room. I wondered if I had a fever.

2. When Tony got into his car this morning. He discovered that he had left the car windows open. The seats and rug were soaked. Since it had rained overnight.

   _____

   _____

   _____

3. After cutting fish at the restaurant all day. Jenny smelled like a cat food factory. She couldn't wait to take a hot, perfumed bath.

   _____

   _____

   _____

4. Franco raked out the soggy leaves. That were at the bottom of the cement fishpond. When two bullfrogs jumped out at him. He dropped the rake and ran.

   _____

   _____

   _____

5. Because he had eaten and drunk too much. He had to leave the party early. His stomach was like a volcano. That was ready to erupt.

   _____

   _____

   _____

-*ing* and *to* Fragments

When a word ending in -*ing* or the word *to* appears at or near the start of a word group, a fragment may result. Such fragments often lack a subject and part of the verb.

Underline the word groups in the examples below that contain -*ing* words. Each is an -*ing* fragment.

Example 1

I spent all day in the employment office. Trying to find a job that suited me. The prospects looked bleak.

Example 2

Lola surprised Tony on the nature hike. Picking blobs of resin off pine trees. Then she chewed them like bubble gum.

Example 3

Mel took an aisle seat on the bus. His reason being that he had more legroom.

People sometimes write *-ing* fragments because they think the subject in one sentence will work for the next word group as well. In Example 1, they might think the subject *I* in the opening sentence will also serve as the subject for "Trying to find a job that suited me." But the subject must actually be *in* the sentence.

How to | Correct *-ing* Fragments

1. Attach the fragment to the sentence that comes before it or to the sentence that comes after it, whichever makes sense. Example 1 could read, "I spent all day in the employment office, trying to find a job that suited me." (Note that here a comma is used to set off "trying to find a job that suited me," which is extra material placed at the end of the sentence.)

2. Add a subject and change the *-ing* verb part to the correct form of the verb. Example 2 could read, "She picked blobs of resin off pine trees."

3. Change *being* to the correct form of the verb *be (am, are, is, was, were)*. Example 3 could read, "His reason was that he had more legroom."

How to | Correct *to* Fragments

As noted on the previous page, when *to* appears at or near the start of a word group, a fragment sometimes results.

> To remind people of their selfishness. Otis leaves handwritten notes on cars that take up two parking spaces.

The first word group in the example above is a *to* fragment. It can be corrected by adding it to the sentence that comes after it.

> To remind people of their selfishness, Otis leaves handwritten notes on cars that take up two parking spaces.

(Note that here a comma is used to set off "To remind people of their selfishness," which is introductory material in the sentence.)

Practice

3

Underline the *-ing* fragment in each of the following selections. Then make the fragment a sentence by rewriting it, using the method described in parentheses.

EXAMPLE

The dog eyed me with suspicion. <u>Not knowing whether its master was at home.</u> I hesitated to open the gate.

(Add the fragment to the sentence that comes after it.)

Not knowing whether its master was at home, I hesitated to open the gate.

_____

1. Eli lay in bed after the alarm rang. Wishing that he had $100,000. Then he would not have to go to work.
   (Add the fragment to the preceding sentence.)

   _____

   _____

2. Investigating the strange, mournful cries in his neighbor's yard. George found a puppy tangled in its leash.
   (Add the fragment to the sentence that comes after it.)

   _____

   _____

3. I had to drive to the most remote parking lot to get a space. As a result, being late for class.
   (Add the subject *I* and change *being* to the correct form of the verb *was*.)

   _____

   _____

Practice

4

Underline the *-ing* or *to* fragment in each item. Then rewrite the item correctly, using one of the methods of correction described on page 85.

1. Glistening with dew. The gigantic web hung between the branches of the tree. The spider waited patiently for a visitor.

   _____

   _____

   _____

2. Kevin loves his new puppy. Claiming that the little dog in his best friend.

   _____

   _____

3. Noah picked through the box of chocolates. Removing the kinds he didn't like. He saved these for his wife and ate the rest.

_____

_____

4. The grass I was walking on suddenly became squishy. Having hiked into a marsh of some kind.

_____

_____

_____

5. Steve drove quickly to the bank. To cash his paycheck. Otherwise, he would have had no money for the weekend.

_____

_____

_____

Added-Detail Fragments

Added-detail fragments lack a subject and a verb. They often begin with one of the following words or phrases.

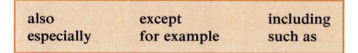

also	**except**	**including**
especially	**for example**	**such as**

See if you can underline the one added-detail fragment in each of these examples:

Example 1

Tony has trouble accepting criticism. Except from Lola. She has a knack for tact.

Example 2

My apartment has its drawbacks. For example, no hot water in the morning.

Example 3

I had many jobs while in school. Among them, busboy, painter, and security guard.

People often write added-detail fragments for much the same reason they write *-ing* fragments. They think the subject and verb in one sentence will serve for the next word group as well. But the subject and verb must be in *each* word group.

> **How to** Correct Added-Detail Fragments
>
> **1.** Attach the fragment to the complete thought that precedes it. Example 1 could read, "Tony has trouble accepting criticism, except from Lola." (Note that here a comma is used to set off "except from Lola," which is extra material placed at the end of the sentence.)
>
> **2.** Add a subject and a verb to the fragment to make it a complete sentence. Example 2 could read, "My apartment has its drawbacks. For example, there is no hot water in the morning."
>
> **3.** Change words as necessary to make the fragment part of the preceding sentence. Example 3 could read, "Among the many jobs I had while in school were busboy, painter, and security guard."

Practice

5

Underline the fragment in each selection below. Then make it a sentence by rewriting it, using the method described in parentheses.

EXAMPLE

My husband and I share the household chores. <u>Including meals.</u> I do the cooking and he does the eating.
(Add the fragment to the preceding sentence.)

My husband and I share the household chores, including meals.

1. Hakeem is very accident-prone. For example, managing to cut his hand while crumbling a bar of shredded wheat.
(Correct the fragment by adding the subject *he* and changing *managing* to *managed.*)

_____

_____

2. Tina's job in the customer service department depressed her. All day, people complained. About missing parts, rude salespeople, and errors on bills.
(Add the fragment to the preceding sentence.)

_____

_____

3. My mother is always giving me household hints. For example, using club
    soda on stains. Unfortunately, I never remember them.
    (Correct the fragment by adding the subject and verb *she suggests.*)

    _____

    _____

Underline the added-detail fragment in each selection. Then rewrite that part of
the selection needed to correct the fragment. Use one of the three methods of correction described on page 88.

Practice

6

1. My little boy is constantly into mischief. Such as tearing the labels off all
    the cans in the cupboard.

    _____

    _____

2. The old house was filled with expensive woodwork. For example, a hand-
    carved mantel and a mahogany banister.

    _____

    _____

3. Andy used to have many bad eating habits. For instance, chewing with his
    mouth open.

    _____

    _____

4. I put potatoes in the oven without first punching holes in them. A half hour
    later, there were several explosions. With potatoes splattering all over the
    walls of the oven.

    _____

    _____

5. Janet looked forward to seeing former classmates at the high school reunion.
    Including the football player she had had a wild crush on. She wondered if
    he had grown fat and bald.

    _____

    _____

Missing-Subject Fragments

In each example below, underline the word group in which the subject is missing.

Example 1

One example of my father's generosity is that he visits sick friends in the hospital. And takes along get-well cards with a few dollars folded in them.

Example 2

The weight lifter grunted as he heaved the barbells into the air. Then, with a loud groan, dropped them.

People write missing-subject fragments because they think the subject in one sentence will apply to the next word group as well. But the subject, as well as the verb, must be in *each* word group to make it a sentence.

How to **Correct Missing-Subject Fragments**

1. Attach the fragment to the preceding sentence. Example 1 could read, "One illustration of my father's generosity is that he visits sick friends in the hospital and takes along get-well cards with a few dollars folded in them."

2. Add a subject (which can often be a pronoun standing for the subject in the preceding sentence). Example 2 could read, "Then, with a loud groan, he dropped them."

Practice

7

Underline the missing-subject fragment in each selection. Then rewrite that part of the selection needed to correct the fragment. Use one of the two methods of correction described above.

1. Fred went to the refrigerator to get milk for his breakfast cereal. And discovered about one tablespoon of milk left in the carton.

   _____

   _____

2. At the laundromat, I loaded the dryer with wet clothes. Then noticed the "Out of order" sign taped over the coin slot.

   _____

   _____

3. Our neighborhood's most eligible bachelor got married this weekend. But did not invite us to the wedding. We all wondered what the bride was like.

   _____

   _____

4. Larry's father could not accept his son's lifestyle. Also, was constantly criticizing Larry's choice of friends.

   _____

   _____

5. Wanda stared at the blank page in desperation. And decided that the first sentence of a paper is always the hardest to write.

   _____

   _____

A REVIEW

How to Check for Fragments

1. Read your paper aloud from the *last* sentence to the *first*. You will be better able to see and hear whether each word group you read is a complete thought.

2. If you think any word group is a fragment, ask yourself, Does this contain a subject and a verb and express a complete thought?

3. More specifically, be on the lookout for the most common fragments.

   • Dependent-word fragments (starting with words like *after, because, since, when,* and *before*)

   • *-ing* and *to* fragments (*-ing* or *to* at or near the start of a word group)

   • Added-detail fragments (starting with words like *for example, such as, also,* and *especially*)

   • Missing-subject fragments (a verb is present but not the subject)

www.mhhe.com/langan

Collaborative Activity

Editing and Rewriting

Working with a partner, read the short paragraph below and underline the five fragments. Then correct the fragments. Feel free to discuss the rewrite quietly with your partner and refer back to the chapter when necessary.

[1]I am only thirty, but a trip to the movies recently made me realize that my youth is definitely past. [2]The science-fiction movie had attracted a large audience of younger kids and teenagers. [3]Before the movie began. [4]Groups of kids ran up and down the aisles, laughing, giggling, and spilling popcorn. [5]I was annoyed with them. [6]But thought, "At one time I was doing the same thing. [7]Now I'm acting like one of the adults." [8]The thought was a little depressing, for I remembered how much fun it was not to care what the adults thought. [9]Soon after the movie began, a group of teenagers walked in and sat in the first row. [10]During the movie, they vied with each other. [11]To see who could make the loudest comment. [12]Or the most embarrassing noise. [13]Some of the adults in the theater complained to the usher, but I had a guilty memory about doing the same thing myself a few times. [14]In addition, a teenage couple was sitting in front of me. [15]Occasionally, these two held hands or the boy put his arm around the girl. [16]A few times, they sneaked a kiss. [17]Realizing that my wife and I were long past this kind of behavior in the movies. [18]I again felt like an old man.

Collaborative Activity

Creating Sentences

Working with a partner, make up your own short fragments test as directed. Write one or more of your sentences about the photo shown here.

1. Write a dependent-word fragment in the space below. Then correct the fragment by making it into a complete sentence. You may want to begin your fragment with the word *before, after, when, because,* or *if*.

    Fragment _____

    Sentence _____

    _____

2. Write a fragment that begins with a word that has an *-ing* ending in the space below. Then correct the fragment by making it into a complete sentence. You may want to begin your fragment with the word *laughing, walking, shopping,* or *talking*.

    Fragment _____

    Sentence _____

    _____

3. Write an added-detail fragment in the space below. Then correct the fragment by making it into a complete sentence. You may want to begin your fragment with the word *also, especially, except,* or *including*.

    Fragment _____

    Sentence _____

    _____

Reflective Activity

1. Look at the paragraph about going to the movies that you revised. How has removing fragments affected the reading of the paragraph? Explain.

2. Explain what it is about fragments that you find most difficult to remember and apply. Use an example to make your point clear. Feel free to refer to anything in this chapter.

Review Test 1

Turn each of the following word groups into a complete sentence. Use the space provided.

EXAMPLES

Feeling very confident

Feeling very confident, I began my speech.

Until the rain started

We played softball until the rain started.

1. Before you sit down

2. When the noise stopped

3. To get to the game on time

4. During my walk along the trail

5. Because I was short on cash

6. Lucy, whom I know well

7. Up in the attic

_____

8. Through hard work

_____

9. Which I agreed to do

_____

10. Was ready for a change

_____

Review Test   2

Underline the fragment in each selection. Then correct the fragment in the space provided.

EXAMPLE

Sam received all kinds of junk mail. <u>Then complained to the post office.</u> Eventually, some of the mail stopped coming.

*Then he complained to the post office.*_____

1. After seeing an offensive mouthwash ad on television. I resolved never to buy that brand again.

_____

_____

2. People worked together on the assembly line. Moving quickly and efficiently. They wanted to make as much money as possible.

_____

_____

3. Mark was offered several different jobs. And accepted one that featured a four-day workweek.

_____

_____

4. Our yard sale was an enormous success. We sold everything. Except the self-portrait of my grandfather.

_____

_____

5. While they were taking a midnight walk. Tony and Lola saw hundreds of lightning bugs flickering over the lake. They were also attacked by hundreds of man-of-war mosquitoes.

   _____

   _____

6. Andy always wins at hide-and-seek. Peeking through his fingers as he counts to one hundred. The other kids will soon catch on.

   _____

   _____

7. Tamika has worked on the crossword puzzle all day. All the while mumbling each clue out loud. I hope she finishes soon.

   _____

   _____

8. Italian food is mouth-watering. Especially pizza. Spaghetti is delicious, too.

   _____

   _____

9. Lola looked at the enormous diamond on Holly's finger. And decided it was fake. The diamond was the size of a small headlight.

   _____

   _____

10. I often take pictures in my backyard. For instance, of a squirrel stealing sunflower seeds from a bird feeder.

    _____

    _____

Review Test 3

In the space provided, write *C* in front of the four word groups that are complete sentences; write *frag* in front of the six fragments. The first two items are done for you.

frag   1. When Lola prepares for a day at the beach.

_C_   2. She first selects a colorful bikini with a matching coverup.

_____   3. Second, gathering together a pair of large, dark sunglasses, a beach bag and towel, suntan lotion, and a very comfortable lounge chair.

_____ 4. Also, a large-brimmed hat in an unusual bright color.

_____ 5. In addition, she takes along a radio to listen to her favorite music.

_____ 6. Occasionally bringing along a good book to read as well.

_____ 7. She also tucks into the beach bag some fattening snacks.

_____ 8. Such as potato chips and oatmeal cookies.

_____ 9. Before leaving, she checks to make sure her fingernail polish matches her toenail polish.

_____ 10. Then on her way to a great afternoon at the beach.

Now correct the fragments you have found. Attach each fragment to the sentence that comes before or after it, or make whatever other change is needed to turn the fragment into a sentence. Use the space provided. The first one is corrected for you.

1. *When Lola prepares for a day at the beach, she first selects a colorful bikini with a matching coverup.*

2. _____

_____

3. _____

_____

4. _____

_____

5. _____

_____

6. _____

_____

Review Test 4

Write quickly for five minutes about the high school you attended. Don't worry about spelling, punctuation, finding exact words, or organizing your thoughts. Just focus on writing as many words as you can without stopping.

After you have finished, go back and make whatever changes are needed to correct any fragments in your writing.

NAME: _____

DATE: _____

Fragments

Each word group in the student paragraph below is numbered. In the space provided, write *C* if a word group is a complete sentence; write *frag* if it is a fragment. You will find ten fragments in the paragraph.

1. _____
2. _____
3. _____
4. _____
5. _____
6. _____
7. _____
8. _____
9. _____
10. _____
11. _____
12. _____
13. _____
14. _____
15. _____
16. _____
17. _____
18. _____
19. _____
20. _____

[1]I was seventeen on the night I died. [2]In the spring of 2002 [3]I had a severe case of the flu. [4]And had spent the first three days of may illness in bed. [5]Running a temperature between 102° and 106°. [6]Getting up only to take care of the necessities of life. [7]On Friday, the sixth day of my illness, rain from early morning on. [8]The wind howled outside, the house was damp and chilly, and my fever seemed higher than ever. [9]In late afternoon, I took my pillow and blanket into the living room. [10]Because I was sick of bed and had decided to lie on the sofa and watch television. [11]I watched Oprah Winfrey and read a magazine for a while. [12]Then I must have fallen asleep. [13]When I was suddenly conscious again. [14]I was in the middle of total darkness. [15]And total silence. [16]I was absolutely terrified. [17]Because I was sure that I had died. [18]Then, somewhere in the blackness ahead of me, I saw and recognized a small, dissolving spot of light. [19]I slowly realized that it was coming from the television set. [20]And that there had been a power failure.

Fragments MASTERY TEST 2

Underline the fragment in each item. Then make whatever changes are needed to turn the fragment into a sentence.

EXAMPLE

In grade school, I didn't want to wear glasses. *a*nd avoided having to get them by memorizing the Snellen eye chart.

1. I rang their doorbell for ten minutes. Finally deciding no one was home. I stalked away in disgust.

2. According to the latest weather report. Heavy rains will fall for the next twenty-four hours. Flash floods are expected.

3. A ceiling should be painted a very light color. Such as white or pale beige. Then the room will seem larger.

4. My classes all being in the afternoon this semester. I can sleep until noon every day. My roommate hates me for it.

5. The plumber told us he could fix the leak in our shower. But would not be able to come until next month.

6. I spent an hour in the mall parking lot yesterday. Looking for my gray compact car. There were hundreds of other cars just like it in the lot.

7. Tony filled in the three-page application. Then he waited to see the personnel manager. Who would interview him for the position.

8. Suddenly the pitcher turned around. And threw to first base. But the runner was already standing on second.

9. Staggering under the weight of the heavy laundry basket. Nick stumbled down the basement steps. Then he discovered the washer was not working.

10. My brother spends a lot of time at the mall. There is an arcade there called Space Port. Where he meets his friends and plays video games.

NAME: _____

DATE: _____

MASTERY TEST 3 | # Fragments

Underline the fragment in each item. Then make whatever changes are needed to turn the fragment into a sentence.

1. Susie turned in her exam book. Then she walked out of the room. Wondering if she had passed.

2. The manager was fined $10,000. He had knocked the umpire's cap off his head. And kicked it across the infield.

3. Lola's printer was giving her trouble. All the *y*'s were losing their tails. And looked like *v*'s.

4. My little brother enjoys playing practical jokes. On anyone who visits our house. He even tells people that our house is haunted.

5. Because she had not studied for the exam. Susie was very nervous. If she got a passing grade, it would be a miracle.

6. Customers were lined up ten-deep at every entrance. Waiting for the store to open. Everything was on sale at 50 percent off.

7. Eva often gets up very early. Sometimes as early as 6 A.M. She says she thinks most clearly in the mornings.

8. We loaded the car with camping gear. Including a four-burner Coleman stove and a portable television.

9. James has a terrible problem. Unless he can scrape together three hundred dollars for his monthly installment. He will lose his new Honda.

10. The unusual meeting began at 3 P.M. But adjourned at 3:05 P.M. Nobody could think of anything to talk about.

NAME: _____

DATE: _____

Fragments MASTERY TEST 4

Underline and then correct the ten fragments in the following passage.

When my mother was a young girl. She spent several summers on her aunt and uncle's farm. To this day she has vivid memories of the chores she did on the farm. Such as shucking corn for dinners and for canning. As she pulled off the moist brown cornsilk. Yellow worms would wiggle on the ear or drop off into her lap. Another task was preparing string beans. Which had to be picked over before the beans would be cooked. My mother and her aunt spent hours snapping the ends off the beans. And tossing each one into a large basin. But the chore my mother remembers most clearly is preparing a chicken for Sunday dinner. Her aunt would head for the chicken yard. Somehow, the chickens seemed to know her purpose. They ran wildly in all directions. Fluttering and squawking, or fleeing into the henhouse. When Aunt Helen found the right chicken. She picked it up and gave its neck a quick twist. Killing it instantly. Back in the kitchen, she and my mother would gut the chicken. And pluck its feathers out, down to the last tiny pinfeather. One special treat came out of this bloody chore. My mother always got the chicken feet to play with. Their long white tendons still attached. As my mother pulled on the tendons, the claws opened and closed like mechanical toys. My mother loved to terrorize her friends with these moving claws.

NAME: _____

DATE: _____

MASTERY TEST 5 | # Fragments

The passage that follows contains five fragments. Underline the fragments and then correct them in the space provided.

[1]If you have ever gone to a casino, club, or a neighborhood bar. [2]You probably have inhaled secondhand smoke. [3]In most states, nonsmokers must tolerate smoke in public places. [4]Treating it as if it were just a smelly annoyance. [5]However, research proves that secondhand smoke is linked to serious health problems. [6]One study shows that nonsmokers who live with smokers have a 30 percent greater chance of getting lung cancer. [7]And are at a higher risk for heart disease. [8]Children who live with smokers have increased chances of life-threatening medical conditions. [9]Including lung infections, severe asthma, and sudden infant death syndrome. [10]Even those who don't live with smokers can be harmed by brief exposures to secondhand smoke, which quickly affects the arteries and threatens people at high risk of heart disease. [11]To date, only fifteen states have comprehensive laws. [12]That protect people from secondhand smoke.

1. _____

   _____

2. _____

   _____

3. _____

   _____

4. _____

   _____

5. _____

   _____

Run-Ons

Introductory Activity

A run-on occurs when two sentences are run together with no adequate sign given to mark the break between them. Shown below are four run-on sentences and four correctly marked sentences. See if you can complete the statement that explains how each run-on is corrected.

1. A student yawned in class the result was a chain reaction of copycat yawning.

    A student yawned in class. The result was a chain reaction of copycat yawning.

The run-on has been corrected by using a _____ and a capital letter to separate the two complete thoughts.

2. I placed an ad in the paper last week, no one has replied.

    I placed an ad in the paper last week, but no one has replied.

The run-on has been corrected by using a joining word, _____, to connect the two complete thoughts.

3. A bus barreled down the street, it splashed murky rainwater all over the pedestrians.

    A bus barreled down the street; it splashed murky rainwater all over the pedestrians.

continued

The run-on has been corrected by using a _____ to connect the two closely related thoughts.

4. I had a campus map, I still could not find my classroom building.

Although I had a campus map, I still could not find my classroom building.

The run-on has been corrected by using the dependent word _____ to connect the two closely related thoughts.

Answers are on page 560.

What Are Run-Ons?

www.mhhe.com/langan

A *run-on* is two complete thoughts that are run together with no adequate sign given to mark the break between them. As a result of the run-on, the reader is confused, unsure of where one thought ends and the next one begins. Two types of run-ons are fused sentences and comma splices.

Some run-ons have no punctuation at all to mark the break between the thoughts. Such run-ons are known as *fused sentences:* they are fused or joined together as if they were only one thought.

Fused Sentence

Rosa decided to stop smoking she didn't want to die of lung cancer.

Fused Sentence

The exam was postponed the class was canceled as well.

In other run-ons, known as *comma splices*, a comma is used to connect or "splice" together the two complete thoughts.* However, a comma alone is *not enough* to connect two complete thoughts. Some connection stronger than a comma alone is needed.

---

*Notes:
1. Some instructors feel that the term *run-ons* should be applied only to fused sentences, not to comma splices. But for many other instructors, and for our purposes in this book, the term *run-on* applies equally to fused sentences and comma splices. The bottom line is that you do not want either fused sentences or comma splices in your writing.
2. Some instructors refer to each complete thought in a run-on as an *independent clause*. A *clause* is simply a group of words having a subject and a verb. A clause may be *independent* (expressing a complete thought and able to stand alone) or *dependent* (not expressing a complete thought and not able to stand alone). A run-on is two independent clauses that are run together with no adequate sign given to mark the break between them.

Comma Splice

Rosa decided to stop smoking, she didn't want to die of lung cancer.

Comma Splice

The exam was postponed, the class was canceled as well.

Comma splices are the most common kind of run-on. Students sense that some kind of connection is needed between thoughts, and so they put a comma at the dividing point. But the comma alone is *not sufficient.* A stronger, clearer mark is needed between the two thoughts.

A Warning: Words That Can Lead to Run-Ons

People often write run-ons when the second complete thought begins with one of the following words:

I	we	there	now
you	they	this	then
he, she, it		that	next

Remember to be on the alert for run-ons whenever you use these words in your writing.

Correcting Run-Ons

Here are four common methods of correcting a run-on:

1. Use a period and a capital letter to separate the two complete thoughts. (In other words, make two separate sentences of the two complete thoughts.)

   Rosa decided to stop smoking. She didn't want to die of lung cancer.

   The exam was postponed. The class was canceled as well.

2. Use a comma plus a joining word (*and, but, for, or, nor, so, yet*) to connect the two complete thoughts.

   Rosa decided to stop smoking, for she didn't want to die of lung cancer.

   The exam was postponed, and the class was canceled as well.

3. Use a semicolon to connect the two complete thoughts.

   Rosa decided to stop smoking; she didn't want to die of lung cancer.

   The exam was postponed; the class was canceled as well.

continued

4. Use subordination (put a dependent word at the beginning of one
    fragment).

    Because Rosa didn't want to die of lung cancer, she decided to stop
    smoking.

    When the exam was postponed, the class was canceled as well.

The following pages will give you practice in all four methods of correcting
run-ons. The use of subordination will be explained further on page 133, in a
chapter that deals with sentence variety.

Method 1: Period and a Capital Letter

One way of correcting a run-on is to use a period and a capital letter at the break
between the two complete thoughts. Use this method especially if the thoughts are
not closely related or if another method would make the sentence too long.

Practice

1

Locate the split in each of the following run-ons. Each is a *fused sentence*—that is,
each consists of two sentences fused or joined together with no punctuation at all
between them. Reading each sentence aloud will help you "hear" where a major
break or split in the thought occurs. At such a point, your voice will probably drop
and pause.

Correct the run-on by putting a period at the end of the first thought and a
capital letter at the start of the second thought.

EXAMPLE
                                              H
Gary was not a success at his job. his mouth moved faster than his hands.

1. Gerald's motorized wheelchair broke down he was unable to go to class.

2. The subway train hurtled through the station a blur of spray paint and
    graffiti flashed in front of my eyes.

3. Jenny panicked the car had stalled on a treacherous traffic circle.

4. Half the class flunked the exam the other half of the students were absent.

5. One reason for the high cost of new furniture is the cost of good wood one
    walnut tree sold recently for $40,000.

6. The wedding reception began to get out of hand guests started to throw cake
    at each other.

7. Jamal's pitchfork turned over the rich earth earthworms poked their heads
    out of new furrows.

8. There were a lot of unusual people at the party a few of the women had shaved heads.

9. Carol talks all the time her tongue is getting calluses.

10. Hundreds of crushed cars were piled in neat stacks the rusted hulks resembled flattened tin cans.

Locate the split in each of the following run-ons. Some of the run-ons are fused sentences, and some of them are *comma splices*—run-ons spliced or joined together only with a comma. Correct each run-on by putting a period at the end of the first thought and a capital letter at the start of the next thought.

Practice

2

1. I wish Carl wouldn't fall asleep in class, his snoring drowns out the lecture.

2. The crime rate in this country is increasing, every eight seconds another home is burglarized.

3. Our car radio is not working properly we get whistling noises and static instead of music.

4. That shopping mall has the smell of death about it half the stores are empty.

5. Cats sleep in all sorts of unusual places, our new cat likes to curl up in the bathroom sink.

6. Every day, Americans use 450 billion gallons of water this amount would cover New York City to a depth of 96 feet.

7. The driver had an unusual excuse for speeding, he said he had just washed his car and was trying to dry it.

8. The telephone rang at least fifteen times nobody felt like getting up to answer it.

9. Some of our foods have misleading names, for example, English muffins were actually invented in America.

10. The soccer star raised his arms in victory his shot sailed into the goal.

Write a second sentence to go with each sentence below. Start the second sentence with the word given in the margin.

Practice

3

EXAMPLE

He   My dog's ears snapped up. *He had heard a wolf howling on television.*

They   1. I could not find my car keys. _____

_____

Then   2. The first thing Marcus ate for dessert was a peach. _____

_____

She   3. My daughter began screaming. _____

_____

It   4. The toaster oven was acting strangely. _____

_____

There   5. Cars had to stop suddenly at the intersection. _____

_____

Method 2: Comma and a Joining Word

Another way of correcting a run-on is to use a comma plus a joining word to connect the two complete thoughts. Joining words (also called *coordinating conjunctions*) include *and, but, for, or, nor, so,* and *yet.* Here is what the four most common joining words mean:

and   in addition, along with

Lola was watching Monday night football, and she was doing her homework as well.

(*And* means *in addition:* Lola was watching Monday night football; *in addition,* she was doing her homework.)

but   however, except, on the other hand, just the opposite

I voted for the president two years ago, but I would not vote for him today.

(*But* means *however:* I voted for the president two years ago; *however,* I would not vote for him today.)

for   because, the reason why, the cause for something

Saturday is the worst day to shop, for people jam the stores.

(*For* means *because:* Saturday is the worst day to shop *because* people jam the stores.) If you are not comfortable using *for,* you may want to use *because* instead of *for* in the activities that follow. If you do use *because,* omit the comma before it.

SO   as a result, therefore

Our son misbehaved again, so he was sent upstairs without dessert.

(*So* means *as a result:* Our son misbehaved again; *as a result,* he was sent upstairs without dessert.)

Insert the comma and the joining word (*and, but, for, so*) that logically connects the two thoughts in each sentence.

Practice

4

EXAMPLE

A trip to the zoo always depresses me, ^{for} I hate to see animals in cages.

1. The telephone was ringing someone was at the front door as well.

2. Something was obviously wrong with the meat loaf it was glowing in the dark.

3. Tia and Nina enjoyed the movie they wished the seats had been more comfortable.

4. Brett moved from Boston to Los Angeles he wanted to get as far away as possible from his ex-wife.

5. I decided to go back to school I felt my brain was turning to slush.

6. Lola loved the rose cashmere sweater she had nothing to wear with it.

7. Art's son has joined the Army his daughter is thinking of joining, too.

8. Lydia began working the second shift she is not able to eat supper with her family anymore.

9. Fred remembered to get the hamburger he forgot to buy the hamburger rolls.

10. My TV wasn't working I walked over to a friend's house to watch the game.

Add a complete, closely related thought to each of the following statements. When you write the second thought, use a comma plus the joining word shown at the left.

EXAMPLE

but I was sick with the flu, _____*but I still had to study for the test.*_____

so 1. The night was hot and humid _____

_____

but 2. Fred wanted to get a pizza _____

_____

and 3. Lola went shopping in the morning _____

_____

for 4. I'm going to sell my car _____

_____

but 5. I expected the exam to be easy _____

_____

Method 3: Semicolon

A third method of correcting a run-on is to use a semicolon to mark the break between two thoughts. A *semicolon* (;) is made up of a period above a comma and is sometimes called a *strong comma.* The semicolon signals more of a pause than a comma alone but not quite the full pause of a period.

Occasional use of semicolons can add variety to sentences. For some people, however, the semicolon is a confusing mark of punctuation. Keep in mind that if you are not comfortable using it, you can and should use one of the first two methods of correcting a run-on sentence.

Semicolon Alone

Here are some earlier sentences that were connected with a comma plus a joining word. Now they are connected with a semicolon. Notice that a semicolon, unlike a comma, can be used alone to connect the two complete thoughts in each sentence.

Lola was watching Monday night football; she was doing her homework as well.

I voted for the president two years ago; I would not vote for him today.

Saturday is the worst day to shop; people jam the stores.

Insert a semicolon where the break occurs between the two complete thoughts in each of the following sentences.

Practice 6

EXAMPLE

She had a wig on; it looked more like a hat than a wig.

1. I just canceled my cell phone service the bill was just too expensive.

2. Reggie wanted to watch a football game the rest of the family insisted on watching a movie.

3. Bonnie put a freshly baked batch of chocolate chip cookies on the counter to cool everyone gathered round for samples.

4. About $25 million worth of pizza is eaten each year an average of 300 new pizza parlors open every week.

5. Nate never heard the third base coach screaming for him to stop he was out at home plate by ten feet.

Semicolon with a Transition

A semicolon is sometimes used with a transitional word and a comma to join two complete thoughts:

I figured that the ball game would cost me about ten dollars; however, I didn't consider the high price of food and drinks.

Fred and Martha have a low-interest mortgage on their house; otherwise, they would move to another neighborhood.

Sharon didn't understand the instructor's point; therefore, she asked him to repeat it.

TIP Sometimes transitional words do not join complete thoughts but are merely interrupters in a sentence (see pages 358–359):

My parents, moreover, plan to go on the trip.
I believe, however, that they'll change their minds.

Transitional Words

Here is a list of common transitional words (also called *adverbial conjunctions*).

Common Transitional Words		
however	moreover	therefore
on the other hand	in addition	as a result
nevertheless	also	consequently
instead	furthermore	otherwise

Practice

7

For each item, choose a logical transitional word from the box above and write it in the space provided. In addition, put a semicolon *before* the transition and a comma *after* it.

EXAMPLE

It was raining harder than ever _; however,_ Bobby was determined to go to the amusement park.

1. The tree must be sprayed with insecticide _____ the spider mites will kill it.

2. I helped the magician set up his props _____ I agreed to let him saw me in half.

3. Fred never finished paneling his basement _____ he hired a carpenter to complete the job.

4. My house was robbed last week _____ I bought a watchdog.

5. Juanita is taking five courses this semester _____ she is working forty hours a week.

Practice

8

Punctuate each sentence by using a semicolon and a comma.

EXAMPLE

Our tap water has a funny taste;consequently,we buy bottled water to drink.

1. I arrived early to get a good seat however there were already a hundred people outside the door.

2. Foul language marred the live boxing match as a result next time the network will probably use a tape delay.

3. The fluorescent lights in the library gave Jan a headache furthermore they distracted her by making a loud humming sound.

4. The broken shells on the beach were like tiny razors consequently we walked along with extreme caution.

5. Ted carefully combed and recombed his hair nevertheless his bald spot still showed.

Method 4: Subordination

A fourth method of joining related thoughts is to use subordination. *Subordination* is a way of showing that one thought in a sentence is not as important as another thought. Here are three sentences in which one idea is subordinated to (made less emphatic than) the other idea:

Because Rosa didn't want to die of lung cancer, she decided to stop smoking.

The wedding reception began to get out of hand when the guests started to throw food at each other.

Although my brothers wanted to watch a *Star Trek* rerun, the rest of the family insisted on turning to the network news.

Dependent Words

Notice that when we subordinate, we use dependent words like *because, when,* and *although.* Following is a brief list of common dependent words (see the complete list on page 128). Subordination is explained in full on pages 133–134.

Common Dependent Words		
after	before	unless
although	even though	until
as	if	when
because	since	while

Choose a logical dependent word from the box above and write it in the space provided.

EXAMPLE

Although going up a ladder is easy, looking down can be difficult.

1. The instructor is lowering my grade in the course _____ because I was late for class three times.

2. _____ the airplane dropped a few feet, my stomach rose a few feet.

3. _____ the football game was being played, we sent out for a pizza.

4. _____ the football game was over, we went out for another pizza.

5. You should talk to a counselor _____ you decide on your courses for next semester.

SECTION 1: SENTENCES

Practice

9

Practice

10

Rewrite the five sentences below, taken from this chapter, so that one idea is sub-ordinate to the other. In each case, use one of the dependent words in the box on page 113.

EXAMPLE

My house was burglarized last week; I bought a watchdog.

Because my house was burglarized last week, I bought a watchdog.

> **HINT** As in the example, use a comma if a dependent statement starts a sentence.

---

1. Sharon didn't understand the instructor's point; she asked him to repeat it.

   _____

   _____

2. Marco remembered to get the hamburger; he forgot to get the hamburger rolls.

   _____

   _____

3. Michael gulped two cups of strong coffee; his heart started to flutter.

   _____

   _____

4. A car sped around the corner; it sprayed slush all over the pedestrians.

   _____

   _____

5. Lola loved the rose cashmere sweater; she had nothing to wear with it.

   _____

   _____

Collaborative Activity

Editing and Rewriting

Working with a partner, read carefully the short paragraph below and underline the five run-ons. Then use the space provided to correct the five run-ons. Feel free to discuss the rewrite quietly with your partner and refer back to the chapter when necessary.

[1]When Mark began his first full-time job, he immediately got a credit card, a used sports car was his first purchase. [2]Then he began to buy expensive clothes that he could not afford he also bought impressive gifts for his parents and his girlfriend. [3]Several months passed before Mark realized that he owed an enormous amount of money. [4]To make matters worse, his car broke down, a stack of bills suddenly seemed to be due at once. [5]Mark tried to cut back on his purchases, he soon realized he had to cut up his credit card to prevent himself from using it. [6]He also began keeping a careful record of his spending he had no idea where his money had gone till then. [7]He hated to admit to his family and friends that he had to get his budget under control. [8]However, his girlfriend said she did not mind inexpensive dates, and his parents were proud of his growing maturity.

_____

_____

_____

_____

_____

_____

_____

_____

_____

Collaborative Activity

Creating Sentences

Working with a partner, make up your own short run-ons test as directed.

1. Write a run-on sentence. Then rewrite it, using a period and capital letter to separate the thoughts into two sentences.

   Run-on _____

   _____

   Rewrite _____

   _____

2. Write a sentence that has two complete thoughts. Then rewrite it, using a comma and a joining word to correctly join the complete thoughts.

   Two complete thoughts _____

   _____

   Rewrite _____

   _____

3. Write a sentence that has two complete thoughts. Then rewrite it, using a semicolon to correctly join the complete thoughts.

   Two complete thoughts _____

   _____

   Rewrite _____

   _____

Reflective Activity

1. Look at the paragraph about Mark that you revised above. Explain how run-ons interfere with your reading of the paragraph.

2. In your own written work, which type of run-on are you most likely to write: comma splices or fused sentences? Why do you tend to make the kind of mistake that you do?

3. Which method for correcting run-ons are you most likely to use in your own writing? Which are you least likely to use? Why?

Review Test 1

Some of the run-ons that follow are *fused sentences,* having no punctuation between the two complete thoughts; others are *comma splices,* having only a comma between the two complete thoughts.

Correct the run-ons by using one of the following three methods:

- Period and a capital letter
- Comma and a joining word (*and, but, for, so*)
- Semicolon

Use whichever method seems most appropriate in each case.

EXAMPLE

Fred pulled the cellophane off the cake, *and* the icing came along with it.

1. I found the cat sleeping on the stove the dog was eating the morning mail.

2. Yoko has a twenty-mile drive to school she sometimes arrives late for class.

3. I lifted the empty water bottle above me a few more drops fell out of it and into my thirsty mouth.

4. These pants are guaranteed to wear like iron they also feel like iron.

5. I saw a black-and-white blob on the highway soon the odor of skunk wafted through my car.

6. She gets A's in her math homework by using her pocket calculator she is not allowed to use the calculator at school.

7. Flies were getting into the house the window screen was torn.

8. Martha moans and groans upon getting up in the morning she sounds like a crazy woman.

9. Lola met Tony at McDonald's they shared a large order of fries.

10. The carpet in their house needs to be replaced the walls should be painted as well.

Review Test 2

Correct the run-on in each sentence by using subordination. Choose from among the following dependent words.

after	before	unless
although	even though	until
as	if	when
because	since	while

EXAMPLE

Tony hated going to a new barber, he was afraid of butchered hair.

Because Tony was afraid of butchered hair, he hated going to a new barber.

1. The meal and conversation were enjoyable, I kept worrying about the check.

_____

_____

2. My wet fingers stuck to the frosty ice cube tray, I had to pry them loose.

_____

_____

3. I take a late afternoon nap, my mind and body are refreshed and ready for my night course.

_____

_____

4. Our daughter jumped up screaming a black spider was on her leg.

_____

_____

5. I wanted badly to cry I remained cold and silent.

_____

_____

6. Lisa does the food shopping every two weeks she first cashes her paycheck at the bank.

_____

_____

7. Follow the instructions carefully, you'll have the computer set up and working in no time.

   _____

   _____

8. Every child in the neighborhood was in the backyard, Frank stepped outside to investigate.

   _____

   _____

9. My first year in college was not a success, I spent most of my time in the game room.

   _____

   _____

10. A burglar was in our upstairs bedroom going through our drawers, we were in the den downstairs watching television.

    _____

    _____

Review Test 3

On separate paper, write six sentences, each of which has two complete thoughts. In two of the sentences, use a period and a capital letter between the thoughts. In another two sentences, use a comma and a joining word (*and, but, or, nor, for, so, yet*) to join the thoughts. In the final two sentences, use a semicolon to join the thoughts.

Review Test 4

Write for five minutes about something that makes you angry. Don't worry about spelling, punctuation, finding exact words, or organizing your thoughts. Just focus on writing as many words as you can without stopping.

   After you have finished, go back and make whatever changes are needed to correct any run-on sentences in your writing.

NAME: _____

DATE: _____

MASTERY TEST 1 | # Run-Ons

In the space provided, write *R-O* beside run-on sentences. Write *C* beside the one sentence that is punctuated correctly. Some of the run-ons have no punctuation between the two complete thoughts; others have only a comma.

Correct each run-on by using (1) a period and a capital letter, (2) a comma and a joining word, or (3) a semicolon. Do not use the same method of correction for every sentence.

EXAMPLES

_____R-O_____ I applied for the job, ^but^ I never got called in for an interview.

_____R-O_____ Carla's toothache is getting worse; she should go to a dentist soon.

_____ 1. I had a very bad headache I felt light-headed and feverish as well.

_____ 2. Our children have the newest electronic games the house sounds like a pinball arcade.

_____ 3. Two men held up the ski shop, they were wearing bank tellers' masks.

_____ 4. Swirls of dust flew across the field good topsoil vanished into the distance.

_____ 5. I cannot get a definite commitment from Beth I decided not to count on her.

_____ 6. The soup was too hot to eat, so I dropped in two ice cubes and cooled it off quickly.

_____ 7. The course on the history of UFOs sounded interesting it turned out to be very dull.

_____ 8. That clothing store is a strange place to visit, you keep walking up to dummies that look like real people.

_____ 9. Luisa throws out old pieces of soap, for she can't stand the sharp edges of the worn-down bars.

_____ 10. The oil warning light came on Gerry foolishly continued to drive the car.

Run-Ons MASTERY TEST 2

In the space provided, write *R-O* beside run-on sentences. Write *C* beside the one sentence that is punctuated correctly. Some of the run-ons have no punctuation between the two complete thoughts; others have only a comma.

Correct each run-on by using (1) a period and a capital letter, (2) a comma and a joining word, or (3) a semicolon. Do not use the same method of correction for every sentence.

_____ 1. This semester Melissa has three different jobs she barely has enough time to sleep.

_____ 2. First Nick grilled three hamburgers, and then he placed a slice of cheese on each one.

_____ 3. Cats make ideal pets they are clean and require less attention than other animals.

_____ 4. Kathy is afraid of snakes she trembles in fear at the thought of seeing one.

_____ 5. I began to get sleepy during the long drive home, so I pulled over and took a short nap.

_____ 6. The batter hit the baseball it rocketed over the fence for a game-winning home run.

_____ 7. The average person needs at least eight hours of sleep each night most people get less than seven hours of sleep nightly.

_____ 8. Residents rejected a plan to build a stadium in their community they feared major traffic problems.

_____ 9. I spoke to the police officer in a friendly tone I hoped to avoid getting a speeding ticket.

_____ 10. Our landlord raised our rent twice in one year we are now looking for a new place to live.

NAME: _____

DATE: _____

Run-Ons

In the space provided, write *R-O* beside run-on sentences. Write *C* beside the two sentences that are punctuated correctly. Some of the run-ons have no punctuation between the two complete thoughts; others have only a comma.

Correct each run-on by using (1) a period and capital letter, (2) a comma and a joining word, or (3) a semicolon. Do not use the same method of correction for every sentence.

_____ 1. Lola does yoga exercises every morning she strongly believes in a healthy body.

_____ 2. Fast cars and fast people can be lots of fun, but they can also be very dangerous.

_____ 3. I wondered why the time was passing so slowly then I realized my watch had stopped.

_____ 4. Bill can crush walnuts with his teeth he is also good at biting the caps off of beer bottles.

_____ 5. At one time Bill used to bend nails with his teeth this practice ended when a wise guy slipped him a hardened nail.

_____ 6. My dentist teaches part-time in a neighborhood clinic he refers to himself as a drill instructor.

_____ 7. An improperly placed goldfish bowl can start a house fire, sunlight reflects and magnifies through the bowl glass.

_____ 8. At the crack of dawn, our neighbors start up their lawn mowers, and the Saturday morning symphony begins.

_____ 9. Kevin had a bad headache yesterday, moreover, his arthritis was bothering him.

_____ 10. As a little girl, she pretended she was a hairdresser her closet was full of bald dolls.

Run-Ons MASTERY TEST 4

In the space provided, write *R-O* beside run-on sentences. Write *C* beside the one sentence that is punctuated correctly. Some of the run-ons have no punctuation between the two complete thoughts; others have only a comma.

Correct each run-on by using (1) a period and capital letter, (2) a comma and a joining word, or (3) a semicolon. Do not use the same method of correction for every sentence.

_____ 1. The supermarket needs to hire more cashiers customers must stand in long checkout lines just to buy a few groceries.

_____ 2. The news reporter said the snowstorm would dump a foot of snow on our city, but all we saw were a few flurries.

_____ 3. Metal detectors are being installed in many high schools this will prevent students from bringing weapons to school.

_____ 4. Critics said the new movie was horrible the large crowd in the theater seemed to disagree.

_____ 5. Dust and cat fur covered the floor of the old attic it was an allergy sufferer's nightmare.

_____ 6. Kendra looked everywhere for her car keys they turned out to be in her pocket.

_____ 7. Honeybees can communicate to each other by "dancing" their movements tell other bees where to find nectar-filled flowers.

_____ 8. The volcano destroyed the surrounding forest thousands of old trees were snapped like dry twigs.

_____ 9. Ken's new dog has a bad habit it likes to eat leather shoes.

_____ 10. Leeches are unpleasant wormlike creatures that drink blood they can also help doctors treat severe injuries.

NAME: _____

DATE: _____

Run-Ons

In the space provided, write *R-O* beside run-on sentences. Write *C* beside the one sentence that is punctuated correctly. Some of the run-ons have no punctuation between the two complete thoughts; others have only a comma.

Correct each run-on by using (1) a period and a capital letter, (2) a comma and a joining word, or (3) a semicolon. Do not use the same method of correction for every sentence.

_____ 1. The cable company increased rates twice this year customers have threatened to cancel their service.

_____ 2. Bill wanted to arrive for the interview early he missed his bus.

_____ 3. The salesperson said the used car was in perfect shape the engine was dotted with rust.

_____ 4. Wind howled through the trees rain pelted loudly against the windows of our house.

_____ 5. A pen exploded in the washing machine all Sara's clothes were stained in blue ink.

_____ 6. In the 1300s, one-third of Europe's population was killed by the bubonic plague this highly contagious disease was spread by fleas.

_____ 7. Kathy spilled soda on her expensive new cell phone, and then it stopped working.

_____ 8. Angry basketball fans yelled at the referee his mistakes cost the team at least six points.

_____ 9. Security cameras filmed the jewelry store robbery police have not been able to catch the thieves.

_____ 10. Today, the average American woman can expect to live seventy-nine years the lifespan of the average man is just seventy-two.

Sentence Variety I

7

This chapter will show you how to write effective and varied sentences. You'll learn more about two techniques—subordination and coordination—you can use to expand simple sentences, making them more interesting and expressive. You'll also reinforce what you have learned in Chapters 5 and 6 about how subordination and coordination can help you correct fragments and run-ons in your writing.

Four Traditional Sentence Patterns

Sentences in English are traditionally described as *simple, compound, complex,* or *compound-complex.* Each is explained below.

The Simple Sentence

A simple sentence has a single subject-verb combination.

> Children play.
>
> The game ended early.
>
> My car stalled three times last week.
>
> The lake has been polluted by several neighboring streams.

A simple sentence may have more than one subject:

> Lola and Tony drove home.
>
> The wind and water dried my hair.

or more than one verb:

The <u>children</u> <u>smiled</u> and <u>waved</u> at us.

The <u>lawn mower</u> <u>smoked</u> and <u>sputtered</u>.

or several subjects and verbs:

<u>Manny</u>, <u>Moe</u>, and <u>Jack</u> ~~lubricated~~ my car, ~~replaced~~ the oil filter, and ~~cleaned~~ the spark plugs.

Practice

1

On separate paper, write:

Three sentences, each with a single subject and verb

Three sentences, each with a single subject and a double verb

Three sentences, each with a double subject and a single verb

In each case, underline the subject once and the verb twice. (See pages 67–68 if necessary for more information on subjects and verbs.)

The Compound Sentence

A compound, or "double," sentence is made up of two (or more) simple sentences. The two complete statements in a compound sentence are usually connected by a comma plus a joining word (*and, but, for, or, nor, so, yet*).

A compound sentence is used when you want to give equal weight to two closely related ideas. The technique of showing that ideas have equal importance is called *coordination.*

Following are some compound sentences. Each sentence contains two ideas that the writer considers equal in importance.

The rain increased, so the officials canceled the game.

Martha wanted to go shopping, but Fred refused to drive her.

Hollis was watching television in the family room, and April was upstairs on the phone.

I had to give up wood carving, for my arthritis had become very painful.

Combine the following pairs of simple sentences into compound sentences. Use a comma and a logical joining word (*and, but, for, so*) to connect each pair.

> **HINT** If you are not sure what *and, but, for,* and *so* mean, review pages 108–109.

EXAMPLE

- We hung up the print.
- The wall still looked bare.

  We hung up the print, but the wall still looked bare.

1. • My cold grew worse.
   • I decided to see a doctor.

   _____

   _____

2. • My uncle always ignores me.
   • My aunt gives me kisses and presents.

   _____

   _____

3. • We played softball in the afternoon.
   • We went to a movie in the evening.

   _____

   _____

4. • I invited Rico to sleep overnight.
   • He wanted to go home.

   _____

   _____

5. • Police raided the club.
   • They had gotten a tip about illegal drugs for sale.

   _____

   _____

Practice
3

On separate paper, write five compound sentences of your own about the photo below. Use a different joining word (*and, but, for, or, nor, so, yet*) to connect the two complete ideas in each sentence.

The Complex Sentence

A complex sentence consists of a simple sentence (a complete statement) and a statement that begins with a dependent word.* Here is a list of common dependent words:

Dependent Words

after	if, even if	when, whenever
although, though	in order that	where, wherever
as	since	whether
because	that, so that	which, whichever
before	unless	while
even though	until	who
how	what, whatever	whose

A complex sentence is used when you want to emphasize one idea over another in a sentence. Look at the following complex sentence:

> Because I forgot the time, I missed the final exam.

---

*The two parts of a complex sentence are sometimes called an independent clause and a dependent clause. A *clause* is simply a word group that contains a subject and a verb. An *independent clause* expresses a complete thought and can stand alone. A *dependent clause* does not express a complete thought in itself and "depends on" the independent clause to complete its meaning. Dependent clauses always begin with a dependent or subordinating word.

The idea that the writer wants to emphasize here—*I missed the final exam*—is expressed as a complete thought. The less important idea—*Because I forgot the time*—is subordinated to the complete thought. The technique of giving one idea less emphasis than another is called *subordination.*

Following are other examples of complex sentences. In each case, the part starting with the dependent word is the less emphasized part of the sentence.

While Aisha was eating breakfast, she began to feel sick.

I checked my money *before* I invited Pedro for lunch.

When Jerry lost his temper, he also lost his job.

Although I practiced for three months, I failed my driving test.

Use logical dependent words to combine the following pairs of simple sentences into complex sentences. Place a comma after a dependent statement when it starts the sentence.

Practice

4

EXAMPLES

- I obtained a credit card.
- I began spending money recklessly.
  When I obtained a credit card, I began spending money recklessly.

- Alan dressed the turkey.
- His brother greased the roasting pan.
  Alan dressed the turkey while his brother greased the roasting pan.

1. • The instructor announced the quiz.
    • The class groaned.

    _____

    _____

2. • Gene could not fit any more groceries into his cart.
    • He decided to go to the checkout counter.

    _____

    _____

3. • Your car is out of commission.
    • You should take it to Otto's Transmission.

    _____

    _____

4. • I received a raise at work.

    • I called my boss to say thank you.

    _____

5. • We owned four cats and a dog.

    • No one would rent us an apartment.

    _____

    _____

Practice

5

Rewrite the following sentences, using subordination rather than coordination. Include a comma when a dependent statement starts a sentence.

EXAMPLE

The hair dryer was not working right, so I returned it to the store.

Because the hair dryer was not working right, I returned it

to the store.

1. Ruth turned on the large window fan, but the room remained hot.

    _____

    _____

2. The plumber repaired the water heater, so we can take showers again.

    _____

    _____

3. I washed the sheets and towels, and I scrubbed the bathroom floor.

    _____

    _____

4. You should go to a doctor, for your chest cold may get worse.

    _____

    _____

5. The fish tank broke, and guppies were flopping all over the carpet.

    _____

    _____

Combine the following simple sentences into complex sentences. Omit repeated words. Use the dependent words *who, which,* or *that.*

> **HINTS**
>
> **a.** The word *who* refers to persons.
> **b.** The word *which* refers to things.
> **c.** The word *that* refers to persons or things.

Use commas around the dependent statement only if it seems to interrupt the flow of thought in the sentence. (See pages 358–359.)

EXAMPLES

- Clyde picked up a hitchhiker.
- The hitchhiker was traveling around the world.

  Clyde picked up a hitchhiker who was traveling around the world.

- Larry is a sleepwalker.
- Larry is my brother.

  Larry, who is my brother, is a sleepwalker.

1. • The magazine article was about abortion.
    • The article made me very angry.

    _____

    _____

2. • The woodshed has collapsed.
    • I built the woodshed myself.

    _____

    _____

3. • The power drill is missing.
    • I bought the power drill at half price.

    _____

    _____

4. • Rita Haber was indicted for bribery.
    • Rita Haber is our mayor.

    _____

5. • The chicken pies contained dangerous preservatives.
    • We ate the chicken pies.

    _____

    _____

Practice

7

On separate paper, write eight complex sentences, using, in turn, the dependent words *unless, if, after, because, when, who, which,* and *that.*

The Compound-Complex Sentence

A compound-complex sentence is made up of two (or more) simple sentences and one (or more) dependent statements. In the following examples, a solid line is under the simple sentences and a dotted line is under the dependent statements.

When the power line snapped, Jack was listening to the stereo, and Linda was reading in bed.

After I returned to school following a long illness, the math teacher gave me makeup work, but the history instructor made me drop her course.

Practice

8

Read through each sentence to get a sense of its overall meaning. Then insert a logical joining word (*and, or, but, for,* or *so*) and a logical dependent word (*because, since, when,* or *although*).

1. _____ he suffered so much during hay fever season, Pete bought

   an air conditioner, _____ he swallowed allergy pills regularly.

2. _____ I put on my new flannel shirt, I discovered that a button

   was missing, _____ I angrily went looking for a replacement

   button in the sewing basket.

3. _____ the computer was just repaired, the screen keeps freezing,

   _____ I have to restart the program.

4. _____ I have lived all my life on the East Coast, I felt uncomfortable during a West Coast vacation, _____ I kept thinking that the ocean was on the wrong side.

5. _____ water condensation continues in your basement, either you should buy a dehumidifier _____ you should cover the masonry walls with waterproof paint.

On separate paper, write five compound-complex sentences.

Practice

9

Review of Subordination and Coordination

www.mhhe.com/langan

Subordination and coordination are ways of showing the exact relationship of ideas within a sentence. Through **subordination** we show that one idea is less important than another. When we subordinate, we use dependent words like *when, although, while, because,* and *after.* (A list of common dependent words has been given on page 128.) Through **coordination** we show that ideas are of equal importance. When we coordinate, we use the words *and, but, for, or, nor, so, yet.*

Use subordination or coordination to combine the following groups of simple sentences into one or more longer sentences. Be sure to omit repeated words. Since various combinations are possible, you might want to jot down several combinations on separate paper. Then read them aloud to find the combination that sounds best.

Keep in mind that, very often, the relationship among ideas in a sentence will be clearer when subordination rather than coordination is used.

Practice

10

EXAMPLE

- My car does not start on cold mornings.
- I think the battery needs to be replaced.
- I already had it recharged once.
- I don't think charging it again would help.

  Because my car does not start on cold mornings, I think the battery needs to be replaced. I already had it recharged once, so I don't think charging it again would help.

  _____

> ### COMMA HINTS
>
> **a.** Use a comma at the end of a word group that starts with a dependent word (as in "Because my car does not start on cold mornings, . . .").
>
> **b.** Use a comma between independent word groups connected by *and, but, for, or, nor, so, yet* (as in "I already had it recharged once, so . . .").

1. • Louise used a dandruff shampoo.
   • She still had dandruff.
   • She decided to see a dermatologist.

   _____

   _____

   _____

2. • Omar's parents want him to be a doctor.
   • Omar wants to be a salesman.
   • He impresses people with his charm.

   _____

   _____

   _____

3. • The instructor conducted a discussion period.
   • Jack sat at his desk with his head down.
   • He did not want the instructor to call on him.
   • He had not read the assignment.

   _____

   _____

   _____

   _____

4. • Lola wanted to get a quick lunch at the cafeteria.
    • All the sandwiches were gone.
    • She had to settle for a cup of yogurt.

    _____

    _____

    _____

5. • I was leaving to do some shopping in town.
    • I asked my son to water the back lawn.
    • He seemed agreeable.
    • I returned three hours later.
    • The lawn had not been watered.

    _____

    _____

    _____

    _____

6. • I had eaten too quickly.
    • My stomach became upset.
    • It felt like a war combat zone.
    • I took two Alka-Seltzer tablets.

    _____

    _____

    _____

7. • Midge is always buying plants and flower seeds.
    • She enjoys growing things.
    • Not many things grow well for her.
    • She doesn't know why.

    _____

    _____

    _____

8. • My car was struck from behind yesterday.
   • I slowed suddenly for a red light.
   • The driver of the truck behind me slammed on his brakes.
   • He didn't quite stop on time.

   _____

   _____

   _____

   _____

9. • Ed skimmed through the help-wanted ads.
   • Nothing was there for him.
   • He desperately needed a job.
   • He would have to sell his car.
   • He could no longer keep up the payments.

   _____

   _____

   _____

   _____

10. • The meat loaf didn't taste right.
    • The mashed potatoes had too much salt in them.
    • We sent out for a pizza.
    • It was delivered late.
    • It was cold.

   _____

   _____

   _____

   _____

Review Test   1

Combine each group of short sentences into one sentence. Various combinations are possible. Choose the combination that reads most smoothly and clearly and that sounds most appropriate in the context of surrounding sentences. Use separate paper.

Here is an example of a group of sentences and some possible combinations:

EXAMPLE

- Martha moved in the desk chair.
- Her moving was uneasy.
- The chair was hard.
- She worked at the assignment.
- The assignment was for her English class.

Martha moved uneasily in the hard desk chair, working at the assignment for her English class.

Moving uneasily in the hard desk chair, Martha worked at the assignment for her English class.

Martha moved uneasily in the hard desk chair as she worked at the assignment for her English class.

While she worked at the assignment for her English class, Martha moved uneasily in the hard desk chair.

> **HINT** In combining short sentences into one sentence, omit repeated words where necessary.

Department Store Sale

- There's a sale at the large department store.
- The department store is in our local shopping mall.

- Shoppers flock to the store.
- They crowd the aisles.

- They find neat piles of sweaters and shirts on special sale tables.
- The clothes are not piled neatly for long.

- People are eager to find a great bargain.
- They paw through the sweaters.
- They flip through the shirts.

- Do not try to buy clothing that needs to be tried on during the sale.
- Do not try this unless you have lots of time.
- There is always a long line of customers at the fitting rooms.

- The store has reduced the prices of sleepwear by 50 percent.
- Stacks of pajamas and nightgowns are quickly snapped up.

- Some people buy things they don't need.
- Others buy things they won't ever use.
- They all enjoy taking home bargains.

- The manager smiles at the sale's success.
- The salespeople don't smile.
- The shoppers behave so badly.

- The shoppers madly hunt for bargains.
- They throw clothes on the floor.
- They push each other.

- At the end of the day, the store has made money.
- At the end of the day, the manager is happy.
- At the end of the day, the salespeople feel like quitting.

Review Test 2

Combine each group of short sentences into one sentence. Various combinations are possible. Choose the combination that reads most smoothly and clearly and that sounds most appropriate in the context of surrounding sentences. In combining short sentences into one sentence, omit repeated words where necessary. Use separate paper.

Life in Winter

- Many people think winter is a dead season.
- It is actually full of hidden life.

- For instance, many insects die in autumn.
- They leave life behind in the form of eggs.

- The eggs hatch the next spring.
- Millions of young insects will emerge.
- They will continue the life cycle.

- Other animals bury themselves alive.
- They can escape winter's cold.

- Frogs and turtles dig into the mud.
- They enter a state of hibernation.

- The pond freezes.
- The frogs and turtles remain alive.

- Woodchucks also go into a deep, months-long sleep.
- Winter is on its way.

- The woodchuck enters its den.
- This happens when it is ready to hibernate.
- It rolls into a tight ball.

- The woodchuck's heart slows to five beats a minute.
- It normally beats eighty times a minute.
- This happens until spring returns.

- The winter may be long and bitter.
- Life goes on.

NAME: _____

DATE: _____

Sentence Variety I  MASTERY TEST 1

Combine each group of short sentences into one sentence. Various combinations are possible. Choose the combination that reads most smoothly and clearly and that sounds most appropriate in the context of surrounding sentences. Use separate paper.

> **HINT** In combining short sentences into one sentence, omit repeated words where necessary.

Cocoa and Donut

- The little boy sat in a high chair.
- He watched his father dunk a white sugar donut into a cup of coffee.
- He watched his father take a bite of the wet donut.

- The boy then picked up a piece of white sugar donut.
- The piece of donut was on his high-chair tray.
- He did not put the donut into his mouth.

- The boy pushed the donut into the cup of cocoa on the tray.
- He did this after he made sure his father wasn't watching.
- He watched it sink.

- Then he pushed on the donut.
- He did so until cocoa flowed over the top of the cup.
- It ran onto the tray.
- It dripped onto a white linen tablecloth.

- Then the boy pulled out the soggy piece of donut from the cup.
- He jammed it into his mouth.

NAME: _____

DATE: _____

MASTERY TEST 2 | # Sentence Variety I

Combine each group of short sentences into one sentence. Various combinations are possible. Choose the combination that reads most smoothly and clearly and that sounds most appropriate in the context of surrounding sentences. Use separate paper.

> **HINT** In combining short sentences into one sentence, omit repeated words where necessary.

Jack Alone

- Jack worked a long day.
- The work was as a delivery man for United Parcel.
- He entered his apartment, hoping to relax.

- He ate his takeout pizza.
- He took off his heavy brown uniform.
- He put on his comfortable flannel pajamas.

- Jack then shuffled back to the kitchen.
- He boiled water.
- He made a large cup of tea.

- Jack added a tablespoon of honey to the tea.
- He also got a few cookies.

- Jack might feel lonely later.
- He was relaxed and comfortable now.
- He was happy to be by himself.

Standard English Verbs

Introductory Activity

Underline what you think is the correct form of the verb in each pair of sentences below.

That radio station once (play, played) top-forty hits.

It now (play, plays) classical music.

When Jean was a little girl, she (hope, hoped) to become a movie star.

Now she (hope, hopes) to be accepted at law school.

At first, my father (juggle, juggled) with balls of yarn.

Now that he is an expert, he (juggle, juggles) raw eggs.

On the basis of the examples above, see if you can complete the following statements.

1. The first sentence in each pair refers to an action in (past time, the present time), and the regular verb has an _____ ending.

2. The second sentence in each pair refers to an action in (past time, the present time), and the regular verb has an _____ ending.

Answers are on page 562.

Many people have grown up in communities where nonstandard verb forms are used in everyday life. Such nonstandard forms include *they be, it done, we has, you was, she don't,* and *it ain't.* Community dialects have richness and power but are a drawback in college and the world at large, where standard English verb forms must be used. Standard English helps ensure clear communication among English-speaking people everywhere, and it is especially important in the world of work.

This chapter compares the community dialect and the standard English forms of a regular verb and three common irregular verbs.

Regular Verbs: Dialect and Standard Forms

The chart below compares community dialect (nonstandard) and standard English forms of the regular verb *talk.*

	Talk		
Community Dialect (Do not use in your writing)		**Standard English** (Use for clear communication)	
Present Tense			
I talks	we talks	I talk	we talk
you talks	you talks	you talk	you talk
he, she, it talk	they talk	he, she, it talks	they talk
Past Tense			
I talk	we talk	I talked	we talked
you talk	you talk	you talked	you talked
he, she, it talk	they talk	he, she, it talked	they talked

One of the most common nonstandard forms results from dropping the endings of regular verbs. For example, people might say "Rose work until ten o'clock tonight" instead of "Rose works until ten o'clock tonight." Or they'll say "I work overtime yesterday" instead of "I worked overtime yesterday." To avoid such nonstandard usage, memorize the forms shown above for the regular verb *talk.* Then do the activities that follow. These activities will help you make it a habit to include verb endings in your writing.

Present Tense Endings

The verb ending -s or -es is needed with a regular verb in the present tense when the subject is *he, she, it,* or any one person or thing.

He	He lifts weights.
She	She runs.
It	It amazes me.
One person	Their son Ted swims.
One person	Their daughter Terry dances.
One thing	Their house jumps at night with all the exercise.

All but one of the ten sentences that follow need -s or -es endings. Cross out the nonstandard verb forms and write the standard forms in the spaces provided. Mark the one sentence that needs no change with a *C*.

Practice

1

www.mhhe.com/langan

EXAMPLE

ends   The sale ~~end~~ tomorrow.

_____ 1. Renée hate it when I criticize her singing.

_____ 2. Whenever my sister tries to tell a joke, she always mess it up.

_____ 3. Ice cream feel good going down a sore throat.

_____ 4. Frank cover his ears every time his baby sister cries.

_____ 5. "Dinner sure smell good," said Fran as she walked into the kitchen.

_____ 6. My brother wants to be an astronaut so he can see stars.

_____ 7. The picture on our television set blur whenever there is a storm.

_____ 8. My mother think women should get equal pay for equal work.

_____ 9. Sometimes Alonso pretend that he is living in a penthouse.

_____ 10. It seem as if we are working more and more but getting paid less and less.

Rewrite the short selection below, adding present tense -*s* verb endings wherever needed.

Charlotte behave rudely when she speak on her cell phone. First of all, she answer the phone anytime it ring, even at a restaurant or the movies. Then she raise her voice and act as if the caller is sitting right next to her. Sometimes she wave her hands or laugh loudly. She never notice how people roll their eyes at her. She even ask others near her to be quiet while she talk. If she keep this up, no one will go anywhere with her—unless she leave the phone at home.

_____

_____

_____

_____

_____

_____

_____

_____

_____

_____

_____

_____

_____

_____

_____

_____

_____

Past Tense Endings

The verb ending -*d* or -*ed* is needed with a regular verb in the past tense.

Yesterday we finished painting the house.

I completed the paper an hour before class.

Fred's car stalled on his way to work this morning.

www.mhhe.com/langan

All but one of the ten sentences that follow need *-d* or *-ed* endings. Cross out the nonstandard verb forms and write the standard forms in the spaces provided. Mark the one sentence that needs no change with a *C*.

Practice

3

EXAMPLE

jumped   The cat ~~jump~~ on my lap when I sat down.

_____ 1. As the burglar alarm went off, three men race out the door.

_____ 2. Lola's new lipstick was so red that it glow in the dark.

_____ 3. Stan smelled gas when he walk into the apartment.

_____ 4. As soon as the pilot sight the runway, he turned on his landing lights.

_____ 5. While the bear stare hungrily at him, the tourist reached for his camera.

_____ 6. Aliya studied for three hours and then decide to get some sleep.

_____ 7. Just as Miss Muffet seated herself, a large spider joined her.

_____ 8. José hurried to cash his paycheck because he need money for the weekend.

_____ 9. The waiter dropped the tray with a loud crash; bits of broken glass scatter all over the floor.

_____ 10. A customer who twisted his ankle in the diner's parking lot decide to sue.

Rewrite this selection, adding past tense *-d* or *-ed* verb endings where needed.

Practice

4

Bill's boss shout at Bill. Feeling bad, Bill went home and curse his wife. Then his wife scream at their son. Angry himself, the son went out and cruelly tease a little girl who live next door until she wail. Bad feelings were pass on as one person wound the next with ugly words. No one manage to break the vicious circle.

_____

_____

_____

_____

_____

_____

Three Common Irregular Verbs: Dialect and Standard Forms

The following charts compare the nonstandard and standard dialects of the common irregular verbs *be, have,* and *do.* (For more on irregular verbs, see the next chapter, beginning on page 157.)

Be

Community Dialect (Do not use in your writing)		Standard English (Use for clear communication)	
Present Tense			
I be (*or* is)	we be	I am	we are
you be	you be	you are	you are
he, she, it be	they be	he, she, it is	they are
Past Tense			
I were	we was	I was	we were
you was	you was	you were	you were
he, she, it were	they was	he, she, it was	they were

Have

Community Dialect (Do not use in your writing)		Standard English (Use for clear communication)	
Present Tense			
I has	we has	I have	we have
you has	you has	you have	you have
he, she, it have	they has	he, she, it has	they have
Past Tense			
I has	we has	I had	we had
you has	you has	you had	you had
he, she, it have	they has	he, she, it had	they had

Do

Community Dialect (Do not use in your writing)		Standard English (Use for clear communication)	
Present Tense			
I does	we does	I do	we do
you does	you does	you do	you do
he, she, it do	they does	he, she, it does	they do
Past Tense			
I done	we done	I did	we did
you done	you done	you did	you did
he, she, it done	they done	he, she, it did	they did

TIP   Many people have trouble with one negative form of *do.* They will say, for example, "She don't listen" instead of "She doesn't listen," or they will say "This pen don't work" instead of "This pen doesn't work." Be careful to avoid the common mistake of using *don't* instead of *doesn't.*

Underline the standard form of the irregular verb *be, have,* or *do.*

Practice

5

1. This week, my Aunt Charlotte (have, has) a dentist's appointment.

2. She (does, do) not enjoy going to the dentist.

3. She (is, are) always frightened by the shiny instruments.

4. The drills (is, are) the worst thing in the office.

5. When Aunt Charlotte (was, were) a little girl, she (have, had) a bad experience at the dentist's.

6. The dentist told her he (was, were) going to pull out all her teeth.

7. Aunt Charlotte (do, did) not realize that he (was, were) only joking.

8. Her parents (was, were) unprepared for her screams of terror.

9. Now, she (has, had) a bad attitude toward dentists.

10. She refuses to keep an appointment unless I (am, are) with her in the waiting room.

Practice 6

Cross out the nonstandard verb form in each sentence. Then write the standard form of *be, have,* or *do* in the space provided.

_____ 1. If it be not raining tomorrow, we're going camping.

_____ 2. You is invited to join us.

_____ 3. You has to bring your own sleeping bag and flashlight.

_____ 4. It don't hurt to bring a raincoat also, in case of a sudden shower.

_____ 5. The stars is beautiful on a warm summer night.

_____ 6. Last year we have a great time on a family camping trip.

_____ 7. We done all the cooking ourselves.

_____ 8. The food tasted good even though it have some dead leaves in it.

_____ 9. Then we discovered that we has no insect repellent.

_____ 10. When we got home, we was covered with mosquito bites.

Practice 7

Fill in each blank with the standard form of *be, have,* or *do.*

My mother sings alto in our church choir. She _____ to go to choir practice every Friday night and _____ expected to know all the music. If she _____ not know her part, the other choir members _____ things like glare at her and _____ likely to make nasty comments, she says. Last weekend, my mother _____ houseguests and _____ not have time to learn all the notes. The music _____ very difficult, and she thought the other people _____ going to make fun of her. But they _____ very understanding when she told them that she _____ laryngitis and couldn't make a sound.

Review Test 1

Underline the standard verb form.

1. Paul (pound, pounded) the mashed potatoes until they turned into glue.

2. The velvety banana (rest, rests) on the shiny counter.

3. My neighbor's daughter (have, has) a brand-new Toyota.

4. It (is, be) fire-engine red with black leather upholstery.

5. The tree in the backyard (have, had) to be cut down.

6. When Rashid (talk, talks) about his ex-wife, his eyes grow hard and cold.

7. Every time my heart (skip, skips) a beat, I worry about my health.

8. My friend Pat (do, does) everything at the last minute.

9. The pattern on the wallpaper (look, looks) like fuzzy brown spiders marching in rows.

10. My hands (tremble, trembled) when I gave my speech in front of the class.

Review Test 2

Cross out the nonstandard verb forms in the sentences that follow. Then write the standard English verb forms in the space above, as shown.

EXAMPLE
              watches   *play*
    She ~~watch~~ closely while the children ~~plays~~ in the water.

1. The stores was all closed by the time the movie were over.

2. If you does your assignment on time, that instructor are going to like you.

3. The boxer pull his punches; the fight were fixed.

4. The tires is whitewalls; they be very good-looking.

5. He typically start to write a research paper the night before it be due.

6. It don't matter to him whether he have to stay up all night.

7. Jeannette anchor the relay team, since she be the fastest runner.

8. I done Bill a favor that I hope he don't forget.

9. Last night I sneak into the kitchen and remove some Hershey's Kisses from the candy jar.

10. I add the figures again and again, but I still weren't able to understand the bank statement.

MASTERY TEST 1 ## Standard English Verbs

Underline the correct words in the parentheses.

1. The radio announcer said that traffic (is, are) tied up for six miles because of an accident that just (happen, happened) on the expressway.

2. My new pen (scratch, scratches) when I write with it; it (make, makes) little cuts in the paper.

3. Before I (mail, mailed) the letter, the postal rate went up, so I (need, needed) an extra stamp.

4. Rodrigo (have, has) a new tuxedo that (make, makes) him look just like a movie star.

5. They (do, does) not plan to give a New Year's Eve party this year, for they (have, has) painful memories of last year's.

6. Tim (is, be) terrific at home repairs; for example, he (fix, fixes) broken appliances just like a professional.

7. Just as Stanley (walk, walked) around the corner, he saw someone trying to steal his bicycle, so he (yell, yelled) for the police.

8. Little Danny (pile, piled) the blocks into a tower, but it (collapse, collapsed) with a loud crash, scattering all over the floor.

9. We (suspect, suspected) from the start that it (was, were) the neighbor's boy who took our lawn furniture.

10. My two sisters (was, were) thrilled when I (turn, turned) up with three tickets to the rock concert.

Standard English Verbs MASTERY TEST 2

NAME: _____

DATE: _____

Cross out the nonstandard verb form and write the correct form in the space provided.

EXAMPLE

seems   The job offer ~~seem~~ too good to be true.

_____   1. When I was learning how to drive, I strip the gears on my father's car.

_____   2. My parents is going to throw me a big party when I graduate.

_____   3. Bill prefer riding his motorcycle to just about any other activity.

_____   4. Vince do well on every exam he takes.

_____   5. Lucille change into comfortable clothes right after she gets home from a day of work.

_____   6. I remember how my mittens used to steam when I place them on the living room radiator.

_____   7. It was so cold that my breath turn into sharp white puffs of smoke when I exhaled.

_____   8. When Ida have her work breaks during the day, she often reads a magazine.

_____   9. Tea contain so much caffeine that it stimulates some people more than coffee.

_____   10. When I were little, my father would punish me just for expressing my opinion.

NAME: _____

DATE: _____

MASTERY TEST 3 # Standard English Verbs

PART 1

Fill in each blank with the appropriate standard verb form of *be, have,* or *do* in present or past tense.

    People _____ really funny at amusement parks. They _____ to prove that

        1   2
they _____ absolutely fearless, so they _____ crazy things such as stand up

        3   4
while the roller coaster _____ on its way downhill at ninety miles per hour. A

                         5
normally careful driver _____ accidents on purpose; he _____ this to see how

                  6   7
many cars he can hit in the Demolition Derby. I wonder if our parents _____

                                            8
equally crazy things when they _____ kids and needed to prove to the world that

                                9
they _____ courage.

       10

PART 2

Fill in each blank with the appropriate form of the regular verb shown in parentheses. Use present or past tense as needed.

    When Joanne (*rush*) _____, she often gets into trouble. Last Monday, while

                                  11
in a hurry to catch her train, she (*park*) _____ her car too close to a shiny green

                                           12
Camaro that was in the next space on the lot. When she (*arrive*) _____ at the sta-

                                         13
tion in the afternoon and (*open*) _____ her car door, Joanne (*realize*) _____ she

                             14   15
could not back out of the parking space without hitting the other car. In addition,
its driver was waiting impatiently and (*scowl*) _____ as she (*watch*) _____

                                      16   17
Joanne struggling with the wheel. Joanne finally got out of the space, but she
(*scrape*) _____ a two-inch strip off the Camaro's fender. The angry driver of

                18
the other car (*calm*) _____ down only when Joanne (*agree*) _____ to pay.

                    19   20

NAME: _____

DATE: _____

Standard English Verbs

PART 1

Fill in each blank with the appropriate standard verb form of *be, have,* or *do* in the present or past tense.

    My cousin Rita _____ determined to lose ten pounds, so she _____ put
                  1   2
herself on a rigid diet that _____ not allow her to eat anything she enjoys. Last
                                  3
weekend while the family _____ at Aunt Agatha's house for dinner, all Rita
                                             4
_____ to eat _____ a can of Diet Delight peaches. We _____ convinced that
  5   6   7
Rita meant business when she joined an exercise club whose members _____ to
                                                      8
work out on enormous machines and _____ fifty sit-ups just to get started. If Rita
                                      9
succeeds, we _____ going to be proud.
            10

PART 2

Fill in each blank with the appropriate form of the regular verb shown in parentheses. Use present or past tense as needed.

    Have you ever (*notice*) _____ what (*happen*) _____ at a children's
                               11   12
playground? Very often one child (*struggle*) _____ with another to be first
                                           13
on the sliding board, while a third child (*compete*) _____ with a fourth for the
                                         14
sandbox. Meanwhile, each parent (*wait*) _____ patiently on a nearby park bench
                                      15
and (*ignore*) _____ his or her offspring. Just yesterday, I saw a young father
          16
whose daughter had (*drag*) _____ him to the playground. He (*stare*) _____
                           17   18
at his watch while she (*scream*) _____ happily from the top of the jungle gym.
                                19
He must have been counting the minutes until they (*return*) _____ home.
                                                                     20

Irregular Verbs

Introductory Activity

You may already have a sense of which common English verbs are regular and which are not. To test yourself, fill in the past tense and past participle of the verbs below. Five are regular verbs and so take *-d* or *-ed* in the past tense and past participle. For these verbs, write *R* under *Verb Type* and then write their past tense and past participle verb forms. Five are irregular verbs and will probably not sound right when you try to add *-d* or *-ed*. For these verbs, write *I* under *Verb Type*. Also, see if you can write in their irregular verb forms.

Present	Verb Type	Past	Past Participle
fall	*I*	*fell*	*fallen*
1. scream			
2. write			
3. steal			
4. ask			
5. kiss			
6. choose			
7. ride			
8. chew			
9. think			
10. dance			

Answers are on page 562.

A Brief Review of Regular Verbs

Every verb has four principal parts: present, past, past participle, and present participle. These parts can be used to build all the verb tenses (the times shown by a verb).

Most verbs in English are regular. The past and past participle of a regular verb are formed by adding *-d* or *-ed* to the present. The *past participle* is the form of the verb used with the helping verbs *have, has,* or *had* (or some form of *be* with passive verbs, which are explained on pages 196–197). The *present participle* is formed by adding *-ing* to the present. Here are the principal forms of some regular verbs:

Present	Past	Past Participle	Present Participle
laugh	laughed	laughed	laughing
ask	asked	asked	asking
touch	touched	touched	touching
decide	decided	decided	deciding
explode	exploded	exploded	exploding

List of Irregular Verbs

Irregular verbs have irregular forms in the past tense and past participle. For example, the past tense of the irregular verb *grow* is *grew;* the past participle is *grown.*

Almost everyone has some degree of trouble with irregular verbs. When you are unsure about the form of a verb, you can check the following list of irregular verbs. (The present participle is not shown on this list, because it is formed simply by adding *-ing* to the base form of the verb.) Or you can check a dictionary, which gives the principal parts of irregular verbs.

Present	Past	Past Participle
arise	arose	arisen
awake	awoke *or* awaked	awoke *or* awaked
be (am, are, is)	was (were)	been
become	became	become
begin	began	begun
bend	bent	bent
bite	bit	bitten
blow	blew	blown

Present	Past	Past Participle
break	broke	broken
bring	brought	brought
build	built	built
burst	burst	burst
buy	bought	bought
catch	caught	caught
choose	chose	chosen
come	came	come
cost	cost	cost
cut	cut	cut
do (does)	did	done
draw	drew	drawn
drink	drank	drunk
drive	drove	driven
eat	ate	eaten
fall	fell	fallen
feed	fed	fed
feel	felt	felt
fight	fought	fought
find	found	found
fly	flew	flown
freeze	froze	frozen
get	got	got *or* gotten
give	gave	given
go (goes)	went	gone
grow	grew	grown
have (has)	had	had
hear	heard	heard
hide	hid	hidden
hold	held	held
hurt	hurt	hurt
keep	kept	kept
know	knew	known
lay	laid	laid
lead	led	led

Present	Past	Past Participle
leave	left	left
lend	lent	lent
let	let	let
lie	lay	lain
light	lit	lit
lose	lost	lost
make	made	made
meet	met	met
pay	paid	paid
ride	rode	ridden
ring	rang	rung
rise	rose	risen
run	ran	run
say	said	said
see	saw	seen
sell	sold	sold
send	sent	sent
shake	shook	shaken
shrink	shrank *or* shrunk	shrunk *or* shrunken
shut	shut	shut
sing	sang	sung
sit	sat	sat
sleep	slept	slept
speak	spoke	spoken
spend	spent	spent
stand	stood	stood
steal	stole	stolen
stick	stuck	stuck
sting	stung	stung
swear	swore	sworn
swim	swam	swum
take	took	taken
teach	taught	taught
tear	tore	torn
tell	told	told

Present	Past	Past Participle
think	thought	thought
wake	woke *or* waked	woken *or* waked
wear	wore	worn
win	won	won
write	wrote	written

Practice 1

Cross out the incorrect verb form in the following sentences. Then write the correct form of the verb in the space provided.

EXAMPLE

began   When the mud slide started, the whole neighborhood ~~began~~ going downhill.

_____ 1. The winner of the reality show has ate three bowls of juicy worms.

_____ 2. The mechanic done an expensive valve job on my engine without getting my permission.

_____ 3. Sheri has wore that ring since the day Clyde bought it for her.

_____ 4. She has wrote a paper that will make you roar with laughter.

_____ 5. The gas station attendant gived him the wrong change.

_____ 6. My sister be at school when a stranger came asking for her at our home.

_____ 7. The basketball team has broke the school record for most losses in a year.

_____ 8. Because I had lended him the money, I had a natural concern about what he did with it.

_____ 9. I seen that stray dog nosing around the yard yesterday.

_____ 10. I knowed her face from somewhere, but I couldn't remember just where.

Practice 2

For each of the italicized verbs in the following sentences, fill in the three missing forms in the order shown in the box:

> a. Present tense, which takes an -*s* ending when the subject is *he, she, it,* or any *one person or thing* (see page 145)
>
> b. Past tense
>
> c. Past participle—the form that goes with the helping verb *have, has,* or *had*

EXAMPLE

My little nephew loves to *break* things. Every Christmas he (a) _breaks_ his new toys the minute they're unwrapped. Last year he (b) _broke_ five toys in seven minutes and then went on to smash his family's new china platter. His mother says he won't be happy until he has (c) _broken_ their hearts.

1. Mary Beth wears contact lenses in order to *see* well. In fact, she (a) _____ so poorly without the lenses that the world is a multicolored blur. Once, when she lost one lens, she thought she (b) _____ a frog in the sink. She had really (c) _____ a lump of green soap.

2. When I was younger, I used to hate it when my gym class had to *choose* sides for a baseball game. Each captain, of course, (a) _____ the better players first. Since I was nearsighted and couldn't see a fly ball until it fell on my head, I would often have to wait half the period until one or the other captain (b) _____ me. If I had had my way, I would have (c) _____ to play chess.

3. My father loves to *take* pictures. Whenever we go on vacation, he (a) _____ at least ten rolls of film along. Last year, he (b) _____ more than two hundred pictures of the same mountain scenery. Only after he had (c) _____ his last shot were we allowed to climb the mountain.

4. Instructors must love to *speak* to their classes. My English instructor (a) _____ so much that he has to get a drink of water midway through his lecture. Last Wednesday, he (b) _____ for the entire class period. I guess he never heard that old expression "Speak only when you're (c) _____ to."

5. Our next-door neighbor's pet poodle loves to *swim*. When there is no lake or pond handy, she (a) _____ in the family bathtub. Two summers ago, Fifi (b) _____ across the river in which the family was fishing. She won't be satisfied until she has (c) _____ the English Channel.

6. Convertibles are not practical, but they are fun to *drive*. My cousin has a sky-blue Chevrolet convertible which she (a) _____ to work. One day she (b) _____ with the top down and then forgot to put it back up again. That night it rained, and the seat was so wet the next day that she has (c) _____ with the top up ever since.

7. Annabelle loves buying new things to *wear*. She (a) _____ a different outfit every day of the year. Last year, she never (b) _____ the same clothing twice. She often complains that she gets tired of her clothes long before they're (c) _____ out.

8. My eight-year-old nephew likes to *blow* up balloons. Every year he (a) _____ up several dozen for his parents' New Year's Eve party. Last year, he (b) _____ up fifty balloons, including one in the shape of an American flag. When he tiptoed downstairs at midnight, he was thrilled to see all the guests saluting the balloon he had (c) _____ up.

9. Every year, I can't wait for summer vacation to *begin*. As soon as it (a) _____, I can get to work on all the things around the house that I had to ignore during school. This past May, the minute my exams were over, I (b) _____ cleaning out the garage, painting the windowsills, and building a bookcase. I must have (c) _____ half a dozen projects. Unfortunately, it's now Labor Day, and I haven't finished any of them.

10. We always have trouble getting our younger son, Teddy, to stop watching television and *go* to sleep. He never (a) _____ to his room until 10 or 11 P.M. In the past, when he finally (b) _____ upstairs, we did not check on him, since there was no TV set in his room. The night we finally did decide to look in on Teddy, we found him reading *TV Guide* with a flashlight under the covers and told him things had (c) _____ too far.

Troublesome Irregular Verbs

Three common irregular verbs that often give people trouble are *be, have,* and *do.* See pages 148–149 for a discussion of these verbs. Three sets of other irregular verbs that can lead to difficulties are *lie-lay, sit-set,* and *rise-raise.*

Lie-Lay

The principal parts of *lie* and *lay* are as follows:

Present	Past	Past Participle
lie	lay	lain
lay	laid	laid

To lie means *to rest* or *recline*. *To lay* means *to put something down.*

To Lie

Tony *lies* on the couch.

This morning he *lay* in the tub.

He has *lain* in bed all week with the flu.

To Lay

I *lay* the mail on the table.

Yesterday I *laid* the mail on the counter.

I have *laid* the mail where everyone will see it.

Underline the correct verb.

Practice

3

> **HINT** Use a form of *lie* if you can substitute *recline.* Use a form of *lay* if you can substitute *place.*

1. Vicky is the sort of person who (lies, lays) her cards on the table.

2. I am going to (lie, lay) another log on the fire.

3. (Lying, Laying) down for an hour after supper helps Fred regain his energy.

4. I have (lain, laid) all the visitors' coats in the master bedroom.

5. Frankenstein's monster (lay, laid) on the table, waiting for lightning to recharge his batteries.

Sit-Set

The principal parts of *sit* and *set* are as follows:

Present	Past	Past Participle
sit	sat	sat
set	set	set

To sit means *to take a seat* or *to rest. To set* means *to put* or *to place.*

To Sit	**To Set**
I *sit* down during work breaks.	Tony *sets* out the knives, forks, and spoons.
I *sat* in the doctor's office for three hours.	His sister already *set* out the dishes.
I have always *sat* in the last desk.	They have just *set* out the dinnerware.

Practice

4

Underline the correct form of the verb. Use a form of *sit* if you can substitute *rest.* Use a form of *set* if you can substitute *place.*

1. During family arguments I try to (sit, set) on the fence instead of taking sides.

2. I walked three blocks before (sitting, setting) down the heavy suitcases.

3. Lorenzo (sat, set) the grapefruit on the teacher's desk.

4. That poor man has not (sat, set) down once today.

5. You can (sit, set) the laundry basket on top of the washer.

Rise-Raise

The principal parts of *rise* and *raise* are as follows:

Present	**Past**	**Past Participle**
rise	rose	risen
raise	raised	raised

To *rise* means *to get up* or *to move up. To raise* (which is a regular verb with simple *-ed* endings) means *to lift up* or *to increase in amount.*

To Rise	**To Raise**
The soldiers *rise* at dawn.	I'm going to *raise* the stakes in the card game.
The crowd *rose* to applaud the batter.	I *raised* the shades to let in the sun.
Dracula has *risen* from the grave.	I would have quit if the company had not *raised* my salary.

Underline the correct verb.

> **HINT** Use a form of *rise* if you can substitute *get up* or *move up*. Use a form of *raise* if you can substitute *lift up* or *increase*.

1. Even though I can sleep late on Sunday if I want to, I usually (rise, raise) early.

2. Some dealers (rise, raise) rather than lower their prices before a sale.

3. After five days of steady rain, the water in the dam had (risen, raised) to a dangerous level.

4. The landlord (rose, raised) the rent in order to force the tenants out of the apartment.

5. The cost of living (rises, raises) steadily from year to year.

Review Test   1

Cross out the incorrect verb form. Then write the correct form of the verb in the space provided.

_____ 1. While I was kneading the meat loaf, someone rung the doorbell.

_____ 2. My first-grade teacher, Ms. Rickstein, teached me the meaning of fear.

_____ 3. Lola brang a sweatshirt, for she knew the mountains got cold at night.

_____ 4. We done the grocery shopping on Thursday evening.

_____ 5. She had went home early from the dance, for she didn't like any of the people she had seen there.

_____ 6. The police officer came with me when I drived home to get my owner's registration card.

_____ 7. The boy next door growed six inches in less than a year.

_____ 8. We had gave the landlord notice three times that our plumbing system needed repairs, and each time he failed to respond.

_____ 9. I had ate so much food at the buffet that I needed to loosen my belt.

_____ 10. Last summer I swum the width of that river and back again.

Review Test   2

Write short sentences that use the form requested for the following irregular verbs.

EXAMPLE

Past of *ride:* _The Lone Ranger rode into the sunset._

1. Past of *break:* _____

2. Past participle of *bring:* _____

3. Past participle of *grow:* _____

4. Past of *choose:* _____

5. Present of *do:* _____

6. Past of *drink:* _____

7. Past participle of *write:* _____

8. Present of *give:* _____

9. Past participle of *begin:* _____

10. Present of *go:* _____

NAME: _____

DATE: _____

Irregular Verbs · MASTERY TEST 1

Underline the correct word in the parentheses.

1. Juan had (wrote, written) me five times before the letters stopped.

2. Did you see the damage that maniac (did, done) to the laundromat?

3. The fever made me hallucinate, and I (saw, seen) monkeys at the foot of my bed.

4. After dicing the vegetables, Sarah (freezed, froze) them.

5. I (drank, drunk) at least six cups of coffee while working on the paper.

6. That last commercial (came, come) close to making me scream.

7. The foreman asked why I had (went, gone) home early from work the day before.

8. I should have (wore, worn) heavier clothes to the picnic.

9. If I hadn't (threw, thrown) away the receipt, I could have gotten my money back.

10. Willy (brang, brought) his volleyball to the picnic.

11. I would have (become, became) very angry if you had not intervened.

12. I was exhausted because I had (swam, swum) two lengths of the pool.

13. Albert (eat, ate) four slices of almond fudge cake before he got sick.

14. How long has your watch been (broke, broken)?

15. If we had (knew, known) how the weather would be, we would not have gone on the trip.

16. The children had (did, done) the dishes as a surprise for their mother.

17. Teresa has (rode, ridden) all over the city looking for an apartment.

18. The burglar (ran, run) like a scared rabbit when he heard the alarm.

19. Someone had (took, taken) the wrong coat from the restaurant rack.

20. The trucker (drived, drove) all night; his eyes looked like poached eggs.

NAME: _____

DATE: _____

MASTERY TEST 2 Irregular Verbs

Cross out the incorrect verb form. Write the correct form in the space provided.

_____ 1. The mop that I left by the door has froze stiff.

_____ 2. My car was stole, and I had no way of getting to school.

_____ 3. Someone leaved a book in the classroom.

_____ 4. Our gym teacher speaked on physical fitness, but we slept through the lecture.

_____ 5. That sweater was tore yesterday.

_____ 6. After I had loosed weight, the pants fit perfectly.

_____ 7. Ellen awaked from a sound sleep with the feeling there was someone in the house.

_____ 8. Life has dealed Lonnell a number of hard moments.

_____ 9. Father begun to yell at me as I walked in the door.

_____ 10. The sick puppy laid quietly on the veterinarian's table.

_____ 11. The instructor didn't remember that I had spoke to him.

_____ 12. While Alvin sung in the church choir, his mother beamed with pride and pleasure.

_____ 13. I would have went on vacation this week, but my boss asked me to wait a month.

_____ 14. When the boys throwed stones at us, we decided to throw some back.

_____ 15. I blowed up the balloon until it exploded in my face.

_____ 16. The body that the men taked out of the water was a terrible thing to see.

_____ 17. Rich breaked the video game that I lent him.

_____ 18. If the phone had rang once more, my mother would have tossed a pot at it.

_____ 19. A sudden banging on the door shaked me out of sleep.

_____ 20. Granny has wore the same dress to every wedding and funeral for twenty tears.

NAME: _____

DATE: _____

Irregular Verbs

Write in the space provided the correct form of the verb shown at the left.

sink

1. The fishing rod slipped out of his hand and _____ to the bottom of the pond.

choose

2. I _____ the blueberry pie for dessert because the pudding looked watery.

write

3. Pat had _____ the essay three times, but it still needed revision.

lie

4. As soon as I _____ down to take a nap, the phone rang.

catch

5. Greg _____ a cold while defrosting the refrigerator.

sell

6. The brothers worked on their old station wagon for a month and then _____ it for twice as much as they paid for it.

ride

7. Eric _____ the bucking bronco for a full thirty seconds before he was tossed into the sawdust.

hide

8. How did my little brother ever guess where his Christmas present was _____?

speak

9. If I _____ only when I was spoken to, I'd never get a word in edgewise.

shake

10. Susie's hands _____ as she handed in her paper.

NAME: _____

DATE: _____

MASTERY TEST 4 | # Irregular Verbs

Write in the space provided the correct form of the verb shown at the left.

ring
1. Sometimes the doorbell has _____ for several minutes before my grand-father notices the sounds.

shrink
2. My brand-new jeans _____ three sizes in the wash.

lend
3. Stella _____ someone her notebook and then forgot who had borrowed it.

rise
4. If taxes had not _____ so much this year, I could have afforded a vacation.

sleep
5. I turned in my term paper and then _____ for ten hours.

sting
6. Kim didn't see the bee in her sleeve and was _____ the moment she put her jacket on.

wear
7. Nick-jogs five miles a day and has _____ out three pairs of running shoes this year.

burst
8. Lola blew the biggest bubble I have ever seen. Then it _____ leaving shreds of pink bubble gum all over her face.

keep
9. I should have _____ my old coat instead of contributing it to the church rummage sale.

drive
10. We _____ for fifteen miles without seeing a single McDonald's.

Subject-Verb Agreement

Introductory Activity

As you read each pair of sentences below, write a check mark beside the sentence that you think uses the underlined word correctly.

The results of the election is very surprising. ____
The results of the election are very surprising. ____

There was many complaints about the violent TV show. ____
There were many complaints about the violent TV show. ____

Everybody usually gather at the waterfront on the Fourth of July. ____
Everybody usually gathers at the waterfront on the Fourth of July. ____

On the basis of the examples above, see if you can complete the following statements.

1. In the first two pairs of sentences, the subjects are _____ and _____. Since both these subjects are plural, the verb must be plural.

2. In the last pair of sentences, the subject, *Everybody,* is a word that is always (singular, plural), and so its accompanying verb must be (singular, plural).

Answers are on page 563.

www.mhhe.com/langan

A verb must agree with its subject in number. A *singular subject* (one person or thing) takes a singular verb. A *plural subject* (more than one person or thing) takes a plural verb. Mistakes in subject-verb agreement are sometimes made in the following situations:

1. When words come between the subject and the verb
2. When a verb comes before the subject
3. With indefinite pronouns
4. With compound subjects
5. With *who*, *which*, and *that*

Each situation is explained on the following pages.

Words between the Subject and the Verb

Words that come between the subject and the verb do not change subject-verb agreement.

The breakfast cereals in the pantry are made mostly of sugar.

In the example above, the subject (*cereals*) is plural and so the verb (*are*) is plural. The words *in the pantry* that come between the subject and the verb do not affect subject-verb agreement. To help find the subject of certain sentences, you should cross out prepositional phrases (explained on page 70):

One ~~of the crooked politicians~~ was jailed for a month.

The posters ~~on my little brother's wall~~ include hip-hop stars, athletes, and models in bathing suits.

Following is a list of common prepositions.

Common Prepositions				
about	before	by	inside	over
above	behind	during	into	through
across	below	except	of	to
among	beneath	for	off	toward
around	beside	from	on	under
at	between	in	onto	with

Draw one line under the subject. Then lightly cross out any words that come between the subject and the verb. Finally, draw two lines under the correct verb in parentheses.

EXAMPLE

The price of the stereo speakers (is, are) too high for my wallet.

1. The blue stain on the sheets (comes, come) from the cheap dish towel that I put in the washer with them.

2. The sport coat, along with the two pairs of pants, (sells, sell) for just fifty dollars.

3. The roots of the apple tree (is, are) very shallow.

4. Amir's sisters, who wanted to be at his surprise party, (was, were) unable to come because of flooded roads.

5. The dust-covered photo albums in the attic (belongs, belong) to my grandmother.

6. The cost of personal calls made on office telephones (is, are) deducted from our pay.

7. Two cups of coffee in the morning (does, do) not make up a hearty breakfast.

8. The moon as well as some stars (is, are) shining brightly tonight.

9. The electrical wiring in the apartment (is, are) dangerous and needs replacing.

10. Chapter 4 of the psychology book, along with six weeks of class notes, (is, are) to be the basis of the test.

Verb before the Subject

A verb agrees with its subject even when the verb comes *before* the subject. Words that may precede the subject include *there, here,* and, in questions, *who, which, what,* and *where.*

Inside the storage shed are the garden tools.

At the street corner were two panhandlers.

There are times I'm ready to quit my job.

Where are the instructions for the DVD player?

> **TIP** If you are unsure about the subject, ask *who* or *what* of the verb. With the first sentence above, you might ask, "What are inside the storage shed?" The answer, garden *tools,* is the subject.

www.mhhe.com/langan

Practice

2

Underline the subject in each sentence. Then double-underline the correct verb in parentheses.

1. There (is, are) long lines at the checkout counter.

2. Scampering to the door to greet Martha Grencher (was, were) her two little dogs.

3. Filling the forest floor (was, were) dozens of pine cones.

4. There (is, are) pretzels if you want something to go with the cheese.

5. At the end of the line, hoping to get seats for the movie, (was, were) Janet and Maureen.

6. There (is, are) rats nesting under the backyard woodpile.

7. Swaggering down the street (was, were) several tough-looking boys.

8. On the very top of that mountain (is, are) a house for sale.

9. At the soap opera convention, there (was, were) fans from all over the country.

10. Under a large plastic dome on the side of the counter (lies, lie) a single gooey pastry.

Indefinite Pronouns

The following words, known as *indefinite pronouns,* always take singular verbs.

Indefinite Pronouns			
(*-one* words)	(*-body* words)	(*-thing* words)	
one	nobody	nothing	each
anyone	anybody	anything	either
everyone	everybody	everything	neither
someone	somebody	something	

> **TIP** *Both* always takes a plural verb.

Write the correct form of the verb in the space provided.

hope, hopes   1. Everyone in our neighborhood _____ the farm stays open.

dances, dance   2. Nobody _____ the way he does.

deserves, deserve   3. Either of our football team's guards _____ to be an all-state guard.

was, were   4. Both of the race drivers _____ injured.

appears, appear   5. Everyone who received an invitation _____ to be here.

offers, offer   6. No one ever _____ to work on that committee.

owns, own   7. One of my sisters _____ a VW convertible.

has, have   8. Somebody _____ been taking shopping carts from the supermarket.

thinks, think   9. Everyone that I talked to _____ the curfew is a good idea.

has, have   10. Each of the candidates _____ talked about withdrawing from the race.

Compound Subjects

Subjects joined by *and* generally take a plural verb.

> Yoga and biking are Lola's ways of staying in shape.

> Ambition and good luck are the keys to his success.

When subjects are joined by *or*, *either... or*, *neither... nor*, *not only... but also*, the verb agrees with the subject closer to the verb.

> Either the restaurant manager or his assistants deserve to be fired for the spoiled meat used in the stew.

The nearer subject, *assistants*, is plural, and so the verb is plural.

www.mhhe.com/langan

Write the correct form of the verb in the space provided.

matches, match   1. This tie and shirt _____ the suit, but the shoes look terrible.

has, have   2. The kitchen and the bathroom _____ to be cleaned.

is, are   3. A good starting salary and a bonus system _____ the most attractive features of my new job.

plan, plans   4. Neither Ellen nor her brothers _____ to work at a temporary job during their holiday break from college.

is, are   5. For better or worse, working on his van and playing video games _____ Pete's main interests in life.

www.mhhe.com/langan

Who, Which, and That

When *who*, *which*, and *that* are used as subjects, they take singular verbs if the word they stand for is singular and plural verbs if the word they stand for is plural. For example, in the sentence

Gary is one of those people <u>who</u> <u>are</u> very private.

the verb is plural because *who* stands for *people*, which is plural. On the other hand, in the sentence

Gary is a person <u>who</u> <u>is</u> very private.

the verb is singular because *who* stands for *person*, which is singular.

Practice

5

Write the correct form of the verb in the space provided.

was, were 1. I removed the sheets that _____ jamming my washer.

stumbles, stumble 2. This job isn't for people who _____ over tough decisions.

blares, blare 3. The radio that _____ all night belongs to my insomniac neighbor.

gives, give 4. The Saturn is one of the small American cars that _____ high gasoline mileage.

appears, appear 5. The strange smell that _____ in our neighborhood on rainy days is being investigated.

Collaborative Activity

Editing and Rewriting

Working with a partner, read the short paragraph below and mark off the five mistakes in subject-verb agreement. Then use the space provided to correct the five agreement errors. Feel free to discuss the rewrite quietly with your partner and refer back to the chapter when necessary.

When most people think about cities, they do not thinks about wild animals. But in my city apartment, there is enough creatures to fill a small forest. In the daytime, I must contend with the pigeons. These unwanted guests of my apartment makes a loud feathery mess on my bedroom windowsill. In the evening, my apartment is visited by roaches. These large insects creep onto my kitchen floor and walls after dark and frighten me with their shiny glistening bodies. Later at night, my apartment is invaded by mice. Waking from sleep, I can hear their little feet tapping as they scurry behind walls and above my ceiling. Everybody I know think I should move into a new apartment. What I really need is to go somewhere that have less wild creatures—maybe a forest!

_____   _____

_____   _____

_____

Collaborative Activity

Creating Sentences

Working with a partner, write sentences as directed. With each item, pay special attention to subject-verb agreement.

1. Write a sentence in which the words *in the cafeteria* or *on the table* come between the subject and verb. Underline the subject of your sentence and circle the verb.

2. Look at the photo and write a sentence that begins with the words *there is* or *there are*. Underline the subject of your sentence and circle the verb.

3. Write a sentence in which the indefinite pronoun *nobody* or *anything* is the subject.

4. Write a sentence with the compound subjects *manager* and *employees*. Underline the subject of your sentence and circle the verb.

Reflective Activity

1. Look at the paragraph about the apartment that you revised above. Which rule involving subject-verb agreement gave you the most trouble? How did you figure out the correct answer?

2. Explain which of the five subject-verb agreement situations discussed in this chapter is most likely to cause you problems.

Review Test 1

Complete each of the following sentences, using *is*, *are*, *was*, *were*, *have*, or *has*. Underline the subject of each of these verbs.

EXAMPLE

The <u>hot dogs</u> in that luncheonette *are hazardous to your health.* _____

1. Neither of the songs _____

    _____

2. The new state tax on alcohol and cigarettes _____

    _____

3. The shadowy figure behind the cemetery walls _____

    _____

4. The movie actress and her agent _____

    _____

5. Larry is one of those people who _____

    _____

6. The football coach, along with ten of his assistants, _____

    _____

7. The students in the computer lab _____

   _____

8. Someone sitting in the left-field bleachers of the ballpark _____

   _____

9. The first several weeks that I spent in college _____

   _____

10. Tony's gentle voice and pleasant smile _____

   _____

Review Test   2

Underline the correct word in the parentheses.

1. Excessive use of alcohol, caffeine, or cigarettes (damages, damage) a mother's unborn child.

2. Neither of the newspaper articles (gives, give) all the facts of the murder case.

3. There (is, are) five formulas that we have to memorize for the test.

4. The rug and the wallpaper in that room (has, have) to be replaced.

5. The old man standing under the park trees (does, do) not look happy.

6. The scratch on the record (was, were) there when I bought it.

7. Heavy snows and months of subfreezing temperatures (is, are) two reasons why I moved to Florida.

8. I don't enjoy people who (likes, like) to play pranks.

9. The price of the set of dishes you like so much (is, are) $345.

10. What time in the morning (does, do) planes leave for Denver?

Review Test 3

There are eight mistakes in subject-verb agreement in the following passage. Cross out each incorrect verb and write the correct form above it. In addition, underline the subject of each of the verbs that must be changed.

There are several things that makes Tracy want to quit her job as a waitress. First of all, she is never permitted to sit down. Even when there is no customers seated at her tables, she must find something useful to do, such as folding napkins or refilling ketchup bottles. By the end of the night, her feet feel like two chunks of raw hamburger. Second, she finds it difficult to be cheerful all of the time, but cheerfulness is one of the qualities that is expected of her. People who go out to eat in a restaurant wants to enjoy themselves, and they don't like their spirits dampened by a grouchy waitress. This means that when Tracy feels sick or depressed, she can't let her feelings show. Instead, she has to pretend that the occasion is as pleasant for her as it is for her customers, night after night. Neither of these problems, however, bother her as much as people who are fussy. Both the child who demands extra fudge sauce on her ice cream and the adult who asks for cleaner silverware has to be satisfied. In addition, each night at least one of the customers at her tables insist on being a perfectionist. As Tracy learned her first day on the job, the customer is always right—even if he complains that the peas have too many wrinkles. Though she may feel like dumping the peas into the customer's lap, Tracy must pretend that each of her customers are royalty and hurry to find some less wrinkled peas. Sometimes she wishes people would just stay home and eat.

Subject-Verb Agreement   MASTERY TEST 1

Underline the correct verb in the parentheses. Note that you will first have to determine the subject in each sentence. To help find subjects in certain sentences, you may find it helpful to cross out prepositional phrases.

1. The four flights of stairs up to my apartment (is, are) as steep as Mount Everest sometimes.

2. The sweater and the books on the table (belongs, belong) to Keiko.

3. One of their sons (has, have) been expelled from school.

4. My brother and I (has, have) season tickets to the games.

5. Jake and Eva (enjoys, enjoy) watching old movies on television.

6. Either of the television sets (gives, give) excellent picture quality.

7. There (is, are) about ten things I must get done today.

8. Hurrying down the street after their father (was, were) two small children.

9. Here (is, are) the screwdriver you were looking for all weekend.

10. No one in this world (is, are) going to get out alive.

11. The plywood under your carpets (is, are) rotting.

12. Sex and violence (is, are) the mainstays of many popular movies.

13. Tamara and her sister Teresa (goes, go) to the gym to work out three times per week.

14. Not only the manager but also the owners of the ball club (is, are) responsible for the poor performance of the team.

15. There (is, are) a great deal of work yet to be done.

16. One of the women on the bowling team (has, have) won a million dollars in the state lottery.

17. The study of statistics (is, are) important for a psychology major.

18. My father is a person who (cares, care) more about time with his family than about success in his job.

19. The carpenter and the electrician (is, are) working at the house today.

20. I tug and pull, but the line of supermarket carts (seems, seem) welded together.

NAME: _____

DATE: _____

MASTERY TEST 2 | Subject-Verb Agreement

In the space provided, write the correct form of the verb shown in the margin.

is, are
1. The chain-link fence surrounding the school grounds _____ ready to collapse.

plays, play
2. I envy people who _____ a musical instrument well.

is, are
3. Inside the bakery shop carton _____ your favorite pastries.

has, have
4. Someone on the team _____ forgotten her warm-up jacket.

wants, want
5. Because I spilled a beaker of sulfuric acid, nobody in my chemistry lab _____ to work with me.

is, are
6. At the end of the long movie line _____ about twenty people who will not get into the next show.

looks, look
7. Neither of the coats _____ good on you.

is, are
8. A little time for rest and relaxation _____ what I need right now.

was, were
9. The shirts that she thought _____ too expensive are now on sale.

shops, shop
10. Raquel and her mother _____ together on Thursday nights.

NAME: _____

DATE: _____

Subject-Verb Agreement   **MASTERY TEST 3**

Cross out the incorrect form of the verb. In addition, underline the subject
that goes with the verb. Then write the correct form of the verb in the space
provided. Mark the one sentence that is correct with a *C*.

_____ 1. The price of the computer games have been reduced.

_____ 2. The marigolds that was planted yesterday were accidentally mowed over today.

_____ 3. Many tables at the auction was covered with very old books.

_____ 4. Brenda checked with the employment agencies that was helping her look
for a job.

_____ 5. Trucks and cars uses our street heavily since road construction began.

_____ 6. The old woman rooting through those trash baskets have refused to enter
a nursing home.

_____ 7. The vicious gossip about our new neighbor have begun to anger me.

_____ 8. Donovan plays two sports and are good at both of them.

_____ 9. The plastic slipcovers on their furniture has started to turn yellow.

_____ 10. Either my willpower or my lust for chocolate has to win out.

NAME: _____

DATE: _____

MASTERY TEST 4 | # Subject-Verb Agreement

Cross out the incorrect form of the verb. In addition, underline the subject that goes with the verb. Then write the correct form of the verb in the space provided. Mark the one sentence that is correct with a *C*.

_____ 1. Why has Cindy and Karen quit their jobs as telephone repair persons?

_____ 2. One actress at the rehearsals have become ill from the heat.

_____ 3. The buildings across the street is all going to be demolished.

_____ 4. Those old coats in your closet has dust lying on their shoulders.

_____ 5. Archery and soccer is the new sports at our school.

_____ 6. If only there was more hours in the day, I could get all my work done.

_____ 7. Two pieces of dry toast and a soft-boiled egg is all Rita is allowed to eat for breakfast.

_____ 8. One of the waitresses at the diner have just won a free trip to Las Vegas.

_____ 9. Lola's long red silk scarf and her lipstick match perfectly.

_____ 10. Anything that parents tell their children usually get ignored.

NAME: _____

DATE: _____

Subject-Verb Agreement

Underline the correct verb in the parentheses. Note that you will first have to determine the subject in each sentence. To help find subjects in certain sentences, you may find it helpful to cross out prepositional phrases.

1. All the animals for sale in that pet store (looks, look) unhealthy.

2. The extra fees on may new cell phone bill (is, are) too high.

3. One of my instructors (has, have) a hybrid car.

4. Wet roads and dangerous driving (was, were) to blame for the accident.

5. Not one cash register in the store (is, are) working correctly.

6. Once a year, Jim and his buddies (goes, go) fishing.

7. The books in the library (was, were) damaged by the flood.

8. Crawling across the kitchen floor (was, were) three hairy spiders.

9. The employees of the hospital (wants, want) a pay raise.

10. Neither Kevin nor Denise (wants, want) to talk about their relationship.

11. A stack of folded shirts in the Laundromat (was, were) stolen.

12. Someone once said, "Politics (is, are) a dirty business."

13. A few kids on the high school team (hopes, hope) to play college football.

14. Hakeem is one of those guys who (knows, know) how to fix anything.

15. The buttons on the old keyboard (is, are) dirty from use.

16. The executives of that company (makes, make) ten times as much as any of their employees.

17. The old houses across the street on our block (needs, need) major repairs.

18. Shoppers in the long line at the closeout sale in the mall (was, were) muttering angrily to themselves.

19. Physics (is, are) a subject that requires strong math skills.

20. The chrome wheels on the classic Ford Mustang (shines, shine).

Consistent Verb Tense

Introductory Activity

See if you can find and underline the two mistakes in verb tense in the following selection.

When Computer Warehouse had a sale, Alex decided to buy a new personal computer. He planned to set up the machine himself and hoped to connect it to the Internet right away. When he arrived home, however, Alex discovers that hooking up the wires to the computer could be complicated and confusing. The directions sounded as if they had been written for electrical engineers. After two hours of frustration, Alex gave up and calls a technician for help.

Now try to complete the following statement:

Verb tenses should be consistent. In the selection above, two verbs have to be changed because they are mistakenly in the (*present, past*) _____ tense while all the other verbs in the selection are in the (*present, past*) _____ tense.

Answers are on page 564.

Keeping Tenses Consistent

Do not shift tenses unnecessarily. If you begin writing a paper in the present tense, don't shift suddenly to the past. If you begin in the past, don't shift without reason to the present. Notice the inconsistent verb tenses in the following example:

> Smoke <u>spilled</u> from the front of the overheated car. The driver <u>opens</u> up the hood, then <u>jumped</u> back as steam <u>billows</u> out.

The verbs must be consistently in the present tense:

> Smoke <u>spills</u> from the front of the overheated car. The driver <u>opens</u> up the hood, then <u>jumps</u> back as steam <u>billows</u> out.

Or the verbs must be consistently in the past tense:

> Smoke <u>spilled</u> from the front of the overheated car. The driver <u>opened</u> up the hood, then <u>jumped</u> back as steam <u>billowed</u> out.

www.mhhe.com/langan

In each item, one verb must be changed so that it agrees in tense with the other verbs. Cross out the incorrect verb and write the correct form in the space at the left.

Practice 1

EXAMPLE

looked   I gave away my striped sweater after three people told me I ~~look~~ like a giant bee.

_____ 1. Mike peels and eats oranges at movies; the smell caused other people to move away from him.

_____ 2. The nursing program attracted Juanita, but she weighed the pluses and minuses and then decides to enroll in the x-ray technician course instead.

_____ 3. I grabbed for the last bag of pretzels on the supermarket shelf. But when I pick it up, I discovered there was a tear in the cellophane bag.

_____ 4. Ruby waits eagerly for the mail carrier each day. Part of her hoped to get a letter in which someone declares he is madly in love with her and will cherish her forever.

_____ 5. The first thing Jerry does every day is weigh himself. The scale informed him what he can eat that day.

_____ 6. My sister sprinkles detergent flakes on my head and then ran around telling everyone that I had dandruff.

_____ 7. When Norm peeled back the old shingles, he discovers that the roof was rotted through.

_____   8. My father knocked on the bedroom door. When he asks me if he could come in, I said, "Not right now."

_____   9. Omar is so unaggressive that when a clerk overcharged him for an item, he pays the money and makes no comment.

_____   10. When my doctor told me I needed an operation, I swallow hard and my stomach churned.

Review Test 1

Change the verbs where needed in the following selection so that they are consistently in the past tense. Cross out each incorrect verb and write the correct form above it, as shown in the example. You will need to make nine corrections.

[1]Last week, I began driving to work, as usual. [2]I drove up the expressway ramp and ~~merge~~ *merged* into three lanes of speeding cars. [3]I turned on the radio and settle in for another twenty-five minutes of tension and pressure. [4]Then, about five miles on, I saw something unusual. [5]Up ahead, stranded on the narrow concrete island that separated three lanes of eastbound traffic from three lanes of westbound traffic, was a small brown dog. [6]Streams of zooming cars pass the animal like two rushing rivers. [7]Several times, the dog attempt to cross the road. [8]He moves gingerly onto the highway, only to jump back at the approach of a car. [9]I realize it was only a matter of time before the panicky dog bolt into the traffic and kill itself. [10]I didn't know what to do. [11]I slow my car down a little and wondered if I should pull onto the shoulder. [12]Then, I heard a welcome sound—a police siren. [13]Someone must have called the state police about the dog. [14]In my rearview mirror, I saw the patrol car and a white van labeled "Animal Control." [15]I drove on, confident that the dog would be rescued and relieve that someone had cared enough to save its small life.

Review Test 2

Change verbs as necessary in the following selection so that they are consistently in the past tense. Cross out each incorrect verb and write the correct form above it. You will need to make ten corrections in all.

[1]The first time I tried to parallel park on my own was a memorable experience. [2]My first mistake was trying to move into the parking place hood first. [3]I got the car's front end close to the curb, but the rear end remains out in the street. [4]I then backed out and pull up beside the car in front of the parking place. [5]This is where I make my second mistake. [6]Because I was worried that someone might steal my place, I fail to pull up enough alongside the car. [7]So when I backed in, my rear wheels are against the curb while the car's hood was out in the street blocking traffic. [8]I then had to pull out, and I attempt to park once more. [9]As I backed in the second time, I remember my teacher's advice. [10]She trained me not to turn the wheels in until the steering wheel of my car is even with the rear bumper of the car in front of the parking place. [11]I did this and the car slips neatly into the space, with only a few inches left between the tires and the curb. [12]As I was congratulating myself on my success, the car behind me pulls out, leaving a parking space big enough for a Mack truck.

NAME: _____

DATE: _____

MASTERY TEST 1   # Consistent Verb Tense

In each item, one verb must be changed so that it agrees in tense with the other verbs. Cross out the inconsistent verb and write the correct form in the space provided.

_____ 1. After he bought a CD player and collects a lot of CDs, my brother wound up listening mostly to his FM radio.

_____ 2. The little boy raced his Lionel train too fast, so that it topples off the track when it rounded a curve.

_____ 3. She let her mother cut her hair until her friends began saying that her hairstyle looks very strange.

_____ 4. The air pollution is so bad that the weather bureau urges people not to exercise outside until it cleared.

_____ 5. Sandy greeted the mailman and flips quickly through the letters he handed her to see if there was a letter from her boyfriend.

_____ 6. After the truck overturned, passing motorists parked their cars on the side of the road and walk back to look at the damage.

_____ 7. The lights went out and we all jump because we were watching a horror movie at the time.

_____ 8. The wind came up quickly, knocks down a lot of dead tree branches, and blew in the front window of the bank across the street.

_____ 9. After the wolf unsuccessfully huffed and puffed at the little pigs' brick house, he realizes he would have to hire a demolition contractor.

_____ 10. While in the hospital, she read lots of magazines, watched daytime television, shuffles up and down the corridor, and generally felt very bored.

Consistent Verb Tense   MASTERY TEST 2

In each item, one verb must be changed so that it agrees in tense with the other verb or verbs. Cross out the inconsistent verb and write the correct form in the space provided.

_____ 1. Lola likes to use lip gloss but hates the way it stains her fingers and never seemed to come off.

_____ 2. Tony reached way down into the bread bag. He skipped the first couple of pieces and grabs one of the fresher, bigger pieces from the middle.

_____ 3. Darrell believes he is smarter than we are; he tried to show this all the time.

_____ 4. When I noticed the way my mother cocked her head, I realize that she had an earache.

_____ 5. When we asked for a fresh tablecloth, the waiter looks as though we were speaking Russian.

_____ 6. As the tourists walked through the forest, they cheek the trail markers that were posted along the way.

_____ 7. My eyes always close and my fingers get numb when I listened to an afternoon lecture in Professor Snorrel's class.

_____ 8. Leon graduated from Camden High School, works as a plumber's assistant for two years, and then returned to school.

_____ 9. At holiday dinners, many people continue to stuff themselves even when it seemed obvious that they are already full.

_____ 10. I wiped my hands on my trousers before I walk in for the job interview. I did not want the personnel officer to know my palms were sweating.

Additional Information about Verbs

The purpose of this special chapter is to provide additional information about verbs. Some people will find the grammatical terms here a helpful reminder of earlier school learning about verbs. For them, these terms will increase their understanding of how verbs function in English. Other people may welcome more detailed information about terms used elsewhere in the text. In either case, remember that the most common mistakes people make when using verbs have been treated in earlier sections of the book.

Verb Tense

Verbs tell us the time of an action. The time that a verb shows is usually called *tense.* The most common tenses are the simple present, past, and future. In addition, there are nine other tenses that enable us to express more specific ideas about time than we could with the simple tenses alone. In the box on the facing page are the twelve verb tenses, and examples of each tense. Read them to increase your sense of the many different ways of expressing time in English.

Tenses	Examples
Present	I *work*.
	Tanya *works*.
Past	Howard *worked* on the lawn.
Future	You *will work* overtime this week.
Present perfect	Gail *has worked* hard on the puzzle.
	They *have worked* well together.
Past perfect	They *had worked* eight hours before their shift ended.
Future perfect	The volunteers *will have worked* many unpaid hours.
Present progressive	I *am* not *working* today.
	You *are working* the second shift.
	The clothes dryer *is* not *working* properly.
Past progressive	She *was working* outside.
	The plumbers *were working* here this morning.
Future progressive	The sound system *will be working* by tonight.
Present perfect progressive	Married life *has* not *been working* out for that couple.
Past perfect progressive	I *had been working* overtime until recently.
Future perfect progressive	My sister *will have been working* at that store for eleven straight months by the time she takes a vacation next week.

www.mhhe.com/langan

The perfect tenses are formed by adding *have, has,* or *had* to the past participle (the form of the verb that ends, usually, in *-ed*). The progressive tenses are formed by adding *am, is, are, was,* or *were* to the present participle (the form of the verb that ends in *-ing*). The perfect progressive tenses are formed by adding *have been, has been,* or *had been* to the present participle.

Certain tenses are explained in more detail on the following pages.

Present Perfect
(*have* or *has* + past participle)

The present perfect tense expresses an action that began in the past and has recently been completed or is continuing in the present.

> The city *has* just *agreed* on a contract with the sanitation workers.
>
> Tony's parents *have lived* in that house for twenty years.
>
> Lola *has enjoyed* vampire novels since she was a little girl.

Past Perfect
(*had* + past participle)

The past perfect tense expresses a past action that was completed before another past action.

> Lola *had learned* to dance by the time she was five.
>
> The class *had* just *started* when the fire bell rang.
>
> Bad weather *had* never *been* a problem on our vacations until last year.

Present Progressive
(*am, is,* or *are* + *-ing* form)

The present progressive tense expresses an action still in progress.

> I *am taking* an early train into the city every day this week.
>
> Karl *is playing* softball over at the field.
>
> The vegetables *are growing* rapidly.

Past Progressive
(*was* or *were* + *-ing* form)

The past progressive expresses an action that was in progress in the past.

> I *was spending* twenty dollars a week on cigarettes before I quit.
>
> Last week, the store *was selling* many items at half price.
>
> My friends *were driving* over to pick me up when the accident occurred.

Practice

1

For the sentences that follow, fill in the present or past perfect or the present or past progressive of the verb shown. Use the tense that seems to express the meaning of each sentence best.

EXAMPLE

park   This summer, Mickey _____*is parking*_____ cars at a French restaurant.

walk   1. We _____ for five miles before we realized we were lost.

feel   2. The new mail carrier _____ good about his job until the first dog bit him.

place   3. After an hour, the waiter _____ only a basket of stale rolls on our table.

try   4. All last winter, my little brother _____ to get a job carrying groceries at the supermarket.

grow   5. This year, Aunt Agatha _____ tomatoes—she must have about five hundred already.

look   6. I _____ everywhere for the paper; finally, I found it under the cat.

study   7. Miriam _____ French for three years so she can talk to her poodle.

see   8. James loves karate; he _____ every Bruce Lee movie in existence.

watch   9. Nilsa _____ soap operas for four hours a day in the two months she was unemployed.

throw   10. The pitcher _____ to second; unfortunately, the runner was on third.

Verbals

Verbals are words formed from verbs. Verbals, like verbs, often express action. They can add variety to your sentences and vigor to your writing style. The three kinds of verbals are *infinitives, participles,* and *gerunds.*

www.mhhe.com/langan

Infinitive

An infinitive is *to* plus the base form of the verb.

> I started *to practice.*
>
> Don't try *to lift* that table.
>
> I asked Russ *to drive* me home.

Participle

A participle is a verb form used as an adjective (a descriptive word). The present participle ends in *-ing*. The past participle ends in *-ed* or has an irregular ending.

> *Favoring* his *cramped* leg, the *screaming* boy waded out of the pool.
>
> The *laughing* child held up her *locked* piggy bank.
>
> *Using* a shovel and a bucket, I scooped water out of the *flooded* basement.

Gerund

A gerund is the *-ing* form of a verb used as a noun.

> *Studying* wears me out.
>
> *Playing* basketball is my main pleasure during the week.
>
> Through *jogging,* you can get yourself in shape.

Practice

2

In the space beside each sentence, identify the italicized word as a participle (*P*), an infinitive (*I*), or a gerund (*G*).

_____ 1. The *sobbing* child could not find his parents.

_____ 2. *Gossiping* with neighbors is my favorite pastime.

_____ 3. *Painting* the front porch is a chore Fred promises to get to every spring.

_____ 4. All my brother ever wants *to do* is play video games.

_____ 5. Lola always liked *to race* through a pile of dead leaves.

_____ 6. My boss's *graying* hair gives him a look of authority.

_____ 7. *Glowing* embers were all that remained of the fire.

_____ 8. It doesn't matter if you win or lose—just try *to break* even.

_____ 9. *Holding* her nose, my mother asked, "What's that awful smell?"

_____ 10. *Wearing* glasses makes that man look intelligent.

Active and Passive Verbs

When the subject of a sentence performs the action of a verb, the verb is in the *active voice*. When the subject of a sentence receives the action of a verb, the verb is in the *passive voice*.

The passive form of a verb consists of a form of the verb *be* plus the past participle of the main verb. Look at the active and passive forms of the verbs below.

Active

Lola *ate* the vanilla pudding.
(The subject, *Lola*, is the doer of the action.)

The plumber *replaced* the water heater.
(The subject, *plumber,* is the doer of the action.)

Passive

The vanilla pudding *was eaten by* Lola.
(The subject, *pudding*, does not act. Instead, something happens to it.)

The water heater *was replaced by* the plumber.
(The subject, *heater,* does not act. Instead, something happens to it.)

In general, active verbs are more effective than passive ones. Active verbs give your writing a simpler and more vigorous style. The passive form of verbs is appropriate, however, when the performer of the action is unknown or is less important than the receiver of the action. For example:

My house was vandalized last night.
(The performer of the action is unknown.)

Troy was seriously injured as a result of your negligence.
(The receiver of the action, *Troy,* is being emphasized.)

Change the following sentences from the passive to the active voice. Note that you may have to add a subject in some cases.

Practice 3

EXAMPLE

The moped bicycle was ridden by Tony.
Tony rode the moped bicycle.

The basketball team was given a standing ovation.
The crowd gave the basketball team a standing ovation.

(Here a subject had to be added.)

1. The surprise party was organized by Eliza.

2. Many people were offended by the comedian.

3. The old woman's groceries are paid for by the neighbors.

4. The horse chestnuts were knocked off the trees by the boys.

_____

5. The devil was driven out of Regan by the exorcist.

_____

6. The huge moving van was loaded by four perspiring men.

_____

7. A tray of glasses was dropped by the inexperienced waiter.

_____

8. Umbrellas are always being lost by my forgetful Aunt Agatha.

_____

9. Babe Ruth's home run record was finally broken by Barry Bonds.

_____

10. A bomb was found in the suitcase by the airport security staff.

_____

Review Test 1

On separate paper, write three sentences apiece that use:

1. Present perfect tense

2. Past perfect tense

3. Present progressive tense

4. Past progressive tense

5. Infinitive

6. Participle

7. Gerund

8. Passive voice (when the subject is unknown or is less important than the receiver of an action—see page 196–197)

NAME: _____

DATE: _____

SCORE
Number Correct

_____ x 10

_____ %

Additional Information about Verbs MASTERY TEST 1

PART A

In each space, write the **present perfect tense** form of the verb shown.

practice   1. Carlos _____ his speech each night for the past week.

search   2. Divers _____ the sunken ship looking for lost treasure.

clean   3. As of today, volunteers _____ three vacant lots for the new neighborhood garden.

PART B

In each space, write the **past perfect tense** form of the verb shown.

hike   4. Ray _____ for an hour when he noticed a bear following him.

inspect   5. My father _____ the old car twice before he agreed to buy it.

PART C

In each space, write the **present progressive tense** form of the verb shown.

sing   6. Our neighbors _____ in the church choir tonight.

run   7. Sandra _____ in the New York City marathon.

PART D

In each space, write the **past progressive tense** form of the verb shown.

talk   8. Last night, Jessica _____ for hours on the phone.

plan   9. Until he was severely injured in a car bombing, the soldier _____ to get married this summer.

eat   10. Before he started his diet, Phil _____ ice cream after each meal.

199

MASTERY TEST 2 Additional Information about Verbs

PART 1

In the space provided, identify the italicized word as a participle (*P*), an infinitive (*I*), or a gerund (*G*).

_____ 1. The *blaring* siren woke up the entire neighborhood.

_____ 2. *Cooking* helps Mimi relax when she is stressed.

_____ 3. After school, the boys wanted *to play* video games.

_____ 4. Too much *drinking* ruined Paul's first semester of college.

_____ 5. *Crumbling* walls are all that remains of the homes in the abandoned neighborhood.

PART 2

Change the following sentences from the passive to the active voice. Note that you may have to add a subject in some cases.

1. The wooden floor in our living room was eaten by termites.

   _____

2. A small bonus was given to each employee by the store manager.

   _____

3. Food and shelter were donated to the survivors of the storm.

   _____

4. Tomatoes and peppers were planted in the backyard by Maria.

   _____

5. A threat to bomb the high school was made by an angry student.

   _____

Pronoun Reference, Agreement, and Point of View

13

Introductory Activity

Read each pair of sentences below, noting the underlined pronouns. Then see if you can circle the correct letter in each of the statements that follow.

1. a. Only one of the nominees for "best actress" showed their anxiety as the names were being read.

   b. Only one of the nominees for "best actress" showed her anxiety as the names were being read.

2. a. At the mall, they are already putting up Christmas decorations.

   b. At the mall, shop owners are already putting up Christmas decorations.

3. a. I go to the steak house often because you can get inexpensive meals there.

   b. I go to the steak house often because I can get inexpensive meals there.

In the first pair, (a, b) uses the underlined pronoun correctly because the pronoun refers to *one*, which is a singular word.

In the second pair, (a, b) is correct because otherwise the pronoun reference would be unclear.

In the third pair, (a, b) is correct because the pronoun point of view should not be shifted unnecessarily.

Answers are on page 564.

Pronouns are words that take the place of nouns (words for persons, places, or things). In fact, the word *pronoun* means *for a noun.* Pronouns are shortcuts that keep you from unnecessarily repeating words in writing. Here are some examples of pronouns:

Martha shampooed *her* dog. (*Her* is a pronoun that takes the place of *Martha's.*)

As the door swung open, *it* creaked. (*It* replaces *door.*)

When the motorcyclists arrived at McDonald's, *they* removed *their* helmets. (*They* replaces *motorcyclists; their* replaces *motorcyclists'.*)

This chapter presents rules that will help you avoid three common mistakes people make with pronouns. The rules are as follows:

1. A pronoun must refer clearly to the word it replaces.
2. A pronoun must agree in number with the word or words it replaces.
3. Pronouns should not shift unnecessarily in point of view.

www.mhhe.com/langan

Pronoun Reference

A sentence may be confusing and unclear if a pronoun appears to refer to more than one word, as in this sentence:

I locked my suitcase in my car, and then it was stolen.

What was stolen? It is unclear whether the suitcase or the car was stolen.

I locked my suitcase in my car, and then my car was stolen.

A sentence may also be confusing if the pronoun does not refer to any specific word. Look at this sentence:

We never buy fresh vegetables at that store because they charge too much.

Who charges too much? There is no specific word that *they* refers to. Be clear.

We never buy fresh vegetables at that store because the owners charge too much.

Here are additional sentences with unclear pronoun reference. Read the explanations of why they are unclear and look carefully at the ways they are corrected.

Unclear

Lola told Gina that she had gained weight.

(*Who* had gained weight: Lola or Gina? Be clear.)

My older brother is an electrician, but I'm not interested in it.

(There is no specific word that *it* refers to. It would not make sense to say, "I'm not interested in electrician.")

Our instructor did not explain the assignment, which made me angry.

(Does *which* mean that the instructor's failure to explain the assignment made you angry or that the assignment itself made you angry? Be clear.)

Clear

Lola told Gina, "You've gained weight."

(Quotation marks, which can sometimes be used to correct an unclear reference, are explained in Chapter 25.)

My older brother is an electrician, but I'm not interested in becoming one.

I was angry that our instructor did not explain the assignment.

Rewrite each of the following sentences to make clear the vague pronoun reference. Add, change, or omit words as necessary.

Practice

1

EXAMPLE

Lana thanked Rita for the gift, which was very thoughtful of her.

Lana thanked Rita for the thoughtful gift.

1. Mario insisted to Harry that it was his turn to drive.

   _____

   _____

2. I failed two of my courses last semester because they graded unfairly.

   _____

   _____

3. Don was offered an accounting job, which pleased his parents very much.

   _____

   _____

4. When Tony questioned the mechanic, he became very upset.

_____

_____

5. I was very nervous about the biology exam, which was unexpected.

_____

_____

6. Paul told his younger brother that the dog had chewed his new running shoes.

_____

_____

7. My cousin is an astrologer, but I don't believe in it.

_____

_____

8. Liz told Elaine that she had been promoted.

_____

_____

9. Whenever I start enjoying a new television show, they take it off the air.

_____

_____

10. When the center fielder heard the crack of the bat, he raced toward the fence but was unable to catch it.

_____

_____

www.mhhe.com/langan

Pronoun Agreement

A pronoun must agree in number with the word or words it replaces. If the word a pronoun refers to is singular, the pronoun must be singular; if the word is plural, the pronoun must be plural. (Note that the word a pronoun refers to is known as the *antecedent.*)

Lola agreed to lend me her Billie Holiday CDs.

The gravediggers sipped coffee during their break.

In the first example, the pronoun *her* refers to the singular word *Lola;* in the second example, the pronoun *their* refers to the plural word *gravediggers.*

Write the appropriate pronoun (*they, their, them, it*) in the blank space in each of the following sentences.

Practice

2

EXAMPLE

My credit cards got me into debt, so I burned _____*them*_____.

1. After the hikers arrived at the camp, _____ removed _____ heavy packs.

2. That breakfast cereal is delicious, but _____ has almost no nutrients.

3. I never buy gifts in stores anymore, for I use my computer to purchase _____ on the Internet.

4. The heat was so oppressive during the race that _____ caused several runners to pass out.

5. Anna's parents went to a marriage counselor, and _____ are getting along better now.

www.mhhe.com/langan

Indefinite Pronouns

The following words, known as *indefinite pronouns,* are always singular.

Indefinite Pronouns		
(-*one* words)	**(-*body* words)**	
one	nobody	each
anyone	anybody	either
everyone	everybody	neither
someone	somebody	

Either of the apartments has *its* drawbacks.

One of the girls lost *her* skateboard.

Everyone in the class must hand in *his* paper tomorrow.

In each example, the pronoun is singular because it refers to one of the indefinite pronouns. There are two important points to remember about indefinite pronouns.

Point 1 The last example above suggests that everyone in the class is male. If the students were all female, the pronoun would be *her*. If the students were a mixed group of males and females, the pronoun form would be *his or her*.

Everyone in the class must hand in *his or her* paper tomorrow.

Some writers still follow the traditional practice of using *his* to refer to both men and women. Many now use *his or her* to avoid an implied sexual bias. Perhaps the best practice, though, is to avoid using either *his* or the somewhat awkward *his or her*. This can often be done by rewriting a sentence in the plural:

All students in the class must hand in *their* papers tomorrow.

Here are some examples of sentences that can be rewritten in the plural.

A young child is seldom willing to share her toys with others.
Young children are seldom willing to share their toys with others.

Anyone who does not wear his seat belt will be fined.
People who do not wear their seat belts will be fined.

A newly elected politician should not forget his or her campaign promises.
Newly elected politicians should not forget their campaign promises.

Point 2 In informal spoken English, *plural* pronouns are often used with indefinite pronouns. Instead of saying

Everybody has *his or her* own idea of an ideal vacation.

we are likely to say

Everybody has *their* own idea of an ideal vacation.

Here are other examples:

Everyone in the class must pass in *their* papers.
Everybody in our club has *their* own idea about how to raise money.
No one in our family skips *their* chores.

In such cases, the indefinite pronouns are clearly plural in meaning. Also, the use of such plurals helps people avoid the awkward *his or her*. In time, the plural pronoun may be accepted in formal speech or writing. Until that happens, however, you should use the grammatically correct singular form in your writing.

Underline the correct pronoun.

EXAMPLE

   Neither of those houses has (its, their) own garage.

1. Neither of the boys brought (his, their) homework in today.
2. Each waitress is responsible for (her, their) own section.
3. It seems as though no one in my fraternity wants to pay (his, their) dues these days.
4. Only one of the boys remembered to bring (his, their) cell phone.
5. Each of my sisters has (her, their) own room.
6. Any man who purchased one of those ill-made suits probably wasted (his, their) money.
7. Almost every woman on our street leaves for (her, their) job about the same time each morning.
8. Before a discussion in our women's club, each member must decide on one question that (she, they) wants to ask.
9. Either of the travel routes has (their, its) share of places to see.
10. Any player on the men's team who gains weight is in danger of losing (his, their) job.

Pronoun Point of View

Pronouns should not shift their point of view unnecessarily. When writing a paper, be consistent in your use of first-, second-, or third-person pronouns.

Type of Pronoun	Singular	Plural
First-person pronouns	I (my, mine, me)	we (our, us)
Second-person pronouns	you (your)	you (your)
Third-person pronouns	he (his, him) she (her) it (its)	they (their, them)

> **TIP** Any person, place, or thing, as well as any indefinite pronoun like *one,* *anyone, someone,* and so on (page 205), is a third-person word.

For instance, if you start writing in the first-person *I*, don't jump suddenly to the second-person *you*. Or if you are writing in the third-person *they*, don't shift unexpectedly to *you*. Look at the examples.

Inconsistent

One reason that *I* like living in the city is that *you* always have a wide choice of sports events to attend. (The most common mistake people make is to let a *you* slip into their writing after they start with another pronoun.)

Someone who is dieting should have the help of friends*; you* should also have plenty of willpower.

Students who work while *they* are going to school face special problems. For one thing, *you* seldom have enough study time.

Consistent

One reason that *I* like living in the city is that *I* always have a wide choice of sports events to attend.

Someone who is dieting should have the help of friends; *he* or *she* should also have plenty of willpower.

Students who work while *they* are going to school face special problems. For one thing, *they* seldom have enough study time.

Practice

4

Cross out inconsistent pronouns in the following sentences and write the correction above the error.

EXAMPLE

I work much better when the boss doesn't hover over ~~you~~ *me* with instructions on what to do.

1. What I don't like about eating Chinese food is that you always feel hungry an hour later.

2. Students may not leave the exam room unless you have finished the exam.

3. These days people never seem to get the recognition they deserve, no matter how hard you work.

4. If our pets could talk, we would find it easier to take care of them. As it is, you can never be sure what a pet means by a bark or a meow.

5. Whenever a woman feels she is being discriminated against, you should register a complaint.

6. If a person plans to make a complaint, you should check all the facts first.

7. I work at a shop where you do not get paid for all the holidays you should.

8. If you think you're coming down with cold symptoms, one should take action right away.

9. Once we were at the campsite, you had only a radio as contact with the outside world.

10. In our office, we can have a long coffee break anytime you want it.

Review Test   1

Underline the correct word in the parentheses.

1. When the moon and stars come out, (it, the night) is beautiful.

2. If a person drives defensively, (he or she, they) will be constantly aware of other drivers' actions on the road.

3. Hitting the wall with her skateboard, she chipped (it, the skateboard).

4. Persons wanting old furniture should check the newspaper classified section; also, (they, you) might stop at yard sales.

5. We drove for hours, and (we, you) got scared by the heavy fog.

6. Lonnie is the kind of player that always gives (his, their) best for the team.

7. Although we had a delightful vacation, (you, we) are always glad to get home.

8. I've always loved butterfly exhibits, so I decided to start collecting (them, butterflies).

9. When Vanessa asked why she was being given a ticket, (he, the officer) said she had run a stop sign.

10. I buy my clothes at the outlet store because (it has, they have) the best prices.

Review Test 2

Cross out the pronoun error in each sentence and write the correction in the space provided at the left. Then circle the letter that correctly describes the type of error that was made.

EXAMPLES

_____*Students*_____ ~~Anyone~~ turning in their papers late will be penalized.

Mistake in: a. pronoun reference   (b.) pronoun agreement

_____*Paul*_____ When Clyde takes his son Paul to the park, ~~he~~ enjoys himself.

Mistake in: (a.) pronoun reference   b. pronoun point of view

_____*we*_____ From where we stood, ~~you~~ could see three states.

Mistake in: a. pronoun agreement   (b.) pronoun point of view

_____ 1. After throwing the dog a stick, I took it home.

   Mistake in: a. pronoun reference   b. pronoun agreement

_____ 2. Everyone on the women's team was in the locker room packing their travel bag.

   Mistake in: a. pronoun agreement   b. pronoun point of view

_____ 3. Ralph walks the dog so he won't get fat.

   Mistake in: a. pronoun reference   b. pronoun point of view

_____ 4. One of the children forgot to put on their gloves.

   Mistake in: a. pronoun agreement   b. pronoun point of view

_____ 5. I've been taking allergy pills, and now it doesn't bother me as much.

   Mistake in: a. pronoun reference   b. pronoun agreement

_____ 6. When people face a common problem, your personal relationship often becomes stronger.

   Mistake in: a. pronoun agreement   b. pronoun point of view

_____ 7. Everyone who was at the dance has their own memories of the sudden fire.

   Mistake in: a. pronoun reference   b. pronoun agreement

HINT You may want to rewrite item 7 in the plural, using the lines below.

_____

_____

_____ 8. Sometimes our instructor has Ted write on the board because chalk dust makes him sneeze.

Mistake in: a. pronoun reference   b. pronoun point of view

_____ 9. Even though I closed the bedroom door, you could still hear the television downstairs.

Mistake in: a. pronoun agreement   b. pronoun point of view

_____ 10. If a person walks through those woods, you will see at least ten kinds of nesting birds.

Mistake in: a. pronoun agreement   b. pronoun point of view

HINT You may want to rewrite item 10 in the plural, using the lines below.

_____

_____

NAME: _____

DATE: _____

MASTERY TEST 1 Pronoun Reference, Agreement, and Point of View

Underline the correct word in the parentheses.

1. I realized that each of the coaches had done (her, their) best to motivate me.

2. Either of the television sets has (its, their) good and bad features.

3. I hated my job as an office mail boy because (I, you) got taken advantage of by everyone.

4. A player on the ice hockey team broke (his, their) arm last week.

5. I quit my pottery classes because (it, the ceramic dust) made me sneeze.

6. If (a person goes, people go) barefoot through the store, he or she can expect to meet a security guard.

7. We went to Disney World on a Sunday, and (you, we) had to wait an hour for every ride.

8. My cat got hold of a lollipop, and (it, the cat) got very sticky.

9. When Jack argues with Ted, (he, Ted) always gets in the last word.

10. One of my sisters has decided to separate from (her, their) husband.

11. I've been taking cold medicine, and now (it, the cold) is better.

12. The ten girls in our cabin developed a closeness that (you, we) could feel grow as the summer at camp progressed.

13. Sarah was nervous about her speech, but (it, the nervousness) didn't show.

14. Each of the men was asked to put (his, their) name on the petition.

15. When we reached the station, (you, we) realized that the train had left.

16. Has everybody in the sorority finished (her, their) work for the committee?

17. I went fishing yesterday and caught three (of them, fish).

18. No one in the men's dorm felt (he, they) had taken very good notes at the lecture.

19. When the Dolphins met the Cowboys in the playoff game, (they, the Dolphins) won.

20. If students work with irresponsible lab partners, (you, they) will find it difficult to get a good grade.

NAME: _____

DATE: _____

Pronoun Reference, Agreement, and Point of View

In the space provided, write *PE* beside the sentences that contain pronoun errors.
Write *C* beside the two sentences that use pronouns correctly. Then cross out
each pronoun error and write the correction above it.

EXAMPLE

_____*PE*_____   Each of the boys explained ~~their~~ *his* project.

_____   1. Lola loves to run, but Tony's not interested in it.

_____   2. My deepest thoughts and feelings are ones that you can hide easily.

_____   3. If I don't have my activities for the day planned in advance, I waste too much time deciding what to do next.

_____   4. My cousin is a religious man and has devoted much of his life to it.

_____   5. They take too many taxes out of my weekly paycheck.

_____   6. I have a carton full of pencils and pens here; where do you want me to put them?

_____   7. One of the best swimmers on the team has badly sprained her back.

_____   8. As we watched the lightning storm, you were in awe.

_____   9. Elaine told Sue that she was being selfish.

_____   10. Each of the women had pinned a gardenia in their hair.

NAME: _____

DATE: _____

MASTERY TEST 3 | # Pronoun Reference, Agreement, and Point of View

In the space provided, write *PE* beside sentences that contain pronoun errors. Write *C* beside the two sentences that use pronouns correctly. Then cross out each pronoun error and write the correction above it.

_____ 1. A person should always be extremely careful when using their chainsaw.

_____ 2. Many people flick on the television as soon as they get in the house; this is a bad habit for you to get into.

_____ 3. After I joined the shopping club, they began sending me stacks of junk mail.

_____ 4. Many toys on the market today can both entertain children and educate them as well.

_____ 5. The custard pie was so good that you kept going back for more.

_____ 6. Lola told her mother that she was too impatient.

_____ 7. A student in a late-afternoon class often has difficulty attending to their instructor.

_____ 8. No one except a police officer is allowed to turn their car around on a toll road.

_____ 9. When my broken wrist was set, I could feel the bones grinding against each other.

_____ 10. At the bookstore in the mall, they have all the best sellers in racks at the front.

NAME: _____

DATE: _____

Pronoun Reference, Agreement, and Point of View  MASTERY TEST 4

In the spaces provided, write *PE* beside sentences that contain pronoun errors. Write *C* beside the two sentences that use pronouns correctly. Then cross out each pronoun error and write the correction above it.

_____ 1. When a tire went flat on his car, my brother had to replace it.

_____ 2. People will enjoy the movie if they don't mind a sentimental ending.

_____ 3. Everyone who donates their time for the project will receive free admission to the union picnic.

_____ 4. People should never go for a job interview if you don't prepare in advance.

_____ 5. If a person intends to pass a chemistry course, you have to be good at math.

_____ 6. Tisha told her mother she needed a new pair of shoes.

_____ 7. We wanted to see the exhibit, but you couldn't push through the crowds.

_____ 8. Everyone in the class should be ready to deliver her report by next Monday.

_____ 9. I enjoyed the volleyball match even though I'm not very good at it.

_____ 10. I wanted a free pencil sharpener, but you first had to buy five dozen pencils.

Pronoun Types

Introductory Activity

In each pair, write a check beside the sentence that you think uses pronouns correctly.

Ali and *I* enrolled in a computer course. _____
Ali and *me* enrolled in a computer course. _____

The police officer pointed to my sister and *me*. _____
The police officer pointed to my sister and *I*. _____

Lola prefers men *whom* take pride in their bodies. _____
Lola prefers men *who* take pride in their bodies. _____

The players are confident that the league championship is *theirs'*. _____
The players are confident that the league championship is *theirs*. _____

Them concert tickets are too expensive. _____
Those concert tickets are too expensive. _____

Our parents should spend some money on *themself* for a change. _____
Our parents should spend some money on *themselves* for a change. _____

Answers are on page 565.

This chapter describes some common types of pronouns: subject and object pronouns, possessive pronouns, demonstrative pronouns, and reflexive pronouns.

Subject and Object Pronouns

Pronouns change their form depending on the place they occupy in a sentence. Here is a list of subject and object pronouns:

Subject Pronouns	Object Pronouns
I	me
you	you (no change)
he	him
she	her
it	it (no change)
we	us
they	them

Subject Pronouns

Subject pronouns are subjects of verbs.

They are getting tired. (*They* is the subject of the verb *are getting*.)

She will decide tomorrow. (*She* is the subject of the verb *will decide*.)

We women organized the game. (*We* is the subject of the verb *organized*.)

Several rules for using subject pronouns, and mistakes people sometimes make, are explained starting below.

Rule 1

Use a subject pronoun in a sentence with a compound (more than one) subject.

Incorrect	Correct
Dwayne and *me* went shopping yesterday.	Dwayne and *I* went shopping yesterday.
Him and *me* spent lots of money.	*He* and *I* spent lots of money.

If you are not sure which pronoun to use, try each pronoun by itself in the sentence. The correct pronoun will be the one that sounds right. For example, "*Me* went shopping yesterday" does not sound right; "*I* went shopping yesterday" does.

www.mhhe.com/langan

Rule 2

Use a subject pronoun after forms of the verb *be*. Forms of *be* include *am, are, is, was, were, has been, have been,* and others.

> It was *I* who telephoned.
>
> It may be *they* at the door.
>
> It is *she*.

The sentences above may sound strange and stilted to you, since this rule is seldom actually followed in conversation. When we speak with one another, forms such as "It was me," "It may be them," and "It is her" are widely accepted. In formal writing, however, the grammatically correct forms are still preferred. You can avoid having to use a subject pronoun after *be* simply by rewording a sentence. Here is how the preceding examples could be reworded:

> *I* was the one who telephoned.
>
> *They* may be at the door.
>
> *She* is here.

Rule 3

Use subject pronouns after *than* or *as* when a verb is understood after the pronoun.

> You read faster than I (read). (The verb *read* is understood after *I.*)
>
> Tom is as stubborn as I (am). (The verb *am* is understood after *I.*)
>
> We don't go out as much as they (do). (The verb *do* is understood after *they.*)

TIPS

1. Avoid mistakes by mentally adding the "missing" verb at the end of the sentence.

2. Use object pronouns after *as* or *than* when a verb is not understood after the pronoun.

> The law applies to you as well as me.
>
> Our boss paid Monica more than me.

Object Pronouns

Object pronouns (*me, him, her, us, them*) are the objects of verbs or prepositions. (Prepositions are connecting words like *for, at, about, to, before, by, with,* and *of.* See also page 70.)

Nika chose *him*. (*Him* is the object of the verb *chose*.)

We met *them* at the ball park. (*Them* is the object of the verb *met*.)

Don't mention UFOs to *us*. (*Us* is the object of the preposition *to*.)

Between you and *me*, don't trust that woman. (*Me* is the object of the preposition *between*.)

People are sometimes uncertain about what pronoun to use when two objects follow the verb.

Incorrect	**Correct**
I spoke to George and *he*.	I spoke to George and *him*.
She pointed at Hana and *I*.	She pointed at Hana and *me*.

TIP If you are not sure which pronoun to use, try each pronoun by itself in the sentence. The correct pronoun will be the one that sounds right. For example, "I spoke to he" doesn't sound right; "I spoke to him" does.

Underline the correct subject or object pronoun in each of the following sentences. Then show whether your answer is a subject or an object pronoun by circling the *S* or *O* in the margin. The first one is done for you as an example.

Practice

1

S Ⓞ 1. I left the decision to (her, she).

S O 2. My sister and (I, me) decided to combine funds to buy our parents' Christmas present.

S O 3. He arrived sooner than (they, them).

S O 4. Give more spaghetti to Hal and (her, she).

S O 5. Sonia and (she, her) gave the car an oil change.

S O 6. The two people failed for cheating on the test were Mary and (he, him).

S O 7. (She, Her) and Luisa are jealous of my success.

S O 8. (We, Us) fellows decided to get up a football game.

S O 9. I don't feel he is a better volleyball player than (me, I).

S O 10. (Her, She) and (I, me) are not talking to each other.

For each sentence, in the space provided, write an appropriate subject or object pronoun. Try to use as many different pronouns as possible. The first one is done for you as an example.

1. Lola ran after Sue and _____*me*_____ to return the books she had borrowed.

2. Mr. Spud, our football coach, asked Gary and _____ to play on both offense and defense.

3. Pull the map out of the glove compartment and give it to _____.

4. The bowling team presented _____ with a bronze trophy.

5. The instructor caught Ted and _____ whispering during the exam.

6. No one was dressed up as much as _____ was.

7. My sister and _____ decided to care for the stray puppy.

8. I'm tired of _____ and their polite artificial smiles.

9. The block party was organized by _____ and our neighbors.

10. My uncle entertained _____ kids with his scary ghost stories.

Relative Pronouns

Relative pronouns do two things at once. First, they refer to someone or something already mentioned in the sentence. Second, they start a short word group that gives additional information about this someone or something. Here is a list of relative pronouns, followed by some example sentences:

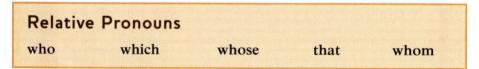

Relative Pronouns				
who	which	whose	that	whom

The only friend *who* really understands me is moving away.
The child *whom* Ben and Arlene adopted is from Korea.
Chocolate, *which* is my favorite food, upsets my stomach.
I guessed at half the questions *that* were on the test.

In the example sentences, *who* refers to *friend,* *whom* refers to *child,* *which* refers to *chocolate,* and *that* refers to *questions.* In addition, each of these relative pronouns begins a group of words that describes the person or thing being referred to. For example, the words *whom Ben and Arlene adopted* tell which child the sentence is about, and the words *which is my favorite food* give added information about chocolate.

Points to Remember about Relative Pronouns

Point 1

Whose means *belonging to whom.* Be careful not to confuse *whose* with *who's,* which means *who is.*

Point 2

Who, whose, and *whom* all refer to people. *Which* refers to things. *That* can refer to either people or things.

> I don't know *whose* book this is.
>
> Don't sit on the chair *which* is broken.
>
> Let's elect a captain *that* cares about winning.

Point 3

Who, whose, whom, and *which* can also be used to ask questions. When they are used in this way, they are called *interrogative* pronouns:

> *Who* murdered the secret agent?
>
> *Whose* fingerprints were on the bloodstained knife?
>
> To *whom* have the detectives been talking?
>
> *Which* suspect is going to confess?

TIP In informal usage, *who* is generally used instead of *whom* as an interrogative pronoun. Informally, we can say or write, "*Who* are you rooting for in the game?" or "*Who* did the instructor fail?" More formal usage would use *whom:* "Whom are you rooting for in the game?" and "Whom did the instructor fail?"

Point 4

Who and *whom* are used differently. *Who* is a subject pronoun. Use *who* as the subject of a verb:

> Let's see *who* will be teaching the course.

Whom is an object pronoun. Use *whom* as the object of a verb or a preposition:

> Dr. Kelsey is the instructor *whom* I like best.
>
> I haven't decided for *whom* I will vote.

You may want to review the material on subject and object pronouns on pages 217–220.

Here is an easy way to decide whether to use *who* or *whom.* Find the first verb after the place where the *who* or *whom* will go. See if it already has a subject. If it does have a subject, use the object pronoun *whom.* If there is no subject, give it one by using the subject pronoun *who.* Notice how *who* and *whom* are used in the sentences that follow:

I don't know *who* sideswiped my car.

The suspect *whom* the police arrested finally confessed.

In the first sentence, *who* is used to give the verb *sideswiped* a subject. In the second sentence, the verb *arrested* already has a subject, *police.* Therefore, *whom* is the correct pronoun.

Practice 3

Underline the correct pronoun in each of the following sentences.

1. My grandfather, (who, which) is seventy-nine, goes bowling every Friday.

2. The plant (who, that) Nita got for her birthday finally died.

3. I wish I had a relative (who, whom) would give me a million dollars.

4. I don't know to (who, whom) I should send my complaint letter.

5. Nobody knew (who, whom) was responsible for the mistake.

Practice 4

On separate paper, write five sentences using *who, whose, whom, which,* and *that.*

Possessive Pronouns

Possessive pronouns show ownership or possession.

Clyde shut off the engine of *his* motorcycle.

The keys are *mine.*

Here is a list of possessive pronouns:

www.mhhe.com/langan

Possessive Pronouns	
my, mine	our, ours
your, yours	your, yours
his	their, theirs
her, hers	
its	

Possessive pronouns show ownership or possession.

> Clyde revved up *his* motorcycle and blasted off.
>
> The keys are *mine.*

Points to Remember about Possessive Pronouns

Point 1

A possessive pronoun *never* uses an apostrophe. (See also page 326.)

Incorrect	Correct
That coat is *hers'*.	That coat is *hers.*
The card table is *theirs'*.	The card table is *theirs.*

Point 2

Do not use any of the following nonstandard forms to show possession.

Incorrect	Correct
I met a friend of *him.*	I met a friend of *his.*
Can I use *you* car?	Can I use *your* car?
Me sister is in the hospital.	*My* sister is in the hospital.
That magazine is *mines.*	That magazine is *mine.*

Cross out the incorrect pronoun form in each of the sentences that follow. Write the correct form in the space at the left.

Practice

5

EXAMPLE

___My___   ~~Me~~ car has broken down again.

_____ 1. That car won't be safe until you get its' brakes fixed.

_____ 2. If you are a friend of him, you're welcome to stay with us.

_____ 3. The seat you are sitting on is mines.

_____ 4. The neighbors called they dogs to chase the cat off the lawn.

_____ 5. The coffeepot is ours'.

Demonstrative Pronouns

Demonstrative pronouns point to or single out a person or thing. There are four demonstrative pronouns:

Demonstrative Pronouns	
this	these
that	those

Generally speaking, *this* and *these* refer to things close at hand; *that* and *those* refer to things farther away.

Is anyone using *this* spoon?

I am going to throw away *these* magazines.

I just bought *that* silver Honda at the curb.

Pick up *those* toys in the corner.

> **TIP** Do not use *them, this here, that there, these here,* or *those there* to point out. Use only *this, that, these,* or *those.*

Incorrect	Correct
Them tires are badly worn.	*Those* tires are badly worn.
This here book looks hard to read.	*This* book looks hard to read.
That there candy is delicious.	*That* candy is delicious.
Those there squirrels are pests.	*Those* squirrels are pests.

Practice

6

Cross out the incorrect form of the demonstrative pronoun and write the correct form in the space provided.

EXAMPLE

Those   ~~Them~~ clothes need washing.

_____ 1. That there dog will bite you if it gets a chance.

_____ 2. This here fingernail is not growing straight.

_____ 3. Them girls cannot be trusted.

_____ 4. Carry in those there shopping bags if you want to help.

_____ 5. The place where I'd like to live is that there corner house.

Look at the photo above and write four sentences about it using *this, that, these,* and *those.*

_____

_____

_____

_____

Reflexive Pronouns

Reflexive pronouns are pronouns that refer to the subject of a sentence. Here is a list of reflexive pronouns.

Reflexive Pronouns		
myself	herself	ourselves
yourself	itself	yourselves
himself		themselves

Sometimes the reflexive pronoun is used for emphasis:

You will have to wash the dishes *yourself.*

We *ourselves* are willing to forget the matter.

The president *himself* turns down his living room thermostat.

Points to Remember about Reflexive Pronouns

Point 1

In the plural *-self* becomes *-selves*.

> Lola washes *herself* in lavender bath oil.
>
> They treated *themselves* to a Bermuda vacation.

Point 2

Be careful that you do not use any of the following incorrect forms as reflexive pronouns.

Incorrect	Correct
He believes in *hisself*.	He believes in *himself*.
We drove the children *ourself*.	We drove the children *ourselves*.
They saw *themself* in the fun house mirror.	They saw *themselves* in the fun house mirror.
I'll do it *meself*.	I'll do it *myself*.

Practice

8

Cross out the incorrect form of the reflexive pronoun and write the correct form in the space at the left.

EXAMPLE

themselves   She believes that God helps those who help ~~themself~~.

_____ 1. Tony considers hisself the strongest wrestler in the class.

_____ 2. The striking players are only making theirselves look greedy.

_____ 3. You must carry your luggage yourselfs.

_____ 4. Many firefighters themself do not have smoke detectors in their homes.

_____ 5. We decided to finish the basement by ourself.

Review Test 1

Underline the correct word in the parentheses.

1. I'm going to leave if (that, that there) waiter doesn't come over here soon.

2. Though secured by a chain, the snarling German shepherd still terrified Lee and (I, me).

3. That iPod is (mine, mines).

4. Watching Alan and (I, me) dancing made him grit his teeth.

5. My aunts promised (us, we) girls a trip to Canada for graduation.

6. The service manager did not remember (who, whom) worked on my car.

7. I think (those, those there) people should be kicked out of the theater for talking.

8. The giggling boys only made (themself, themselves) look foolish.

9. If the decision were up to (they, them), my position in the company would be that of full-time pencil sharpener.

10. If (she, her) and Sandy had reported the leak, the cellar would not have flooded.

Review Test 2

Cross out the pronoun error in each sentence and write the correct form above it.

EXAMPLE

Terry and ~~me~~ *I* have already seen the movie.

1. Our friends have gotten theirselves into debt by overusing credit cards.

2. This here heat pump will lower your energy bill.

3. Watching the football game, us fans soon realized that our team would lose.

4. If you and her get confused about directions, stop and check at a service station.

5. Dimitri felt both sorry for and angry at the drug addict whom tried to steal his car.

6. Before he took a foul shot, the basketball player crossed hisself for good luck.

7. Jane and me refused to join the union.

8. The parents theirselfs must share the blame for their child's failure in school.

9. Our class painted more colorful posters than them.

10. You and me have got to have a talk.

Review Test 3

On separate paper, write sentences that use correctly each of the following words or word groups.

EXAMPLE

Peter and him   *The coach suspended Peter and him.*

1. those

2. Sue and she

3. faster than I

4. ours

5. Lola and me

6. whom

7. yourselves

8. with Linda and him

9. you and I

10. the neighbors and us

NAME: _____

DATE: _____

Pronoun Types MASTERY TEST 1

Underline the correct word in parentheses.

1. Harold pretended to be at ease, but he didn't fool Susan or (me, I).

2. (This, This here) tree is full of sparrows at night.

3. I believe that coat is (hers', hers).

4. Talking intimately, Zoe and (I, me) didn't see Earl walking up to our front porch.

5. The two of you must give (yourself, yourselves) another chance.

6. Al and (I, me) are equally poor in math.

7. My car's front tires, (who, which) vibrate at high speeds, need to be realigned.

8. (Those, Them) newspapers have to be carried down to the incinerator.

9. That last hamburger on the grill is (yours', yours) if you want it.

10. Though the furry black tarantula was in a cage, it still scared Manuel and (I, me).

11. Whenever our neighbor sees me on the porch, he invites (hisself, himself) over.

12. You are getting more of your work done than (I, me).

13. Ted (hisself, himself) takes full responsibility for the accident.

14. The instructor glared at Sarah and (I, me) and then dismissed the class.

15. Though younger than (I, me), Andrea acts like my superior.

16. When I miss class, I get together later with a student (who, whom) takes good notes.

17. Of all the children in the class, Dora and (he, him) are the least reliable.

18. The professor asked Chico and (I, me) to volunteer.

19. I recently met a friend of (her, hers).

20. (Those, Them) boots weren't made for walking.

NAME: _____

DATE: _____

MASTERY TEST 2 **Pronoun Types**

Cross out the incorrect pronoun in each sentence and write the correct form in the space provided at the left.

_____ 1. The coach's decision didn't suit Charlie or I.

_____ 2. Our instructor gave us homework in all of those there books.

_____ 3 That rabbit of yours' just became a mother again.

_____ 4. Joel won because he has played chess much longer than her.

_____ 5. Our brothers were very proud of themself when they caught the vandal in our neighborhood.

_____ 6. The women whom filed the class action suit were initially fired by the company.

_____ 7. The mail carrier says that Tyrell and me get more mail than all the other people on the block combined.

_____ 8. Lee never gets tired of talking about hisself.

_____ 9. Even the United States mail gets things done faster than her.

_____ 10. This here toothbrush looks as if someone used it to scrub potatoes.

_____ 11. Angela and me go hiking together each fall.

_____ 12. The firefighters theirselfs were puzzled by the source of the smoke in my basement.

_____ 13. Our garden is better cared for than theirs'.

_____ 14. The stone barely missed we and the children.

_____ 15. Them mosquitoes will bite you faster than you can blink your eyes.

_____ 16. If you want that old garden shovel, it's yours'.

_____ 17. I heard that her and her sister were expelled from school.

_____ 18. Julio is looking for someone to who he can sell his car.

_____ 19. Pete jogs on a more regular basis than me.

_____ 20. The pages are torn in many of them books.

Adjectives and Adverbs

Introductory Activity

Write in an appropriate word or words to complete each of the sentences below.

1. The teenage years were a _____ time for me.

2. The mechanic listened _____ while I described my car problem.

3. Basketball is a _____ game than football.

4. My brother is the _____ person in our family.

Now see if you can complete the following sentences.

The word inserted in the first sentence is an (adjective, adverb); it describes the word *time*.

The word inserted in the second sentence is an (adjective, adverb); it probably ends in the two letters _____ and describes the word *listened*.

The word inserted in the third sentence is a comparative adjective; it may be preceded by *more* or end in the two letters _____.

The word inserted in the fourth sentence is a superlative adjective; it may be preceded by *most* or end in the three letters _____.

Answers are on page 565.

Adjectives and adverbs are descriptive words. Their purpose is to make the meaning of the words they describe more specific.

www.mhhe.com/langan

Adjectives

What Are Adjectives?

Adjectives describe nouns (names of persons, places, or things) or pronouns.

> Charlotte is a *kind* woman. (The adjective *kind* describes the noun *woman*.)
>
> He is *tired*. (The adjective *tired* describes the pronoun *he*.)

An adjective usually comes before the word it describes (as in *kind woman*). But it can also come after forms of the verb *be (is, are, was, were,* and so on). Less often, an adjective follows verbs such as *feel, look, smell, sound, taste, appear, become,* and *seem.*

> The bureau is *heavy*. (The adjective *heavy* describes the bureau.)
>
> These pants are *itchy*. *(*The adjective *itchy* describes the pants.)
>
> The children seem *restless*. (The adjective *restless* describes the children.)

How many adjectives can you think of to describe the artwork pictured here? Use these adjectives to write at least two sentences describing the artwork.

Using Adjectives to Compare

For most short adjectives, add *-er* when comparing two things and *-est* when comparing three or more things.

> I am *taller* than my brother, but my father is the *tallest* person in the house.

> The farm market sells *fresher* vegetables than the corner store, but the *freshest* vegetables are the ones grown in my own garden.

For most *longer* adjectives (two or more syllables), add *more* when comparing two things and *most* when comparing three or more things.

> Backgammon is *more enjoyable* to me than checkers, but chess is the *most enjoyable* game of all.

> My mother is *more talkative* than my father, but my grandfather is the *most talkative* person in the house.

Points to Remember about Adjectives

Point 1

Be careful not to use both an *-er* ending and *more*, or both an *-est* ending and *most*.

Incorrect	**Correct**
Football is a *more livelier* game than baseball.	Football is a *livelier* game than baseball.
Tod Traynor was voted the *most likeliest* to succeed in our high school class.	Tod Traynor was voted the *most likely* to succeed in our high school class.

Point 2

Pay special attention to the following words, each of which has irregular forms.

	Comparative (Two)	**Superlative (Three or More)**
bad	worse	worst
good, well	better	best
little	less	least
much, many	more	most

Practice

1

Fill in the comparative or superlative forms for the following adjectives. Two are done for you as examples.

	Comparative (Two)	**Superlative (Three or More)**
fast	*faster*	*fastest*
timid	*more timid*	*most timid*
kind		
ambitious		
generous		
fine		
likable		

Practice

2

Add to each sentence the correct form of the word in the margin.

EXAMPLE

bad

The _____*worst*_____ day of my life was the one when my house caught fire.

comfortable   1. My jeans are the _____ pants I own.

difficult   2. My biology exam was the _____ of my five exams.

easy   3. The _____ way to get a good grade in the class is to take effective notes.

little   4. I made _____ money in my job as a delivery boy than I made as a golf caddy.

good   5. The _____ pay I ever made was as a drill press operator in a machine shop.

long   6. The ticket lines for the rock concert were the _____ I had ever seen.

memorable   7. The _____ days of my childhood were the ones I spent on trips with my grandfather.

experienced   8. I am a _____ driver than my sister, but my brother is the _____ driver in the family.

bad   9. This year's drought is _____ than last year's; forecasters are saying that next year's drought may be the _____ of this century.

good   10. The diner's cheesecake is _____ than its custard pie.

www.mhhe.com/langan

Adverbs

What Are Adverbs?

Adverbs describe verbs, adjectives, or other adverbs. An adverb usually ends in *-ly.*

Charlotte spoke *kindly* to the confused man. (The adverb *kindly* describes the verb *spoke.*)

The man said he was *completely* alone in the world. (The adverb *completely* describes the adjective *alone.*)

Charlotte listened *very* sympathetically to his story. (The adverb *very* describes the adverb *sympathetically.*)

A Common Mistake with Adjectives and Adverbs

Perhaps the most common mistake that people make with adjectives and adverbs is to use an adjective instead of an adverb after a verb.

Incorrect	**Correct**
Tony breathed *heavy.*	Tony breathed *heavily.*
I rest *comfortable* in that chair.	I rest *comfortably* in that chair.
She learned *quick.*	She learned *quickly.*

Underline the adjective or adverb needed.

Practice

3

1. Her pink top clashed (violent, violently) with her orange skirt.

2. If I had not run (quick, quickly), the dog would have caught me.

3. The crowd pushed (angry, angrily) toward the box office window.

4. Sam peered with (considerable, considerably) effort through the grimy cellar window.

5. The trees swayed (gentle, gently) in the wind.

6. I was (real, really) tired.

7. I exercise (regular, regularly), and my eating habits are also (regular, regularly).

8. Sarah sat very (quiet, quietly) on the stairs, listening to her parents quarrel (angry, angrily) in the kitchen.

9. I listened (careful, carefully) to the doctor's (exact, exactly) instructions.

10. (Slow, Slowly) but (sure, surely), I improved my grades in school.

Well and *Good*

Two words often confused are *well* and *good*. *Good* is an adjective; it describes nouns. *Well* is usually an adverb; it describes verbs. *Well* (rather than *good*) is also used as an adjective when referring to a person's health. Here are some examples:

I became a *good* swimmer. (*Good* is an adjective describing the noun *swimmer.*)

For a change, two-year-old Rodney was *good* during the church service. (*Good* is an adjective describing Rodney and comes after *was*, a form of the verb *be*.)

Maryann did *well* on that exam. (*Well* is an adverb describing the verb *did*.)

I explained that I wasn't feeling *well*. (*Well* is used in reference to health.)

Practice

4

Write *well* or *good* in the sentences that follow.

1. He writes _____ enough to pass the course.

2. We always have a _____ time at the county fair.

3. The mayor and district attorney know each other very _____.

4. Jim has not been feeling _____ lately.

5. I did not do _____ when I took the typing test.

Review Test 1

Cross out the adjective or adverb error in each sentence and write the correction in the space at the left.

EXAMPLES

frequently   My boss ~~frequent~~ tells me to slow down.

___*harder*___   For me, the country is a ~~more harder~~ place to live than the city.

_____   1. Make sure the job is done safe.

_____   2. He was found guilty of the charges, and the judge lectured him harsh.

SECTION 3:
MODIFIERS AND
PARALLELISM

_____ 3. I am the taller of the five children in my family.

_____ 4. Theo swam effortless through the water, not making a single awkward movement.

_____ 5. At this time it is importanter to be in school than to have a full-time job.

_____ 6. His eyes are his most attractivest feature.

_____ 7. I slept light, for the stereo blared noisily upstairs.

_____ 8. Mr. Scott is the helpfulest of my instructors.

_____ 9. Despite reforms, conditions at the prison are more worse than before.

_____ 10. Tony didn't feel good after eating diced eggplant in clam sauce.

Review Test 2

Write a sentence that uses each of the following adjectives and adverbs correctly.

1. nervous _____

2. nervously _____

3. good _____

4. well _____

5. carefully_____

6. most honest _____

7. easier _____

8. best _____

9. more useful _____

10. loudest _____

NAME: _____

DATE: _____

Adjectives and Adverbs

PART 1

Cross out the incorrect adjectival or adverbial form in each sentence. Then write the correct form in the space provided.

_____ 1. My mother spoke bluntly to the salesperson, and he responded aggressive.

_____ 2. The spade cut sharp and severed the tree root.

_____ 3. Because the children were quietly during the movie, their parents were happy to buy them some ice cream.

_____ 4. Our powerful singing rang out noisy in the packed theater.

_____ 5. Your cupcakes taste so well that they are rapidly disappearing.

PART 2

Cross out the error in comparison in each sentence. Then write the correct form in the space provided.

_____ 6. Andy considers himself importanter than other people.

_____ 7. Lola's hair is the most shortest that she has ever worn it.

_____ 8. Despite the reviews, I think *The Killer Frogs* was the entertainingest movie released this year.

_____ 9. Earthworms are less likelier to make me squeamish than are spiders.

_____ 10. I always do a more good job in preparing a meal than my brother does.

Adjective and Adverbs MASTERY TEST 2

PART 1

Cross out the incorrect adjectival and adverbial form in each sentence. Then write the correct form in the space provided.

_____ 1. For a week after his accident, Carlos could not walk steady.

_____ 2. I didn't think the instructor had graded my paper fair.

_____ 3. The sharp blade slipped easy between the chicken's bumpy skin and satiny flesh.

_____ 4. My father was thoughtfully as he looked at the pictures in the old family album.

_____ 5. Waitressing was easy for Marge, but since my coordination was not as well as hers, I was fired.

PART 2

Add to each sentence the correct form of the word at the left.

strong   6. Jerry, whose nickname is Goliath, is probably the _____ player on the football team.

graceful   7. The _____ sport at the Olympics is the figure skating competition.

hard   8. My science exam was the _____ of my two tests.

little   9. That is the _____ of my many worries.

bad   10. I can't decide what to do; the _____ thing, though, would be to do nothing.

Misplaced Modifiers

16

Introductory Activity

Because of misplaced words, each of the sentences below has more than one possible meaning. In each case, see if you can explain both the intended meaning and the unintended meaning.

1. The farmers sprayed the apple trees wearing masks.

   Intended meaning: _____

   Unintended meaning: _____

2. The woman reached out for the faith healer who had a terminal disease.

   Intended meaning: _____

   Unintended meaning: _____

Answers are on page 566.

What Misplaced Modifiers Are
and How to Correct Them

Misplaced modifiers are words that, because of awkward placement, do not describe the words the writer intended them to describe. Misplaced modifiers often confuse the meaning of a sentence. To avoid them, place words as close as possible to what they describe.

Misplaced Words

They could see the Goodyear blimp *sitting on the front lawn.*

(The *Goodyear blimp* was sitting on the front lawn?)

We had a hamburger after the movie, *which was too greasy for my taste.*

(The *movie* was too greasy for your taste?)

Our phone *almost rang* fifteen times last night.

(The phone *almost rang* fifteen times, but in fact did not ring at all?)

Correctly Placed Words

Sitting on the front lawn, they could see the Goodyear blimp.

(The intended meaning—that the Goodyear blimp was visible from the front lawn—is now clear.)

After the movie, we had a hamburger, which was too greasy for my taste.

(The intended meaning—that the hamburger was greasy—is now clear.)

Our phone rang almost fifteen times last night.

(The intended meaning—that the phone rang a little under fifteen times—is now clear.)

Other single-word modifiers to watch out for include *only, even, hardly, nearly,* and *often.* Such words should be placed immediately before the word they modify.

Underline the misplaced word or words in each sentence. Then rewrite the sentence, placing related words together to make the meaning clear.

Practice

1

EXAMPLE

Anita returned the hamburger to the supermarket that was spoiled.

Anita returned the hamburger that was spoiled to

the supermarket.

1. They finally found a Laundromat driving around in their car.

_____

_____

2. I read that Chuck Yeager was a pilot who broke the sound barrier in the library.

_____

_____

3. Evelyn was thinking about her lost chemistry book taking the elevator.

_____

_____

4. Lola selected a donut from the bakery filled with banana cream.

_____

_____

5. Howard almost worked twenty hours overtime to pay some overdue bills.

_____

_____

6. Tickets have gone on sale for next week's championship game in the college bookstore.

_____

_____

7. I returned the orange socks to the department store that my uncle gave me.

_____

_____

8. The camper saw the black bear looking through the binoculars.

_____

_____

9. I nearly earned two hundred dollars last week.

_____

_____

10. Mushrooms should be stored in the refrigerator enclosed in a paper bag.

_____

_____

Rewrite each sentence, adding the *italicized* words. Make sure that the intended meaning is clear and that two different interpretations are not possible.

EXAMPLE

I borrowed a pen for the essay test. (Insert *that ran out of ink.*)

For the essay test, I borrowed a pen that ran out of ink.

1. We agreed to go out to dinner tonight. (Insert *in our science class.*)

   _____

   _____

2. Bob and I decided to get married. (Insert *on a rainy day in June* to show when the decision was made.)

   _____

   _____

3. Suki decided to hail a taxi. (Insert *weighed down with heavy packages.*)

   _____

   _____

4. I've looked everywhere for an instruction book on how to play the guitar. (Insert *without success.*)

   _____

   _____

5. Mother told me to wash the car. (Insert *over the phone.*)

   _____

   _____

Review Test   1

Write *M* for *misplaced* or *C* for *correct* in front of each sentence.

_____ 1. Josh spotted the missing dog on his way to the bank.

_____ 2. Josh, while on his way to the bank, spotted the missing dog.

_____ 3. Mona brought a casserole right out of the oven to the new neighbors.

_____ 4. Mona brought a casserole to the new neighbors right out of the oven.

_____   5. My sister smiled at the usher in the theater with long sideburns.

_____   6. My sister smiled at the usher with long sideburns in the theater.

_____   7. A cheerful man with one leg hopped onto the bus.

_____   8. A cheerful man hopped onto the bus with one leg.

_____   9. The weary hunter shot at the ducks sitting in his car.

_____   10. Sitting in his car, the weary hunter shot at the ducks.

_____   11. Steven saw a kangaroo at the window under the influence of
whiskey.

_____   12. Steven saw a kangaroo under the influence of whiskey at the
window.

_____   13. Under the influence of whiskey, Steven saw a kangaroo at
the window.

_____   14. I was attacked by a stray dog working in the yard.

_____   15. While working in the yard, I was attacked by a stray dog.

_____   16. He remembered with dismay that he had to wash the windows.

_____   17. He remembered that he had to wash the windows with dismay.

_____   18. With dismay, he remembered that he had to wash the windows.

_____   19. Ana received a sports car for her birthday that has a sun roof.

_____   20. Ana received a sports car that has a sun roof for her birthday.

Review Test 2

Underline the five misplaced modifiers in the passage below. Then, in the spaces
that follow, show how you would correct them.

   [1]Before heading to work in the morning, joggers almost fill all the streets.
[2]They quietly pound the sidewalks wearing brightly colored sweatsuits and
sneakers. [3]Groups of early feeding pigeons and squirrels scatter as the
joggers move easily down the streets. [4]The joggers are gazed at by people
who are waiting at bus stops wearing expressions of wonder and envy.
[5]Occasionally, a jogger stops to tie a shoelace kneeling on the cement. [6]The

joggers pass supermarkets and vegetable trucks parked at loading ramps. [7]On rainy days, the runners watch for slick spots on the sidewalk, but they don't worry about the rain or cold. [8]Pushing on at a steady pace, they count the number of miles traveled. [9]Finally, the joggers take quick showers and think about the workday ahead back at their homes. [10]They will return to their special world of running the next morning.

1. _____

_____

2. _____

_____

3. _____

_____

4. _____

_____

5. _____

_____

NAME: _____

DATE: _____

MASTERY TEST 1 | Misplaced Modifiers

Underline the misplaced word or words in each sentence. Then rewrite the sentence, placing related words together and making the meaning clear.

1. Every six hours the doctor told me to take a pill.

_____

_____

2. I bought a watch at the flea market that I wear every day.

_____

_____

3. Lola dozed by the pool growing redder by the minute.

_____

_____

4. We need another player on the team who can catch badly.

_____

_____

5. Elena almost got an A in every subject.

_____

_____

6. Mike signed a letter of intent to play football at Penn State in the family kitchen.

_____

_____

7. I threw the potatoes into the pot and tore open a bag of peas in a bad mood.

_____

_____

8. My uncle bought a house from an elderly real estate agent with a large bay window.

_____

_____

NAME: _____

DATE: _____

Misplaced Modifiers   MASTERY TEST 2

Underline the misplaced word or words in each sentence. Then rewrite the sentence, placing related words together and making the meaning clear.

1. Fran was attacked by a stray dog working in the yard.

   _____

   _____

2. I will never ride another horse wearing shorts.

   _____

   _____

3. Everyone we invited almost came to the party.

   _____

   _____

4. The boy struggled to reel in the large fish with shaking hands.

   _____

   _____

5. I bought a tire from an auto shop that flattened overnight.

   _____

   _____

6. Judy bought sheepskin seat covers for her Toyota that cost only thirty dollars.

   _____

   _____

7. Breakfast is served at the school cafeteria from 8 A.M. until the end of the school year.

   _____

   _____

8. Finding their house burglarized, the Murphys called the police when they came back from vacation.

   _____

   _____

Dangling Modifiers

17

Introductory Activity

Because of dangling words, each of the sentences below has more than one possible meaning. In each case, see if you can explain both the intended meaning and the unintended meaning.

1. Munching leaves from a tall tree, the children were fascinated by the eighteen-foot-tall giraffe.

   Intended meaning: _____

   _____

   Unintended meaning: _____

   _____

2. Arriving home after ten months in the army, Michael's neighbors threw a block party for him.

   Intended meaning: _____

   _____

   Unintended meaning: _____

   _____

Answers are on page 566.

What Dangling Modifiers Are and How to Correct Them

A modifier that opens a sentence must be followed immediately by the word it is meant to describe. Otherwise, the modifier is said to be *dangling,* and the sentence takes on an unintended meaning. For example, look at this sentence:

While sleeping in his backyard, a Frisbee hit Bill on the head.

The unintended meaning is that the *Frisbee* was sleeping in his backyard. What the writer meant, of course, was that *Bill* was sleeping in his backyard. The writer should have placed *Bill* right after the modifier, revising the rest of the sentence as necessary:

While sleeping in his backyard, *Bill* was hit on the head by a Frisbee.

The sentence could also be corrected by adding the missing subject and verb to the opening word group:

While *Bill* was sleeping in his backyard, a Frisbee hit him on the head.

Other sentences with dangling modifiers follow. Read the explanations of why they are dangling, and look carefully at how they are corrected.

Dangling	**Correct**
Having almost no money, my survival depended on my parents.	Having almost no money, *I* depended on my parents for survival.
(*Who* has almost no money? The answer is not *survival* but *I*. The subject *I* must be added.)	*Or:* Since *I* had almost no money, I depended on my parents for survival.
Riding his bike, a German shepherd bit Tony on the ankle.	Riding his bike, *Tony* was bitten on the ankle by a German shepherd.
(*Who* is riding the bike? The answer is not *German shepherd*, as it unintentionally seems to be, but *Tony*. The subject *Tony* must be added.)	*Or:* While *Tony* was riding his bike, a German shepherd bit him on the ankle.
When trying to lose weight, all snacks are best avoided.	When trying to lose weight, *you* should *avoid* all snacks.
(*Who* is trying to lose weight? The answer is not *snacks* but *you*. The subject *you* must be added.)	*Or:* When *you* are trying to lose weight, *avoid* all snacks.

These examples make clear two ways of correcting a dangling modifier. Decide on a logical subject and do one of the following:

1. **Place the subject *within* the opening word group:**

   Since *I* had almost no money, I depended on my parents for survival.

In some cases an appropriate subordinating word such as *since* must be added, and the verb may have to be changed slightly as well.

2. **Place the subject right *after* the opening word group:**

   Having almost no money, *I* depended on my parents for survival.

Sometimes even more rewriting is necessary to correct a dangling modifier. What is important to remember is that a modifier must be placed as close as possible to the word that it modifies.

Practice 1

Rewrite each sentence to correct the dangling modifier. Mark the one sentence that is correct with a *C*.

1. Folded into a tiny square, I could not read the message.

   _____

   _____

2. Wading into the lake, tadpoles swirled around my ankles.

   _____

   _____

3. Soaked to the skin, Chris was miserable waiting in the unsheltered doorway.

   _____

   _____

4. Hanging on the wall, I saw a photograph of my mother.

   _____

   _____

5. Settling comfortably into the chair, the television captured my attention for the next hour.

   _____

   _____

6. Driving home after a tiring day at work, the white line became blurry.

    _____

    _____

7. Soaring high over the left-field fence, the batter hit his first home run.

    _____

    _____

8. Threadbare and dirty, Myrna knew the time had come to replace the rug.

    _____

    _____

9. After spending most of the night outdoors in a tent, the sun rose and we went into the house.

    _____

    _____

10. Hot and sizzling, we bit into the apple tarts.

    _____

    _____

Complete the following sentences. In each case, a logical subject should follow the opening words.

Practice

2

EXAMPLE

   Checking the oil stick, _I saw that my car was a quart low._ _____

1. Since failing the first test, _____

2. Before learning how to dance, _____

3. While flying the kite, _____

4. After taking my coffee break, _____

5. Though very tired, _____

Review Test   1

Write *D* for *dangling* or *C* for *correct* in front of each sentence. Remember that the opening words are a dangling modifier if they are not followed immediately by a logical subject.

_____   1. Hanging in the closet for a year, Lola forgot she owned an aqua dress.

_____   2. Lola forgot she owned an aqua dress that had been hanging in the closet for a year.

_____   3. Having just watched the frightening movie, my hosue suddenly felt haunted.

_____   4. Having just watched the frightening movie, I suddenly felt my house was haunted.

_____   5. Hitching a ride, I was picked up by a Mack truck.

_____   6. Hitching a ride, a Mack truck picked me up.

_____   7. While waiting for the bus, rain began to fall.

_____   8. While waiting for the bus, it began to rain.

_____   9. While I was waiting for the bus, rain began to fall.

_____   10. Being tired, my chores were not finished.

_____   11. Because I was tired, I did not finish my chores.

_____   12. While I was practicing yoga exercises, a mail carrier rang the doorbell.

_____   13. While practicing yoga exercises, a mail carrier rang the doorbell.

_____   14. Containing dangerous chemicals, people are not swimming in the lake.

_____   15. Containing dangerous chemicals, the lake is not open for swimming.

_____   16. Because the lake contains dangerous chemicals, it is not open for swimming.

_____   17. Falling heavily, Toshio broke his arm.

_____   18. Falling heavily, Toshio's arm was broken.

_____   19. Just before finishing the book, the power failed.

_____   20. Just before I finished the book, the power failed.

Review Test   2

Underline the five dangling modifiers in this passage. Then correct them in the spaces provided.

[1]When my brother Rick gets hold of a best seller, he forgets that the rest of the world exists. [2]Absorbed in his book, dinner is forgotten. [3]He must be reminded to eat even when we have meat loaf, his favorite meal. [4]Rick not only ignores the other people in the family but also forgets his chores. [5]Reading after breakfast, lunch, and dinner, a lot of dishes pile up and wastebaskets are not emptied. [6]We try to understand; in fact, we think he's lucky. [7]Sitting in the middle of a room, his book seems to drown out the television, radio, and screaming children. [8]Never wanting any sleep, his book still has his attention at 1 A.M. [9]We bought a new rocking chair once when Rick was in the middle of a best seller. [10]Rocking away, his eyes never left the pages long enough to notice it. [11]Only after finishing the book did he ask, "When did we get the new chair?"

1. _____

   _____

2. _____

   _____

3. _____

   _____

4. _____

   _____

5. _____

   _____

NAME: _____

DATE: _____

Dangling Modifiers

Underline the dangling modifier in each sentence. Then rewrite the sentence, correcting the dangling modifier.

1. Feeling extra lucky, the black cat didn't scare Diana.

   _____

   _____

2. After waiting all day, the moving truck finally arrived at our apartment.

   _____

   _____

3. Hot and sizzling, Lola bit into the apple tart.

   _____

   _____

4. Having faulty plumbing, we decided not to rent the apartment.

   _____

   _____

5. Waiting in line to be seated, the hostess finally called our names.

   _____

   _____

6. Out late the night before, Rania's eyes were red and strained.

   _____

   _____

7. Having won the championship game, the locker room was filled with cheering players.

   _____

   _____

8. While walking through the shopping mall, my head suddenly began to pound.

   _____

   _____

Dangling Modifiers  MASTERY TEST 2

Underline the dangling modifier in each sentence. Then rewrite the sentence, correcting the dangling modifier.

1. While cutting the lawn, five mosquitoes bit me.

   _____

   _____

2. Smoking in the rest room, my math teacher caught Fred and me.

   _____

   _____

3. Shortly before giving birth, the doctor gave his wife a sedative.

   _____

   _____

4. Quickly taking the sheets off the clothesline, rain pelted our faces.

   _____

   _____

5. Dripping with perspiration, the air-conditioned store offered us relief.

   _____

   _____

6. While shopping at the store, my bike was stolen.

   _____

   _____

7. Hurrying to class, my English paper fell out of my notebook into a puddle.

   _____

   _____

8. After watching two movies at the drive-in, my stomach began rumbling for pizza.

   _____

   _____

Faulty Parallelism

Introductory Activity

Read aloud each pair of sentences below. Write a check mark beside the sentence that reads more smoothly and clearly and sounds more natural.

Pair 1

_____ I use my computer to write papers, to search the Internet, and for playing video games.

_____ I use my computer to write papers, to search the Internet, and to play video games.

Pair 2

_____ One option Sonja had was to stay in the Air Force; the other was returning to college.

_____ One option Sonja had was to stay in the Air Force; the other was to return to college.

Pair 3

_____ Dad's favorite chair has a torn cushion, the armrest is stained, and a musty odor.

_____ Dad's favorite chair has a torn cushion, a stained armrest, and a musty odor.

Answers are on page 567.

Parallelism Explained

Words in a pair or a series should have parallel structure. By balancing the items in a pair or a series so that they have the same kind of structure, you will make the sentence clearer and easier to read. Notice how the parallel sentences that follow read more smoothly than the nonparallel ones.

www.mhhe.com/langan

Nonparallel (Not Balanced)	Parallel (Balanced)
Fran spends her free time reading, listening to music, and she works in the garden.	Fran spends her free time reading, listening to music, and working in the garden.
	(A balanced series of *-ing* words: *reading, listening, working.*)
After the camping trip I was exhausted, irritable, and wanted to eat.	After the camping trip I was exhausted, irritable, and hungry.
	(A balanced series of descriptive words: *exhausted, irritable, hungry.*)
My hope for retirement is to be healthy, to live in a comfortable house, and having plenty of money.	My hope for retirement is to be healthy, to live in a comfortable house, and to have plenty of money.
	(A balanced series of *to* verbs: *to be, to live, to have.*)
Nightly, Alexei puts out the trash, checks the locks on the doors, and the burglar alarm is turned on.	Nightly, Alexei puts out the trash, checks the locks on the doors, and turns on the burglar alarm.
	(Balanced verbs and word order: *puts out the trash, checks the locks, turns on the burglar alarm.*)

Balanced sentences are not a skill you need to worry about when you are writing first drafts. But when you rewrite, you should try to put matching words and ideas into matching structures. Such parallelism will improve your writing style.

The unbalanced part of each sentence is italicized. Rewrite this part so that it matches the rest of the sentence.

EXAMPLE

In the afternoon, I changed two diapers, ironed several shirts, and *was watching* soap operas. _watched_____

1. After the exercise class, I woke up with stiff knees, throbbing legs, and *arms that ached.* _____

2. Our favorite restaurant specializes in delicious omelets, *soups that are freshly made,* and inexpensive desserts. _____

3. The man running the checkout counter was tall, thin, and *having a bad temper.*

    _____

4. Caulking the windows, *to replace weather stripping,* and painting the garage are my chores for the weekend. _____

5. With her pale skin and *her eyes that were green,* she appeared ghostly in the moonlight. _____

6. As an Oprah Winfrey fan, I love to watch her show and *reading her magazine.*

    _____

7. After calling the police, checking the area hospitals, and *we prayed,* we could only wait. _____

8. The stars appeared on talk shows, signed autographs, and *were attending* opening nights in order to promote their latest movie. _____

9. Our teenage daughter ties up the phone for hours, giggling with her girlfriends, deciding what to wear, and *complaints about her strict parents.*

    _____

10. In Allan's nightmare, he was audited by the IRS, investigated by the police, and *bill collectors were chasing him.* _____

    _____

Complete the following statements. The first two parts of each statement are parallel in form; the part that you add should be parallel in form as well.

Practice

2

EXAMPLE

Three things I like about myself are my sense of humor, my thoughtfulness, and *my self-discipline.* _____

1. Among the drawbacks of apartment living are noisy neighbors, yearly rent increases, and _____

2. Three bad habits I have resolved to change are losing my temper, showing up late for appointments, and _____

3. The best features of my part-time job are good pay, flexible hours, and

   _____

4. Cigarette smoking is expensive, disgusting, and _____

5. Lessons I had to learn after moving from my parents' home included how to budget my money, how to take care of my own laundry, and _____

   _____

Collaborative Activity

Editing and Rewriting

Working with a partner, read carefully the short paragraph below and mark the five instances of faulty parallelism. Then use the space provided to correct the instances of faulty parallelism. Feel free to discuss the rewrite quietly with your partner and refer back to the chapter when necessary.

[1]Human beings attempt to protect themselves psychologically as well as in physical ways. [2]If someone harms you physically, you may want to fight back. [3]To guard yourself psychologically, you may use defense mechanisms. [4]You may be unaware of your real motives in adjusting to a situation that is undesirable or a threat. [5]Three common defense mechanisms are regression, rationalization, and trying to compensate.

continued

[6]Regression means returning to an earlier form of behavior. [7]A person who regresses temporarily rejects the "hard cruel world" and is seeking the greater security of childhood. [8]Rationalization is making excuses. [9]A student not wanting to study for a test decides that she doesn't know what to study. [10]Compensation is a form of substitution. [11]If a person wants a better education but cannot attend school, she may try studying on her own or to learn more through experience.

_____

_____

_____

_____

_____

_____

_____

_____

_____

_____

_____

_____

_____

_____

_____

_____

_____

Collaborative Activity

Creating Sentences

Working with a partner, make up your own short test on faulty parallelism, as directed.

1. Write a sentence that includes three things you want to do tomorrow. One of those things should not be in parallel form. Then correct the faulty parallelism.

    Nonparallel _____

    _____

    Parellel _____

    _____

2. Write a sentence that names three positive qualities of a person you like or three negative qualities of a person you don't like.

    Nonparallel _____

    _____

    Parellel _____

    _____

3. Write a sentence that includes three everyday things that annoy you.

    Nonparallel _____

    _____

    Parellel _____

    _____

Reflective Activity

1. Look at the paragraph on defense mechanisms that you revised above. How has the attention to parallel form improved the paragraph?

2. How would you evaluate your use of parallel form in your writing? Do you use it almost never, at times, or often? How would you benefit from using it more?

Review Test 1

Cross out the unbalanced part of each sentence. Then rewrite the unbalanced part so that it matches the other item or items in the sentence.

EXAMPLE

I enjoy watering the grass and ~~to work~~ in the garden.

working
_____

1. Our production supervisor warned Jed to punch in on time, dress appropriately for the job, and he should stop taking extra breaks.

_____

2. On his ninetieth birthday, the old man mused that his long life was due to hard work, a loving wife, and because he had a sense of humor.

_____

3. The philosopher's advice is to live for the present, find some joy in each day, and by helping others.

_____

4. Freshly prepared food, an attractive decor, and having prompt service are signs of a good restaurant.

_____

5. Tarah has tickets for reckless driving, speeding, and she parked illegally.

_____

6. Washing clothes, cooking meals, and to take care of children used to be called "women's work."

_____

7. Our compact car provides better mileage; more comfort is provided by our station wagon.

_____

8. As the first bartender to arrive each day, Elena must slice lemons, get ice, and she has to check the inventory.

_____

9. Last week I finished my term paper, took all my final exams, and an interview for a summer job.

_____

10. On our ideal vacation, I enjoy lazing in the sun, eating delicious food, and to be with special friends.

_____

Review Test   2

On separate paper, write five sentences of your own that use parallel structure. Each sentence should contain three items in a series.

Review Test   3

There are six nonparallel parts in the following passage. The first is corrected for you as an example. Underline and correct the other five.

   [1]My sister used to drive an old VW "Bug." [2]With its dented body, torn upholstery, and <u>fenders that were rusted</u>, the car was a real eyesore. [3]Worse, though, the car was in terrible shape mechanically. [4]The engine coughed, the tailpipe rattled, and there were squealing brakes. [5]My father spent many hours searching for cures for the car's many ailments. [6]He often spoke about pushing the car off a cliff or to explode it and put it out of its misery. [7]He wasn't serious, of course, but one day the little car saved my father the trouble. [8]As Kathy was driving one afternoon, smoke began pouring through the backseat of the car. [9]My sister parked on the side of the road and began to check the engine. [10]Quickly, another motorist pulled over, jumped out of his car, and pushing my sister away from the VW. [11]The car smoldered a few minutes and then bursting into flames. [12]Firefighters arrived in about ten minutes but were too late. [13]The car's tires had melted, its body was black, the glass popping out of the windows, and the

steering wheel was twisted. [14]When Kathy told the family what had happened, everyone was sympathetic. [15]I suspect, however, that my father shed no tears that the Bug was gone from our lives.

1. *rusty fenders* _____

2. _____

3. _____

4. _____

5. _____

6. _____

Faulty Parallelism

The unbalanced part of each sentence is italicized. Rewrite this part so that it matches the rest of the sentence.

1. Long ticket lines, *fans that are rude,* and overpriced food—these are what I dislike about going to football games.

   _____

2. My sister can do her math homework, cut my hair, and *be planning a party* while she watches television.

   _____

3. The sky got dark, a wind sprang up, and *there was a drop in the temperature.*

   _____

4. My magazines sometimes arrive torn, dirty, and *being late.*

   _____

5. Between work and dinner, she picked up her son at school, *was stopping at the drugstore,* and dropped the dog off at the vet's office.

   _____

6. The flowers that Robin entered in the show were healthy-looking, brilliantly colored, and *smelled sweet.*

   _____

7. I'd play golf day and night if it weren't for eating and *to have to sleep.*

   _____

8. The crowd showed excitement, happiness, and *there was patriotic spirit.*

   _____

9. If it weren't for Marie's indecision and *being insecure,* she could accomplish great things in the business world.

   _____

10. My nephew's career plans center on becoming a state trooper, training as a police officer, or *to join the FBI.*

   _____

NAME: _____

DATE: _____

MASTERY TEST 2 | # Faulty Parallelism

Draw a line under the unbalanced part of each sentence. Then rewrite the unbalanced part so that it matches the other items in the sentence.

1. My bedridden little brother asked for a bowl of cereal, a glass of orange juice, and to have a comic book to read.

   _____

2. Science fiction, popular music, and sports that are on television are the things my father enjoys most.

   _____

3. My sister's peculiar habits included yelling in her sleep and to do her homework in the bathtub.

   _____

4. That new blond boy is both handsome as he is personable.

   _____

5. Lola enjoys novels, shopping for new clothes, and meeting new men.

   _____

6. Shoppers stop in pet stores to buy a pet, to pick up pet supplies, or just looking at the animals.

   _____

7. Our children can watch television, talk on the phone, and their homework all at the same time.

   _____

8. Frustrated, annoyed, and feeling depression, Steve returned to work after the strike.

   _____

9. Thelma likes people who have thoughtfulness and are unselfish.

   _____

10. His headache was so bad that Andy was ready to give all his money or the confessing of all his secrets to anyone who would stop the pain.

   _____

Sentence Variety II

Like Chapter 7, this chapter will show you several ways to write effective and varied sentences. You will increase your sense of the many ways available to you for expressing your ideas. The practices here will also reinforce much of what you have learned in this section about modifiers and the use of parallelism.

-ing Word Groups

Use an *-ing* word group at some point in a sentence. Here are examples:

The doctor, *hoping* for the best, examined the X-rays.

Jogging every day, I soon raised my energy level.

More information about *-ing* words, also known as *present participles,* appears on page 196.

Combine each pair of sentences below into one sentence by using an *-ing* word and omitting repeated words. Use a comma or commas to set off the *-ing* word group from the rest of the sentence.

Practice

1

EXAMPLE

- The diesel truck chugged up the hill.
- It spewed out smoke.

  Spewing out smoke, the diesel truck chugged up the hill.

or *The diesel truck, spewing out smoke, chugged up the hill.*

1. • Ginger refused to get out of bed.
   • She pulled the blue blanket over her head.

   _____

   _____

2. • Dad is able to forget the troubles of the day.
   • He putters around in his basement workshop.

   _____

   _____

3. • The crowd of dancers moved as one.
   • They swayed to the music.

   _____

   _____

4. • George tried to protect himself from the dampness of the room.
   • He wrapped a scarf around his neck.

   _____

   _____

5. • The woman listened intently to the earnest young man.
   • She caressed her hair.

   _____

   _____

Practice

2

On separate paper, write five sentences of your own that contain *-ing* word groups.

-ed Word Groups

Use an *-ed* word group at some point in a sentence. Here are examples:

> *Tired* of studying, I took a short break.
>
> Mary, *amused* by the joke, told it to a friend.
>
> I opened my eyes wide, *shocked* by the red "F" on my paper.

More information about *-ed* words, also known as *past participles,* appears on page 196.

Combine each of the following pairs of sentences into one sentence by using an *-ed* word and omitting repeated words. Use a comma or commas to set off the *-ed* word group from the rest of the sentence.

EXAMPLE

- Tim woke up with a start.
- He was troubled by a dream.

  Troubled by a dream, Tim woke up with a start.

or *Tim, troubled by a dream, woke up with a start.*

1. • I called an exterminator.
   • I was bothered by roaches.

   _____

   _____

2. • Sam grew silent.
   • He was baffled by what had happened.

   _____

   _____

3. • The crowd began to file slowly out of the stadium.
   • They were stunned by the last-minute touchdown.

   _____

   _____

4. • I tried to stifle my grin.
   • I was amused but reluctant to show how I felt.

   _____

   _____

5. • Cindy lay on the couch.
   • She was exhausted from working all day.

   _____

   _____

On separate paper, write five sentences of your own that contain *-ed* word groups.

-*ly* Openers

Use an -*ly* word to open a sentence. Here are examples:

Gently, he mixed the chemicals together.

Anxiously, the contestant looked at the game clock.

Skillfully, the quarterback rifled a pass to his receiver.

More information about -*ly* words, which are also known as *adverbs,* appears on page 235.

More information about -*ly* words, which are also known as *adverbs,* appears on page 235.

Practice

5

Combine each of the following pairs of sentences into one sentence by starting with an -*ly* word and omitting repeated words. Place a comma after the opening -*ly* word.

EXAMPLE

- I gave several yanks to the starting cord of the lawn mower.
- I was angry.

Angrily, I gave several yanks to the starting cord of the lawn mower.

1. • The burglars carried the television out of the house.
   • They were quiet.

   _____

   _____

2. • Janelle squirmed in her seat as she waited for her turn to speak.
   • She was nervous.

   _____

   _____

3. • I reinforced all the coat buttons with strong thread.
   • I was patient.

   _____

   _____

4. • He finished answering the last question on the test.
    • He was quick.

    _____

    _____

5. • I tore the wrapping off the present.
    • I was excited.

    _____

    _____

On separate paper, write five sentences of your own that begin with -*ly* words.

Practice

6

To Openers

Use a *to* word group to open a sentence. Here are examples.

> *To* succeed in that course, you must attend every class.
>
> *To* help me sleep better, I learned to quiet my mind through meditation.
>
> *To* get good seats, we went to the game early.

The *to* in such a group is also known as an *infinitive,* as explained on page 195.

Practice 7

Combine each of the following pairs of sentences into one sentence by starting with a *to* word group and omitting repeated words. Use a comma after the opening *to* word group.

EXAMPLE

- I fertilize the grass every spring.
- I want to make it greener.

  To make the grass greener, I fertilize it every spring.

1. • Doug ran five miles a day all summer.
   • He wanted to prepare for the track season.

   _____

   _____

2. • You should meet Al's parents.
   • This will help you understand him better.

   _____

   _____

3. • She wants to get the stain off her hand.
   • She will have to use an abrasive soap.

   _____

   _____

4. • I left the house early.
   • I had to get to the church on time.

   _____

   _____

5. • I punched in my code number.
   • I did this to make the automatic banking machine work.

   _____

   _____

Practice 8

On separate paper, write five sentences of your own that begin with *to* word groups.

Prepositional Phrase Openers

Use prepositional phrase openers. Here are examples:

From the beginning, I disliked my boss.

In spite of her work, she failed the course.

After the game, we went to a movie.

> **TIP** Prepositional phrases include words like *in, from, of, at, by,* and *with*. A full list is on page 70.

Combine each of the following groups of sentences into one sentence by omitting repeated words. Start each sentence with a suitable prepositional phrase and put the other prepositional phrases in places that sound right. Generally, you should use a comma after the opening prepositional phrase.

Practice

9

EXAMPLE

- A fire started.
- It did this at 5 A.M.
- It did this inside the garage.

  At 5 A.M., a fire started inside the garage.

  _____

1. • I sat napping.
   • I did this during my work break.
   • I did this in the lunchroom corner.
   • I did this with my head on my arm.

   _____

   _____

2. • We played basketball.
   • We did this in the church gym.
   • We did this during the winter.
   • We did this on many evenings.

   _____

   _____

3. • Fred Grencher studies his bald spot.
   • He does this with grave concern.
   • He does this in the bathroom mirror.
   • He does this before going to bed.

   _____

   _____

4. • The car skidded.
   • It did this on an oil slick.
   • It did this on a sharp curve.
   • It did this during the race.

   _____

   _____

5. • The teenage driver raced his car to the busy intersection.
   • He did this without slowing down.
   • The intersection is in the heart of town.

   _____

   _____

Practice

10

On separate paper, write five sentences of your own, each beginning with a prepositional phrase and containing at least one other prepositional phrase.

Series of Items

Use a series of items. Following are two of the many items that can be used in a series: adjectives and verbs. The section on parallelism (page 257) gives you practice in some of the other kinds of items that can be used in a series.

Adjectives in Series

Adjectives are descriptive words. Here are examples:

The *husky young* man sanded the *chipped, weather-worn* paint off the fence.

Husky and *young* are adjectives that describe *man; chipped* and *weather-worn* are adjectives that describe *paint*. More information about adjectives appears on page 232.

Combine each of the following groups of sentences into one sentence by using adjectives in a series and omitting repeated words. Use a comma between adjectives only when *and* inserted between them sounds natural.

EXAMPLE

- I sewed a set of buttons onto my coat.
- The buttons were shiny.
- The buttons were black.
- The coat was old.
- The coat was green.

I sewed a set of shiny black buttons onto my old green coat.

1. • The boy stomped on the bug.
    • The boy was little.
    • The boy was angry.
    • The bug was tiny.
    • The bug was red.

    _____

    _____

2. • The man slowly wiped his forehead with a bandanna.
    • The man was tall.
    • The man was thin.
    • His forehead was sweaty.
    • His bandanna was dirty.
    • His bandanna was blue.

    _____

    _____

3. • My sister is intelligent.
    • My sister is good-natured.
    • My sister is humorous.

    _____

    _____

4. • The boy looked at the girl.
   • The boy was shy.
   • The boy was timid.
   • The girl was grinning.
   • The girl was curly-haired.

   _____

   _____

5. • A man wearing work clothes strode into the tavern.
   • The man was short.
   • The man was muscular.
   • The man was bald.
   • The work clothes were wrinkled.
   • The work clothes were green.
   • The tavern was noisy.
   • The tavern was smoke-filled.

   _____

   _____

Practice

12

On separate paper, write five sentences of your own that contain a series of adjectives.

Verbs in Series

Verbs are words that express action. Basic information about verbs appears on pages 68–73. Here are examples:

   In my job as a cook's helper, I *prepared* salads, *sliced* meat and cheese, and *made* all kinds of sandwiches.

Practice

13

Combine each group of sentences below into one sentence by using verbs in a series and omitting repeated words. Use a comma between verbs in a series.

EXAMPLES

• In the dingy bar Sam shelled peanuts.
• He sipped a beer.
• He talked up a storm with friends.

   In the dingy bar, Sam shelled peanuts, sipped a beer, and talked up a storm with friends.

1. • When the popular comedian walked from behind the curtain, the crowd applauded.
   • The crowd stomped their feet.
   • The crowd shouted, "Hi … oh!"

   _____

   _____

2. • Everywhere in the cafeteria students were pulling on their coats.
   • They were scooping up their books.
   • They were hurrying off to class.

   _____

   _____

3. • By 6 A.M., I had read the textbook chapter.
   • I had taken notes on it.
   • I had studied the notes.
   • I had drunk eight cups of coffee.

   _____

   _____

4. • I pressed the Rice Krispies into the bowl.
   • I poured milk on them.
   • I waited for the milk to soak the cereal.

   _____

   _____

5. • I am afraid the dentist's drill will slip off my tooth.
   • I am afraid it will bite into my gum.
   • I am afraid it will make me jump with pain.

   _____

   _____

On separate paper, write five sentences of your own that use verbs in a series.

Practice

14

Review Test   1

Combine each group of short sentences into one sentence. Various combinations are possible. Choose the combination that reads most smoothly and clearly and that sounds most appropriate in the context of surrounding sentences. Use separate paper.

> **HINT** In combining short sentences into one sentence, omit repeated words where necessary.

Writing a Paper

- Martha is trying to write a paper.
- The paper is for her English class.
- Martha can think of nothing to write.

- She scribbles words.
- The words do not develop her paper's subject.
- This is unfortunate.

- She wishes the paper were finished.
- Her wishing is desperate.
- The paper seems stupid.
- The paper is annoying.

- Martha thinks of calls she could make to friends.
- Martha thinks of shows she could be watching on television.
- She is irritated.

- She sighs.
- She gets back to work.
- She then does two things.

- She first writes whatever comes into her head about her subject.
- She does this for twenty minutes.

- She then reads what she has written.
- She does this to decide on her main point.
- She does this to decide on her support for that point.

- She soon discovers the point of her paper.
- She soon discovers how to support that point.
- She soon discovers how to organize the support.

- She finally has a draft of her paper.
- It is the first draft.
- It is a rough draft.
- She has it after working hard for more than an hour.

- She still has to write a second draft.
- She even has to write a third draft.
- But the worst part is over.
- That is clear.

Review Test 2

Combine each group of short sentences into one sentence. Various combinations are possible. Choose the combination that reads most smoothly and clearly and that sounds most appropriate in the context of surrounding sentences. Use separate paper.

> **HINT** In combining short sentences into one sentence, omit repeated words where necessary.

April Fool's Day

- April Fool's Day is an occasion.
- It is a playful occasion.
- But it is a sometimes annoying occasion.

- Jokers play tricks on their friends.
- Jokers send them unordered pizzas.
- They tell them their cars were stolen.

- They also put salt in the sugar bowl.
- They put sugar in the salt shaker.
- They do so full of glee.

- Practical jokers also like to make phone calls.
- The calls are to the zoo.
- The practical jokers are determined to make the most of the day.

- The caller asks for someone with the name of an animal.
- The caller acts seriously.

- The caller may ask to speak to Mr. Lion.
- The caller may ask to speak to Mr. Bear.
- The caller may ask to speak to Ms. Fish.

- A joker once asked for Mr. Tad Pole.
- The joker wanted to ask for a new name.
- The joker wanted to ask for a silly name.

- The local zoo is trying an approach this year.
- The approach is clever.
- The approach is friendly.
- The approach is meant to discourage such calls.

- The zoo will play a recorded message.
- The recorded message will be played on April Fool's Day.
- The recorded message will say, "Mr. Lion and his friends are busy. They can't come to the phone."

- The recording will also say, "They would prefer a visit."
- "The visit will be from you and your family."
- "The visit will be in the near future."

NAME: _____

DATE: _____

MASTERY TEST 1 | # Sentence Variety II

Combine each group of short sentences into one sentence. Various combinations are possible. Choose the combination that reads most smoothly and clearly and that sounds most appropriate in the context of surrounding sentences. Use separate paper.

> **HINT** In combining short sentences into one sentence, omit repeated words where necessary. The story about Dracula continues in the next mastery test.

A Surprise for Dracula

- Lola had a dream.
- The dream was about Dracula.
- This happened recently.

- Dracula slipped through a window.
- The window was open.
- He approached Lola.
- Lola was sleeping.

- Dracula's lip curled back.
- His fangs were revealed.
- The fangs were long.
- The fangs were pointed.
- The pointing was cruel.

- He stood over Lola.
- He grinned down at her.
- He assumed his victim was powerless.

- He bent down to her neck.
- The bending was slow.
- But then something happened.
- What happened was unexpected.

282

Sentence Variety II

Follow the directions given with Mastery Test 1.

A Surprise for Dracula (continued)

- Lola's eyes opened.
- Lola's hand flew out.
- She gave Dracula a karate chop.
- The karate chop was quick.
- The karate chop was on the side of his head.

- Dracula was knocked to the floor.
- He then sprang up.
- He made a cry.
- The cry was terrible.
- The cry was chilling.

- He leaped at Lola.
- She held up a crucifix.
- The crucifix was small.
- The crucifix was shining.

- Dracula came to a stop.
- The stop was abrupt.
- He began to shrink.
- This happened rapidly.
- He finally disappeared.
- Only a bat remained.

- The bat was squeaking.
- It flew out of the room.
- Its going was quick.

Paper Format

Introductory Activity

This chapter will discuss the guidelines for preparing a paper. Which of the paper openings below seems clearer and easier to read?

A

	Finding Faces
	It takes just a little imagination to find faces in the
	objects around you. For instance, clouds are sometimes
	shaped like faces. If you lie on the ground on a partly

B

	"finding faces"
	It takes just a little imagination to find faces in the objects
	around you. For instance, clouds are sometimes shaped like
	faces. If you lie on the ground on a partly cloudy day, chan-
	ces are you will be able to spot many well-known faces

What are three reasons for your choice?

_____

_____

_____

_____

Answers are on page 568.

Guidelines for Preparing a Paper

Here are guidelines to follow in preparing a paper for an instructor.

1. Use full-sized theme or printer paper, 8½ by 11 inches.

2. Leave wide margins (1 to 1½ inches) all around the paper. In particular, do not crowd the right-hand or bottom margin. This white space makes your paper more readable; also, the instructor has room for comments.

3. If you write by hand,
   - Use a pen with blue or black ink (*not* a pencil).
   - Be careful not to overlap letters and not to make decorative loops on letters.
   - On narrow-ruled paper, write on every other line.
   - Make all your letters distinct. Pay special attention to *a, e, i, o,* and *u*—five letters that people sometimes write illegibly.

4. Center the title of your paper on the first line of the first page. Do not put quotation marks around the title. Do not underline the title. Capitalize all the major words in a title, including the first word. Short connecting words within a title, such as *of, for, the, in,* and *to,* are not capitalized.

5. Skip a line between the title and the first line of your text. Indent the first line of each paragraph about five spaces (half an inch) from the left-hand margin.

6. Make commas, periods, and other punctuation marks firm and clear. Leave a slight space after each period.

7. If you break a word at the end of a line, break only between syllables (see page 383). Do not break words of one syllable.

8. Put your name, date, and course number where your instructor asks for them.

Remember these points about the title and the first sentence of your paper.

9. The title should be several words that tell what the paper is about. It should usually *not* be a complete sentence. For example, if you are writing a paper about your jealous sister, the title could simply be "My Jealous Sister."

10. Do not rely on the title to help explain the first sentence of your paper. The first sentence must be independent of the title. For instance, if the title of your paper is "My Jealous Sister," the first sentence should *not* be "She has been this way as long as I can remember." Rather, the first sentence might be "My sister has always been a jealous person."

Practice

1

Identify the mistakes in format in the following lines from a student theme. Explain the mistakes in the spaces provided. One mistake is described for you as an example.

		"The generation gap in our house"
		When I was a girl, I never argued with my parents about
		differences between their attitude and mine. My father
		would deliver his judgment on an issue and that was alw-
		ays the end of the matter. There was no discussion permit-
		ted, so I gradually began to express my disagreement in other

1. *Hyphenate only between syllables (al-ways).* _____

2. _____

3. _____

4. _____

5. _____

6. _____

Practice

2

As already stated, a title should tell in several words what a paper is about. Often a title can be based on the sentence that expresses the main idea of a paper.

Following are five main-idea sentences from student papers. Write a suitable and specific title for each paper, basing the title on the main idea.

EXAMPLE

Title: *Aging Americans as Outcasts*
Our society treats aging Americans as outcasts in many ways.

1. Title: _____
   Selfishness is a common trait in young children.

2. Title: _____
   Exercising every morning offers a number of benefits.

3. Title: _____
   My teenage son is a stubborn person.

4. Title: _____
   To survive in college, a person must learn certain essential study skills.

5. Title: _____
   Only after I was married did I fully realize the drawbacks and values of single life.

In four of the five following sentences, the writer has mistakenly used the title to help explain the first sentence. But as has already been stated, you must *not* rely on the title to help explain your first sentence.

Rewrite the sentences so that they stand independent of the title. Write *Correct* under the one sentence that is independent of the title.

EXAMPLE

Title: Flunking an Exam
First sentence: I managed to do this because of several bad habits.

Rewritten: *I managed to flunk an exam because of several bad habits.*
_____

1. Title: The Worst Day of My Life
    First sentence: It began when my supervisor at work gave me a message to call home.

    Rewritten: _____
    _____

2. Title: Catholic Church Services
    First sentence: They have undergone many changes in the last few decades.

    Rewritten: _____
    _____

3. Title: An Embarrassing Incident
    First sentence: This happened to me when I was working as a waitress at the Stanton Hotel.

    Rewritten: _____
    _____

4. Title: The Inability to Share
    First sentence: The inability to share can cause great strains in a relationship.

    Rewritten: _____
    _____

5. Title: Offensive Television Commercials
    First sentence: Many that I watch are degrading to human dignity.

    Rewritten: _____
    _____

Review Test

Use the space provided below to rewrite the following sentences from a student paper, correcting the mistakes in format.

	"my nursing home friends"
	I now count some of them among my good friends. I fi-
	rst went there just to keep a relative of mine company.
	That is when I learned some of them rarely got any visitors.
	Many were starved for conversation and friendship.
	At the time, I did not want to get involved. But what I

Paper Format MASTERY TEST 1

Identify the five mistakes in paper format in the student paper that follows. From the box below, choose the letters that describe the five mistakes and write those letters in the spaces provided in the order in which they appear in the paper.

---

a. The title should not be underlined.

b. The title should not be set off in quotation marks.

c. There should not be a period at the end of a title.

d. All the major words in a title should be capitalized.

e. The title should just be several words and not a complete sentence.

f. The first sentence of a paper should stand independent of the title.

g. A line should be skipped between the title and the first line of the paper.

h. The first line of a paper should be indented.

i. The right-hand margin should not be crowded.

j. Hyphenation should occur only between syllables.

	"Nervous times"
	There are three different times that I feel nervous. First of all, if
	I'm in a classroom full of students I don't know and I'm asked to
	answer a question, I may begin to stutter. Or I may know the
	answer, but my mind will just block out. Second, if I'm going out
	on a date with a guy for the first time, I won't eat. Eating when
	I'm nervous makes my fork tremble, and I'm likely to drop food on
	my clothes. Finally if I'm going to a job interview, I will practice
	at home what I'm going to say. But as soon as I'm alone with the
	interviewer, and he asks me if there's anything I'd like to say, I
	say something dumb like "I'm a people person, you know." One day
	I hope to overcome my nervousness.

1. _____   2. _____   3. _____   4. _____   5. _____

MASTERY TEST 2   # Paper Format

Identify the five mistakes in paper format in the student paper that follows. From the box below, choose the letters that describe the five mistakes and write those letters in the spaces provided in the order in which they appear in the paper.

---

a. The title should not be underlined.

b. The title should not be set off in quotation marks.

c. There should not be a period at the end of a title.

d. All the major words in a title should be capitalized.

e. The title should just be several words and not a complete sentence.

f. The first sentence of a paper should stand independent of the title.

g. A line should be skipped between the title and the first line of the paper.

h. The first line of a paper should be indented.

i. The right-hand margin should not be crowded.

j. Hyphenation should occur only between syllables.

---

	coming down with the flu
	I could tell that I was coming down with it. For one th-
	ing, my nose and throat were shutting down. I could not breathe
	through my nose at all, while my nose was running nonstop, so
	that I soon went through a box of tissues. My throat was sore,
	and when I was brave enough to speak, my voice sounded horrible.
	Another reason I knew I had the flu was fever and chills. The
	thermometer registered 102 degrees. My chills were so bad that
	to get warm I had to put on sweat socks, flannel pajamas, and a
	heavy robe, and I then had to get under two blankets and a
	sheet. Finally, I was extremely fatigued. After I got into bed, I
	slept for eight hours straight. When I woke up I was still so tired
	that I couldn't get out of bed. My eyelids felt as if they weighed
	a hundred pounds each, and I could not lift my head off the pillow.
	Too tired to think, I drifted back to sleep with hazy thoughts of
	my mother's homemade chicken soup.

1. _____   2. _____   3. _____   4. _____   5. _____

Capital Letters

21

Introductory Activity

You probably already know a good deal about the uses of capital letters. Answering the questions below will help you check your knowledge before you begin the chapter.

1. Write the full name of a good friend: _____

2. In what city and state were you born? _____

3. What is your present street address? _____

4. Name a country where you would like to travel: _____

5. Name a school that you attended: _____

6. Give the name of a store where you buy food: _____

7. Name a company where you or anyone you know works:

   _____

8. Which day of the week gives you the best chance to relax? _____

9. What holiday is your favorite? _____

10. Which brand of toothpaste do you use? _____

11. Give the brand name of candy or chewing gum you like: _____

12. Name a song or a television show you enjoy: _____

13. Write the title of a magazine or newspaper you read:

    _____

continued

Three capital letters are needed in the example below. Underline the words you think should be capitalized. Then write them, capitalized, in the spaces provided.

on the final night of the NBA Playoffs, my roommate said, "let's buy some snacks and invite a few friends over to watch the game." i knew my plans to write a term paper would have to be changed.

14. _____   15. _____   16. _____

Answers are on page 569.

Main Uses of Capital Letters

www.mhhe.com/langan

Capital letters are used with:

1. First word in a sentence or direct quotation
2. Names of persons and the word *I*
3. Names of particular places
4. Names of days of the week, months, and holidays
5. Names of commercial products
6. Titles of books, magazines, articles, films, television shows, songs, poems, stories, papers that you write, and the like
7. Names of companies, associations, unions, clubs, religious and political groups, and other organizations

Each use is illustrated on the pages that follow.

First Word in a Sentence or Direct Quotation

Our company has begun laying people off.

The doctor said, "This may hurt a bit."

"My husband," said Sheryl, "is a light eater. When it's light, he starts to eat."

In the third example above, *My* and *When* are capitalized because they start new sentences. But *is* is not capitalized, because it is part of the first sentence.

Names of Persons and the Word *I*

At the picnic, I met Tony Curry and Lola Morrison.

Names of Particular Places

After graduating from Gibbs High School in Houston, I worked for a summer at a nearby Holiday Inn on Clairmont Boulevard.

But Use small letters if the specific name of a place is not given.

After graduating from high school in my hometown, I worked for a summer at a nearby hotel on one of the main shopping streets.

Names of Days of the Week, Months, and Holidays

This year, Memorial Day falls on the last Thursday in May.

But Use small letters for the seasons—summer, fall, winter, spring.

In the early summer and fall, my hay fever bothers me.

Names of Commercial Products

The consumer magazine gave high ratings to Cheerios breakfast cereal, Breyer's ice cream, and Progresso chicken noodle soup.

But Use small letters for the *type* of product (breakfast cereal, ice cream, chicken noodle soup, and the like).

Titles of Books, Magazines, Articles, Films, Television Shows, Songs, Poems, Stories, Papers That You Write, and the Like

My oral report was on *The Diary of a Young Girl,* by Anne Frank.

While watching *The Young and the Restless* on television, I thumbed through *Cosmopolitan* magazine and *The New York Times*.

Names of Companies, Associations, Unions, Clubs, Religious and Political Groups, and Other Organizations

A new bill before Congress is opposed by the National Rifle Association.

My wife is Jewish; I am Roman Catholic. We are both members of the Democratic Party.

My parents have life insurance with Prudential, auto insurance with Allstate, and medical insurance with Blue Cross and Blue Shield.

Write a paragraph describing the advertisement shown here so that a person who has never seen it will be able to visualize it and fully understand it. Once you have written your paragraph, check to make sure you have used capital letters properly throughout.

Practice

1

In the sentences that follow, cross out the words that need capitals. Then write the capitalized forms of the words in the space provided. The number of spaces tells you how many corrections to make in each case.

EXAMPLE

Rhoda said, "~~Why~~ should I bother to *eat* this ~~hershey~~ bar? I should just apply it directly to my hips." _____*Why*_____   _____*Hershey*_____

1. Vince wanted to go to the halloween party dressed as a thanksgiving turkey, but he was afraid someone might try to carve him.

   _____   _____

2. Laurie called upstairs, "if you're not ready in five minutes, i'm leaving without you."

   _____   _____

3. The old ford rattled its way from connecticut to florida on four balding goodyear tires.

   _____   _____   _____   _____

4. Patients read *newsweek, time,* and *people* magazines while they waited for the dentist to examine them.

   _____   _____   _____

5. Juanita King, a member of the northside improvement association, urged the city to clean up the third Street neighborhood.

   _____   _____   _____   _____

6. At soundworks, a discount store on washington boulevard, she purchased a panasonic stereo amplifier.

   _____   _____   _____   _____

7. Tom finished basic training at fort gordon and was transferred to a base near Stuttgart, germany.

   _____   _____   _____

8. On thursday nights Terri goes to the weight watchers' meeting at a nearby high school.

   _____   _____   _____

9. The two films they enjoyed most during the horror film festival held in february were *return of dracula* and *alien.*

   _____   _____   _____   _____

10. My sister bought jeans at old navy and got lunch at taco bell.

    _____   _____   _____   _____

Other Uses of Capital Letters

Capital letters are also used with

1. Names that show family relationships
2. Titles of persons when used with their names
3. Specific school courses
4. Languages
5. Geographic locations
6. Historical periods and events
7. Races, nations, and nationalities
8. Opening and closing of a letter

Each use is illustrated on the pages that follow.

Names That Show Family Relationships

Aunt Fern and Uncle Jack are selling their house.

I asked Grandfather to start the fire.

Is Mom feeling better?

But Do not capitalize words like *mother, father, grandmother, grandfather, uncle, aunt,* and so on when they are preceded by *my* or another possessive word.

My aunt and uncle are selling their house.

I asked my grandfather to start the fire.

Is my mom feeling better?

Titles of Persons When Used with Their Names

I wrote an angry letter to Senator Blutt.

Can you drive to Dr. Stein's office?

We asked Professor Bushkin about his attendance policy.

But Use small letters when titles appear by themselves, without specific names.

I wrote an angry letter to my senator.

Can you drive to the doctor's office?

We asked our professor about his attendance policy.

Specific School Courses

My courses this semester include Accounting I, Introduction to Web Design, Business Law, General Psychology, and Basic Math.

But Use small letters for general subject areas.

This semester I'm taking mostly business courses, but I have a psychology course and a math course as well.

Languages

Yasmin speaks English and Spanish equally well.

Geographic Locations

I lived in the South for many years and then moved to the West Coast.

But Use small letters in giving directions.

Go south for about five miles and then bear west.

Historical Periods and Events

One essay question dealt with the Battle of the Bulge in World War II.

Races, Nations, Nationalities

The census form asked whether I was Caucasian, African American, Native American, Latino, or Asian.

Last summer I hitchhiked through Italy, France, and Germany.

The city is a melting pot for Koreans, Vietnamese, and Mexican Americans.

But Use small letters when referring to *whites* or *blacks*.

Both whites and blacks supported our mayor in the election.

Opening and Closing of a Letter

Dear Sir: Sincerely yours,

Dear Madam: Truly yours,

TIP Capitalize only the first word in a closing.

Cross out the words that need capitals in the following sentences. Then write the capitalized forms of the words in the spaces provided. The number of spaces tells you how many corrections to make in each case.

1. When aunt esther died, she left all her money to her seven cats and nothing to my uncle.

   _____   _____

2. This fall I'm taking night courses in spanish and aerobic exercise I.

   _____   _____   _____

3. Tony was referred to dr. purdy's office because his regular dentist was on vacation.

   _____   _____

4. The latino family in the apartment upstairs has just moved here from the southwest.

   _____   _____

5. My accounting courses are giving me less trouble than intermediate math 201.

   _____   _____

Unnecessary Use of Capitals

Many errors in capitalization are caused by adding capitals where they are not needed. Cross out the incorrectly capitalized letters in the following sentences and write the correct forms in the spaces provided. The number of spaces tells you how many corrections to make in each sentence.

1. During the Summer I like to sit in my backyard, Sunbathe, and read Magazines like *Glamour* and *People*.

   _____   _____   _____

2. Every Week I seem to be humming another Tune. Lately I have been humming the Melody for the latest Pepsi commercial on television.

   _____   _____   _____

3. After High School I traveled to twenty States, including Alaska, and then I decided to enroll in a local College.

   _____   _____   _____   _____

4. The Title of my Paper was "The End of the Civil War." My Instructor did not give me a good Grade for it.

_____ _____ _____ _____

5. My Friend Jesse said, "People no longer have to go to College and get a Degree in order to find a good job and succeed in Life."

_____ _____ _____ _____

Collaborative Activity

Editing and Rewriting

Working with a partner, read the short paragraph that follows and mark off the sixteen words with missing capital letters. Then use the space provided to rewrite the passage, adding capital letters where needed. Feel free to discuss the passage quietly with your partner and refer back to the chapter when necessary.

[1]Red Riding Hood decided to visit her grandmother in brooklyn. [2]Old Mrs. Hood had just been released from bayshore hospital, where she had spent the entire month of september recovering from a broken hip. [3]Red Riding Hood's mother gave her daughter a container of campbell's vegetable soup and ritz crackers to bring to Grandma Hood. [4]Red entered the subway entrance on third avenue, and when the train roared in, she boarded a car. [5]Suddenly, a young man approached red. [6]He resembled a wolf with his long, greasy hair and beard, and he said, "what a foxy face you've got, little girl. [7]I'd like to eat you up." [8]"Leave me alone," said Red. [9]"I'm a part-time Guardian angel and I know how to defend myself." [10]When he tried to touch Red, she flipped the new york times she was reading into his face to distract him. [11]Then she delivered a quick karate chop with her hand. [12]the man staggered backward, and an elderly woman then batted him with a large box of reynolds aluminum foil from her shopping bag. [13]The train entered the station and Red Riding Hood stepped over the wolflike man, who lay groaning on the floor. [14]"Maybe this will teach you to let people ride the subway in peace," she said as she stepped through the doors.

continued

_____

_____

_____

_____

_____

_____

_____

_____

_____

_____

_____

_____

Collaborative Activity

Creating Sentences

Working with a partner, write a sentence (or two) as directed. Pay special attention to capital letters.

1. Write a sentence (or two) about a place you like (or want) to visit. Be sure to include the name of the place, including the city, state, or country where it is located.

2. Write a sentence (or two) in which you state the name of your elementary school, your favorite teacher or subject, and your least favorite teacher or subject.

3. Write a sentence (or two) which includes three brand-name products that you often use. You may begin the sentence with the words, "Three brand-name products I use every day are . . ."

4. Think of the name of your favorite musical artist or performer. Then write a sentence in which you include the musician's name and the title of one of his or her songs.

5. Write a sentence in which you describe something you plan to do two days from now. Be sure to include the date and day of the week in your sentence.

Reflective Activity

1. What would writing be like without capital letters? Use an example or two to help show how capital letters are important to writing.

2. What three uses of capital letters are most difficult for you to remember? Explain, giving examples.

Review Test 1

Cross out the words that need capitals in the following sentences. Then write the capitalized forms of the words in the spaces provided. The number of spaces tells you how many corrections to make in each sentence.

EXAMPLE

During halftime of the ~~saturday~~ afternoon football game, my sister said, "~~let's~~ get some hamburgers from ~~wendy's~~ or put a pizza in the oven."

   Saturday   _Let's_   _Wendy's_

1. Stanley was disgusted when he was told he couldn't order lipton tea at the chinese restaurant.

   _____   _____

2. When my grandfather came to america from the ukraine, which was then a part of russia, he spoke no english.

   _____   _____   _____   _____

3. Nikki said, "i've been working as a waitress at the red lobster since last march."

   _____   _____   _____   _____

4. My math 101 course meets on tuesdays in wister hall.

   _____   _____   _____   _____

5. Every election Day, my mother takes a day off from her job as a nurse at memorial hospital to serve as a poll watcher for the democrats.

   _____   _____   _____   _____

6. "At my age," grandma rose said, "i'm just glad to wake up each morning."

   _____   _____   _____

7. At the corner of thirteenth and market streets is a newsstand where people can buy magazines from as far away as france.

   _____   _____   _____   _____

8. When aunt esther's pontiac finally broke down, she decided to get a toyota.

   _____   _____   _____   _____

9. The college is showing the movie *stagecoach* on friday night as part of its john wayne film festival.

   _____   _____   _____   _____

10. On our trip to washington, we visited the lincoln memorial, sat through a session of the United States senate, and then fell asleep at a concert at the kennedy center.

   _____   _____   _____

   _____   _____   _____

Review Test   2

On separate paper, write

- Seven sentences demonstrating the seven main uses of capital letters.
- Eight sentences demonstrating the eight other uses of capital letters.

NAME: _____

DATE: _____

Capital Letters

Cross out the two capitalization errors in each of the following sentences. Then write the corrections in the spaces provided.

_____   1. That fancy new restaurant, fork, requires all men to wear a shirt and Tie.

_____

_____   2. Lisa complained, "this pearl bracelet I bought at woolworth's has started to turn green."

_____

_____   3. Though howard no longer lives on third Street, he likes to return there on weekends to visit old friends.

_____

_____   4. Joe and Leslie love arizona, but we prefer colorado.

_____

_____   5. The statue in Boyle's Square is supposed to represent all the soldiers killed during the revolutionary war.

_____

_____   6. I hired a lawyer after my Ford Focus was sideswiped by a united parcel delivery truck.

_____

_____   7. Yuri often works overtime on saturdays and sundays to help keep up with his bills.

_____

_____   8. Our neighbor, mr. charles Reynolds, accidentally backed into our maple tree today.

_____

_____   9. "last week I bought Adidas sneakers and a jogging sweatshirt," Janey said. "But my asthma is so bad that my Doctor won't let me start running."

_____

_____   10. I don't like instant coffee, but that's all that's served at the weight watchers' meetings on Wednesday nights.

_____

NAME: _____

DATE: _____

Capital Letters

Cross out the two capitalization errors in each of the following sentences. Then write the corrections in the spaces provided.

_____

_____

1. I asked the clerk, "do you have any italian olives?"

_____

_____

2. the third-grade children sang "Jingle Bells" during the school christmas ceremony.

_____

_____

3. I drove lance to the auto shop to get the estimate on repairs to his 2000 mustang.

_____

_____

4. "because of the bad weather," said the manager, "our Store will be closing at four o'clock."

_____

_____

5. I can't decide whether to buy the boots I saw at butler's or to see if I can find a better pair at Florsheim's on hudson Street.

_____

_____

6. I am so brainwashed by Advertising that I always want to buy both skippy and Peter Pan peanut butter.

_____

_____

7. Linda works at the farmers' National Bank in williamstown on Mondays, Wednesdays, and Fridays.

_____

_____

8. He got low grades in his Math courses but straight A's in English and spanish.

_____

_____

9. When the company transferred Rick's mother to the West coast, he wound up as a student at Beverly Hills High school.

_____

_____

10. The epitaph on W. C. Fields's tombstone reads, "on the whole, I'd rather be in philadelphia."

NAME: _____

DATE: _____

Capital Letters **MASTERY TEST 3**

Cross out the two capitalization errors in each of the following sentences. Then write the corrections in the spaces provided.

_____ 1. My Uncle, a ranger at Olympia National Park, wrote a pamphlet titled *a Guide to Olympia's Wildflowers.*

_____ 2. Last summer I visited my aunt in israel and had a chance to learn some Hebrew and French, since she spoke both Languages.

_____ 3. During the college's festival of marx brothers movies, Jean saw *Duck Soup* for the first time.

_____ 4. The book titled *A Study in Human Dignity* tells the story of john merrick, a terribly deformed young man.

_____ 5. Dave studied at the Culinary Institute of America before joining the staff at the greenbrier inn.

_____ 6. As soon as his father came in the door, Frankie cried, "Who won, Dad? i'll bet the dodgers did."

_____ 7. After visiting the smithsonian institution in Washington, we headed for a Chinese restaurant recommended by friends.

_____ 8. Although he is a christian scientist, Harold Phipps decided to let the doctors treat his son with antibiotics.

_____ 9. After the game we stopped off to get an early supper at a nearby burger king.

_____ 10. U2's "One" is tony's all-time favorite Song.

MASTERY TEST 4 # Capital Letters

Cross out the two capitalization errors in each of the following sentences. Then write the corrections in the spaces provided.

_____

_____

1. "Why subscribe to *TV guide*," said Fara to Tyrell, "when there's a perfectly good TV listing in the sunday paper?"

_____

2. Someone smashed into Claude's toyota when it was parked on Pine street and stole all his CDs.

_____

_____

3. Sherry came home from work hungry and devoured three hershey bars and a bag of fritos; then she asked what was for supper.

_____

_____

4. "You ought to quit smoking those camels," said Martha to her husband. "Even tiparillos would be less harmful."

_____

_____

5. Corey was watching a soap opera, *General hospital*, on TV when a woman from bell Telephone called.

_____

_____

6. I had no sooner sat down in dr. Stein's office last tuesday evening than his beeper began to sound.

_____

7. My Mother's first job was as a real estate salesperson for century 21.

_____

_____

8. To Sam, labor day means staying up all night to watch the Jerry Lewis Telethon.

_____

_____

9. Until the remodeling work is completed, our psychology classes will be held in wister hall.

_____

_____

10. The dirty Sign on the back of the speeding truck read, "this driver is a professional."

Numbers and Abbreviations

Introductory Activity

This chapter will introduce you to the specific rules using numbers and abbreviations in your writing. Write a check mark beside the item in each pair that you think uses numbers correctly.

_____ I finished the exam by 8:55, but my grade was only 65 percent.

_____ I finished the exam by eight-fifty-five, but my grade was only sixty-five percent.

_____ 9 people are in my biology lab, but there are 45 in my lecture group.

_____ Nine people are in my biology lab, but there are forty-five in my lecture group.

Write a check mark beside the item in each pair that you think uses abbreviations correctly.

_____ Both of my bros. were treated by Dr. Lewis after the mt. climbing accident.

_____ Both of my brothers were treated by Dr. Lewis after the mountain climbing accident.

continued

_____ I spent two hrs. finishing my Eng. paper and handed it to my teacher, Ms. Peters, right at the deadline.

_____ I spent two hours finishing my English paper and handed it to my teacher, Ms. Peters, right at the deadline.

Answers are on page 569.

www.mhhe.com/langan

Numbers

Rule 1 Spell out numbers that take no more than two words. Otherwise, use numerals—the numbers themselves.

Last year Tina bought nine new CDs.

Ray struck out fifteen batters in Sunday's softball game.

But

Tina now has 114 CDs in her collection.

Already this season Ray has recorded 168 strikeouts.

You should also spell out a number that begins a sentence:

One hundred fifty first-graders throughout the city showed flu symptoms today.

Rule 2 Be consistent when you use a series of numbers. If some numbers in a sentence or paragraph require more than two words, then use numerals throughout the selection.

This past spring, we planted 5 rhodos, 15 azaleas, 50 summersweet, and 120 myrtle around our house.

Rule 3 Use numbers to show dates, times, addresses, percentages, exact sums of money, and parts of a book.

John Kennedy was killed on November 22, 1963.

My job interview was set for 10:15. (*But:* Spell out numbers before *o'clock*. For example: The time was then changed to eleven o'clock.)

Lee's new address is 118 North 35th Street.

Almost 40 percent of my meals are eaten at fast-food restaurants.

The cashier rang up a total of $18.35. (*But:* Round amounts may be expressed as words. For example: The movie has a five-dollar admission charge.)

Read Chapter 6 in your math textbook and answer questions 1 to 5 on page 250.

Use the three rules to make the corrections needed in these sentences.

1. Why do I always wind up with 5 exams in 3 days?

2. 2 teenage girls were responsible for the shoplifting.

3. My appointment was for eight-thirty in the evening.

4. However, the doctor didn't arrive until 9 o'clock.

5. I worked overtime last week and received a paycheck for two hundred and eighty-two dollars.

6. Steve lives at twenty-three West Pine Street.

7. Devon and Crystal were married on May thirty-first, nineteen-seventy-six.

8. Our son has decorated his room with two wall posters, five compact disc covers, and over 215 baseball cards.

9. Sears' fifty percent off sale on certain items ends on Friday.

10. Our team was penalized 5 yards for having 12 players on the field.

Practice

1

Abbreviations

While abbreviations are a helpful time-saver in note taking, you should avoid most abbreviations in formal writing. Listed below are some of the few abbreviations that can acceptably be used in compositions. Note that a period is used after most abbreviations.

www.mhhe.com/langan

1. **Mr., Mrs., Ms., Jr., Sr., and Dr. when used with proper names:**

    Mr. Rollin   Ms. Peters   Dr. Coleman

2. **Time references:**

    A.M., or A.M., or a.m.   P.M., or P.M., or p.m.   B.C., or B.C.   A.D. or A.D.

3. **First or middle initial in a signature:**

    T. Alan Parker   Trina M. Evans

4. **Organizations, technical words, and trade names known primarily by their initials:**

    ABC   CIA   UNESCO   GM   AIDS   DNA

Cross out the words that should not be abbreviated and correct them in the spaces provided.

1. My cous. moved into her own apt. after she had a fight with her parents.

_____   _____

2. Next Wed. I finish my last class of the semester.

_____

3. Linda gets depressed when all her charge acct. bills arrive before the first of the mo.

_____   _____

4. After the mov. men broke my recliner, I wrote an angry letter to the pres. of the co.

_____   _____   _____

5. Inez has lost fifteen lbs. on the diet she started three wks. ago.

_____   _____

6. My favor. actor is Tom Hanks, esp. in the movie *Saving Private Ryan*.

_____   _____

7. That sec. from the temp. agency can type seventy-eight words a min.

_____   _____   _____

8. My younger bro. is a drum major with his h. s. marching band.

_____   _____   _____

9. Our new Honda gets twenty-eight miles a gal. on city sts.

_____   _____

10. At 11:15 A.M., Dr. Liu came out of the hosp. operating rm. and told me that my wife was fine.

_____   _____

Review Test

Cross out the mistake or mistakes in numbers and abbreviations and correct them in the spaces provided.

1. Nothing was left in the refrigerator except 2 overripe pears.

   _____

2. As usual, the train pulled into the sta. forty min. late.

   _____   _____

3. On Saturdays, the hardware store on Central Avenue doesn't open until ten-fifteen.

   _____

4. Even though I had paid all my premiums on time, my insur. co. refused to reimburse me for my loss.

   _____   _____

5. Dr. Engler's driver's lic. was revoked after he got into a traffic accident on Wayne Ave.

   _____   _____

6. I can still remember when it cost only 8 cents to mail a first-class letter and three cents for a postcard.

   _____

7. Last Wed. I fell asleep at 9 P.M. watching the pres. address a joint session of Congress on television.

   _____   _____

8. My little brother has had bronchitis six times this year and has missed 32 days of school.

   _____

9. The nice thing about double feat. is that you can see two mov. for the price of one.

   _____   _____

10. Can you believe that the thrift shop on Seventeenth Street is selling two-hundred-and-fifty-dollar down coats for $49.95?

   _____

NAME: _____

DATE: _____

MASTERY TEST 1 # Numbers and Abbreviations

Cross out the mistake in numbers or abbreviations in each sentence and correct it in the space provided.

_____ 1. In a panic, William grabbed the phone book and looked in the inside cover for the emergency number of the fire dept.

_____ 2. Did you know that an eight-ounce glass of tomato juice has only 50 calories?

_____ 3. Rod finally entered the ladies' room to investigate after he had waited a half hr. for his girlfriend.

_____ 4. By the time I graduated from high school, I had written 3 term papers, thirty-two book reports, and 120 spelling tests.

_____ 5. The federal govt. agreed to reimburse the citizens whose land was being incorporated into a protected wilderness area.

_____ 6. The basketball ref. called a technical foul on the screaming coach who had run out onto the court.

_____ 7. It took Saul all evening to do the twenty problems on page eighty-seven.

_____ 8. In Floyd's backyard were 125 old tires, 263 yards of rusty barbed wire, and three cast-iron bathtubs.

_____ 9. To discourage burglars, our automatic timer turns on a light and radio at 8 o'clock every night.

_____ 10. The overjoyed couple had won a thousand dollars a wk. for life in the state lottery.

NAME: _____

DATE: _____

Numbers and Abbreviations

Cross out the mistake in numbers or abbreviations in each sentence and correct it
in the space provided. Mark the one sentence that is correct with a *C*.

_____ 1. A delivery van was carelessly blocking the entrance to the hosp. emergency
room.

_____ 2. From five potted tomato plants on the patio, Ruth harvested over ninety-five
tomatoes.

_____ 3. Whenever I catch a cold, I take 2 aspirins every four hours.

_____ 4. Mrs. Ramirez stood patiently in line at the P.O. waiting to mail a package
and several letters.

_____ 5. As she did, she studied the faces of the "Ten Most Wanted" crim. on the
FBI poster.

_____ 6. After joining Weight Watchers, Kendra lost thirty-two pounds in only
17 weeks.

_____ 7. I hurried to answer the phone, but it was only someone from the Rescue
Squad requesting a contrib.

_____ 8. One of the actual questions on the test was when the War of Eighteen-
Twelve was fought.

_____ 9. Global warming may cause the ice in Montana's Glacier National Park to
disappear by mid-two thousand thirty.

_____ 10. The trouble with Ms. Ryder, my history prof., is that she never gives any
examples when she lectures.

End Marks

A sentence always ends with a period, a question mark, or an exclamation point. Each of these will be discussed in turn on the following pages. First, see if you can add the end mark needed in each of the following sentences.

1. All week I have been feeling depressed

2. What is the deadline for handing in the paper

3. The man at the door wants to know whose car is double-parked

4. That truck ahead of us is out of control

Answers are on page 569.

www.mhhe.com/langan

Period (.)

Use a period after a sentence that makes a statement.

> More single parents are adopting children.
> It has rained for most of the week.

Use a period after most abbreviations.

Mr. Brady	B.A.	Dr. Ballard
Ms. Peters	A.M.	Tom Ricci, Jr.

Question Mark (?)

Use a question mark after a *direct* question.

When is your paper due?

How is your cold?

Tom asked, "When are you leaving?"

"Why doesn't everyone take a break?" Rosa suggested.

Do not use a question mark after an *indirect* question (a question not in the speaker's exact words).

She asked when the paper was due.

He asked how my cold was.

Tom asked when I was leaving.

Rosa suggested that everyone take a break.

www.mhhe.com/langan

Exclamation Point (!)

Use an exclamation point after a word or sentence that expresses strong feeling.

Come here!

Ouch! This pizza is hot!

That truck just missed us!

www.mhhe.com/langan

> **TIP** Be careful not to overuse exclamation points.

Is the exclamation point used correctly in this sign? If not, what should be done to fix the sign?

Practice

1

Add a period, a question mark, or an exclamation point, as needed, to each of the following sentences.

1. How long will the store sale continue

2. Watch out for that bump in the road

3. The copper bracelet on her arm helps her arthritis

4. Does Barbara's room always look as if a hurricane came for a visit

5. Dr. Kirby specializes in acupuncture of the wallet

6. Manny, Moe, and Jack are always working on their cars

7. Watch out or you'll step on my sunglasses

8. He asked if I had read Tolkien's *The Lord of the Rings*

9. "It will take hours to clean up this mess" Ellen cried.

10. Little Alan asked his uncle, "Is your mustache a wig "

Review Test

Add a period, question mark, or exclamation point as needed to each of the following sentences.

1. Our mechanic said the old car needs an oil change and two new tires

2. Did you know that the average person should drink two quarts of water each day

3. The manager surprised everyone when he announced that the factory would be closing

4. That man just stole my wallet

5. What was your score on the math test

6. On Friday nights, noisy teenagers gather in the park behind my apartment

7. That child is waving a loaded handgun

8. If you could travel to any place in the world, where would you go

9. I wonder if the bad weather will cause the baseball game to be canceled

10. My computer is on fire

NAME: _____

DATE: _____

End Marks

Add a period, a question mark, or an exclamation point, as needed, to each of the following sentences.

> **HINT** End marks go *inside* the quotation marks that appear in some sentences.

1. Even today women earn, on the average, only 59 percent of men's salaries

2. Are you going to watch the Miss America pageant this year

3. After interrupting the program, the radio announcer hurried to assure us, "This was only a test "

4. The strange meal consisted of sausage, potato chips, and watermelon

5. When will daylight saving time end this year

6. Karen screamed, "I don't ever want to see you again "

7. That tree has been attacked by some kind of insect

8. Watch out for an incoming Frisbee

9. Sometimes I get depressed and wonder if I will ever get my degree

10. Do you know how many cups of coffee it took me to finish this paper

11. The man threw open the window and yelled, "I'm mad at the world, and I'm not going to take it anymore "

12. My little brother is always working on ways to be more obnoxious

13. In bold red letters, the ad proclaimed, "You too can be a star "

14. My Uncle Jack is so budget-conscious that the only book he ever reads is his bankbook

15. How much time do we have left to finish the test

16. Lewis yelled at the top of his voice, "Turn down that radio before I smash it "

17. Elaine asked, "Ivan, will you type my sociology paper "

18. Get inside quickly or that dog will bite you—hurry

19. "One of the strangest phobias people have," said the professor, "is the fear of peanut butter sticking to the roof of the mouth "

20. Have you heard the one about the fellow at the shopping mall who wanted to buy the escalator because it was marked down

End Marks MASTERY TEST 2

Add a period, a question mark, or an exclamation point, as needed, to each of the following sentences.

> **HINT** End marks go *inside* the quotation marks that appear in some sentences.

1. Uncle Arthur's mustache makes him look like a walrus

2. Do coleslaw and French fries come with every order

3. From the airplane window, the clouds looked like mashed potatoes

4. A voice from the stands screamed, "Strike the bum out "

5. How can you hold down two jobs and still go to college

6. With a loud crack, the rotted branch broke and fell from the tree

7. "On your way over," asked Fran, "could you pick up a case of Cokes "

8. Every time I take a shower, the kitchen ceiling begins to drip

9. The instructor asked me whether I had studied for the exam

10. "Somebody's been squeezing the bottom of the chocolates without eating them " Mariah cried.

11. Annie wanted to know if I had finished bathing the dog

12. Why do I always get thirsty in the middle of the night

13. You're going to knock the vase off the table—watch out

14. I often wonder why more people don't buy live Christmas trees and plant them in their yards afterward

15. Must all our house guests bring screaming kids with them

16. The minute Aunt Agatha thought she had won, she jumped out of her seat and yelled "Bingo "

17. I'd think twice before I took one of his courses again

18. The water company wants to know if it can replace the meter in our basement

19. Have you tried that new Indian fast-food restaurant, Cash and Curry

20. It is better to keep one's mouth closed and be thought a fool than to open it and remove all doubt

Apostrophe

Look over carefully the three items below. Then see if you can answer the questions that follow each item.

1. She is my best friend.   =   She's my best friend.

    I am afraid of snakes.   =   I'm afraid of snakes.

    Do not watch too much TV.   =   Don't watch too much TV.

    They are a perfect match.   =   They're a perfect match.

    It is a terrible movie.   =   It's a terrible movie.

What is the purpose of the apostrophe in the examples above?

_____

_____

2. the desk of the editor   =   the editor's desk

    the car of Giovanni   =   Giovanni's car

    the teeth of my cat   =   my cat's teeth

    the smile of the child   =   the child's smile

    the briefcase of my mother   =   my mother's briefcase

What is the purpose of the apostrophe in the examples above?

_____

_____

3. Several families were affected by the flood. One family's car floated
    away and was found in a field more than a mile away.

    Why does the apostrophe belong in the second sentence but not the first?

    _____

    _____

Answers are on page 570.

The two main uses of the apostrophe are

1. To show the omission of one or more letters in a contraction.

2. To show ownership or possession.

Each use is explained on the pages that follow.

Apostrophe in Contractions

A contraction is formed when two words are combined to make one word. An
apostrophe is used to show where letters are omitted in forming the contraction.
Here are two contractions:

www.mhhe.com/langan

have + not = haven't (the *o* in *not* has been omitted)

I + will = I'll (the *wi* in *will* has been omitted)

The following are some other common contractions:

I + am	= I'm		it + is	= it's
I + have	= I've		it + has	= it's
I + had	= I'd		is + not	= isn't
who + is	= who's		could + not	= couldn't
do + not	= don't		I + would	= I'd
did + not	= didn't		they + are	= they're
let + us	= let's		there + is	= there's

> **TIP** *will* + *not* has an unusual contraction: *won't.*

Practice

1

Combine the following words into contractions. Two are done for you.

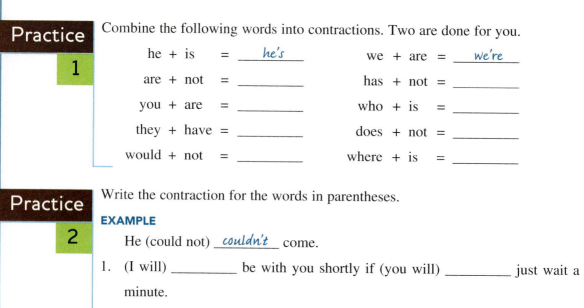

he + is   = ___he's___   we + are = ___we're___

are + not   = _____   has + not = _____

you + are   = _____   who + is   = _____

they + have = _____   does + not = _____

would + not = _____   where + is   = _____

Practice

2

Write the contraction for the words in parentheses.

EXAMPLE

He (could not) ___couldn't___ come.

1. (I will) _____ be with you shortly if (you will) _____ just wait a
    minute.

2. (It is) _____ such a long drive to the ballpark that Luan (would not)
    _____ go there if you paid him.

3. You (should not) _____ drink any more if (you are) _____ hoping
    to get home safely.

4. Alisha's husband (is not) _____ the aggressive type, and her former hus-
    bands (were not) _____ either.

5. (I would) _____ like to know (who is) _____ in charge of the cash
    register and why (it is) _____ taking so long for this line to move.

> **TIP** Even though contractions are common in everyday speech and in
> written dialogue, usually it is best to avoid them in formal writing.

3

Write five sentences using the apostrophe in different contractions.

1. _____

2. _____

3. _____

4. _____

5. _____

Four Contractions to Note Carefully

Four contractions that deserve special attention are *they're, it's, you're,* and *who's.* Sometimes these contractions are confused with the possessive words *their, its, your,* and *whose.* The list below shows the difference in meaning between the contractions and the possessive words.

Contractions	**Possessive Words**
they're (means *they are*)	their (means *belonging to them*)
it's (means *it is* or *it has*)	its (means *belonging to it*)
you're (means *you are*)	your (means *belonging to you*)
who's (means *who is*)	whose (means *belonging to whom*)

Possessive words are explained further on page 326.

Underline the correct form (the contraction or the possessive word) in each of the following sentences. Use the contraction whenever the two words of the contraction (*they are, it is, you are, who is*) would also fit.

Practice

4

1. (They're, Their) going to hold the party in (they're, their) family room.

2. (You're, Your) not going to be invited if you insist on bringing (you're, your) accordion.

3. (Who's, Whose) going with us, and (who's, whose) car are we taking?

4. (It's, Its) too early to go to bed and (it's, its) too late in the day to take a nap.

5. If (your, you're) not going to drive by (they're, their) house, (it's, its) going to be impossible for them to get home tonight.

Apostrophe to Show Ownership or Possession

To show ownership or possession, we can use such words as *belongs to, owned by,* or (most commonly) *of.*

the knapsack *that belongs to* Lola

the grades *possessed by* Travis

the house *owned by* my mother

the sore arm *of* the pitcher

But the apostrophe plus *s* is often the quickest and easiest way to show possession. Thus we can say:

Lola's knapsack

Travis's grades

my mother's house

the pitcher's sore arm

Points to Remember

1. The *'s* goes with the owner or possessor (in the examples given, *Lola, Travis, mother,* and *pitcher*). What follows is the person or thing possessed (in the examples given, *knapsack, grades, house,* and *sore arm*). An easy way to determine the owner or possessor is to ask the question "Who owns it?" In the first example, the answer to the question "Who owns the knapsack?" is *Lola*. Therefore, the *'s* goes with *Lola*.

2. In handwriting, there should always be a break between the word and the *'s.*

Lola's   not   Lola's
Yes   No

3. A singular word ending in *-s* (such as *Travis*) also shows possession by adding an apostrophe plus *s* (Travis's).

Practice

5

Rewrite the italicized part of each of the sentences below, using the *'s* to show possession. Remember that the *'s* goes with the owner or possessor.

EXAMPLES

The motorcycle owned by Clyde is a frightening machine.

Clyde's motorcycle
_____

The roommate of my brother is a sweet and friendly person.

My brother's roommate
_____

1. The *sneakers owned by Lola* were stolen.

_____

2. As a joke, he put on *the lipstick that belongs to Veronica*.

_____

3. *The house of his brother* was burglarized.

_____

4. *The tires belonging to the car* are badly worn.

_____

5. *The bicycle owned by Joe* was stolen from the bike rack outside school.

_____

6. I discovered the *nest of the blue jay* while pruning the tree.

_____

7. I don't like *the title of my paper.*

_____

8. *The arthritis of my mother* gets progressively worse.

_____

9. *The boyfriend belonging to my sister* is a gorgeous-looking man.

_____

10. It is *a game belonging to anybody* at this point.

_____

Underline the word in each sentence that needs an 's. Then write the word correctly in the space at the left. One is done for you as an example.

Practice 6

children's 1. The children voices carried downstairs.

_____ 2. Georgia husband is not a take-charge guy.

_____ 3. My friend computer is also a typewriter.

_____ 4. When the teacher anger became apparent, the class quickly grew quiet.

_____ 5. His girlfriend apple pie made his stomach rebel.

_____ 6. Albert dog looks like a porcupine without its quills.

_____ 7. Under the couch were several of our daughter toys.

_____ 8. My boss car was stolen.

_____ 9. That wine tastes like last night rain.

_____ 10. The dentist charged $75 to fix our son tooth.

Add an *'s* to each of the following words to make it the possessor or owner of something. Then write sentences using the words. Your sentences can be serious or playful. One is done for you as an example.

1. Cary _____*Cary's*_____

   _____*Cary's hair is bright red.*_____

2. neighbor_____

   _____

3. car _____

   _____

4. sister _____

   _____

5. doctor _____

   _____

Apostrophe versus Possessive Pronouns

Do not use an apostrophe with possessive pronouns. They already show ownership. Possessive pronouns include *his, hers, its, yours, ours,* and *theirs.*

Incorrect	**Correct**
The bookstore lost its' lease.	The bookstore lost its lease.
The racing bikes were theirs'.	The racing bikes were theirs.
The change is yours'.	The change is yours.
His' problems are ours', too.	His problems are ours, too.
Her' cold is worse than his'.	Her cold is worse than his.

Apostrophe versus Simple Plurals

When you want to make a word plural, just add an *s* at the end of the word. Do *not* add an apostrophe. For example, the plural of the word *movie* is *movies,* not *movie's* or *movies'.* Look at this sentence:

When Korie's cat began catching birds, the neighbors called the police.

The words *birds* and *neighbors* are simple plurals, meaning more than one bird, more than one neighbor. The plural is shown by adding *-s* only. (More information about plurals starts on page 396.) On the other hand, the *'s* after *Korie* shows possession—that Korie owns the cat.

Copyright © Richard Jolley. Reprinted by permission of CartoonStock.com.

Why is this cartoon funny?

In the spaces provided under each sentence, add the one apostrophe needed and explain why the other words ending in *s* are simple plurals.

Practice

8

EXAMPLE

Originally, the cuffs of mens pants were meant for cigar ashes.

cuffs: *simple plural meaning more than one cuff*

mens: *men's, meaning "belonging to men"*

ashes: *simple plural meaning more than one ash*

1. The sharp odor of the cheese and onions made Rons eyes water.

   onions: _____

   Rons: _____

   eyes: _____

2. My mothers recipe for chicken pot pie is famous among our relatives and friends.

   mothers: _____

   relatives: _____

   friends: _____

3. Sailors ran to their battle stations; the ships alarm had sounded.

   Sailors: _____

   stations: _____

   ships: _____

4. The kites string broke when it got caught in the branches of a tree.

   kites: _____

   branches: _____

5. We met two guys after our colleges football game and went with them to the movies that night.

   guys: _____

   colleges: _____

   movies: _____

6. My daughters prayers were answered when the heavy snow caused all the schools in the area to close for the rest of the week.

   daughters: _____

   prayers: _____

   schools: _____

7. We almost drowned when our inner tubes turned over in the rivers rushing currents.

   tubes: _____

   rivers: _____

   currents: _____

8. That movie directors specialty is films about vampires.

   directors: _____

   films: _____

   vampires: _____

9. The secretary made copies of the companys tax returns for the previous three years.

copies: _____

companys: _____

returns: _____

years: _____

10. Scientists are exploring Africas Congo region for living relatives of the dinosaurs.

Scientists: _____

Africas: _____

relatives: _____

dinosaurs: _____

Apostrophe with Plural Words Ending in -s

Plurals that end in -s show possession simply by adding the apostrophe, rather than an apostrophe plus s.

Both of my *neighbors'* homes have been burglarized recently.

The many *workers'* complaints were ignored by the company.

All the *campers'* tents were damaged by the hailstorm.

www.mhhe.com/langan

In each sentence, cross out the one plural word that needs an apostrophe. Then write the word correctly, with the apostrophe, in the space provided.

Practice

9

EXAMPLE

_____bosses'_____ My two ~~bosses~~ tempers are much the same: explosive.

_____ 1. Icy water from the hose froze on many of the firefighters coats.

_____ 2. Other drivers mistakes have led to my three car accidents.

_____ 3. Two of my friends cars have been stolen recently.

_____ 4. My grandparents television has a fifty-inch screen.

_____ 5. All of the soldiers uniforms will be replaced.

Collaborative Activity

Editing and Rewriting

Working with a partner, read the short paragraph below. Then use the space provided to rewrite the paragraph, adding ten apostrophes where needed to indicate contractions and possessives. Feel free to discuss the rewrite quietly with your partner and refer back to the chapter when necessary.

[1]In a small park near the center of Millville, several bronze statues stand in a circle. [2]Most of them are models of the individual rich men who provided money for the towns beginning. [3]The center of the circle is occupied by a nameless man. [4]Citizens call him Joe because hes a symbol of the common man. [5]Joes clothes appear tattered, but his body seems strong. [6]His face looks tired, but his eyes look proud. [7]Each person Joe represents couldnt give money to the town but gave strength and sweat instead. [8]A farmers back worked to supply food to the town. [9]A womans hands wove, knitted, and sewed clothes. [10]A blacksmiths arms struggled to provide horseshoes and tools. [11]Joes eyes must talk to passersby. [12]People seem to realize that without the ordinary persons help, the circle of rich men wouldnt exist.

_____

_____

_____

_____

_____

_____

_____

_____

_____

_____

Collaborative Activity

Creating Sentences

Working with a partner, write sentences that use apostrophes as directed.

1. Write a sentence describing something a friend owns. For instance, you might mention a pet or a material possession.

   _____

   _____

2. Using an apostrophe to show a contraction, write a sentence about something at school or work that you feel is wrong and needs to be changed.

   _____

   _____

3. Write a sentence that correctly uses the word *teachers*. Then write a second sentence that correctly uses the word *teacher's*.

   _____

   _____

Reflective Activity

1. Look at the paragraph about "Joe" that you revised above. How has adding apostrophes affected the reading of the paragraph?

2. Explain what it is about apostrophes that you find most difficult to remember and apply. Use an example to make your point clear.

Review Test 1

In each sentence cross out the two words that need apostrophes. Then write the words correctly in the spaces provided.

1. Youre right and Im wrong, though I hate to admit it.

   _____   _____

2. The divers stomach began to cramp as he struggled to the waters surface.

   _____   _____

3. A baby birds throat muscles wont work when its stomach is full.

   _____   _____

4. In the rabbits frenzy to escape the traps hold, it chewed off its hind leg.

   _____   _____

5. If youre rich and caught speeding in Finland, youll pay a stiffer fine than someone who is poorer.

   _____   _____

6. Marlons motorcycle gang roared down Main Street and terrorized the small towns inhabitants.

   _____   _____

7. Im amazed by my sisters perfect recall of how much she has weighed for every important social event.

   _____   _____

8. A golfers chance of making a hole in one is nearly ten times better than a bowlers chance of bowling a perfect game.

   _____   _____

9. If youre thinking of entering the contest, youll need to pay an admission fee of $10.

   _____   _____

10. I flinched as someones hands covered my eyes and a voice said, "Dont turn around."

    _____   _____

Review Test 2

Rewrite the following sentences, changing the underlined words into either a contraction or a possessive.

1. I do not think the diet of Sarita has helped her lose weight.

_____

_____

2. I have been warned by friends about the false charms of Michael.

_____

_____

3. The house of the Murphys uses the rays of the sun as a heating source.

_____

_____

4. The bill of the plumber was very high, but his work was not very good.

_____

_____

5. The menu of the restaurant is not very extensive.

_____

_____

NAME: _____

DATE: _____

MASTERY TEST 1   # Apostrophe

In each sentence, cross out the word that needs an apostrophe. Then write the word correctly in the space provided.

_____   1. I walked casually around the parking lot, trying to conceal the fact that Id no idea where I left my car.

_____   2. Thea ignored the police motorcycle officers siren and ended up in jail last night.

_____   3. The man insisted that his name was Elmer Fudd, but I didnt believe him.

_____   4. The blue whales tongue weighs about as much as forty men.

_____   5. Lolas mother put on some old jeans and helped Lola paint her new apartment.

_____   6. Tony had to remove wood ticks from his hair after a walk through the field behind his uncles house.

_____   7. The womens room in that service station is always clean.

_____   8. Youre going to cause trouble for yourself if your temper gets out of hand.

_____   9. Some of the most violent crime years in our nations history occurred during the Great Depression.

_____   10. Because Russias population is declining, many of its small towns are gradually being abandoned.

Apostrophe  MASTERY TEST 2

In the space provided under each sentence, add the one apostrophe needed and explain why the other word ending in *s* is a simple plural.

EXAMPLE

Joans hair began to fall out two days after she dyed it.

Joans: *Joan's meaning "hair belonging to Joan"*

days: *simple plural meaning more than one day*

1. The students gradually got used to the professors Japanese accent.

   students: _____

   professors: _____

2. Our tough sheriffs campaign promise is that he'll replace the electric chair with electric bleachers.

   sheriffs: _____

   bleachers: _____

3. My little sisters habit of sucking in noodles makes her an unpleasant dining companion.

   sisters: _____

   noodles: _____

4. When the students complained about the instructors assignment, he said, "You're not in high school anymore."

   students: _____

   instructors: _____

5. A football-sized nest of yellow jackets hung menacingly under the roofs rain gutter.

   jackets: _____

   roofs: _____

NAME: _____

DATE: _____

MASTERY TEST 3 ## Apostrophe

In each sentence two apostrophes are missing or are used incorrectly. Cross out the two errors and write the corrections in the spaces provided.

_____
_____

1. Terrences day started going sour when he noticed that everyone in the donut shop had gotten fatter donuts' than he got.

_____
_____

2. While the team was in the showers, someone tied all the players sneakers' together.

_____
_____

3. If youll check the noise in the attic, Ill stand by the phone in case you scream.

_____
_____

4. Despite the drivers warning that smoking was not allowed, several people lit cigarettes' in the back of the bus.

_____
_____

5. When I sat on the fender of Hassans car, he stared darts' at me until I slid off.

_____
_____

6. My brothers cell phone was stolen by vandals' who broke his car window.

_____
_____

7. Melissas typing might improve if shed cut an inch off her nails.

_____
_____

8. Anna has been on Andys blacklist since she revealed that he sleeps with his' socks on.

_____
_____

9. The troopers face was stern as he told me that my drivers license had expired.

_____
_____

10. I never ride anymore in my uncles station wagon; its like being on a roller coaster.

NAME: _____

DATE: _____

Apostrophe MASTERY TEST 4

In each sentence two apostrophes are missing or are used incorrectly. Cross out the two errors and write the corrections in the spaces provided.

_____   1. I was shocked when the movie stars toupee blew off; I hadnt realized he was
_____   completely bald.

_____   2. The skirts cheap lining puckered and scorched even though Eileens iron was
_____   set at the lowest possible heat level.

_____   3. The two boys boat capsized in the rivers rushing current.

_____

_____   4. Teds work always ends up on someone elses desk.

_____

_____   5. People in the dentists waiting room squirmed uneasily as a childs cries
_____   echoed down the hall.

_____   6. When Jeans voice cracked during her solo, I thought shed faint with
_____   embarrassment.

_____   7. Didnt you know that school will be closed next week because of a teachers
_____   conference?

_____   8. My youngest sisters goldfish has jumped out of its' bowl many times.

_____

_____   9. "Its the muffler," the mechanic explained, crawling out from under Freds
_____   car.

_____   10. Kevin knew he was headed for trouble when his dates father said that hed
_____   like to come along.

Quotation Marks

Introductory Activity

Read the following scene and underline all the words enclosed within
quotation marks. Your instructor may also have you dramatize the scene
with one person reading the narration and three persons acting the speaking
parts—Len, Tina, and Mario. The two speakers should imagine the scene
as part of a stage play and try to make their words seem as real and true-
to-life as possible.

At a party that Len and his wife Tina recently hosted, Len got
angry at a guy named Mario who kept bothering Tina. "Listen, man,"
Len said, "what's this thing you have for my wife? There are lots of
other women at this party."

"Relax," Mario replied. "Tina is very attractive, and I enjoy talking with her."

"Listen, Mario," Tina said. "I've already told you three times that
I don't want to talk to you anymore. Please leave me alone."

"Look, there's no law that says I can't talk to you if I want to,"
Mario challenged.

"Mario, I'm only going to say this once," Len warned. "Lay off
my wife, or leave this party *now*."

Mario grinned at Len smugly. "You've got good liquor here. Why
should I leave? Besides, I'm not done talking with Tina."

Len went to his basement and was back a minute later holding a
two-by-four. "I'm giving you a choice," Len said. "Leave by the door
or I'll slam you out the window."

Mario left by the door.

1. On the basis of the above selection, what is the purpose of quotation marks?

   _____

2. Do commas and periods that come after a quotation go inside or outside the quotation marks?

   _____

Answers are on page 571.

The two main uses of quotation marks are:

1. To set off the exact words of a speaker or writer
2. To set off the titles of short works

Each use is explained on the pages that follow.

Quotation Marks to Set Off the Words of a Speaker or Writer

Use quotation marks when you want to show the exact words of a speaker or writer:

www.mhhe.com/langan

"Who left the cap off the toothpaste?" Lola demanded. (Quotation marks set off the exact words that Lola spoke.)

Ben Franklin wrote, "Keep your eyes wide open before marriage, half shut afterward." (Quotation marks set off the exact words that Ben Franklin wrote.)

"You're never too young," my Aunt Fern often tells me, "to have a heart attack." (Two pairs of quotation marks are used to enclose the aunt's exact words.)

Maria complained, "I look so old some days. Even makeup doesn't help. I feel as though I'm painting a corpse!" (Note that the end quotes do not come until the end of Maria's speech. Place quotation marks before the first quoted word of a speech and after the last quoted word. As long as no interruption occurs in the speech, do not use quotation marks for each new sentence.)

Complete the following statements that explain how capital letters, commas, and periods are used in quotations. Refer to the four examples on the previous page as guides.

> **HINT** In the four preceding examples, notice that a comma sets off the quoted part from the rest of the sentence. Also observe that commas and periods at the end of a quotation always go *inside* quotation marks.

- Every quotation begins with a _____ letter.
- When a quotation is split (as in the sentence about Aunt Fern), the second part does not begin with a capital letter unless it is a _____ sentence.
- _____ are used to separate the quoted part of a sentence from the rest of the sentence.
- Commas and periods that come at the end of a quote go _____ quotation marks.

The answers are *capital, new, Commas,* and *inside.*

Practice 1

Insert quotation marks where needed in the sentences that follow.

1. Have more trust in me, Lola said to her mother.
2. The instructor asked Sharon, Why are your eyes closed?
3. Christ said, I come that you may have life, and have it more abundantly.
4. I refuse to wear those itchy wool pants! Ralph shouted at his parents.
5. His father replied, We should give all the clothes you never wear to the Salvation Army.
6. The nervous boy whispered hoarsely over the telephone, Is Linda home?
7. When I was ten, Lola said, I spent my entire summer playing Monopoly.
8. Tony said, When I was ten, I spent my whole summer playing basketball.
9. The critic wrote about the play, It runs the gamut of emotions from A to B.
10. The best way to tell if a mushroom is poisonous, the doctor solemnly explained, is if you find it in the stomach of a dead person.

Rewrite the following sentences, adding quotation marks where needed. Use a capital letter to begin a quotation, and use a comma to set off a quoted part from the rest of the sentence.

Practice

2

EXAMPLE

I'm getting tired Sally said.

"I'm getting tired," Sally said.
_____

1. Greg said I'm going with you.

    _____

2. Everyone passed the test the instructor informed the class.

    _____

3. My parents asked where were you?

    _____

4. I hate that commercial he muttered.

    _____

5. If you don't leave soon, he warned, you'll be late for work.

    _____

1. Write three quotations that appear in the first part of a sentence.

Practice

3

EXAMPLE

"Let's go shopping," I suggested.
_____

a. _____

b. _____

c. _____

2. Write three quotations that appear at the end of a sentence.

EXAMPLE

Bob asked, " Have you had lunch yet?"
_____

a. _____

b. _____

c. _____

3. Write three quotations that appear at the beginning and end of a sentence.

EXAMPLE

"If the bus doesn't come soon," Mary said, "we'll freeze."

a. _____

b. _____

c. _____

Indirect Quotations

An indirect quotation is a rewording of someone else's comments rather than a word-for-word direct quotation. The word *that* often signals an indirect quotation.

Direct Quotation	**Indirect Quotation**
George said, "My son is a daredevil."	George said that his son is a daredevil.
(George's exact spoken words are given, so quotation marks are used.)	(We learn George's words *indirectly*, so no quotation marks are used.)
Carol's note to Arnie read, "I'm at the neighbors' house. Give me a call."	Carol left a note for Arnie that said that she would be at the neighbors' house and he should give her a call.
(The exact words that Carol wrote in the note are given, so quotation marks are used.)	(We learn Carol's words *indirectly*, so no quotation marks are used.)

Practice

4

Rewrite the following sentences, changing words as necessary to convert the sentences into direct quotations. The first one is done for you as an example.

1. Eric asked Lynn if she had mailed the party invitations.

    Eric asked Lynn, "Have you mailed the party invitations?"

2. Lynn replied that she thought Eric was going to write them this year.

    _____

3. Eric said that writing invitations was a woman's job.

    _____

4. Lynn exclaimed that Eric was crazy.

_____

5. Eric replied that she had much better handwriting than he did.

_____

Rewrite the following sentences, converting each direct quotation into an indirect statement. In each case you will have to add the word *that* or *if* and change other words as well.

EXAMPLE

The barber asked Reggie, "Have you noticed how your hair is thinning?"

The barber asked Reggie if he had noticed how his hair was thinning.

1. He said, "As the plane went higher, my heart sank lower."

_____

2. The designer said, "Shag rugs are back in style."

_____

3. The foreman asked Jake, "Have you ever operated a lift truck?"

_____

4. My nosy neighbor asked, "Were Ed and Ellen fighting?"

_____

5. Mei Lin complained, "I married a man who eats Tweeties cereal for breakfast."

_____

_____

Quotation Marks to Set Off the Titles of Short Works

Titles of short works are usually set off by quotation marks, while titles of long works are underlined. Use quotation marks to set off the titles of such short works as articles in books, newspapers, or magazines; chapters in a book; short stories; poems; and songs. On the other hand, you should underline the titles of books, newspapers, magazines, plays, movies, compact discs, and television shows. See the following examples.

www.mhhe.com/langan

Quotation Marks	**Underlines**
the article "The Toxic Tragedy"	in the book <u>Who's Poisoning America</u>
the article "New Cures for Head-aches"	in the newspaper <u>The New York Times</u>
the article "When the Patient Plays Doctor"	in the magazine <u>Family Health</u>
the chapter "Connecting with Kids"	in the book <u>Straight Talk</u>
the story "The Dead"	in the book <u>Dubliners</u>
the poem "Birches"	in the book <u>The Complete Poems of Robert Frost</u>
the song "Some Enchanted Evening"	in the album <u>South Pacific</u>
	the television show <u>Jeopardy</u>
	the movie <u>Rear Window</u>

TIP In printed form, the titles of long works are set off by italics—slanted type that looks *like this.*

Practice 6

Use quotation marks or underlines as needed.

1. The young couple opened their brand-new copy of Cooking Made Easy to the chapter titled Meat Loaf Magic.

2. Annabelle borrowed Hawthorne's novel The Scarlet Letter from the library because she thought it was about a varsity athlete.

3. Did you know that the musical West Side Story is actually a modern version of Shakespeare's tragedy Romeo and Juliet?

4. I used to think that Richard Connell's short story The Most Dangerous Game was the scariest piece of suspense fiction in existence—until I began reading Bram Stoker's classic novel Dracula.

5. Every year at Easter, we watch a movie such as The Robe on television.

6. During the past year, Time featured an article about DNA titled Building Blocks of the Future.

7. My father still remembers the way Sarah Brightman sang "Think of Me" in the original production of The Phantom of the Opera.

8. As I stand in the supermarket checkout line, I read a feature story in the National Enquirer titled Mother Gives Birth to Alien Baby.

9. My favorite song by Aretha Franklin is the classic Respect, which has been included in the CD Aretha's Best.

10. Absentmindedly munching a Dorito, Hana opened the latest issue of Newsweek to its cover story, The Junk Food Explosion.

Other Uses of Quotation Marks

1. **To set off special words or phrases from the rest of a sentence:**

   Many people spell the words "all right" as one word, "alright," instead of correctly spelling them as two words.

   I have trouble telling the difference between "principal" and "principle."

www.mhhe.com/langan

2. **To mark off a quote within a quote. For this purpose, single quotes (' ') are used:**

   Ben Franklin said, "The noblest question in the world is, 'What good may I do in it?' "

   "If you want to have a scary experience," Eric told Lynn, "read Stephen King's story 'The Mangler' in his book *Night Shift.*"

Collaborative Activity

Editing and Rewriting

Working with a partner, read the short passage below and circle the ten sets of quotation mark mistakes. Then use the space provided to rewrite the passage, adding the ten sets of quotation marks. Feel free to discuss the rewrite quietly with your partner and refer back to the chapter when necessary.

¹Holding a container of milk and a bag of potatoes, Tony and Lola were standing in the express line at the Safeway supermarket. ²Lola pointed to a sign above the checkout counter that read, Express line—ten items or less. ³She then said to Tony, Look at that guy ahead of us. ⁴He shouldn't be in the express lane.

⁵Be quiet, said Tony. ⁶If you're not, he'll hear you.

⁷I don't mind if he does hear me, Lola replied. ⁸People like that think the world owes them a favor. ⁹I hope the cashier makes him go to another lane. ¹⁰The man in front of them suddenly turned around. ¹¹Stop acting as if I've committed a federal crime, he said. ¹²See those five cans of Alpo—that counts as one item. ¹³See those four packs of Twinkies—that's one item. ¹⁴Let's just say this, Lola replied. ¹⁵You have an interesting way of counting.

_____

_____

_____

_____

_____

_____

_____

_____

_____

_____

_____

_____

_____

Collaborative Activity

Creating Sentences

Working with a partner, write sentences that use quotation marks as directed.

1. Write a sentence in which you quote a favorite expression of someone you know. Identify the person's relationship to you.

   EXAMPLE

   My brother Sam often says after a meal, "That wasn't bad at all."

   _____

   _____

   _____

2. Write a quotation that contains the words *Tony asked Lola*. Write a second quotation that includes the words *Lola replied*.

   _____

   _____

   _____

3. Write a sentence that interests or amuses you from a book, magazine, or newspaper. Identify the title and author of the book, magazine, or newspaper article.

   EXAMPLE

   In her book <u>At Wit's End</u>, Erma Bombeck advises, "Never go to a doctor whose office plants have died."

   _____

   _____

   _____

Reflective Activity

1. Look at the passage about the checkout line that you revised above. Explain how adding quotation marks has affected the reading of the passage.

2. What would writing be like without quotation marks? Explain, using an example, how quotation marks are important to understanding writing.

3. Explain what it is about quotation marks that is most difficult for you to remember and apply. Use an example to make your point clear. Feel free to refer back to anything in this chapter.

Review Test   1

Place quotation marks around the exact words of a speaker or writer in the sentences that follow.

1. Is something wrong with your car again? the mechanic asked Fred.

2. Murphy's law states, Whatever can go wrong, will.

3. John Kennedy once said, Ask not what your country can do for you; ask what you can do for your country.

4. The sign read, Be careful how you drive. You may meet a fool.

5. Martha said, Turn on the burglar alarm when you leave the house, Fred.

6. Tony asked the struggling old lady if he could help with her heavy bag. Go to blazes, you masher, she said.

7. Listen, I confided to my sister, Neil told me he is going to ask you to go out with him.

8. The sign in the tough Western saloon read, Carry out your own dead.

9. When the ball hit Willie Wilson in the head and bounced into the outfield, Eric remarked, That was a heads-up play.

10. A woman who was one of Winston Churchill's political enemies once remarked to him, If you were my husband, I would put poison in your coffee. Churchill's reply was, Madam, if I were your husband, I would drink it.

Review Test 2

Go through the comics section of a newspaper to find a comic strip that amuses you. Be sure to choose a strip where two or more characters are speaking to each other. Write a full description that will enable people who have not read the comic strip to visualize it clearly and appreciate its humor. Describe the setting and action in each panel and enclose the words of the speakers in quotation marks.

NAME: _____

DATE: _____

Quotation Marks

Place quotation marks where needed.

1. A friend of mine used to say, There's nothing wrong with you that a few birthdays won't cure.

2. The food critic wrote, The best test of a fast-food hamburger is to eat it after all the trimmings have been taken off.

3. After I finished James Thurber's story The Secret Life of Walter Mitty, I started to write a paper on it.

4. When I'm done exercising in the morning, said Lola, there's a smoky fragrance to my skin.

5. Well, this is just fine, he mumbled. The recipe calls for four eggs and I have only two.

6. Eating Lola's chili, Tony whispered, is a breathtaking experience.

7. After Bill pulled the flip-top cap off the can, he noticed that the label said, Shake well before drinking.

8. How would you feel, the instructor asked the class, if I gave you a surprise quiz today?

9. In a tired voice, Clyde asked, Did you ever wonder why kids have more energy at the end of a long day than they had when they got up?

10. When Dick Cavett first met Groucho Marx on a street corner, he said, Hello, Groucho, I'm a big fan of yours. Groucho's response was, If it gets any hotter, I could use a big fan.

Quotation Marks MASTERY TEST 2

Place quotation marks or underlines where needed.

1. The tag on the pillow read, Do not remove under penalty of law.

2. You two kids had better stop fighting this minute! ordered Aunt Esther in her most severe tone of voice.

3. If we don't hurry, we'll miss the beginning of the movie, Joe reminded Liz.

4. Honest men, said the cranky old man, are scarcer than the feathers on a frog.

5. The most famous line from George Orwell's novel 1984 is Big Brother is watching you.

6. It never fails, complained Martha. Just as I lie down to take a nap, the telephone rings.

7. I know I'm getting old, Grandfather said. When I walked past the cemetery today, two guys ran after me with shovels.

8. There is a sign in the grocery store that reads, In God we trust. All others pay cash.

9. When Clyde got home from work, he said, At times I feel I'm in a rat race and the rats are winning. Charlotte consoled him by saying that everyone feels that way from time to time.

10. In a Consumer Reports article titled What's Inside Frozen Pot Pies? the editors write, The filth we discovered is not a health hazard. But it's unpleasant to discover that these pies contain big and little parts of aphids, flies, moths, weevils, cereal beetles, and rodent hairs.

MASTERY TEST 3   ## Quotation Marks

Place quotation marks or underlines where needed.

1. Martin Luther King, Jr., once said, Hate cannot drive out hate; only love can do that.

2. Diana Ross's song It's My Turn is one of my all-time favorites.

3. Are you positive you locked the front door? asked Vince for the third time.

4. You know, William said to the bartender, there are times in my life when I kind of panic. I want to go to bed and never get up again.

5. When I know I have a long day ahead, Judy said, I always have trouble sleeping well the night before.

6. Cracking his knuckles, Herschel complained, I wish people didn't have so many annoying habits.

7. Look out, you idiot! screamed the frightened pedestrian. Are you trying to kill somebody?

8. Immanuel Kant once wrote: Two things fill me with constantly increasing admiration and awe the longer and more earnestly I reflect on them—the starry heavens without and the moral law within.

9. The saying we learned in school was, Do unto others as you would have them do unto you. The saying that I now have on the wall of my study reads, Remember the golden rule: he who has the gold makes the rules.

10. One of the questions in Sharon's American literature test was to identify the book in which the following line appears: You don't know about me without you have read a book by the name of The Adventures of Tom Sawyer, but that ain't no matter.

Quotation Marks MASTERY TEST 4

Place quotation marks or underlines where needed.

1. Tony's uncle likes to say to him, You're never too young to have a heart attack.

2. The preacher began his sermon with the words, Nobody will ever get out of this world alive.

3. I won't get nervous. I won't get nervous, Terry kept repeating to herself as she walked into the exam room.

4. The honest politician proclaimed to the crowd, I haven't the slightest idea of what I'm talking about.

5. Tony said to Lola, Guess how many jelly beans I can hold in my mouth at one time.

6. Ved complained, No one wants to go with me to Maniac for Hire, the new movie at the multiplex.

7. If an infielder makes a mistake during a softball game, Darryl yells from the bench, You're a disgrace to your base!

8. As a child I was ugly, said the comedian. Once my old man took me to the zoo. The guy at the gate thanked him for returning me.

9. Don't let your paintbrushes dry up, advises the book Saving Money around the House. Instead, store them in motor oil.

10. I agree that the public has a right to know what is in a hot dog, said the president of the meat company. But does the public really want to know what's in a hot dog?

Comma

Introductory Activity

Commas often (though not always) signal a minor break or pause in a sentence. Each of the six pairs of sentences below illustrates one of six main uses of the comma. Read each pair of sentences and choose the rule that applies from the box on the next page. Each of these rules will be discussed in detail in the pages that follow.

_____ 1. We stocked up on batteries, water, and canned food before the snowstorm.

You can use a credit card, write out a check, or provide cash.

_____ 2. To open the medicine bottle, press down on the cap and turn it to the right.

Before you lounge in the sun, apply suntan lotion to your body and face.

_____ 3. Leeches, creatures which suck human blood, are valuable to medical science.

John Nelson, the famous actor, was a classmate of mine.

_____ 4. Kira said the exam was easy, but I thought it was very difficult.

Wind howled through the alleys, and rain pounded against the roof.

_____ 5. Terrence asked, "Why is it so hard to remember your dreams the next day?"

"I am so tired after school," Lily said, "that I fall asleep right away."

_____ 6. Kyle has driven 1,500,000 accident-free miles in his job as a trucker.

The Wynn Trucking Company of Jersey City, New Jersey, gave Kyle an award on September 26, 2007, for his superior safety record.

---

a. separate items in a list
b. separate introductory material from the sentence
c. separate words that interrupt the sentence
d. separate complete thoughts in a sentence
e. separate direct quotations from the rest of the sentence
f. separate numbers, addresses, and dates in everyday writing

---

Answers are on page 572.

www.mhhe.com/langan

Six Main Uses of the Comma

Commas are used mainly as follows:

1. To separate items in a series

2. To set off introductory material

3. On both sides of words that interrupt the flow of thought in a sentence

4. Between two complete thoughts connected by *and, but, for, or, nor, so, yet*

5. To set off a direct quotation from the rest of a sentence

6. For certain everyday material

You may find it helpful to remember that the comma often marks a slight pause, or break, in a sentence. These pauses or breaks occur at the points where the six main comma rules apply. Read aloud the sentence examples given on the following pages for each of the comma rules and listen for the minor pauses or breaks that are signaled by commas.

At the same time, you should keep in mind that commas are far more often overused than underused. As a general rule, you should *not* use a comma unless a given comma rule applies or unless a comma is otherwise needed to help a sentence read clearly. A good rule of thumb is that "when in doubt" about whether to use a comma, it is often best to "leave it out."

After reviewing each of the comma rules that follow, you will practice adding commas that are needed and omitting commas that are not needed.

Comma between Items in a Series

Use a comma to separate items in a series.

Magazines, paperback novels, and textbooks crowded the shelves.

Hard-luck Harold needs a loan, a good-paying job, and a close friend.

Pat sat in the doctor's office, checked her watch, and chewed gum nervously.

Lola bit into the ripe, juicy apple.

More and more people entered the crowded, noisy stadium.

A comma is used between two descriptive words in a series only if *and* inserted between the words sounds natural. You could say:

Lola bit into the ripe *and* juicy apple.

More and more people entered the crowded *and* noisy stadium.

But notice in the following sentences that the descriptive words do not sound natural when *and* is inserted between them. In such cases, no comma is used.

The model wore a light sleeveless blouse. ("A light *and* sleeveless blouse" doesn't sound right, so no comma is used.)

Dr. Van Helsing noticed two tiny puncture marks on his patient's neck. ("Two *and* tiny puncture marks" doesn't sound right, so no comma is used.)

Practice

1

Place commas between items in a series.

1. Becky brought a cake iced with red white and blue frosting to the Fourth of July picnic.

2. My brother did the laundry helped clean the apartment waxed the car and watched an old episode of HBO's *The Sopranos*.

3. You can make a Big Mac by putting two all-beef patties special sauce lettuce cheese pickles and onions on a sesame-seed bun.

Practice

2

For each item, cross out the one comma that is not needed. Add the one comma that is needed between items in a series.

1. Cold eggs burnt bacon and watery orange juice are the reasons, I've never returned to that diner for breakfast.

2. Andy relaxes, by reading Donald Duck Archie, and Bugs Bunny comic books.

3. Tonight I've got to work at the restaurant for three hours finish writing a paper, and study, for an exam.

Comma after Introductory Material

Use a comma to set off introductory material.

Fearlessly, Lola picked up the slimy slug.

Just to annoy Tony, she let it crawl along her arm.

Although I have a black belt in karate, I decided to go easy on the demented bully who had kicked sand in my face.

Mumbling under her breath, the woman picked over the tomatoes.

TIPS

a. If the introductory material is brief, the comma is sometimes omitted. In the activities here, however, you should include the comma.

b. A comma is also used to set off extra material placed at the end of a sentence. Here are two sentences where this comma rule applies:

I spent all day at the employment office, trying to find a job that suited me.

Tony has trouble accepting criticism, except from Lola.

Place commas after introductory material.

Practice

3

1. When I didn't get my paycheck at work I called up the business office. According to the office computer I was dead.

2. After seeing the accident Susan wanted to stop driving forever. Even so she went driving to work next morning over the ice-covered roads.

3. To get her hair done Faye goes to a beauty salon all the way across town. Once there she enjoys listening to the gossip in the beauty shop. Also she likes looking through *Elle* and other magazines in the shop.

For each item, cross out the one comma that is not needed. Add the one comma that is needed after introductory material.

Practice

4

1. Even though Tina had an upset stomach she went bowling, with her husband.

2. Looking back over the last ten years I can see several decisions I made, that really changed my life.

3. Instead of going with my family to the mall I decided to relax at home, and to call up some friends.

Comma around Words Interrupting the Flow of Thought

Use a comma before and after words that interrupt the flow of thought in a sentence.

> The car, cleaned and repaired, is ready to be sold.

> Joanne, our new neighbor, used to work as a bouncer at Rexy's Tavern.

> Taking long walks, especially after dark, helps me sort out my thoughts.

Usually you can "hear" words that interrupt the flow of thought in a sentence. However, when you are not sure if certain words are interrupters, remove them from the sentence. If it still makes sense without the words, you know the words are interrupters and that the information they give is nonessential. Such nonessential information is set off with commas. In the following sentence,

> Susie Hall, who is my best friend, won a new car in the *Reader's Digest* sweepstakes.

the words *who is my best friend* are extra information, not needed to identify the subject of the sentence, *Susie Hall.* Put commas around such nonessential information. On the other hand, in the sentence

> The woman who is my best friend won a new car in the *Reader's Digest* sweepstakes.

the words *who is my best friend* supply essential information needed for us to identify the woman. If the words were removed from the sentence, we would no longer know which woman won the sweepstakes. Commas are not used around such essential information.

Here is another example:

> *The Shining,* a novel by Stephen King, is the scariest book I've ever read.

Here the words *a novel by Stephen King* are extra information, not needed to identify the subject of the sentence, *The Shining.* Commas go around such nonessential information. On the other hand, in the sentence

> Stephen King's novel *The Shining* is the scariest book I've ever read.

the words *The Shining* are needed to identify the novel. Commas are not used around such essential information.

Most of the time you will be able to "hear" words that interrupt the flow of thoughts in a sentence and will not have to think about whether the words are essential or nonessential.*

---

*Some instructors refer to nonessential or extra information that is set off by commas as a *nonrestrictive* clause. Essential information that interrupts the flow of thought is called a *restrictive* clause. No commas are used to set off a restrictive clause.

Add commas to set off interrupting words.

1. Friday is the deadline the absolute final deadline for your papers to be turned in.

2. The nursery rhyme told how the cow a weird creature jumped over the moon. The rhyme also related how the dish who must also have been strange ran away with the spoon.

3. Tod voted the most likely to succeed in our high school graduating class has just made the front page of our newspaper. He was arrested with other members of the King Kongs a local motorcycle gang for creating a disturbance in the park.

For each item, cross out the one comma that is not needed. Add the two commas that are needed to set off interrupting words.

1. My sister's cat which she got from the animal shelter woke her, when her apartment caught fire.

2. A bulging biology textbook its pages stuffed with notes, and handouts lay on the path to the college parking lot.

3. A baked potato with its crispy skin and soft inside rates as one of my all-time favorite, foods.

Comma between Complete Thoughts Connected by a Joining Word

Use a comma between two complete thoughts connected by *and, but, for, or, nor, so, yet.*

My parents threatened to throw me out of the house, so I had to stop playing the drums.

The polyester bed sheets had a gorgeous design on them, but they didn't feel as comfortable as plain cotton sheets.

The teenage girls walked the hot summer streets, and the teenage boys drove by in their shined-up cars.

The comma is optional when the complete thoughts are short:

Calvin relaxed but Robert kept working.

The soda was flat so I poured it away.

We left school early for the furnace broke down.

Be careful not to use a comma in sentences having *one* subject and a *double* verb. The comma is used only in sentences made up of two complete thoughts (two subjects and two verbs). In the sentence

> Dawn lay awake that stormy night and listened to the thunder crashing.

there is only one subject (*Dawn*) and a double verb (*lay* and *listened*). No comma is needed. Likewise, the sentence

> The quarterback kept the ball and plunged across the goal line for a touchdown.

has only one subject (*quarterback*) and a double verb (*kept* and *plunged*); therefore, no comma is needed.

Practice

7

Place a comma before a joining word that connects two complete thoughts (two subjects and two verbs). The four sentences that have only one subject and a double verb do not need commas; mark these *C* for "correct."

1. The outfielder raced to the warning track and caught the fly ball over his shoulder.
2. The sun set in a golden glow behind the mountain and a single star sparkled in the night sky.
3. Arturo often tries to cut back on his eating but he always gives up after a few days.
4. Her voice became very dry during the long speech and beads of perspiration began to appear on her forehead.
5. Cheryl learned two computer languages in high school and then began writing her own programs.
6. I spent all of Saturday morning trying to fix my car but I still wound up taking it to a garage in the afternoon.
7. She felt like shouting but didn't dare open her mouth.
8. He's making a good living selling cosmetics to beauty shops but he still has regrets about not having gone to college.
9. Crazy Bill often goes into bars and asks people to buy him a drink.
10. He decided not to take the course in advanced math for he wanted to have time for a social life during the semester.

Comma with Direct Quotations

Use a comma to set off a direct quotation from the rest of a sentence.

"Please take a number," said the deli clerk.

Fred told Martha, "I've just signed up for a Dale Carnegie course."

"Those who sling mud," a famous politician once said, "usually lose ground."

"Reading this book," complained Stan, "is about as interesting as watching paint dry."

> **TIP** A comma or a period at the end of a quotation goes inside quotation marks. See also pages 339–340.

In each sentence, add the one or more commas needed to set off the quoted material.

Practice 8

1. "I can't wait to have a fish filet and some fries" said Lola to Tony as she pulled into the order lane at the fast-food restaurant. She asked "What can I get you, Tony?"

2. "Two quarter-pounders with cheese, two large fries, and a large Coke" responded Tony.

3. "Good grief" said Lola. "It's hard to believe you don't weigh three hundred pounds. In fact" she continued "how much do you weigh?"

In each item, cross out the one comma that is not needed to set off a quotation. Add the comma that is needed to set off a quotation from the rest of the sentence.

Practice 9

1. "You better hurry" Thelma's mother warned "or you're going to miss the last bus, of the morning."

2. "It really worries me" said Marty "that you haven't seen a doctor, about that strange swelling under your arm."

3. The student sighed in frustration, and then raised his hand. "My computer has crashed again" he called out to the instructor.

Comma with Everyday Material

Use a comma with certain everyday material as shown in the following sections.

Persons Spoken To

Sally, I think that you should go to bed.

Please turn down the stereo, Mark.

Please, sir, can you spare a dollar?

Dates

My best friend got married on April 29, 2005, and he became a parent on January 7, 2007.

Addresses

Lola's sister lives at Greenway Village, 342 Red Oak Drive, Los Angeles, California 90057.

> **TIP** No comma is used before the zip code.

Openings and Closings of Letters

Dear Vanessa,   Sincerely,

Dear John,   Truly yours,

> **TIP** In formal letters, a colon is used after the opening:
>
> Dear Sir:
>
> Dear Madam:

Numbers

Government officials estimate that Americans spend about 785,000,000 hours a year filling out federal forms.

Practice

10

Place commas where needed.

1. I am sorry sir but you cannot sit at this table.

2. On May 6 1954 Roger Bannister became the first person to run a mile in under four minutes.

3. Redeeming the savings certificate before June 30 2010 will result in a substantial penalty.

4. A cash refund of one dollar can be obtained by sending proof of purchase to Seven Seas P.O. Box 760 El Paso TX 79972.

5. Leo turn off that TV set this minute!

Unnecessary Use of Commas

Remember that if no clear rule applies for using a comma, it is usually better not to use a comma. As stated earlier, "When in doubt, leave it out." Following are some typical examples of unnecessary commas.

Incorrect

Sharon told me, that my socks were different colors. (A comma is not used before *that* unless the flow of thought is interrupted.)

The union negotiations, dragged on for three days. (Do not use a comma between a simple subject and verb.)

I waxed all the furniture, and cleaned the windows. (Use a comma before *and* only with more than two items in a series or when *and* joins two complete thoughts.)

Sharon carried, the baby into the house. (Do not use a comma between a verb and its object.)

I had a clear view, of the entire robbery. (Do not use a comma before a prepositional phrase.)

Cross out the one comma that does not belong in each sentence. Do not add any commas.

Practice

11

1. When I arrived to help with the moving, Jerome said to me, that the work was already done.

2. After the flour and milk have been mixed, eggs must be added, to the recipe.

3. Because my sister is allergic to cat fur, and dust, our family does not own a cat or have any dust-catching drapes or rugs.

4. The guys on the corner, asked, "Have you ever taken karate lessons?"

5. As the heavy Caterpillar tractor, rumbled up the street, our house windows rattled.

6. Las Vegas, Miami Beach, San Diego, and Atlantic City, are the four places she has worked as a bartender.

7. Thomas Farley, the handsome young man, who just took off his trousers, recently escaped from an institution for the mentally ill.

8. Hal wanted to go to medical school, but he does not have the money, and was not offered a scholarship.

9. Joyce reads, a lot of fiction, but I prefer stories that really happened.

10. Because Mary is single, her married friends do not invite her, to their parties.

Collaborative Activity

Editing and Rewriting

Working with a partner, read carefully the short paragraph below and cross out the five misplaced commas. Then, in the space between the lines, insert the ten additional commas needed. Feel free to discuss the rewrite quietly with your partner and refer back to the chapter when necessary.

[1]If you want to become a better note-taker you should keep in mind the following hints. [2]Most important you should attend class on a regular basis. [3]The instructor will probably develop in class, all the main ideas of the course and you want to be there to write the ideas down. [4]Students often ask "How much, should I write down?" [5]By paying close attention in class you will probably develop an instinct for the material, that you must write down. [6]You should record your notes in outline form. [7]Start main points at the margin indent major supporting details and further indent more subordinate material. [8]When the speaker moves from one aspect of a topic to another show this shift on your paper, by skipping a line or two. [9]A last hint but by no means the least is to write down any points your instructor repeats or takes the time, to put on the board.

Collaborative Activity

Creating Sentences

Working with a partner, write sentences that use commas as directed.

1. Write a sentence mentioning three items that can be found in the photo.

    _____

    _____

    _____

2. Write two sentences describing how you relax after getting home from school or work. Start the first sentence with *After* or *When.* Start the second sentence with *Next.*

    _____

    _____

3. Write a sentence that tells something about your favorite movie, book, television show, or song. Use the words *which is my favorite movie* (or *book, television show,* or *song*) after the name of the movie, book, television show, or song.

    _____

    _____

4. Write two complete thoughts about a person you know. The first thought should mention something that you like about the person. The second thought should mention something you don't like. Join the two thoughts with *but.*

    _____

    _____

5. Invent a line that Lola might say to Tony. Use the words *Lola said* in the sentence. Then include Tony's reply, using the words *Tony responded.*

    _____

    _____

6. Write a sentence about an important event in your life. Include in your sentence the day, month, and year of the event.

    _____

    _____

Reflective Activity

1. Look at the paragraph on note taking that you revised above. Explain how adding commas has affected the reading of the paragraph.

2. What would writing be like without the comma? How do commas help writing?

3. What is the most difficult comma rule for you to remember and apply? Explain, giving an example.

Review Test 1

Insert commas where needed. In the space provided under each sentence, summarize briefly the rule that explains the use of the comma or commas.

1. After I fell and fractured my wrist I decided to sell my skateboard.

   _____

2. She asked her son "Are you going to church with me tomorrow?"

   _____

3. The weather bureau predicts that sleet fire or brimstone will fall on Washington today.

   _____

4. The ignition system in his car as well as the generator was not working properly.

   _____

5. Tony asked Lola "Have you ever had nightmares in which some kind of monster was ready to swallow you?"

   _____

6. They attacked their bathroom with Lysol Comet and Fantastik.

   _____

7. The pan of bacon fat heating on the stove burst into flame and he quickly set a lid on the pan to put out the fire.

   _____

8. Lou's bad cough which he had had for almost a week began to subside.

_____

9. I wear thick socks while hiking but I still return from a trip with blistered feet.

_____

10. When they found pencil shavings in the soup the guests decided they were not hungry.

_____

Review Test 2

Insert commas where needed. One sentence does not need commas; mark this sentence *C* for "correct."

1. Some people think school uniforms are a bad idea but I disagree strongly.

2. When I was in high school I did not have a lot of money.

3. I worked in a shoe store every weekend and then I spent my entire paycheck on school clothes.

4. The money enabled me to buy the latest shirts pants and sneakers.

5. Instead of studying or enjoying my friends I spent my time in high school trying to look stylish.

6. I did this I realize now because I thought it would make me popular.

7. If every school required uniforms students would not have to worry so much about clothes.

8. Opponents of school uniforms say that forcing students to wear the same clothes takes away kids' freedom of expression.

9. I on the other hand feel that uniforms free students from the pressure to conform to expensive styles and trends.

10. More important school uniforms allow rich and poor kids to dress equally.

Review Test 3

On separate paper, write six sentences, with each sentence demonstrating one of the six main comma rules.

MASTERY TEST 1 | # Comma

Add commas where needed. Then refer to the box below and write, in the space provided, the letter of the comma rule that applies in each sentence.

a. Between items in a series	d. Between complete thoughts
b. After introductory material	e. With direct quotations
c. Around interrupters	

_____C_____ 1. The hot dogs that we bought tasted delicious but they reacted later like delayed time bombs.

_____b_____ 2. Because it was the thing to do whenever he talked with the guys Tony pretended he had dated a lot of women.

_____d_____ 3. Angel had no idea what his weight was but Kristina always knew hers.

_____C_____ 4. Lola a good athlete surprised Tony by making forty-six of fifty foul shots.

_____A_____ 5. The child's eyes glowed at the sight of the glittering tree colorful packages and stuffed stockings.

_____e_____ 6. "Before you crack open another walnut" Tony's father warned him "remember that we're going to be eating shortly."

_____A_____ 7. When she got back from the supermarket, she realized she had forgotten to get cereal grape jelly and Drano.

_____A_____ 8. The old graveyard was filled with vampires werewolves crooked politicians and other monsters.

_____b_____ 9. The problem with you David is that you take criticism personally.

_____b_____ 10. Jerome chose the shortest line at the post office but the woman in front of him suddenly began pulling a number of tiny packages out of her pockets.

NAME: _____

DATE: _____

Comma MASTERY TEST 2

Add commas where needed. Then refer to the box below to write, in the space provided, the letter of the comma rule that applies in each sentence.

a. Between items in a series	d. Between complete thoughts
b. After introductory material	e. With direct quotations
c. Around interrupters	

_____ 1. As soon as Yuji finished the difficult problem, he let out a satisfied grunt.

_____ 2. On Saturday, if it doesn't rain, we plan to take the kids to the ball game.

_____ 3. I don't care if I never see you, your family, or your vacation pictures again.

_____ 4. Tony quit his part-time job at a local gas station, for he was being paid only $5.50 an hour.

_____ 5. "Aunt Flo is so forgetful," my mother observed, "that whenever she ties a string around her finger as a reminder, she forgets to look at the string."

_____ 6. The restaurant's special "Italian Omelette" contains eggs, tomato, mozzarella cheese, sausage, and salami.

_____ 7. My Aunt Esther loves watching the silly childish antics of the contestants on some game shows.

_____ 8. Although my classes don't begin until ten o'clock, I still have trouble getting to the lecture hall on time.

_____ 9. A flock of snow geese, their shiny wings flashing in the sun, flew above the marshlands.

_____ 10. Mike brought a cassette tape recorder to class, for he had broken two fingers and couldn't take notes.

NAME: _____

DATE: _____

MASTERY TEST 3 ## Comma

Add commas where needed. Then refer to the box below to write, in the space provided, the letter of the one comma rule that applies in each sentence.

> a. Between items in a series
> b. After introductory material
> c. Around interrupters
> d. Between complete thoughts
> e. With direct quotations

_____ 1. Kevin and Tasha took Paul their son to see Walt Disney's *Bambi*.

_____ 2. The film covers the birth of Bambi the loss of his mother his escape from a forest fire and his growth to young fatherhood.

_____ 3. Just before the film started Kevin decided to get a giant box of Jujyfruits.

_____ 4. While he was at the refreshment counter, the houselights dimmed the stage curtains opened and the movie started.

_____ 5. Kevin hurried back down the dark aisle almost stumbling and slipped into the empty aisle seat that he thought was his.

_____ 6. While Kevin popped Jujyfruits into his mouth the woman next to him rested her head on his shoulder.

_____ 7. Kevin's eyes grew accustomed to the dark and he suddenly became aware of an elderly man standing near him in the aisle.

_____ 8. "Excuse me, Sir" the man said. "You're in my seat."

_____ 9. Hearing the man's voice, the woman looked up saw Kevin next to her and screamed.

_____ 10. "I'm really sorry, Madam," Kevin said. He got up quickly and then saw in front of him waving and laughing his wife and son.

NAME: _____

DATE: _____

Comma MASTERY TEST 4

Do three things: (1) cross out the one comma that is not needed; (2) add the one comma that is needed; and (3) in the space provided, write the letter of the rule that applies for each comma you added.

a. Between items in a series	d. Between complete thoughts
b. After introductory material	e. With direct quotations
c. Around interrupters	

_____ 1. On Friday, my day off I went, to get a haircut.

_____ 2. "When I have a headache" my aunt explained, "I simply close my eyes, and take several deep breaths."

_____ 3. The aliens in the science-fiction film visited our planet in peace but we greeted them, with violence.

_____ 4. A neat appearance warm smile, and positive attitude, will make an employer respond to you.

_____ 5. "Even, the greatest creations," the sign said "start from small seeds."

_____ 6. Frank does not like, cooked carrots and he cares even less for lima beans.

_____ 7. According to rumors our school janitor has made himself a millionaire, through real estate investments.

_____ 8. Hilda was not happy, about having to drop the math course but there were too many other demands being made on her time.

_____ 9. A jar of split-pea soup, which was all Bruce had in the refrigerator did not make, for a very satisfactory meal.

_____ 10. Although Sela is normally, a careful and defensive driver she drives recklessly if she is in a bad mood.

MASTERY TEST 5   # Comma

Add commas where needed. Then refer to the box below to write, in the space provided, the letter of the comma rule that applies in each sentence.

a. Between items in a series	d. Between complete thoughts
b. After introductory material	e. With direct quotations
c. Around interrupters	

_____ 1. Teachers angry at the school board's decision decided to go on strike.

_____ 2. Driving too fast on the wet highway Donald lost control of his car at a sharp turn in the road.

_____ 3. The accident left Donald with a broken arm bruised chest and a scratched face.

_____ 4. "It would have been worse" Donald explained "if I didn't wear my seatbelt."

_____ 5. A computer which contained private information on thousands of patients was stolen from the hospital.

_____ 6. After the loud teenagers repeatedly interrupted the movie a security guard escorted them to the exit.

_____ 7. Denise's wedding ring fell down the drain of her bathtub so she hired a plumber to retrieve it.

_____ 8. The developers cleared the woods to build a fast-food restaurant a gas station and a new parking lot.

_____ 9. The words carved on the gravestone said "Don't weep for me. You'll be here soon enough."

_____ 10. Marcus liked the location of the apartment but the rent was more than he could afford.

Other Punctuation Marks

Introductory Activity

The main purpose of this chapter is to explain and illustrate five other punctuation marks not previously discussed. They are the colon (:), semicolon (;), dash (—), hyphen (-), and parentheses ( ).

Each sentence below needs one of these punctuation marks. See if you can insert the correct mark in each case.

1. The following items were on my mother's grocery list eggs, tomatoes, milk, and cereal.

2. A life size statue of her cat adorns the living room of Diana's penthouse.

3. Sigmund Freud, the pioneer of psychoanalysis 1856–1939, was a habitual cocaine user.

4. As children, we would put pennies on the railroad track we wanted to see what they would look like after being run over by a train.

5. The stuntwoman was battered, broken, barely breathing but alive.

Answers are on page 573.

www.mhhe.com/langan

Colon (:)

The colon is a mark of introduction. Use the colon at the end of a complete statement to do the following:

1. **Introduce a list.**

   My little brother has three hobbies: playing video games, racing his Hot Wheels cars all over the floor, and driving me crazy.

2. **Introduce a long quotation.**

   Janet's paper was based on a passage from George Eliot's novel *Middlemarch:* "If we had a keen vision and feeling of all ordinary human life, it would be like hearing the grass grow and the squirrel's heart beat, and we should die of that roar which lies on the other side of silence. As it is, the quickest of us walk about well wadded with stupidity."

3. **Introduce an explanation.**

   There are two ways to do this job: the easy way and the right way.

Two minor uses of the colon are after the opening in a formal letter (*Dear Sir or Madam:*) and between the hour and the minute when writing the time (*The bus will leave for the game at 11:45*).

Practice

1

Place colons where needed.

1. Lin had an excellent excuse for being late for work an early-morning power failure that stopped her alarm clock.

2. I ordered the following items from Sears two pairs of jeans, four plaid flannel shirts, and a wide leather belt.

3. In her speech, Mrs. Wagner quoted William Hazlitt "Man is the only animal that laughs and weeps, for he is the only animal that is struck with the difference between what things are and what they ought to be."

www.mhhe.com/langan

Semicolon (;)

The semicolon signals more of a pause than the comma alone but not quite the full pause of a period. Use a semicolon to do the following. (Note: The first two uses of the semicolon are treated in more detail on pages 110–111.)

1. **Join two complete thoughts that are not already connected by a joining word such as *and, but, for,* or *so.***

   The chemistry lab blew up; Professor Thomas was fired.

   I once stabbed myself with a pencil; a black mark has been under my skin ever since.

2. **Join two complete thoughts that include a transitional word such as *however, otherwise, moreover, furthermore, therefore,* or *consequently.***

   I cut and raked the grass; moreover, I weeded the lawn.

   Sally finished typing the paper; however, she forgot to bring it to class.

3. **Mark off items in a series when the items themselves contain commas.**

   This fall I won't have to work on Labor Day, September 7; Veterans Day, November 11; or Thanksgiving Day, November 26.

   At the final Weight Watchers' meeting, prizes were awarded to Sally Johnson, for losing 20 pounds; Irving Ross, for losing 26 pounds; and Betty Mills, the champion loser, who lost 102 pounds.

Place semicolons where needed.

Practice

2

1. There's an old saying about law school: in the first year, they scare you to death in the second year, they work you to death and in the third year, they bore you to death.

2. I find some television commercials for soap ads ridiculous for example, people are always grinning as the shower spray pelts their teeth.

3. The following persons have been elected to the National Board of Bank Executives: Ellen Green, First National Bank Jay Hunt, Fidelity State Bank and M. O. Granby, Farmers' Regional Bank.

Dash (—)

A dash signals a degree of pause longer than a comma but not as complete as a period. Use the dash to set off words for dramatic effect.

I suggest—no, I insist—that you stay for dinner.

The prisoner walked toward the electric chair—grinning.

A meaningful job, a loving wife, and a car that wouldn't break down all the time—these are the things he wanted in life.

www.mhhe.com/langan

Practice

3

Place dashes where needed.

1. The car is in excellent condition except that the brakes don't always work.

2. I can be ready in ten minutes in fact, I'm ready now.

3. Hunting, fishing, and doing odd jobs around the house rather than going to work these are the activities I enjoy.

Hyphen (-)

Use a hyphen in the following ways:

1. With two or more words that act as a single unit describing a noun.

The society ladies nibbled at the deep-fried grasshoppers.

A white-gloved waiter then put some snails on their table.

> **TIP** Your dictionary will often help when you are unsure about whether to use a hyphen between words.

2. To divide a word at the end of a line of writing or typing.

Although it had begun to drizzle, the teams decided to play the champion-ship game that day.

> **TIPS**
>
> **1.** Divide a word between syllables. Use your dictionary (see page 383) to be sure of correct syllable divisions.
>
> **2.** Do not divide words of one syllable.
>
> **3.** Do not divide a word if you can avoid dividing it.

Place hyphens where needed.

Practice

4

1. I went food shopping with about sixty five dollars in my pocket and came back with about sixty five cents.

2. The ten year old girl was remarkably self confident when she was giving her speech.

3. My wife's aunt and uncle, who live in a split level house, have been unable to prevent mildew from forming on the walls of the lower level.

Parentheses ( )

Use parentheses to do the following:

www.mhhe.com/langan

1. Set off extra or incidental information from the rest of a sentence.

The chapter on drugs in our textbook (pages 142–178) contains some frightening statistics.

The normal body temperature of a cat (101 to 102°) is 3° higher than the temperature of its owner.

2. Enclose letters or numbers that signal items in a series.

Three steps to follow in previewing a textbook are to (1) study the title, (2) read the first and last paragraphs, and (3) study the headings and subheadings.

TIP Do not use parentheses too often in your writing.

Add parentheses where needed.

Practice

5

1. For tomorrow we must study the charts pages 16–20 in the first chapter of our biology text.

2. To make better use of your time, you should prepare 1 a daily list of things to do and 2 a weekly study schedule.

3. A recent study revealed that people who are heavy coffee drinkers five or more cups a day suffer many more ill effects than those whose coffee intake is less.

Review Test 1

At the appropriate spot or spots, place the punctuation mark shown in the margin.

EXAMPLE

;   The singles dance was a success; I met several people I wanted to see again.

:   1. Before you go anywhere, finish your chores the laundry, the dishes, and the vacuuming.

—   2. The Easter Bunny, Santa Claus, and the Tooth Fairy these were the idols of my youth.

-     3. Tom's self important manner makes him boring to be with.

( )   4. The two most important steps in writing an effective paper are 1 to make a point of some kind and 2 to provide specific evidence to support that point.

:   5. Albert Einstein once said "It is in fact nothing short of a miracle that the modern methods of instruction have not yet entirely strangled the holy curiosity of inquiry; for this delicate little plant, aside from stimulation, stands mainly in need of freedom; without this it goes to wrack and ruin without fail."

;   6. Abby bought a second remote-control unit for the television set as a result, she can change the channels as often as her husband does.

—   7. I asked the waiter to return the steak which seemed to consist of more fat than meat to the kitchen.

-     8. Tom always brings a pair of wide angle binoculars to the football games.

( )   9. The television set is relatively new having been bought only a year ago but has been to the repair shop three times.

;   10. Angelo had a lot of studying to do: for sociology, he had to read two articles for his math course, he had to interpret an entire page of graphs and for English, he had to catch up on his journal.

Review Test 2

On separate paper, write two sentences for each of the following punctuation marks: colon, semicolon, dash, hyphen, parentheses.

NAME: _____

DATE: _____

Other Punctuation Marks MASTERY TEST 1

At the appropriate spot (or spots), place the punctuation mark shown in the margin.

—   1. Martha screamed when she saw a water bug the kind that can travel sixty miles an hour race across her bathroom floor.

;   2. A canary's claws must be carefully clipped it is important not to nick the little veins in each one.

—   3. The town is so far north that it has only two seasons winter and August.

:   4. A search of Danny's pockets revealed these items an inch-long piece of wire, a crumpled baseball card, three small stones, and a dead grasshopper.

( )   5. The incoming line section should be a rigid dead-front type, completely encased with metal and self-supporting see diagram A.

-      6. "Seventy Six Trombones" is a toe tapping, finger snapping march from the Broadway classic *The Music Man*.

( )   7. Our country's national parks especially famous ones like Yosemite and Yellowstone must now deal with major crimes committed by summer visitors.

;   8. Native Americans used poetic names for the months of the year for instance, December was "Moon When the Deer Shed Their Horns."

-      9. The slightly built burglar was well known as the most talented "second story" man in town.

:   10. *Consumer Reports* concludes its article on wood stoves by stating "You should first ask yourself if you *need* a wood stove to help lower your home-heating costs. Are you sure you've done as much as you can to save energy in other ways? Are you prepared for the inconveniences, major and minor, that a wood stove entails?"

NAME: _____

DATE: _____

MASTERY TEST 2 | # Other Punctuation Marks

Each sentence below needs one of the following punctuation marks:

colon :	hyphen -	semicolon ;
dash —	parentheses ( )	

1. Bargain hunters swarmed around the entrance to the store the manager quickly opened the doors.

2. The diagram of the reproductive cycle pages 24–25 must also be studied for the test.

3. Self centered people are often very insecure.

4. There is one sure way to get in trouble with that instructor ask too many questions.

5. Tarzan, Superman, the Lone Ranger these were the heroes of his boyhood.

6. George Orwell has written "On the whole, human beings want to be good, but not too good, and not quite all the time. . . . Society has always to demand a little more from human beings than it will get in practice."

7. Two squirrels there they are on top of the fence are building a nest in the storage shed.

8. The three required books on our psychology reading list are *Toward a Psychology of Being,* by Abraham Maslow *On Becoming a Person,* by Carl Rogers and *Love and Will,* by Rollo May.

9. I don't know why the door to the gas station restroom is locked perhaps the owner is afraid someone will get inside to clean it.

10. This do it yourself repair book will save homeowners a lot of money.

Dictionary Use

28

Introductory Activity

The dictionary is an indispensable tool, as will be apparent if you try to answer the following questions *without* using the dictionary.

1. Which one of the following words is spelled incorrectly?

   fortutious   macrobiotics   stratagem

2. If you wanted to hyphenate the following word correctly, at which points would you place the syllable divisions?

   h i e r o g l y p h i c s

3. What common word has the sound of the first *e* in the word *chameleon*?

   _____

4. Where is the primary accent in the following word?

   o c / t o / g e / n a r / i / a n

5. What are the two separate meanings of the word *earmark*?

   _____

   _____

Your dictionary is a quick and sure authority on all these matters: spelling, syllabication, pronunciation, and word meanings. And as this chapter will show, it is also a source for many other kinds of information.

Answers are on page 573.

But Dr Johnson ov wat yuse wil this dicshunary of yors be?

The dictionary is a valuable tool. To take advantage of it, you need to understand the main kinds of information that a dictionary gives about a word. Look at the information provided for the word *dictate* in the following entry from the *American Heritage Dictionary,* fourth paperback edition.*

Spelling and syllabication   Pronunciation   Part of speech

dic•tate (dĭk′tāt′, dĭk-tāt) *v.* **-tat•ed, -tat•ing.** **Meanings**
1. To say or read aloud for transcription.
2. To prescribe or command with authority.
—*n.* (dĭk′tāt′) **1.** A directive; command.
2. A guiding principle: *the dictates of*— **Example**
conscience. [< Lat. *dictāre.* < *dīcere, say*]
—**dic•ta′tion** *n.* **Etymology**

Other form of the word

_____

Spelling

The first bit of information, in the boldface (heavy type) entry itself, is the spelling of *dictate.* You probably already know the spelling of *dictate,* but if you didn't, you could find it by pronouncing the syllables in the word carefully and then looking it up in the dictionary.

Use your dictionary to correct the spelling of the following words:

alright _____   elavater _____

assosiation _____   plesure _____

awkwerd _____   balence _____

diferent _____   beleiving _____

omited _____   libary _____

opinyon _____   apetite _____

critikal _____   happyness _____

embarasment _____   usualy _____

probaly _____   suprise _____

Syllabication

The second bit of information that the dictionary gives, also within the boldface entry, is the syllabication of *dic•tate.* Note that a dot separates each syllable (or part) of the word. Use your dictionary to mark the syllable divisions in the following words. Also indicate how many syllables are in each word.

v e n t u r e   (_____ syllables)

o b s e s s i o n   (_____ syllables)

e n e r g e t i c   (_____ syllables)

i n s p i r a t i o n a l   (_____ syllables)

Noting syllable divisions will enable you to *hyphenate* a word: divide it at the end of one line of writing and complete it at the beginning of the next line. You can correctly hyphenate a word only at a syllable division, and you may have to check your dictionary to make sure of the syllable divisions for a particular word.

Pronunciation

The third bit of information in the dictionary entry is the pronunciation of *dictate:* *(dik´tat´)* or *(dik-tat´).* You already know how to pronounce *dictate,* but if you did not, the information within the parentheses would serve as your guide. Use your dictionary to complete the pronunciation exercises on page 385.

Vowel Sounds

You will probably use the pronunciation key in your dictionary mainly as a guide to pronouncing different vowel sounds (*vowels* are the letters *a, e, i, o,* and *u*). Here is the pronunciation key that appears in the front of the paperback *American Heritage Dictionary**:

> ă pat ā pay â care ä father ě pet ē be ĭ pit ī tie î pier ŏ pot ō toe ô paw, for oi noise o͝o took o͞o boot ou out th thin *th* this ŭ cut û urge yo͞o abuse zh vision ə about, item, edible, gallop, circus

This key tells you, for example, that the short *a* is pronounced like the *a* in *pat,* the long *a* is like the *a* in *pay,* and the short *i* is like the *i* in *pit.*

Now look at the pronunciation key in your own dictionary. The key is probably located in the front of the dictionary or at the bottom of every page. What common word in the key tells you how to pronounce each of the following sounds?

ě _____   ō _____

ī _____   ŭ _____

ŏ _____   o͞o _____

> **TIP** Note that a long vowel always has the sound of its own name.

The Schwa (ə)

The symbol ə looks like an upside-down *e.* It is called a *schwa,* and it stands for the unaccented sound in such words as *about, item, edible, gallop,* and *circus.* More approximately, it stands for the sound *uh*—like the *uh* that speakers sometimes make when they hesitate. Perhaps it would help to remember that *uh,* as well as ə, could be used to represent the schwa sound.

Here are three of the many words in which the schwa sound appears: *social-ize* (sō´shə līz or sō´shuh līz); *legitimate* (lə jĭt´ə mĭt or luh jĭt´uh mĭt); *oblivious*

(ə blĭv′ē əs or uh blĭv′ē uhs). Open your dictionary to any page, and you will almost surely be able to find three words that make use of the schwa in the pronunciation in parentheses after the main entry. Write three such words and their pronunciations in the following spaces:

1. _____

2. _____

3. _____

Accent Marks

Some words contain both a primary accent, shown by a heavy stroke ('), and a secondary accent, shown by a lighter stroke ('). For example, in the word *vicissitude* (vĭ sĭs′ĭ tōōd′), the stress, or accent, goes chiefly on the second syllable (sĭs′), and, to a lesser extent, on the last syllable (tōōd′).

Use your dictionary to add stress marks to the following words:

soliloquy (sə lĭl ə kwē)

diatribe (dī ə trīb)

rheumatism (rōō mə tīz əm)

representation (rĕp rĭ zĕn tā shən)

Full Pronunciation

Use your dictionary to write out the full pronunciation (the information given in parentheses) for each of the following words:

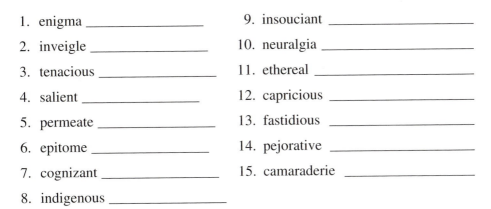

1. enigma _____
2. inveigle _____
3. tenacious _____
4. salient _____
5. permeate _____
6. epitome _____
7. cognizant _____
8. indigenous _____

9. insouciant _____
10. neuralgia _____
11. ethereal _____
12. capricious _____
13. fastidious _____
14. pejorative _____
15. camaraderie _____

Now practice pronouncing each word. Use the pronunciation key in your dictionary as an aid to sounding out each syllable. Do *not* try to pronounce a word all at once; instead, work on mastering *one syllable at a time*. When you can pronounce each of the syllables in a word successfully, then say them in sequence, add the accent, and pronounce the entire word.

Note: Online dictionaries offer spoken pronunciations of words. For example, if you go to www.merriam-webster.com, you will see a speaker icon next to each word entry. If you click on this icon, the word will be pronounced for you.

Other Information about Words

Parts of Speech

The dictionary entry for *dictate* includes the abbreviation *v.* This means that the meanings of *dictate* as a verb will follow. The abbreviation *n.* is then followed by the meaning of *dictate* as a noun.

At the front of your dictionary, you will probably find a key that will explain the meanings of abbreviations used in the dictionary. Use the key to fill in the meanings of the following abbreviations:

pl. = _____   adj. = _____

sing. = _____   adv. = _____

Principal Parts of Irregular Verbs

Dictate is a regular verb and forms its principal parts by adding *-d, -d,* and *-ing* to the stem of the verb. When a verb is irregular, the dictionary lists its principal parts. For example, with *begin* the present tense comes first (the entry itself, *begin*). Next comes the past tense (*began*), and then the past participle (*begun*)—the form of the verb used with such helping words as *have, had,* and *was.* Then comes the present participle (*beginning*)—the *-ing* form of the word.

Look up the principal parts of the following irregular verbs and write them in the spaces provided. The first one has been done for you.

Present	Past	Past Participle	Present Participle
see	*saw*	*seen*	*seeing*
go	_____	_____	_____
ride	_____	_____	_____
speak	_____	_____	_____

Plural Forms of Irregular Nouns

The dictionary supplies the plural forms of all irregular nouns (regular nouns form the plural by adding -*s* or -*es*). Give the plurals of the following nouns:

cemetery   _____

knife   _____

veto   _____

neurosis   _____

See page 396 for more information about plurals.

Meanings

When a word has more than one meaning, the meanings are numbered in the dictionary, as with the verb *dictate*. In many dictionaries, the most common meanings are presented first. The introductory pages of your dictionary will explain the order in which meanings are presented.

Use the sentence context to try to explain the meaning of the underlined word in each of the following sentences. Write your definition in the space provided. Then look up and record the dictionary meaning of the word. Be sure you pick out the meaning that fits the word as it is used in the sentence.

1. The surgeons first <u>flushed</u> the patient's chest cavity with sterile fluid.

   Your definition: _____

   Dictionary definition: _____

   _____

2. Several well-known actors make <u>cameo</u> appearances in the director's first movie.

   Your definition: _____

   Dictionary definition: _____

   _____

3. The spy story was so <u>riveting</u> I stayed awake till 2 A.M. reading it.

   Your definition: _____

   Dictionary definition: _____

   _____

Etymology

Etymology refers to the history of a word. Many words have origins in foreign languages, such as Greek (abbreviated Gk in the dictionary) or Latin (L). Such information is usually enclosed in brackets and is more likely to be present in a hardbound desk dictionary than in a paperback one. A good desk dictionary will tell you, for example, that the word *cannibal* derives from the name of the man-eating tribe, the Caribs, that Christopher Columbus discovered on Cuba and Haiti.

The following are good desk dictionaries:

The American Heritage Dictionary
Random House College Dictionary
Merriam-Webster's Collegiate Dictionary
Webster's New World Dictionary

See if your dictionary says anything about the origins of the following words.

bikini _____

_____

sandwich _____

_____

tantalize _____

_____

breakfast _____

_____

Usage Labels

As a general rule, use only standard English words in your writing. If a word is not standard English, your dictionary will probably give it a usage label such as *informal, nonstandard, slang, vulgar, obsolete, archaic,* or *rare.*

Look up the following words and record how your dictionary labels them. Remember that a recent hardbound desk dictionary will always be the best source of information about usage.

break (meaning *a stroke of luck*) _____

ain't _____

uptight _____

well-heeled _____

cop-out _____

Synonyms

A *synonym* is a word that is close in meaning to another word. Using synonyms helps you avoid unnecessary repetition of the same word in a paper. A paperback dictionary is not likely to give you synonyms for words, but a good desk dictionary will. (You might also want to own a *thesaurus,* a book that lists synonyms and antonyms. An *antonym* is a word approximately opposite in meaning to another word.)

Consult a desk dictionary that gives synonyms for the following words, and write some of the synonyms in the spaces provided.

fear _____

answer _____

love _____

Review Test

Use your dictionary to answer the following questions.

1. How many syllables are in the word *cinematography?* _____

2. Where is the primary accent in the word *domesticity?* _____

3. In the word *oppressive,* the *o* is pronounced like

   a. schwa.

   b. short *o.*

   c. long *u.*

   d. long *o.*

4. In the word *culpable,* the *a* is pronounced like

   a. short *a.*

   b. long *a.*

   c. short *i.*

   d. schwa.

5. In the word *negotiate,* the first *e* is pronounced like

   a. short *e.*

   b. long *e.*

   c. schwa.

   d. short *i.*

There are five misspelled words in the following sentence. Cross out each misspelled word and write the correct spelling in the spaces provided.

> The college I plan to transferr to will accept my psikology credits, the counseler told me, but I will not recieve credit for my courses in introductory mathamatics and basic English.

6. _____

7. _____

8. _____

9. _____

10. _____

NAME: _____

DATE: _____

Dictionary Use

ITEMS **1–5**

Use your dictionary to answer the following questions.

1. How many syllables are in the word *decontaminate?* _____

2. Where is the primary accent in the word *interpretation?* _____

3. In the word *posterity,* the *i* is pronounced like

   a. short *e.*

   b. short *i.*

   c. long *i.*

   d. schwa.

4. In the word *secularize,* the *u* is pronounced like

   a. schwa.

   b. short *a.*

   c. short *u.*

   d. long *u.*

5. In the word *erratic,* the *e* is pronounced like

   a. short *e.*

   b. long *e.*

   c. short *i.*

   d. schwa.

ITEMS **6–10**

There are five misspelled words in the following sentence. Cross out each misspelled word and write in the correct spelling in the spaces provided.

> The canidate for mayor promised to reduce subway fares by a nickle, to crack down on criminels, and to bring new businesses to the city by ofering tax breaks.

6. _____   8. _____   10. _____

7. _____   9. _____

NAME: _____

DATE: _____

MASTERY TEST 2 | # Dictionary Use

ITEMS 1–5

Use your dictionary to answer the following questions.

1. How many syllables are in the word *rationalize?*_____

2. Where is the primary accent in the word *dilapidated?*_____

3. In the word *vicarious,* the second *i* is pronounced like

    a. long *e.*

    b. short *i.*

    c. long *i.*

    d. schwa.

4. In the word *cumbersome,* the *o* is pronounced like

    a. schwa.

    b. short *a.*

    c. short *o.*

    d. long *o.*

5. In the word *esoteric,* the second *e* is pronounced like

    a. short *e.*

    b. long *e.*

    c. short *i.*

    d. schwa.

ITEMS 6–10

There are five misspelled words in the following sentence. Cross out each misspelled word and write the correct spelling in the space provided.

My mother's most precious possesion is her collection of crystel animals; she keeps them in a specal cabinet in the dineeing room and won't allow anyone to handel them.

6. _____   8. _____   10. _____

7. _____   9. _____

Spelling Improvement

Introductory Activity

See if you can circle the word that is misspelled in each of the following pairs:

akward	*or*	awkward
exercise	*or*	exercize
business	*or*	buisness
worried	*or*	worryed
shamful	*or*	shameful
begining	*or*	beginning
partys	*or*	parties
sandwichs	*or*	sandwiches
heroes	*or*	heros

Answers are on page 573.

Poor spelling often results from bad habits developed in the early school years. With work, such habits can be corrected. If you can write your name without misspelling it, there is no reason why you can't do the same with almost any word in the English language. Following are seven steps you can take to improve your spelling.

Step 1: Using the Dictionary

Get into the habit of using the dictionary. When you write a paper, allow yourself time to look up the spelling of all the words you are unsure about. Do not under-estimate the value of this step just because it is such a simple one. By using the dictionary, you can probably make yourself a 95 percent better speller.

Step 2: Keeping a Personal Spelling List

Keep a list of words you misspell and study those words regularly.

> **TIP**
>
> When you have trouble spelling long words, try to break each word into syllables and see whether you can spell the syllables. For example, *misdemeanor* can be spelled easily if you can hear and spell in turn its four syllables: *mis-de-mean-or*. The word *formidable* can be spelled easily if you hear and spell in turn its four syllables: *for-mi-da-ble*. Remember, then: try to see, hear, and spell long words in terms of their syllables.

Step 3: Mastering Commonly Confused Words

Master the meanings and spellings of the commonly confused words on pages 411–427. Your instructor may assign twenty words for you to study at a time and give you a series of quizzes until you have mastered all the words.

Step 4: Using a Computer's Spell-Checker

Most word-processing programs feature a *spell-checker* that will identify incorrect words and suggest correct spellings. If you are unsure how to use yours, consult the program's "help" function. Spell-checkers are not foolproof; they will fail to catch misused homonyms like the words *your* and *you're*.

Step 5: Understanding Basic Spelling Rules

Explained briefly here are three rules that may improve your spelling. While exceptions sometimes occur, these rules hold true most of the time.

1. **Changing y to i.**

   When a word ends in a consonant plus *y*, change *y* to *i* when you add an ending.

   try   + ed = tried   marry + es   = marries

   worry + es = worries   lazy   + ness = laziness

   lucky + ly = luckily   silly   + est = silliest

2. **Final silent e.**

   Drop a final *e* before an ending that starts with a vowel (the vowels are *a, e, i, o,* and *u*).

   hope + ing = hoping   sense + ible = sensible

   fine + est = finest   hide + ing = hiding

   Keep the final *e* before an ending that starts with a consonant.

   use + ful = useful   care   + less = careless

   life + like = lifelike   settle + ment = settlement

3. **Doubling a final consonant.**

   Double the final consonant of a word when all the following are true:

   a. The word is one syllable or is accented on the last syllable.
   b. The word ends in a single consonant preceded by a single vowel.
   c. The ending you are adding starts with a vowel.

   sob   + ing = sobbing   big   + est = biggest

   drop   + ed   = dropped   omit   + ed   = omitted

   admit + ing = admitting   begin + ing = beginning

Combine the following words and endings by applying the three rules above.

1. study   + ed   = _____
2. advise + ing = _____
3. carry   + es   = _____
4. stop   + ing = _____
5. terrify + ed   = _____

6. compel + ed   = _____
7. retire   + ing = _____
8. hungry + ly   = _____
9. expel   + ing = _____
10. judge   + es   = _____

Step 6: Understanding Plurals

Most words form their plurals by adding *-s* to the singular.

Singular	Plural
blanket	blankets
pencil	pencils
street	streets

Some words, however, form their plurals in special ways, as shown in the rules that follow.

1. **Words ending in *-s, -ss, -z, -x, -sh,* or *-ch* usually form the plural by adding *-es*.**

kiss	kisses	inch	inches
box	boxes	dish	dishes

2. **Words ending in a consonant plus *y* form the plural by changing *y* to *i* and adding *-es*.**

party	parties	county	counties
baby	babies	city	cities

3. **Some words ending in *f* change the *f* to *v* and add *-es* in the plural.**

leaf	leaves	life	lives
wife	wives	yourself	yourselves

4. **Some words ending in *o* form their plurals by adding *-es*.**

potato	potatoes	mosquito	mosquitoes
hero	heroes	tomato	tomatoes

5. **Some words of foreign origin have irregular plurals. When in doubt, check your dictionary.**

antenna	antennae	crisis	crises
criterion	criteria	medium	media

6. **Some words form their plurals by changing letters within the word.**

man	men	foot	feet
tooth	teeth	goose	geese

7. **Combined words (words made up of two or more words) form their plurals by adding -*s* to the main word.**

brother-in-law	brothers-in-law
passerby	passersby

Complete these sentences by filling in the plural of the word at the left.

grocery   1. I carried six bags of _____ into the house.

town   2. How many _____ did you visit during the tour?

policy   3. The president's new _____ are making many voters angry.

body   4. Because the grave diggers were on strike, _____ piled up in the morgue.

lottery   5. She plays two state _____ in hopes of winning a fortune.

pass   6. Hank caught six _____ in a losing cause.

tragedy   7. That woman has had to endure many _____ in her life.

watch   8. I have found that cheap _____ work better for me than expensive ones.

suit   9. To help himself feel better, he went out and bought two _____.

boss   10. I have not one but two _____ to worry about every day.

Step 7: Mastering a Basic Word List

Make sure you can spell all the words in the following list. They are some of the words used most often in English. Again, your instructor may assign twenty words for you to study at a time and give you a series of quizzes until you have mastered the words.

ability	bargain	daily
absent	beautiful	danger
accident	because	daughter
across	become	death
address	before	decide
advertise	begin	deposit
advice	being	describe
after	believe	different
again	between	direction
against	bottom **40**	distance
all right	breathe	doubt
almost	building	dozen
a lot	business	during
although	careful	each
always	careless	early
among	cereal	earth
angry	certain	education
animal	change	either
another	cheap	English
answer **20**	chief	enough **80**
anxious	children	entrance
apply	church	everything
approve	cigarette	examine
argue	clothing	exercise
around	collect	expect
attempt	color	family
attention	comfortable	flower
awful	company	foreign
awkward	condition	friend
balance	conversation **60**	garden

general

grocery

guess

happy

heard

heavy

height

himself

holiday

house   **100**

however

hundred

hungry

important

instead

intelligence

interest

interfere

kitchen

knowledge

labor

language

laugh

leave

length

lesson

letter

listen

loneliness

making   **120**

marry

match

matter

measure

medicine

middle

might

million

minute

mistake

money

month

morning

mountain

much

needle

neglect

newspaper

noise

none   **140**

nothing

number

ocean

offer

often

omit

only

operate

opportunity

original

ought

pain

paper

pencil

people

perfect

period

personal

picture

place   **160**

pocket

possible

potato

president

pretty

problem

promise

property

psychology

public

question

quick

raise

ready

really

reason

receive

recognize

remember

repeat   **180**

restaurant

ridiculous

said

same

sandwich

send

sentence

several

shoes

should

since

sleep

smoke

something

soul

started	through	usual
state	ticket	value
straight	tired	vegetable
street	today	view
strong **200**	together	visitor
student	tomorrow	voice
studying	tongue	warning
success	tonight	watch
suffer	touch	welcome
surprise	travel **220**	window
teach	truly	would
telephone	understand	writing
theory	unity	written
thought	until	year
thousand	upon	yesterday **240**

Can you find the sentence-skills mistake in the sign pictured here?

Review Test

Use the three spelling rules to spell the following words.

1. cry   + es   = _____

2. believe + able = _____

3. bury   + ed   = _____

4. date   + ing = _____

5. lonely   + est = _____

6. large   + er   = _____

7. skim   + ed   = _____

8. rare   + ly   = _____

Circle the correctly spelled plural in each pair.

9. beliefs   believs

10. churchs   churches

11. bullys   bullies

12. countries   countrys

13. womans   women

14. potatos   potatoes

Circle the correctly spelled word (from the basic word list) in each pair.

15. foreign   foriegn

16. condicion   condition

17. restarant   restaurant

18. opportunity   oportunity

19. entrance   enterance

20. surprise   surprize

NAME: _____

DATE: _____

MASTERY TEST 1 Spelling Improvement

ITEMS 1–8

Use the three spelling rules to spell the following words.

1. debate + able = _____

2. run + ing = _____

3. thorny + est = _____

4. woe + ful = _____

5. swim + er = _____

6. happy + ly = _____

7. hate + ful = _____

8. infer + ed = _____

ITEMS 9–14

Circle the correctly spelled plural in each pair.

9. knifes	knives	12. stories	storys
10. wishes	wishs	13. heros	heroes
11. decoys	decoies	14. ourselfs	ourselves

ITEMS 15–20

Circle the correctly spelled word (from the basic word list on pages 398–400) in each pair.

15. possible	possable	18. success	sucess
16. exercize	exercise	19. rediculous	ridiculous
17. receive	recieve	20. acident	accident

NAME: _____

DATE: _____

Spelling Improvement   MASTERY TEST 2

ITEMS 1–8

Use the three spelling rules to spell the following words.

1. equip   + ed   = _____

2. excite   + ment = _____

3. heavy   + ly   = _____

4. flat   + est   = _____

5. carry   + ed   = _____

6. begin   + er   = _____

7. surprise + ing   = _____

8. crazy   + ness = _____

ITEMS 9–14

Circle the correctly spelled plural in each pair.

9. issues	issus	12. loaves	loafs
10. partys	parties	13. halfs	halves
11. worries	worrys	14. father-in-laws	fathers-in-law

ITEMS 15–20

Circle the correctly spelled word (from the basic word list on pages 398–400) in each pair.

15. measure	meazure	18. psycology	psychology
16. knowlege	knowledge	19. awkward	akward
17. alright	all right	20. recognize	recognise

Omitted Words and Letters

30

Introductory Activity

See if you can find the six places in the passage below where letters or words have been dropped. Supply whatever is missing.

Two glass bottle of apple juice lie broken the supermarket aisle. Suddenly, a toddler who has gotten away from his parents appears at the head of the aisle. He spots the broken bottles and begins to run toward them. His chubby body lurches along like windup toy, and his arm move excitedly up and down. Luckily, alert shopper quickly reacts to the impending disaster and blocks the toddler's path. Then the shopper waits with crying, frustrated little boy until his parents show up.

Answers are on page 574.

Some people drop small connecting words such as *a, an, in, of,* or *the* when they write. They may also drop the *-s* endings of plural nouns. Be careful not to leave out words or letters when you write, as this may confuse and irritate your readers. They may not want to read what they regard as careless work.

Finding Omitted Words and Letters

Finding omitted words and letters, like finding many other sentence-skills mistakes, is a matter of careful proofreading. You must develop your ability to look carefully at a page to find places where mistakes may exist.

The exercises here will give you practice in finding omitted words and omitted -*s* endings on nouns. Another section of this book (pages 145–146) gives you practice in finding omitted -*s* endings on verbs.

Add the missing word (*a, an, the, of,* or *to*) as needed.

EXAMPLE

Some people regard television as tranquilizer that provides temporary relief from pain and anxiety modern life.

1. When I began eating box of chicken I bought at the fast-food restaurant, I found several pieces that consisted of lot crust covering nothing but chicken bones.

2. Gwen had instructor who tried light a piece of chalk, thinking it was cigarette.

3. In his dream, Ray committed perfect crime: he killed his enemy with icicle, so murder weapon was never found.

4. Dr. Yutzer told me not worry about sore on my foot, but I decided to get second opinion.

5. As little girl ate vanilla sugar cone, ice cream dripped out hole at the bottom onto her pants.

6. When thick black clouds began form and we felt several drops rain, we knew picnic would be canceled.

7. After spending most her salary on new clothes, Susan looks like something out of fashion magazine.

8. As wasps buzzed around room, I ran for can of Raid.

9. Keith put pair wet socks in oven, for he wanted dry them out quickly.

10. Because weather got hot and stayed hot for weeks, my flower garden started look like dried flower arrangement.

The Omitted -s Ending

The plural form of regular nouns usually ends in -s. One common mistake that some people make with plurals is to omit this -s ending. People who drop the ending from plurals when speaking also tend to do it when writing. This tendency is especially noticeable when the meaning of the sentence shows that a word is plural.

> Ed and Mary pay eight hundred dollar a month for an apartment that has only two room.

The -s ending has been omitted from *dollars* and *rooms*.

The activities that follow will help you correct the habit of omitting the -s endings from plurals.

Practice 2

Add -s endings where needed.

EXAMPLE

> Kyle beat me at several game*s* of darts.

1. When Rita's two boyfriend met each other last night, they almost came to blow.

2. My brother let out a choice selection of curse when he dropped his watch in the sand.

3. We were expected to write an essay of several paragraph on key event leading up to the Civil War.

4. Sunlight reflected off the windshield of the many car in the parking lot.

5. A number of house along the elevated subway route have been torn down to make room for two new highway that are being built.

6. Rainy day depress me, especially during those time when I am depressed already.

7. Our drive along the shore was marred by the billboard that seem to have popped up everywhere.

8. There were no folding chair in the room; instead, people were asked to sit on pillow spread around the floor.

9. From the top of either of those watchtower, you can see four state.

10. Motorist waited restlessly as several tow truck worked to remove the tractor trailer spread-eagled across the highway.

Write sentences that use plural forms of the following pairs of words.

EXAMPLE

girl, bike *The little girls raced their bikes down the street.*

1. paper, grade _____

   _____

2. pillow, bed _____

   _____

3. sock, shoe _____

   _____

4. day, night _____

   _____

5. game, loss _____

   _____

TIP People who drop the *-s* ending on nouns also tend to omit endings on verbs. Pages 145–146 will help you correct the habit of dropping endings on verbs.

Review Test   1

In each of the following sentences, two small connecting words are needed. Write them in the spaces provided, and write a caret (∧) at each place in the sentence where a connecting word should appear.

_____   1. Like ostriches, the two men hunched over car's hood buried
_____   their heads in the engine.

_____   2. Each time I put my bare foot down on hot asphalt road, I think
_____   I left layer of skin behind.

_____   3. Lisa sneaked out of diner when the waitress wasn't looking;
_____   she didn't have enough money leave a tip.

_____ 4. Vince held lighted match to his car door, trying unfreeze the
_____   lock.

_____ 5. I can't remember the name the book we were assigned read for
_____   Friday's class.

Review Test 2

Insert the two -s endings needed in each sentence.

_____ 1. Hector keeps two giant jar of multicolored vitamin on the
_____   counter.

_____ 2. The grimy fingerprint of the workers had smudged the electric
_____   switchplate in the living and dining rooms.

_____ 3. If I could just get together a thousand dollar, I think all my
_____   money problem could be solved.

_____ 4. Lola had big plan for the weekend, but all Tony wanted to do
_____   was watch a series of football game on television.

_____ 5. When Emmett opened the package of shirt from the laundry,
_____   he discovered that many button were missing.

Omitted Words and Letters MASTERY TEST 1

PART 1

In the spaces provided, write in the two small connecting words needed in each sentence. Use carets (∧) within the sentences to show where these words belong.

_____   1. With only inning left play, the score was three to two.
_____

_____   2. In middle of the night, I heard a loud crash jumped out of bed, trembling.
_____

_____   3. Whenever Fran puts Frank Sinatra record on stereo, Nick goes to sleep.
_____

_____   4. If Martha thinks she is coming down with cold, she drinks a cup tea with honey.
_____

_____   5. The beautiful starlet slowly got out of her limousine, clutching small white
_____   poodle that resembled animated mop.

PART 2

In the spaces provided, write in the two words that need -s endings in each sentence. Be sure to add the s to each word.

_____   6. Our expense were getting out of control, so my husband and I began keeping
_____   a record of all our purchase.

_____   7. All the section of two course Tony wanted were closed.
_____

_____   8. We had forgotten to make extra ice cube, so Melba volunteered to pick up
_____   two bag at the corner store.

_____   9. A young couple in the laundromat started to roll their sock into ball and lob
_____   them at each other.

_____   10. After several attempt, Vince was finally able to bench-press 250 pound.
_____

NAME: _____

DATE: _____

MASTERY TEST 2 | Omitted Words and Letters

PART 1

In the spaces provided, write in the two small connecting words needed in each sentence. Use carets (∧) within the sentences to show where these words belong.

_____

_____

1. Tara called cable company when picture on her set resembled a crazy quilt.

_____

_____

2. When twenty inches rain fell in one day, our backyard resembled swimming pool.

3. I have lost track how many parties our neighbor has given in past year.

_____

_____

4. Even though Bill had eaten three sandwiches lunch, he began eat a bag of donuts at three o'clock.

_____

_____

5. The quarterback would have had better completion record if backs had not dropped so many passes this year.

PART 2

In the spaces provided, write in the two words that need -s endings in each sentence. Be sure to add the s to each word.

_____

_____

6. The music store in the mall has two trade-in day a month when used CD are purchased for cash.

_____

_____

7. The pattern had worn off the linoleum floor in many place, and the wall were water-stained.

_____

_____

8. Like small black freight train, long lines of ant moved across the sidewalk.

_____

_____

9. The director's chair on Larry's porch are imprinted with the name of the family members.

_____

_____

10. Everything from a group of stuffed parrot to several antique bicycle hung from the ceiling of the restaurant.

Commonly Confused Words

Introductory Activity

This chapter will introduce you to words that people often confuse in their writing. Circle the five words that are misspelled in the following passage. Then write their correct spellings in the spaces provided.

If your a resident of a temperate climate, you may suffer from feelings of depression in the winter and early spring. Scientists are now studying people who's moods seem to worsen in winter, and there findings show that the amount of daylight a person receives is an important factor in "seasonal depression." When a person gets to little sunlight, his or her mood darkens. Its fairly easy to treat severe cases of seasonal depression; the cure involves spending a few hours a day in front of full-spectrum fluorescent lights that contain all the components of natural light.

1. _____
2. _____
3. _____
4. _____
5. _____

Answers are on page 574.

Homonyms

The commonly confused words shown below are known as *homonyms;* they have the same sounds but different meanings and spellings. Complete the activities for each set of words, and check off and study the words that give you trouble.

Common Homonyms

all ready	knew	principal	to
already	new	principle	too
brake	know	right	two
break	no	write	wear
coarse	pair	than	where
course	pear	then	weather
hear	passed	their	whether
here	past	there	whose
hole	peace	they're	who's
whole	piece	threw	your
its	plain	through	you're
it's	plane		

all ready	completely prepared
already	previously, before

We were *all ready* to go, for we had eaten and packed *already* that morning.

Fill in the blanks: I was _____ to start ordering breakfast when I found out that the restaurant had _____ shifted to its lunch menu.

Write sentences using *all ready* and *already.*

_____

_____

brake	**stop**
break	**come apart**

Dot slams the *brake* pedal so hard that I'm afraid I'll *break* my neck in her car.

Fill in the blanks: Al tried to put the _____ on his appetite, but the luscious rum cake made him _____ all his resolutions.

Write sentences using *brake* and *break*.

_____

_____

coarse	**rough**
course	**part of a meal; a school subject; direction; certainly (with *of*)**

During the *course* of my career as a waitress, I've dealt with some very *coarse* customers.

Fill in the blanks: Weaving a wall hanging with _____ yarns is part of the arts and crafts _____.

Write sentences using *coarse* and *course*.

_____

_____

hear	**perceive with the ear**
here	**in this place**

If I *hear* another insulting ethnic joke *here,* I'll leave.

Fill in the blanks: My mother always says, "Come _____ if you can't _____ what I'm saying."

Write sentences using *hear* and *here*.

_____

_____

hole	an empty spot
whole	entire

If there is a *hole* in the tailpipe, I'm afraid we will have to replace the *whole* exhaust assembly.

Fill in the blanks: The gaping _____ in the wallboard gives the

_____ living room a neglected look.

Write sentences using *hole* and *whole*.

_____

_____

its	belonging to it
it's	shortened form for *it is* or *it has*

The kitchen floor has lost *its* shine because *it's* been used as a roller skating rink by the children.

Fill in the blanks: _____ the chemistry course with _____

lab requirement that worries me.

Write sentences using *its* and *it's*.

_____

_____

knew	past tense of *know*
new	not old

We *knew* that the *new* television comedy would be canceled quickly.

Fill in the blanks: If you _____ in advance all the _____

turns your life would take, you might give up.

Write sentences using *knew* and *new*.

_____

_____

| know | to understand |
| no | a negative |

I never *know* who might drop in even though *no* one is expected.

Fill in the blanks: When that spoiled boy's parents say _____ to him, we all _____ a temper tantrum is likely to result.

Write sentences using *know* and *no*.

_____

_____

| pair | a set of two |
| pear | a fruit |

The dessert consisted of a *pair* of thin biscuits topped with vanilla ice cream and poached *pear* halves.

Fill in the blanks: The grove of _____ trees is one of the places where the _____ of escaped convicts was spotted last week.

Write sentences using *pair* and *pear*.

_____

_____

> | passed | went by; succeeded in; handed to |
> | --- | --- |
> | past | by, as in "I drove past the house"; a time before the present |

After Emma *passed* the driver's test, she drove *past* all her friends' houses and honked the horn.

Fill in the blanks: In her _____ jobs, Nadia had _____ up several opportunities for promotion because she did not want to seem aggressive.

Write sentences using *passed* and *past.*

_____

_____

> | peace | calm |
> | --- | --- |
> | piece | a part |

The *peace* of the little town was shattered when a *piece* of a human body was found in the town dump.

Fill in the blanks: The judge promised to give the troublemaker more than just a _____ of his mind if the boy ever disturbed the _____ again.

Write sentences using *peace* and *piece.*

_____

_____

plain	simple
plane	aircraft

The *plain* box contained a very expensive model *plane* kit.

Fill in the blanks: That _____ -looking man boarding the

_____ is actually a famous movie director.

Write sentences using *plain* and *plane*.

_____

_____

principal	main; a person in charge of a school; amount of money borrowed
principle	a law or standard

My *principal* goal in child rearing is to give my daughter strong *principles* to live by.

Fill in the blanks: The school _____ defended the school's

_____ regarding a dress code for students.

Write sentences using *principal* and *principle*.

_____

_____

TIP It might help to remember that the *le* in *principle* is also in *rule*—the meaning of *principle*.

> | right | correct; opposite of *left;* privilege |
> |---|---|
> | write | what you do in English |

It is my *right* to refuse to *write* my name on your petition.

Fill in the blanks: Ellen wanted to _____ and thank Steve for his flowers, but she didn't think it _____ to keep leading him on.

Write sentences using *right* and *write.*

_____

_____

> | than | used in comparisons |
> |---|---|
> | then | at that time |

I glared angrily at my boss, and *then* I told him our problems were more serious *than* he suspected.

Fill in the blanks: I went to the front porch to get my newspaper, and _____ I made my breakfast. The news on the front page was no more cheerful _____ it had been the day before.

Write sentences using *than* and *then.*

_____

_____

> **TIP** It might help to remember that *then* is also a time signal.

their	**belonging to them**
there	**at that place; a neutral word used with verbs like** *is,* ***are, was, were, have,*** **and** *had*
they're	**shortened form of** *they are*

The tenants *there* are complaining because *they're* being cheated by *their* landlords.

Fill in the blanks: Indians once lived _____, building a unique culture within _____ cliff cities; now _____ gone.

Write sentences using *their, there,* and *they're.*

_____

_____

threw	**past tense of** *throw*
through	**from one side to the other; finished**

When a character in a movie *threw* a cat *through* the window, I had to close my eyes.

Fill in the blanks: My favorite sweat socks went _____ hundreds of washings before they started to disintegrate; then my mother _____ them away.

Write sentences using *threw* and *through.*

_____

_____

to	a verb part, as in *to smile*; toward, as in "I'm going to heaven."
too	overly, as in "The pizza was too hot"; also, as in "The coffee was hot, too."
two	the number 2

Lola drove *to* the store *to* get some ginger ale. (The first *to* means *toward;* the second *to* is a verb part that goes with *get.*)

The jacket is *too* tight; the pants are tight, *too.* (The first *too* means *overly;* the second *too* means *also.*)

The *two* basketball players leaped for the jump ball. (2)

Fill in the blanks: _____ Arlene, the _____ holidays just meant _____ much company and _____ little rest.

Write sentences using *to, too,* and *two.*

_____

_____

wear	to have on
where	in what place

I work at a nuclear reactor, *where* one must *wear* a radiation-detection badge at all times.

Fill in the blanks: If you _____ your jacket buttoned up, no one will see _____ the stain is.

Write sentences using *wear* and *where.*

_____

_____

weather	atmospheric conditions
whether	if it happens that; in case; if

Because of the threatening *weather,* it's not certain *whether* or not the game will be played.

Fill in the blanks: The _____ today is glorious, but I don't know _____ the water is warm enough for swimming.

Write sentences using *weather* and *whether.*

_____

_____

whose	belonging to whom
who's	shortened form for *who is* and *who has*

The man *who's* the author of the latest diet book is a man *whose* ability to cash in on the latest craze is well known.

Fill in the blanks: Rashad is determined to find out _____ van is in the street and _____ been watching him from it with binoculars.

Write sentences using *whose* and *who's.*

_____

_____

www.mhhe.com/langan

> **your**   belonging to you
>
> **you're**   shortened form of *you are*

Since *your* family has a history of heart disease, *you're* the kind of person who should take extra health precautions.

Fill in the blanks: When _____ always the last person chosen for a

team, _____ self-confidence dwindles away.

Write sentences using *your* and *you're.*

_____

_____

Other Words Frequently Confused

Following is a list of other words that people frequently confuse. Complete the activities for each set of words, and check off and study the ones that give you trouble.

Commonly Confused Words

a	among	desert	learn
an	between	dessert	teach
accept	beside	does	loose
except	besides	dose	lose
advice	can	fewer	quiet
advise	may	less	quite
affect	clothes	former	though
effect	cloths	latter	thought

SECTION 5:
WORD USE

a	Both *a* and *an* are used before other words to mean, approximately, *one*.
an	

Generally you should use *an* before words starting with a vowel (*a, e, i, o, u*):

> an absence   an exhibit   an idol   an offer   an upgrade

Generally you should use *a* before words starting with a consonant (all other letters):

> a pen   a ride   a digital clock   a movie   a neighbor

Fill in the blanks: Lola bought her mother _____ orchid and _____ slinky nightgown for her birthday.

Write sentences using *a* and *an*.

_____

_____

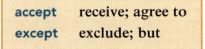

accept	receive; agree to
except	exclude; but

If I *accept* your advice, I'll lose all my friends *except* you.

Fill in the blanks: _____ for one detail, my client is willing to _____ this offer.

Write sentences using *accept* and *except.*

_____

_____

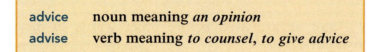

advice	noun meaning *an opinion*
advise	verb meaning *to counsel, to give advice*

Jake never listened to his parents' *advice,* and he ended up listening to a cop *advise* him of his rights.

Fill in the blanks: Nelson's doctor said, "I _____ you to follow my diet rather than take the _____ of the minister who promised you could lose weight through prayer."

Write sentences using *advice* and *advise.*

_____

_____

affect	verb meaning *to influence*
effect	verb meaning *to bring about something*; noun meaning *result*

My sister Nicole cries for *effect,* but my parents caught on and her act no longer *affects* them.

Fill in the blanks: The loud music began to _____ my hearing, creating a high-pitched ringing _____ in my ears.

Write sentences using *affect* and *effect.*

_____

_____

among	implies three or more
between	implies only two

We selfishly divided the box of candy *between* the two of us rather than *among* all the members of the family.

Fill in the blanks: _____ the twenty-five girls on the camping trip, arguments developed only _____ the two counselors.

Write sentences using *among* and *between.*

_____

_____

beside	along the side of
besides	in addition to

Fred sat *beside* Teresa. *Besides* them, there were ten other people at the Tupperware party.

Fill in the blanks: I love this class; _____ the fact that the course has thought-provoking content, I sit _____ a Brad Pitt look-alike.

Write sentences using *beside* and *besides.*

_____

_____

can	refers to the ability to do something
may	refers to permission or possibility

If you *can* work overtime on Saturday, you *may* take Monday off.

Fill in the blanks: When she _____ speak English fluently, she _____ be eligible for that job.

Write sentences using *can* and *may.*

_____

_____

| clothes | articles of dress |
| cloths | pieces of fabric |

I tore up some old *clothes* to use as polishing *cloths*.

Fill in the blanks: I keep some _____ next to me to wipe up any food spills before they reach the baby's _____.

Write sentences using *clothes* and *cloths*.

_____

_____

| desert | noun meaning *a stretch of dry land*; verb meaning to *abandon one's post or duty* |
| dessert | noun meaning *last part of a meal* |

Don't *desert* us now; order a sinful *dessert* along with us.

Fill in the blanks: When it's time to order _____, that man's appetite will never _____ him.

Write sentences using *desert* and *dessert*.

_____

_____

does	form of the verb *do*
dose	an amount of medicine

Elena *does* not realize that a *dose* of brandy is not the best medicine for the flu.

Fill in the blanks: _____ she understand the importance of taking only the prescribed _____?

Write sentences using *does* and *dose*.

_____

_____

fewer	used with things that can be counted
less	refers to amount, value, or degree

I missed *fewer* classes than Rafael, but I wrote *less* effectively than he did.

Fill in the blanks: I've had _____ attacks of nerves since I began drinking _____ coffee.

Write sentences using *fewer* and *less*.

_____

_____

| former | refers to the first of two items named |
| latter | refers to the second of two items named |

I turned down both the service station job and the shipping clerk job; the *former* involved irregular hours and the *latter* offered very low pay.

Fill in the blanks: Howard doesn't like babies or dogs: the _____

cry when they see him and the _____ try to bite him.

Write sentences using *former* and *latter.*

_____

_____

> **TIP** Be sure to distinguish *latter* from *later* (meaning *after some time*).

| learn | to gain knowledge |
| teach | to give knowledge |

After Roz *learns* the new dance, she is going to *teach* it to me.

Fill in the blanks: My dog is very smart; she can _____ any new

trick I _____ her in just minutes.

Write sentences using *learn* and *teach.*

_____

_____

loose	**not fastened; not tight-fitting**
lose	**misplace; fail to win**

I am afraid I'll *lose* my ring: it's too *loose* on my finger.

Fill in the blanks: Lola said to Anthony, "You look dumpy when you wear a

_____ -fitting shirt. You _____ all the wonderful

lines of your chest."

Write sentences using *loose* and *lose*.

_____

_____

quiet	**peaceful**
quite	**entirely; really; rather**

After a busy day, the children were still not *quiet,* and their parents were *quite* tired.

Fill in the blanks: My friends regarded Bob as _____ a catch, but

he was just too _____ for me.

Write sentences using *quiet* and *quite*.

_____

_____

though	despite the fact that
thought	past tense of *think*

Though I enjoyed the dance, I *thought* the cover charge of $5 was too high.

Fill in the blanks: _____ Pam is now content, she once _____ her unhappiness would never end.

Write sentences using *though* and *thought*.

_____

_____

Incorrect Word Forms

Following is a list of incorrect word forms that people sometimes use in their writing. Complete the activities for each word, and check off and study the words that give you trouble.

Incorrect Word Forms

being that	could of	would of
can't hardly	must of	irregardless
couldn't hardly	should of	

being that	Incorrect! Use *because* or *since*.

I'm going to bed now ~~being that~~ *because* I must get up early tomorrow.

Correct the following sentences.

1. Being that she's a year older than I am, Mary thinks she can run my life.
2. I think school will be canceled, being that the bus drivers are on strike.
3. Being that I didn't finish the paper, I didn't go to class.

SECTION 5: WORD USE

| can't hardly | Incorrect! Use *can hardly* or *could hardly*. |
| couldn't hardly | |

can
Small store owners ~~can't~~ hardly afford to offer large discounts.

Correct the following sentences.

1. I can't hardly understand why Nelson would cut class when he's madly in love with the instructor.

2. You can't hardly imagine how I felt when I knocked over my aunt's favorite plant.

3. You couldn't hardly see last night because of the heavy fog.

---

could of	
must of	Incorrect! Use *could have, must have, should have, would have.*
should of	
would of	

have
I should ~~of~~ applied for a loan when my credit was good.

Correct the following sentences.

1. Anita must of gone home from work early.

2. I should of started reading the textbook early in the semester.

3. If the game had been canceled, they would of been very disappointed.

4. If Shirelle had wanted to, she could of come with us.

| irregardless | Incorrect! Use *regardless.* |

Regardless
~~Irregardless~~ of what anyone says, he will not change his mind.

Correct the following sentences.

1. They decided to buy the house irregardless of the price.

2. That company insures people irregardless of their age or state of health.

3. Irregardless of the risk, I started mountain climbing as a hobby.

Review Test 1

These sentences check your understanding of *its, it's; there, their, they're; to, too, two;* and *your, you're.* Underline the correct word in the parentheses. Rather than guess, look back at the explanations of the words when necessary.

1. Some stores will accept (your, you're) credit card but not (your, you're) money.

2. I know (its, it's) late, but (its, it's) important to get this job done properly.

3. (There, Their, They're) is a good baseball game down at the playground, but (there, their, they're) (to, too, two) busy to walk down (there, their, they're).

4. (Its, It's) been two hours since I put the turkey in the oven, but (its, it's) still not ready.

5. (There, Their, They're) going to be away for (to, too, two) weeks and want me to go over to (there, their, they're) yard to water (there, their, they're) rosebushes.

6. (Your, You're) going to have to do a better job on (your, you're) final exam if you expect to pass the course.

7. That issue is (to, too, two) hot for any politician (to, too, two) handle.

8. If (your, you're) hoping to get good grades on (your, you're) essay tests, you need to improve (your, you're) handwriting.

9. (There, Their, They're) planning to trade in (there, their, they're) old car for a new one before taking (there, their, they're) vacation.

10. (Your, You're) going to have to put aside individual differences and play together for the benefit of (your, you're) team.

Review Test 2

The sentences that follow check your understanding of a variety of commonly confused words. Underline the correct word in the parentheses. Rather than guess, look back at the explanations of the words when necessary.

1. I try to get (through, threw) each day without a cigarette. Once I (through, threw) away my latest magazines because their tempting cigarette ads were (affecting, effecting) my resolve.

2. We weren't sure (whether, weather) or not a storm was brewing until several hours had passed. (Then, Than) the air became (quiet, quite), clouds formed, and we (knew, new) enough to run indoors.

3. (Being that, Since) "Stormy (Weather, Whether)" is her favorite song, I (should of, should have) gotten her an album with that song on it.

4. Take my (advice, advise) and hurry down (to, too, two) the radio station. You'll get a (pair, pear) of free tickets to the rock concert.

5. For Lola the (principal, principle) (course, coarse) of the meal—a (desert, dessert) of French vanilla ice cream and blueberry pie—was yet (to, too, two) come.

6. (Its, It's) obvious why people are not eating the cheese; (there, their, they're) frightened by (its, it's) unusual smell.

7. The first (course, coarse) of the meal was soup. Its (principal, principle) ingredient was onion, to which I'm allergic. Trying to be polite, I ate one mouthful, but (than, then) I began to sneeze uncontrollably.

8. As he (passed, past) by the church, he (though, thought) of the Sunday mornings he had spent (there, their, they're) in the (passed, past).

9. The night after I watched the chiller movie, I dreamed that (a, an) gigantic (hole, whole) opened up in the earth, swallowed a whole city, and (than, then) tried to swallow me, (to, too, two).

10. "I'm going to let you be my (knew, new) woman," the man declared. "(Your, You're) my (peace, piece) of property from now on."

   "(Whose, Who's) messed up (your, you're) head?" the woman replied. "I can't believe I (hear, here) you (right, write). (Where, Wear) are you at? I think you have been (affected, effected) by the sun."

Review Test   3

On separate paper, write short sentences using the ten words shown below.

there	then	you're	affect	who's
past	advise	too (meaning *also*)	its	break

MASTERY TEST 1   Commonly Confused Words

Choose the correct words in each sentence and write them in the spaces provided.

_____   1. Last year the (hole, whole) publishing industry seemed to concentrate on
_____   turning out (knew, new) romantic novels.

_____   2. We drove out into the (dessert, desert) (to, too, two) test our dune
_____   buggies.

_____   3. The mechanic did not (know, no) what caused the (break, brake) in the
_____   fuel line of Fred's car.

_____   4. My dog lost (its, it's) tail after being run over by a truck that had lost its
_____   (brakes, breaks).

_____   5. (Irregardless, Regardless) of what her coworkers think, Susan always
_____   wears plain (clothes, cloths) to work.

_____   6. Pete (could of, could have) used the money, but he refused to (accept,
_____   except) the check his parents offered him.

_____   7. Morris can't stand to (hear, here) advice. He lives by the (principal, principle),
_____   "If I make my own decisions, I have only myself to praise or blame."

_____   8. Kevin and Judy have to make (there, their, they're) handwriting neater and
_____   more legible if (there, their, they're) after good grades.

_____   9. Just (among, between) us, I'd advise you not to take Dear Abby's (advice,
_____   advise) as gospel.

_____ 10. That lion over (there, their, they're) clawed at the attendant cleaning (it's,
_____   its) cage.

Commonly Confused Words MASTERY TEST 2

Choose the correct words in each sentence and write them in the spaces provided.

_____   1. Laurie is going to (lose, loose) her job even though she was (among,
_____   between) the ten best salespeople in the company last year.

_____   2. The (affect, effect) of the medication is that all my symptoms (accept,
_____   except) for a slight cough have disappeared.

_____   3. (Its, It's) hard to deny the fact that (there, their, they're) are many fools in
_____   the world.

_____   4. I (would of, would have) tried out for that role, but the director told me
_____   that she had (already, all ready) filled the part.

_____   5. (Being that, Because) you never studied for the course, you (can hardly,
_____   can't hardly) blame the instructor for your F.

_____   6. (There, Their, They're) are only (to, too, two) days left to take advantage
_____   of the store's January white sale.

_____   7. Tony pushed the mower (through, threw) the heavy underbrush on the
_____   back lawn and (than, then) maneuvered it past a huge pile of rocks.

_____   8. (It's, Its) very peaceful and (quite, quiet) along the stretch of the river that
_____   passes near our town.

_____   9. The (weather, whether) was so bad that it caused a one-hour (brake, break)
_____   in the game.

_____   10. Marilyn changed her seat to get away from the (to, too, two) (coarse,
_____   course) people on the bus.

NAME: _____

DATE: _____

Commonly Confused Words

Cross out the two mistakes in usage in each sentence. Then write the correct words in the spaces provided.

_____

_____

1. A stranger in an black suit knocked on my neighbor's door and handed him a plane manila envelope.

_____

_____

2. Its not easy to find food in that refrigerator because it's shelves are crowded and poorly lit.

_____

_____

3. If this cough syrup dose its job, your going to be feeling better very soon.

_____

_____

4. Our psychology instructor should of canceled the last class before the holiday, for less than six students showed up.

_____

_____

5. Do you know that the cactus plant over their is the basis for a delicious desert?

_____

_____

6. When he tries to learn her how to drive, she sets up a mental block and refuses to except his instructions.

_____

_____

7. One affect of the strong wind is that some lose roof shingles have blown off the house.

_____

_____

8. Too get to the Washington Monument, you must ride two buses and take a subway, to.

_____

_____

9. I can't hardly recommend you buy that house, for there are termite wholes in the basement planks.

_____

_____

10. If the principle ingredient in that stew is octopus, I don't know whether I'll accept you're invitation to try it.

NAME: _____

DATE: _____

Commonly Confused Words MASTERY TEST 4

Cross out the two mistakes in usage in each sentence. Then write the correct words in the spaces provided.

_____   1. Beside the twins, the Fosters have three other children—more then anyone
_____   else on the block.

_____   2. Leo should of realized by now that he could have past the course by
_____   studying harder.

_____   3. Its to bad that the pair of you didn't apply for the job there.
_____

_____   4. Nothing was less appealing to Joel then the possibility of excepting the
_____   advice I had given him.

_____   5. Regardless of what you say, I believe we could of learned our collie how
_____   to be a good watchdog.

_____   6. I pursue both rug making and gardening: the latter allows me to be
_____   creative and the former allows me to enjoy the peace of nature.

_____   7. I'll be quiet surprised if the promise of a delicious desert doesn't make my
_____   little sister agree to be quiet.

_____   8. Being that it's sinking into the water, their must be too many people in the
_____   boat.

_____   9. You're new car has been inspected and registered, so it's already to
_____   drive.

_____   10. Whether or not I take that course depends on whose teaching it and how
_____   much righting is required.

Effective Word Choice

Introductory Activity

Write a check mark beside the sentence in each pair that makes more effective and appropriate use of words.

1. After a bummer of a movie, we pigged out on a pizza. _____

   After a disappointing movie, we devoured a pizza. _____

2. Feeling blue about the death of his best friend, Tennyson wrote the tearjerker "In Memoriam." _____

   Mourning the death of his best friend, Tennyson wrote the moving poem "In Memoriam." _____

3. The personality adjustment inventories will be administered on Wednesday in the Student Center. _____

   Psychological tests will be given on Wednesday in the Student Center. _____

4. The referee in the game, in my personal opinion, made the right decision in the situation. _____

   I think the referee made the right decision. _____

Now see if you can circle the correct number in each case:

Pair (1, 2, 3, 4) contains a sentence with slang; pair (1, 2, 3, 4) contains a sentence with a cliché; pair (1, 2, 3, 4) contains a sentence with pretentious words; and pair (1, 2, 3, 4) contains a wordy sentence.

Answers are on page 575.

Choose your words carefully when you write. Always take the time to think about your word choices, rather than simply using the first word that comes to mind. You want to develop the habit of selecting words that are appropriate and exact for your purposes. One way you can show sensitivity to language is by avoiding slang, clichés, pretentious words, and wordiness.

Slang

We often use slang expressions when we talk because they are so vivid and colorful. However, slang is usually out of place in formal writing. Here are some examples of slang expressions:

www.mhhe.com/langan

> Last night's party was a *real train wreck.*
>
> I don't want to *lay a guilt trip* on you.
>
> My boss *dissed* me last night when he said I was a bad employee.
>
> Dad *flipped out* when he learned that Jan had *totaled* the car.
>
> Someone *ripped off* Ken's new Adidas running shoes from his locker.
>
> After the game, we *stuffed our faces* at the diner.
>
> I finally told my parents to *get off my case.*
>
> The movie really *grossed me out.*

Slang expressions have a number of drawbacks. They go out of date quickly, they become tiresome if used excessively in writing, and they may communicate clearly to some readers but not to others. Also, the use of slang can be an evasion of the specific details that are often needed to make one's meaning clear in writing. For example, in "Last night's party was a real train wreck," the writer has not provided the specific details about the party necessary for us to understand the statement clearly. Was it the setting, the food and drink (or lack of them), the guests, the music, or the hosts that made the party such a dreadful experience? In general, then, you should avoid slang in your writing. If you are in doubt about whether an expression is slang, it may help to check a recently published hardbound dictionary.

Rewrite the following sentences, replacing the italicized slang words with more formal ones.

1

EXAMPLE

I was *so beat* Friday night that I decided *to ditch* the birthday party.

I was so exhausted Friday night that I decided not to go to the

birthday party.

1. If you don't *get your act together* in this course, you're going to be *blown away* by the midterm exam.

    _____

    _____

2. Last year, Tarah was *psyched* about her job, but now she's so *fed up* with her boss that she wants to quit.

    _____

    _____

3. The football game was a *real wipeout;* we *got our butts kicked.*

    _____

    _____

4. If people keep *bad-mouthing* Gene, soon no one will *hang out* with him.

    _____

    _____

5. I *pushed the panic button* when the instructor called on me. My brain went *out to lunch.*

    _____

    _____

www.mhhe.com/langan

Clichés

Clichés are expressions that have been worn out through constant use. Some typical clichés are listed on the following page.

Common Clichés

all work and no play	sad but true
at a loss for words	saw the light
better late than never	short and sweet
drop in the bucket	sigh of relief
easier said than done	singing the blues
had a hard time of it	taking a big chance
in the nick of time	time and time again
in this day and age	too close for comfort
it dawned on me	too little, too late
it goes without saying	took a turn for the worse
last but not least	under the weather
make ends meet	where he (*or* she) is coming from
needless to say	word to the wise
on top of the world	work like a dog

Clichés are common in speech but make your writing seem tired and stale. Also, they are often an evasion of the specific details that you must work to provide in your writing. You should, then, avoid clichés and try to express your meaning in fresh, original ways.

Underline the cliché in each of the following sentences. Then substitute specific, fresh words for the trite expression.

Practice 2

EXAMPLE

My parents supported me through some trying times.
rough years

1. The physical exam didn't shed any light on why I was getting headaches.

   _____

2. I heaved a sigh of relief when I learned my final grade for the course was a B.

   _____

3. The record began selling like hotcakes as soon as it was released.

   _____

4. Helen could not have cared less whom Rodney was dating.

_____

5. Since my mother was feeling under the weather, she didn't go to work.

_____

Practice

3
Write a short paragraph describing the kind of day you had. Try to put as many clichés as possible into your writing. For example, "I had a long hard day. I had a lot to get done, and I kept my nose to the grindstone." By making yourself aware of clichés in this way, you should lessen the chance that they will appear in your writing.

Pretentious Words

Some people feel they can improve their writing by using fancy, elevated words rather than more simple, natural words. They use artificial and stilted language that more often obscures their meaning than communicates it clearly. Here are some unnatural-sounding sentences:

The football combatants left the gridiron.

His instructional technique is a very positive one.

At the counter, we inquired about the arrival time of the aircraft.

I observed the perpetrator of the robbery depart from the retail establishment.

The same thoughts can be expressed more clearly and effectively by using plain, natural language, as below:

The football players left the field.

He is a good instructor.

At the counter, we asked when the plane would arrive.

I saw the robber leave the store.

Following is a list of some other inflated words and the simple words that could replace them.

Inflated Words	Simpler Words
component	part
delineate	describe
facilitate	help
finalize	finish
initiate	begin
manifested	shown
subsequent to	after
to endeavor	to try
transmit	send

Cross out the two pretentious words in each sentence. Then substitute clear, simple language for the pretentious words.

Practice

4

EXAMPLE

Sally was ~~terminated~~ from her ~~employment~~.
Sally was fired from her job.

1. My television receiver is not operative.

    _____

2. We made an expedition to the mall to see the new fall apparel.

    _____

3. José indicated an aversion to fish.

    _____

4. The fans expressed their displeasure when the pitcher threw the ball erratically.

    _____

5. How long have you resided in that municipality?

    _____

Wordiness

Wordiness—using more words than necessary to express a meaning—is often a sign of lazy or careless writing. Your readers may resent the extra time and energy they must spend when you have not done the work needed to make your writing direct and concise.

Following is a list of some wordy expressions that could be reduced to single words.

www.mhhe.com/langan

Wordy Form	Short Form
a large number of	many
a period of a week	a week
arrive at an agreement	agree
at an earlier point in time	before
at the present time	now
big in size	big
due to the fact that	because
during the time that	while
five in number	five
for the reason that	because
good benefit	benefit
in every instance	always
in my opinion	I think
in the event that	if
in the near future	soon
in this day and age	today
is able to	can
large in size	large
plan ahead for the future	plan
postponed until later	postponed
red in color	red
return back	return

Here are examples of wordy sentences:

At this point in time in our country, the amount of violence seems to be increasing every day.

I called to the children repeatedly to get their attention, but my shouts did not get any response from them.

Omitting needless words improves these sentences:

Violence is increasing in our country.

I called to the children repeatedly, but they didn't respond.

Rewrite the following sentences, omitting needless words.

EXAMPLE

Starting as of the month of June, I will be working at the store on a full-time basis.

As of June, I will be working at the store full time.

1. Because of the fact that it was raining, I didn't go shopping.

   _____

2. As far as I am concerned, in my opinion I do not feel that prostitution should be legalized.

   _____

3. Please do not hesitate to telephone me if you would like me to come into your office for an interview.

   _____

4. During the time that I was sick and out of school, I missed a total of three math tests.

   _____

5. Well-paying jobs are all too few and far between unless a person has a high degree of training.

   _____

Review Test   1

Certain words are italicized in the following sentences. In the space provided, identify whether the words are slang (*S*), clichés (*C*), or pretentious words (*PW*). Then replace them with more effective words.

_____ 1. If the boss starts *putting heat* on me again, I'm going to quit.

   _____

_____ 2. Because of the rain, I wore a jacket that *has seen better days.*

   _____

_____ 3. Ted won't help us unless we offer *a monetary reward.*

   _____

——————— 4. When my younger brother did not get home from the party until 2 A.M., my mother decided *to put her foot down.*

_____

——————— 5. My upset stomach was *alleviated* by the antacid.

_____

——————— 6. The vacation spot was a *total ripoff;* the weather and the food were both *the pits.*

_____

——————— 7. Phan *saw the error of his ways* and began to work harder.

_____

——————— 8. I needed *a respite from my exertions* after I finished typing the long report.

_____

——————— 9. I *jumped for joy* when I heard about the promotion.

_____

——————— 10. *You could have wiped me off the floor* when I learned that my old girlfriend was on drugs.

_____

Review Test 2

Rewrite the following sentences, omitting needless words.

1. At this point in time, I cannot say with any degree of certainty that I am planning to participate in the blood drive.

_____

_____

2. Due to the fact that there was no consensus of opinion, the committee agreed that it should meet again.

_____

_____

3. As far as Jay is concerned, he thinks that a working day of eight hours of work is too demanding for the average American worker.

_____

_____

4. For the price of $600, you can purchase outright this car of mine.

_____

_____

5. Without a doubt, the importance of the question of abortion as an issue cannot be denied.

_____

_____

NAME: _____

DATE: _____

Effective Word Choice

Certain words are italicized in the following sentences. In the space at the left, identify whether these words are slang (*S*), clichés (*C*), or pretentious words (*PW*). Then replace the words with more effective diction.

_____ 1. The man in the house on the corner *kicked the bucket* last night.

_____

_____ 2. That book is by a millionaire who *didn't have a dime to his name* as a boy.

_____

_____ 3. Marty has always *endeavored* to excel in his college courses.

_____

_____ 4. The boss told Bob to *get his act together* or to resign.

_____

_____ 5. I have a large *quantity* of chores to do this weekend.

_____

_____ 6. Our team's chances of winning the league championship are *as dead as a doornail.*

_____

_____ 7. The players were nervous; they didn't want to *blow* the championship game.

_____

_____ 8. Donna *came out of her shell* after she joined the theater group at school.

_____

_____ 9. When Julie's marriage *hit the rocks,* she decided to see a therapist.

_____

_____ 10. Many people today *entertain anxieties* about our country's economy.

_____

Effective Word Choice MASTERY TEST 2

Certain words are italicized in the following sentences. In the space at the left, identify whether these words are slang (*S*), clichés (*C*), or pretentious words (*PW*). Then replace the words with more effective diction.

_____ 1. Kwan thought it was *too good to be true* when the boss told her to go home early.

_____

_____ 2. I won't be coming; square dancing just *isn't my thing*.

_____

_____ 3. Passing the course *is contingent* upon my grade in the final exam.

_____

_____ 4. I am *sick and tired of* her dog's digging up my backyard.

_____

_____ 5. If the boss starts *putting heat on me* again, I'm going to ask for a transfer.

_____

_____ 6. Long political speeches *bore me to tears*.

_____

_____ 7. I got so tired at Neil's party that I had to *crash* on his living room couch.

_____

_____ 8. Nick scrubbed the countertop with Ajax until it was *clean as a whistle*.

_____

_____ 9. Margery is embarrassed about the fact that, after high school, she did not go on to *an institution of higher learning*.

_____

_____ 10. My husband and I have both lost weight as a result of our *reducing regimens*.

_____

NAME: _____

DATE: _____

Effective Word Choice

The following sentences include examples of wordiness. Rewrite the sentences in the space provided, omitting needless words.

1. The fact of the matter is that I did not remember that I had an appointment to meet with you.

   _____

   _____

2. To make a long story short, my brother and his wife are going to go about getting a divorce.

   _____

   _____

3. At our company there are at present two coffee breaks, with each of them fifteen minutes long.

   _____

   _____

4. At this point in time, Lou would be wise to start working on the paper he has to write for English.

   _____

   _____

5. Permit us to take this opportunity to inform you that your line of credit has been increased.

   _____

   _____

NAME: _____

DATE: _____

Effective Word Choice **MASTERY TEST 4**

The following sentences include examples of wordiness. Rewrite the sentences in the space provided, omitting needless words.

1. In my opinion, I think that all people, men and women both, should be treated exactly alike.

   _____

   _____

2. The exercises that Susan does every day of the week give her more energy with which to deal with everyday life.

   _____

   _____

3. I hereby wish to inform you in this letter that I will not be renewing my lease for the apartment.

   _____

   _____

4. All American citizens should consider it their duty to go out and vote on the day that has been scheduled to be Election Day every year.

   _____

   _____

5. In view of the fact that miracle drugs exist in our science today, our lifetimes will be extended longer than our grandparents'.

   _____

   _____

Reinforcement of the Skills

Introduction

To reinforce the sentence skills presented in Part Two, this part of the book—Part Three—provides combined mastery tests, editing and proofreading tests, and combined editing tests. The *combined mastery tests* will strengthen your understanding of important related skills. *Editing and proofreading tests* offer practice in finding and correcting one kind of error in a brief passage. *Combined editing tests* then offer similar practice—except that each contains a variety of mistakes. Five of these tests feature "real world" documents—résumés, cover letters, and a job application—so you can apply your skills to situations you are likely to encounter outside the classroom. The tests in Part Three will help you become a skilled editor and proofreader. All too often, students can correct mistakes in practice sentences but are unable to do so in their own writing. You must learn to look carefully for sentence-skills errors and to make close checking a habit.

Look at the photos above and think about someone who has helped you in any way. It may be a family member who has always supported you, a friend who helped you through a difficult time, a teacher who inspired you, or even a stranger whose act of kindness you will never forget. Write a letter to this person explaining how he or she made a difference in your life and why you are so grateful. Don't forget to proofread your letter for sentence-skills mistakes. Use the Checklist of Sentence Skills on the inside back cover of your book.

Combined Mastery Tests

Can you find the sentence-skills errors in the two signs above? Rewrite the wording of each sign so that it is grammatically correct. Would you pay less attention to a sign that was confusing or grammatically incorrect? Why or why not?

NAME: _____

DATE: _____

Fragments and Run-Ons

Each of the word groups below is numbered. In the space provided, write *C* if a word group is a complete sentence, write *F* if it is a fragment, and write *R-O* if it is a run-on.

1. _____

2. _____

3. _____

4. _____

5. _____

6. _____

7. _____

8. _____

9. _____

10. _____

11. _____

12. _____

13. _____

14. _____

15. _____

16. _____

17. _____

18. _____

19. _____

20. _____

[1]The cheap motel room smelled musty. [2]As if the window had never been opened. [3]I snapped on the light, a roach sauntered across the floor. [4]Although the bed looked lumpy. [5]I flopped on it gratefully, totally exhausted. [6]I needed about ten hours' sleep. [7]Then I would get something to eat. [8]And start to plan how to get my life going in the right direction again.

[9]As the rest of the class scribbled furiously during the lecture. [10]Gene doodled in his notebook. [11]Weird stick figures marched across the page odd flowers blossomed on its borders. [12]Because he was so involved in his fantasy world. [13]Gene continued to draw. [14]After the lecture had ended.

[15]Gripping the scissors in one hand and her son's shoulder in the other. [16]Margaret attempted to give the squirming toddler a haircut. [17]Waving his fist angrily. [18]The boy knocked the shears out of his mother's hand. [19]The shears skidded across the floor they headed for the family's unsuspecting dog. [20]Who jumped backward suddenly and began to bark loudly.

NAME: _____

DATE: _____

Fragments and Run-Ons

In the space provided, indicate whether each item below contains a fragment (*F*) or a run-on (*R-O*). Then correct the error.

_____ 1. Since the game ended in a tie. The teams had to go into sudden-death over-time. Not a single fan left the stadium.

_____ 2. Nick and Fran buy only name brands at the store, they feel economy brands are lower not just in price but in quality. I disagree with them.

_____ 3. The fire drills in school gave a welcome break to the daily routine. Students moved quickly and obediently. Clearing the building in a hurry.

_____ 4. Because the miracle soles on Fred's shoes have never worn down. He has used the same pair for the last four years. Martha is sick of looking at them.

_____ 5. An astrologer read my chart I didn't believe her. My friend was born on the same day, but we have completely different personalities.

_____ 6. My sister parked her cart in the checkout line at the market. Then dashed off to get final items on her list. I hate people who do that.

_____ 7. When Laurie left for college, her mother was devastated, she was not used to a lonely house. Her solution was to return to school herself.

_____ 8. Trevor and Karen didn't have time to cook dinner. They stopped at McDonald's. To pick up Big Macs.

_____ 9. Because Harvey is only five feet three inches, he has trouble getting dates. He often fantasizes about being a seven-foot-tall basketball player then all the women in the world would look up to him.

_____ 10. Until I was twelve, I believed there really was a tooth fairy. She would leave a dollar under my pillow. Whenever I lost a tooth.

NAME: _____

DATE: _____

Verbs COMBINED MASTERY TEST 1

Each sentence contains a mistake involving (1) standard English or irregular verb forms, (2) subject-verb agreement, or (3) consistent verb tense. Cross out the incorrect verb and write the correct form in the space provided.

_____ 1. The quarterback had broke most of the school's passing records by his senior year.

_____ 2. The cost of the transmission and brake repairs are more than the car's worth.

_____ 3. The more my instructor tried to explain the material and the more he writes on the board, the more confused I got.

_____ 4. Nobody on the police force know the identity of the informer.

_____ 5. Lola likes to use lip gloss but hated the way it stains her fingers and never seems to come off.

_____ 6. Each of Ramona's boyfriends think he is the only man in her life.

_____ 7. The socks I bought at that store have wore thin after only three months.

_____ 8. Out of my little brother's mouth comes some of the most amazing words I have ever heard.

_____ 9. As soon as the store opened, customers race through the doors and hurried to the bargain racks.

_____ 10. We have not ate out at a restaurant since my wife lost her job.

NAME: _____

DATE: _____

Verbs

Each sentence contains a mistake involving (1) standard English or irregular verb forms, (2) subject-verb agreement, or (3) consistent verb tense. Cross out the incorrect verb and write the correct form in the space provided.

_____ 1. Lola was stang by some kind of bug during her hike in the woods.

_____ 2. My sister and I often gets into an argument at the dinner table.

_____ 3. The mechanic told me my car was going to be ready by noon, but he finishes working on it at five o'clock.

_____ 4. I had not did my math homework, so I was sure my instructor would give a surprise quiz.

_____ 5. Roaring down a quiet street at fifty miles an hour were Daisy on her new Honda.

_____ 6. You should have knowed better than to trust your little brother to deliver the message.

_____ 7. Carl watched suspiciously as a strange car drives back and forth in front of his house.

_____ 8. I should have brung an extra pen to the exam.

_____ 9. When Lola saw the children skipping home from school clutching their drawings, she remembered when she use to do the same thing.

_____ 10. Rob Revolting, lead singer of the Deadly Poisons, wears a black satin jumpsuit with a silver skull and crossbones on the front when he perform.

NAME: _____

DATE: _____

Pronouns **COMBINED MASTERY TEST 1**

Choose the sentence in each pair that uses pronouns correctly. Then write the letter of that sentence in the space provided at the left.

_____ 1. a. When I took my son to his first basketball game, he was amazed at how tall they were.

b. When I took my son to his first basketball game, he was amazed at how tall the players were.

_____ 2. a. You can't play the new software on the iMac because it's defective.

b. You can't play the new software on the iMac because the software is defective.

_____ 3. a. Each one of the players on the women's softball team felt proud about her performance in the championship game.

b. Each one of the players on the women's softball team felt proud about their performance in the championship game.

_____ 4. a. I've learned a lot about biking from Eddie, who is a much better biker than me.

b. I've learned a lot about biking from Eddie, who is a much better biker than I.

_____ 5. a. I wanted to browse through the store, but in every department a salesperson came up and asked to help you.

b. I wanted to browse through the store, but in every department a salesperson came up and asked to help me.

Pronouns

In the spaces provided, write *PE* for each of the nine sentences that contain pronoun errors. Write *C* for the sentence that uses pronouns correctly. Then cross out each pronoun error and write the correction above it.

_____ 1. Diane received in the mail an ad that said you could make $1,000 a month addressing envelopes.

_____ 2. We refereed the game ourselfs, for no officials were available.

_____ 3. Before any more time is wasted, you and me must have a serious talk.

_____ 4. One of the Boy Scouts left some live embers burning in his campfire.

_____ 5. Everyone who works in the company must have their chest X-rayed every two years.

_____ 6. The instructor gave George and I a warning look.

_____ 7. Gina wanted to run in for some bread and milk, but it was so crowded that she decided not to bother.

_____ 8. If them eggs have a bad smell, throw them away.

_____ 9. When I visited a friend at the hospital, you had to pay two dollars just to use the parking lot.

_____ 10. Trevor called Franco at work to say that his father had been in an accident.

Faulty Modifiers and Parallelism

In the spaces at the left, indicate whether each sentence contains a misplaced modifier (*MM*), a dangling modifier (*DM*), or faulty parallelism (*FP*). Then correct the error in the space under the sentence.

_____ 1. My parents like to visit auctions, eat Mexican food, and watching horror movies.

_____

_____ 2. An old wreck of wars past, Admiral Hawkeye inspected the ship.

_____

_____ 3. I notified the police that my house had been burglarized by phone.

_____

_____ 4. Dulled by Novocaine, the dentist pulled my tooth.

_____

_____ 5. With sweaty hands and a voice that trembled, Alice read her paper aloud.

_____

_____ 6. At the age of six, my mother bought me a chemistry set.

_____

_____ 7. Cut and infected, Reggie took his dog to the vet.

_____

_____ 8. My neighbor mowed the lawn perspiring heavily.

_____

_____ 9. Midori decided to start a garden while preparing dinner.

_____

_____ 10. To earn extra money, Terry types term papers and is working at the Point Diner.

_____

NAME: _____

DATE: _____

Faulty Modifiers and Parallelism

In the spaces at the left, indicate whether each sentence contains a misplaced modifier (*MM*), a dangling modifier (*DM*), or faulty parallelism (*FP*). Then correct the error in the space under the sentence.

_____ 1. By studying harder, Barry's grades improved.

_____

_____ 2. We put the food back in the knapsack that we had not eaten.

_____

_____ 3. My doctor advised extra sleep, nourishing food, and that I should exercise regularly.

_____

_____ 4. Smelling up the room, I quickly put the trout in the freezer.

_____

_____ 5. Buying a foreign car will cause more family arguments for me than to buy an American car.

_____

_____ 6. Marty is the guy carrying packages with curly brown hair.

_____

_____ 7. My hopes for retirement are good health, having plenty of money, and beautiful companions.

_____

_____ 8. Filled with cigarette butts and used tea bags, I washed the disgusting cups.

_____

_____ 9. I asked Vicky to see a movie with me nervously.

_____

_____ 10. Frightened by the rising crime rate, an alarm system was installed in the house.

_____

SCORE

Number Correct

_____ x 10

_____ %

NAME: _____

DATE: _____

Capital Letters and Punctuation

COMBINED MASTERY TEST 1

Each of the following sentences contains an error in capitalization or punctuation. Refer to the box below to write, in the space provided, the letter identifying the error. Then correct the error.

a. missing capital	c. missing quotation marks
b. missing apostrophe	d. missing comma

_____ 1. I wanted desperately to scratch the scab on my hand but I didn't want to take the risk of infecting it.

_____ 2. "Don't drive too close to the edge of the prairie, the old prospector warned the tourists, "or you're liable to fall off."

_____ 3. Did you know they're going to tear down the old school on second Street and put a McDonald's there?

_____ 4. The hamsters eyes glowed when some fresh lettuce was put into its cage.

_____ 5. Because the electric can opener was broken Fred was unable to make himself some chicken noodle soup.

_____ 6. Its not going to be easy to find a job that both pays well and involves interesting work.

_____ 7. The woman was asked why she wanted to be a mortician. "I enjoy working with people, she replied.

_____ 8. For lonely uncle Russ, holidays are the worst time of the year.

_____ 9. Some people believe that voting should be mandatory not merely encouraged, in the United States.

_____ 10. Florence said to the woman behind her in the theater, "will you shut your mouth, please?"

NAME: _____

DATE: _____

Capital Letters and Punctuation

Each of the following sentences contains an error in capitalization or punctuation. Refer to the box below to write, in the space provided, the letter identifying the error. Then correct the error.

a. missing capital	c. missing quotation marks
b. missing apostrophe	d. missing comma

_____ 1. There is nothing on the menu of that restaurant," Nick said, "that would not cause nausea in laboratory mice."

_____ 2. If you'll hold this package shut for me I'll be able to do a better job of taping it closed.

_____ 3. Lolas yoga class has been canceled this week, so she's decided to go running instead.

_____ 4. Maria said, "the directions called for a pinch of sugar in the stew, but I accidentally added a teaspoonful."

_____ 5. Roger just got a good job offer today so he won't have to stand in the unemployment line anymore.

_____ 6. Unless I start studying soon, I'm going to have to repeat sociology 101.

_____ 7. "Did you hear the news? Tina asked Danny. "A man who was attempting to walk around the world drowned today."

_____ 8. If youre going to stay up late, be sure to turn down the heat before going to bed.

_____ 9. I was able to return the hair dryer, even though I hadn't saved the receipt to the Sears catalog store.

_____ 10. The company has to pay double time when it calls employees in to work an extra shift on sunday.

SCORE
Number Correct

_____ x 10

_____ %

Word Use COMBINED MASTERY TEST 1

Each of the following sentences contains a mistake identified in the left-hand margin. Underline the mistake and then correct it in the space provided.

Slang

1. Ralph was canned from his job yesterday for sleeping at his desk.

_____

Wordiness

2. I'm in college for the purpose of getting a degree in data processing.

_____

Cliché

3. Nick and Fran were able to depend upon their parents in their hour of need.

_____

Pretentious language

4. Eric improved his math skills by utilizing the tutoring center at school.

_____

Adverb error

5. Wilma has not done bad in her math course, even though she missed a week of classes because of illness.

_____

Error in comparison

6. This year my garden has been producing the abundantest crop of weeds in human history.

_____

Confused word

7. It's the second time our dog has broken it's chain and run away.

_____

Confused word

8. The doctor was concerned that the new allergy drug would effect my sense of balance.

_____

Confused word

9. There not too friendly in that store, but their merchandise is sold at bargain prices.

_____

Confused word

10. Whitney plans to move to an efficiency apartment hear in the city.

_____

NAME: _____

DATE: _____

COMBINED MASTERY TEST 2 Word Use

Each of the following sentences contains a mistake identified in the left-hand margin. Underline the mistake and then correct it in the space provided.

Slang

1. That company has spent millions to hype its new shampoo.

_____

Wordiness

2. I plan to quit my job because of the fact that my boss treats me unfairly.

_____

Cliché

3. The catcher and pitcher had a sneaking suspicion that their signs were being stolen.

_____

Pretentious language

4. Bonnie wants to procure a DVD player as soon as she has the money.

_____

Adverb error

5. Phil and Nancy are taking their relationship too serious, considering that they're still teenagers.

_____

Error in comparison

6. The book report for my psychology class is the most bad paper I've ever written.

_____

Confused word

7. Football has always been the principle sport at our school.

_____

Confused word

8. You're children are the ones who broke my front gate, so you're going to pay for the damage.

_____

Confused word

9. Whose the professor whose courses involve a lot of field trips?

_____

Confused word

10. Classes in college are far less regimented then the ones in high school.

_____

Editing and Proofreading Tests

Advertisements, music videos, and many popular TV shows suggest to us that our culture values physical beauty, strength, and wealth. Just look at the images pictured above. But are these the most important qualities a person can have? Can you think of others that are more important? Choose the three qualities that you think are most important for a person to have and write a paragraph in which you show why the three traits you chose are so critical.

The passages in this section can be used in either of two ways:

As Editing Tests

Each passage contains a number of mistakes involving a single sentence skill. For example, the first passage (on page 470) contains five sentence fragments. Your instructor may ask you to proofread the passage to locate the five fragments. Spaces are provided at the bottom of the passage for you to indicate which word groups are fragments. Your instructor may also have you correct the errors, either in the text itself or on separate paper. Depending on how well you do, you may also be asked to edit the second and third passages for fragments.

There are two passages for each skill area, and there are twelve skills covered in all. Here is a list of the skill areas:

Test 1	Fragments
Test 2	Fragments
Test 3	Run-Ons (Fused Sentences)
Test 4	Run-Ons (Comma Splices)
Test 5	Standard English Verbs
Test 6	Irregular Verbs
Test 7	Faulty Parallelism
Test 8	Capital Letters
Test 9	Apostrophes
Test 10	Quotation Marks
Test 11	Commas
Test 12	Commonly Confused Words

As Guided Composition Activities

To give practice in proofreading as well, your instructor may ask you to do more than correct the skill mistakes in each passage. You may be asked to rewrite the passage, correcting it for skill mistakes *and also* copying the rest of the passage perfectly. Should you miss one skill mistake or make even one copying mistake (for example, omitting a word, dropping a verb ending, misspelling a word, or misplacing an apostrophe), you may be asked to rewrite a different passage that deals with the same skill.

Here is how you would proceed. You would start with sentence fragments, rewriting the first passage, proofreading your paper carefully, and then showing it to your instructor. He or she will check it quickly to see that all the fragments have been corrected and that no copying mistakes have been made. If the passage is error-free, you can proceed to run-ons.

If even a single mistake is made, the instructor may question you briefly to see if you recognize and understand it. (Perhaps he or she will put a check beside the line in which the mistake appears, and then ask if you can correct it.) You may then be asked to write the second passage under a particular skill.

You will complete the program in guided composition when you successfully work through all twelve skills. Completing the twelve skills will strengthen your understanding of the skills, increase your ability to transfer the skills to actual writing situations, and markedly improve your proofreading.

In working on the passages, note the following points:

a. For each skill, you will be told how many mistakes appear in the passages. If you have trouble finding the mistakes, turn back and review the pages in this book that explain the skill in question.

b. Here is an effective way to go about correcting a passage. First, read it over quickly. Look for and mark off mistakes in the skill area involved. For example, in your first reading of a passage that has five fragments, you may locate and mark only three fragments. Next, reread the passage carefully so you can find the remaining errors in the skill in question. Finally, make notes in the margin about how to correct each mistake. Only at this point should you begin to rewrite the passage.

c. Be sure to proofread with care after you finish a passage. Go over your writing word for word, looking for careless errors. Remember that you may be asked to do another passage involving the same skill if you make even one mistake.

NAME: _____

DATE: _____

Fragments

Mistakes in each passage: 5

Passage A

¹For her biology class, Ann lay stretched out on the grass in the park. ²Taking notes on the insect life she observed around her. ³First, a clear-winged bug swooped in for a landing. ⁴And swayed on a blade of grass nearby. ⁵Next, landing suddenly on her hand, a ladybug. ⁶Ann could count the number of dots on its tiny, speckled body as it crawled around and under her fingers. ⁷When the ladybug left, Ann picked up a low, flat rock. ⁸Three black crickets slithered quickly away. ⁹Seeking shelter under other rocks or leaves. ¹⁰She watched one camouflage itself under a leaf. ¹¹Carefully, she removed the leaf and watched the cricket dig deeper into the underbrush. ¹²It kept crawling away from the light. ¹³Ann moved her eyes away for a second as a car went by. ¹⁴When she looked back. ¹⁵The cricket had disappeared.

Word groups with fragments: _____   _____   _____   _____   _____

Passage B

[1]One factor that causes you to forget is lack of motivation. [2]If you have no reason for remembering certain information. [3]You will probably forget it. [4]Dr. Joyce Brothers, a prominent psychologist, relates how she memorized facts on boxing. [5]To win $64,000 on a television quiz show. [6]She and her husband were college students at the time. [7]And, like most students, could use some extra money. [8]She was not as interested in boxing as she was in winning the money. [9]After she had won the money and used her memorized information for its purpose. [10]She promptly forgot the facts. [11]Another factor in forgetting is interference. [12]Previous learning can interfere with new learning. [13]Especially if there are similarities between the two. [14]If you have previously studied traditional math, you may experience difficulty learning the new math.

Word groups with fragments: ——— ——— ——— ——— ———

NAME: _____

DATE: _____

Fragments

Mistakes in each passage: 5

Passage A

[1]The best vacation I ever had was when my friends and I rented a big old beach house in Ocean City. [2]Because it had twelve rooms. [3]Each of us had plenty of room to himself. [4]The house was located right on the beach, so all we had to do in the morning was step out the front door. [5]To be right in the middle of the action. [6]As we spent our time playing volleyball and lying in the sun, the days passed by in a blur of contentment. [7]For lunch we strolled up to the boardwalk. [8]To buy hot dogs with sauerkraut heaped on top. [9]After lunch we returned to our spot on the beach to read or take a nap. [10]When the sun got too hot in the afternoon, we retreated to the house. [11]Where we sat in comfortable old rocking chairs on the shady wraparound porch. [12]Sitting there, we could relax and watch the action on the beach. [13]With a cool drink in hand. [14]I felt as though the summer just might last forever.

Word groups with fragments: _____   _____   _____   _____   _____

Passage B

[1]Last Saturday I tried to be a good friend. [2]And agreed to help my friend Lamar move into his new apartment. [3]What was supposed to take only an hour or two ended up lasting the entire day. [4]Although Lamar's idea was to save money by doing the job himself. [5]I think he spent almost as much as it would have cost to hire professionals. [6]I arrived at Lamar's apartment at eight o'clock, but he was still sound asleep. [7]Stumbling around with his eyes half closed. [8]Lamar wasted a half hour before he finally got ready. [9]Then he and I drove to the truck-rental agency. [10]Before he knew what had happened to him, Lamar agreed to buy packing cartons, tape, and twine. [11]He also paid extra for a hand truck to use in moving the refrigerator. [12]Finally seated behind the wheel of the rental truck. [13]Lamar couldn't start it. [14]Forcing the attendant to come out and start it for us. [15]On the way back to the apartment, Lamar stopped at his parents' house to borrow money to pay for the truck. [16]The rest of the day didn't move any faster than the morning. [17]It was dark by the time we finished, and I was left wondering where my Saturday had gone.

Word groups with fragments: _____ _____ _____ _____ _____

NAME: _____

DATE: _____

Run-Ons (Fused Sentences)

Mistakes in each passage: 5

Passage A

¹Someday soon you may not have to get up in the morning and go to work you will, instead, work at home in front of your very own computer. ²Already many American workers are "telecommuters" they do at home what they used to do in the office. ³For instance, one secretary takes dictation from her boss over the telephone. ⁴Then she types the letters on her computer. ⁵Stockbrokers or sales personnel can place orders and keep records right in their living rooms all they need is a computer and Internet connection. ⁶A few banks and consulting firms give their employees a choice of working in the office or at home many other businesses as well plan to try this idea. ⁷Telecommuting has many advantages some of them are no commuting time, no expensive lunch hours, and an extra income tax deduction for a home office. ⁸You also have a chance to do your work without worrying about the boss looking over your shoulder.

Word groups with run-ons: _____   _____   _____   _____   _____

Passage B

[1]Have you ever wondered what the hotels of the future might look like? [2]You need not wonder any longer a hotel in Japan will give you a preview. [3]The name of this hotel is the Capsule Inn its rooms rent for eleven dollars a night. [4]Each room comes with a radio, a television set, and an alarm clock in addition, all the rooms are air-conditioned, but here any resemblance to a twentieth-century hotel ends. [5]The rooms are small plastic capsules each capsule is about five feet high by five feet wide by seven feet deep. [6]The capsules are stacked in a double layer guests have to crawl into bed through a large porthole entrance. [7]Bathrooms and washing facilities, and sofas, chairs, and vending machines are located in common areas in other parts of the hotel. [8]Believe it or not, this hotel is almost always full, perhaps because the price of the rooms is as small as the rooms themselves.

Word groups with run-ons: _____   _____   _____   _____   _____

NAME: _____

DATE: _____

Run-Ons (Comma Splices)

Mistakes in each passage: 5

Passage A

[1]"Typhoid Mary" is the name that was given to a woman who unknowingly spread death throughout New York City at the turn of the century. [2]Typhoid is caused by bacteria and is highly infectious, it causes fever, diarrhea, and often death. [3]Mary was a carrier of the disease, but she herself was unaffected by it. [4]Unfortunately, Mary worked as a cook, so she passed the disease to others through the food she touched. [5]Mary would take a job as cook to a household. [6]A few weeks later, several members of the family would become ill, sometimes typhoid would break out over a whole neighborhood. [7]After this happened several times, Mary became frightened, death appeared wherever she went, but she did not understand why or how. [8]Eventually, Mary was tracked down and arrested by public health authorities. [9]When she promised not to work as a cook again, she was released, she then vanished into the city. [10]But there were rumors that she continued to work as a cook, whenever typhoid broke out in the city for years afterward, "Typhoid Mary" was blamed.

Word groups with run-ons: _____ _____ _____ _____ _____

Passage B

[1]People are fond of pointing out how much there is wrong with television programming, and many shows do leave much to be desired. [2]But there is also much that is good about television, to begin with, television offers us an escape from our daily problems. [3]No matter what is bothering us, we can put our brains on hold for a while and enjoy some mindless fun, this becomes a problem only if we put our brains on hold for hours on end. [4]Another positive aspect of television is the wide choice of programs we have to choose from, it wasn't long ago that there were only three channels. [5]If you didn't find something you liked on one of those three, it was just your tough luck. [6]Since the development of cable television, it is not uncommon for a viewer to have over forty different channels to choose from, this means more interests and tastes are being served. [7]The best thing about television, though, is the service it performs for all of us. [8]It keeps us in touch with what is happening around the world, we have therefore learned more about our fellow citizens and people from other places and cultures. [9]In fact, millions of people have at times worked together to aid others whose misfortunes they learned about on television news.

Word groups with run-ons: _____   _____   _____   _____   _____

NAME: _____

DATE: _____

TEST 5 | Standard English Verbs

Mistakes in each passage: 5

Passage A

¹Sal should have stayed in bed yesterday. ²He knew it when he tried to shut off his alarm and accidentally pushed the clock to the floor. ³Sal decide to brave fate anyway. ⁴He dressed and headed for the breakfast table. ⁵After putting two slices of bread into the toaster, he went out to get the paper. ⁶Rain hurtled down from a dark sky. ⁷The paper was not under the shelter of the porch but was sitting, completely soak with water, on the walk. ⁸"Thanks a lot, paperboy," Sal said to himself as he left the paper where it was and return to the kitchen. ⁹After eating quickly, he gathered his books and ran down to the bus stop. ¹⁰No one was there, which meant he had miss the bus. ¹¹As he stood for twenty minutes waiting for the next bus, his pants were splashed by two cars that went by. ¹²When the bus finally pulled up, Sal reached into his pocket for the fare. ¹³Two dollars slipped out of his fingers and fell into the water at the curb. ¹⁴After fishing out the soggy bills and paying his fare, Sal discovered there were no empty seats on the bus. ¹⁵Standing there, he wonder what other kinds of bad luck awaited him at school.

Sentences with nonstandard verbs: _____ _____ _____ _____ _____

Passage B

[1]Keeping cities clean became more difficult as cities grew larger. [2]Some ancient cities solve the cleanliness problem: for example, inhabitants of ancient Rome had waterborne sewage systems and public baths. [3]But during the Middle Ages, these health-supporting systems disappear from the cities of Europe. [4]Sewage and garbage were dump in yards and streets, and bathing in the river was considered to be bad for one's health. [5]It was not surprising that a great plague, the black death, rage through Europe during this period, killing about one-fourth of its inhabitants. [6]Eventually sanitary facilities improve, and in modern cities, many social agencies take care of removing sewage, disposing of garbage, and sweeping the streets.

Sentences with nonstandard verbs: _____ _____ _____ _____ _____

NAME: _____

DATE: _____

TEST 6 Irregular Verbs

Mistakes in each passage: 10

Passage A

[1]When the game show contestant learned she had chose the box with only a penny in it, she was badly shaken. [2]She begun to cry, and the game show host for a minute was froze with fear. [3]Then he taked her hand and said, "You have not gotten to the end of the line yet, Mrs. Waterby. Cheer up." [4]When she learned she was going to be given one more chance, Mrs. Waterby stopped crying. [5]At the host's signal, a tray was brang onto the stage and placed in front of Mrs. Waterby. [6]On the tray sat three shells. [7]One shell, the host told her, covered the key to a new Lincoln Continental. [8]Mrs. Waterby was to choose the shell she thinked had the key under it. [9]There was a long pause, and she gived her answer, "Number three." [10]The host lifted up the third shell; the key was underneath. [11]Mrs. Waterby danced about the stage, just as she had been instructed to do if she winned. [12]Her husband run up on stage and embraced her. [13]They had realized the great American dream: they had gotten something for nothing.

Sentences with irregular verbs (write down the number of a sentence twice if it contains two irregular verbs):

_____ _____ _____ _____ _____

_____ _____ _____ _____ _____

Passage B

[1]Pete Jenkins had knew the meaning of fear before, like the time he got a cramp while swimming. [2]Luckily, he had been saved from drowning then by a friend he always swum with. [3]But Pete admits that his first job interview brang an even greater fear. [4]On the morning of the interview, his stomach felt as if he had ate a block of cement the night before. [5]In his throat, a lump had grew to the size of a football, and he wondered if he would be able to speak at all. [6]His mother realized Pete was nervous. [7]She drived him to the interview office and then burst out laughing. [8]"Pete," she said, "this is just an interview for a job at McDonald's." [9]At first, Pete was angry with his mother for laughing, but when she apologized he forgived her. [10]He also knowed his mother was right. [11]He was just going to be interviewed for a job making hamburgers. [12]He kepted his composure during the interview and came through it with ease.

Sentences with irregular verbs (write down the number of a sentence twice if it contains two irregular verbs):

_____ _____ _____ _____ _____

_____ _____ _____ _____ _____

NAME: _____

DATE: _____

TEST 7 Faulty Parallelism

Mistakes in each passage: 5

Passage A

¹People who do not want to pay for air conditioning can find other ways to keep a house cool during the hot weather. ²One way is to plant trees and shrubs and the use of awnings. ³As a result, outside walls and windows are kept cool. ⁴Another method is to get rid of the hot air that builds up in attic spaces by installing attic vents and power fans. ⁵In addition, window fans can be used at night to push out the hot daytime air and pull in the air that is cool in the evening. ⁶In the morning, when the house is still cool, the windows should be closed and draw the curtains. ⁷The windows and curtains can be opened if a breeze begins or a sudden drop in temperature. ⁸A final method of keeping the house cool is to water areas outside, such as concrete driveways and patios, that tend to collect heat and reflecting it against the house. ⁹Wet these every hour or so with a sprinkler or hose to prevent heat buildup.

Sentences with faulty parallelism: _____ _____ _____ _____ _____

Passage B

[1]In shopping for a good used car, be cautious and have suspicion. [2]Remember that the previous owner had some reason for getting rid of the car. [3]The reason may have been that he or she wanted to buy a new car or the avoidance of costly repairs. [4]A car that appears to have a "dirt-cheap" price may turn out to have "sky-high" costs. [5]Remember, too, that the older a car is, the chances are better that it will soon require major repairs. [6]If you buy an older car, be sure that repair parts and service facilities are available in your area. [7]Try to pick a used car with the lowest mileage on the odometer, the best overall condition, and that the dealer guarantees for the longest time. [8]There are several ways to protect yourself from a falsified odometer. [9]You should ask for a mileage disclosure statement, examine closely the condition of the vehicle, and contacting the previous owner.

Sentences with faulty parallelism: _____ _____ _____ _____ _____

NAME: _____

DATE: _____

TEST 8 # Capital Letters

Mistakes in each passage: 10

Passage A

[1]Although I'm much older now, I still remember the day I found out santa claus was a fake. [2]I was seven years old, and my brother Neil was five. [3]That evening, Mother told us, "be sure you go to bed early, and don't try any tricks, or you won't get your christmas present till *next* december." [4]So we quickly put on our pajamas, brushed our teeth with colgate toothpaste, and got under the covers. [5]I didn't even finish the Wonder Woman comic book I was halfway through. [6]We whispered for a while about whether we'd get the irish setter puppy we wanted so badly, or if we'd just get another boring game like tinkertoys that was supposed to be "educational." [7]Then we went to sleep, but in the middle of the night I woke up with a horrible thought. [8]What if Santa didn't know that we lived at 7201 springfield avenue? [9]He might bring our puppy to the wrong house! [10]I ran into my parents' bedroom to ask them if he knew where we lived, but they weren't there. [11]Then I heard noises coming from the living room. [12]I tiptoed downstairs—and there were my parents, putting something wrapped in green paper and tied with red ribbon under the tree. [13]To this day, I don't know what hurt more—getting a Scrabble set the next morning or finding out that the jolly fat man in a red suit and white beard was only Mom and Dad.

Sentences with missing capitals (write the number of a sentence as many times as it contains capitalization mistakes):

_____   _____   _____   _____   _____

_____   _____   _____   _____   _____

Passage B

[1]Credit cards have been abused by both the people that own them and the companies that issue them. [2]Some people fall into the habit of using their visa charge card for hotels and meals, their texaco card for gasoline, and other cards for department store purchases. [3]The danger in this, as was pointed out recently on the television program *60 minutes,* is that people can quickly reach a point where they cannot meet the monthly payments on their charge cards. [4]Such people can appreciate the warning in a texas newspaper, "it isn't buying on time that's difficult, it's paying on time." [5]Organizations such as consumers union have published articles alerting people to the high interest charges involved. [6]And magazines such as *time* and *newsweek* have also pointed out how quickly people lose a sense of their financial resources with charge cards. [7]Perhaps charge cards should carry the message, "excessive use of this card may be hazardous to your economic health."

Sentences with missing capitals (write the number of a sentence as many times as it contains capitalization mistakes):

_____ _____ _____ _____ _____

_____ _____ _____ _____ _____

NAME: _____

DATE: _____

TEST 9 | # Apostrophes

Mistakes in each passage: 10

Passage A

[1]Working as a house packer for Jerrys moving service was an enjoyable job for me. [2]First of all, almost no other job allows you to go into peoples houses and see at close range how they live. [3]I encountered a lot of interesting surprises. [4]For example, one womans house was as neat as a display room in a museum, but her basement was as littered as our towns dump. [5]Another person had converted a bedroom into a small library. [6]The rooms four walls contained storage shelves, all filled with books and magazines like *Reader's Digest* and *Time*. [7]I also liked the job because people would give me things they didnt want anymore. [8]For instance, I received a lot of childrens toys and a complete set of tools. [9]In fact, my mothers cellar started filling with items I received from customers cellars. [10]Im planning to work again for Jerry next year.

Sentences with missing apostrophes (write down the number of a sentence twice if it contains two missing apostrophes):

_____   _____   _____   _____   _____

_____   _____   _____   _____   _____

Passage B

[1]Mrs. Bartlett is our towns strangest person. [2]She has lived in the big house on Pine Street, without once setting foot outside, for more years than most people remember. [3]In her yard she keeps several cocker spaniels thatll rip your pants in a second. [4]While the regular mailmans face is familiar to the dogs, they treat a substitute mailman like a juicy bone. [5]In addition to the dogs, there are dozens of tame blackbirds perched in the trees. [6]Hitchcocks movie *The Birds* could have been made using her yard and house as a setting. [7]If you are on her good side, Mrs. B. (everyones name for her) will invite you in for tea. [8]Her gardener, Willy, watches the dogs while you hurry to the porch. [9]Willys job, by the way, is also to serve as night watchman. [10]Since hes almost seven feet tall, its not surprising that no prowlers have troubled the property. [11]Inside the house, a maid named Tina will take your coat. [12]A curiosity-seekers question will get only a scowl from the closemouthed Tina and a short, "Thats not your business." [13]People in general seem to respect this answer, and no ones challenged the right of Mrs. B. to live life her own way.

Sentences with missing apostrophes (write down the number of a sentence twice if it contains two missing apostrophes):

_____ _____ _____ _____ _____

_____ _____ _____ _____ _____

NAME: _____

DATE: _____

Quotation Marks

Quotation marks needed in each passage: 10 pairs

Passage A

[1]When my friend Brad asked me what I wanted to drink at the party, I said, Pepsi, if there is any. I don't drink.

[2]Very funny, Joe. Now what do you want? he asked. [3]He was truly shocked when I repeated my words. [4]I think he was even a little embarrassed that he had brought me to the party. [5]Later the subject of drinking came up when I was talking to a young woman I met.

[6]You must be in training, she assumed. [7]Or is it that you're on medication?

[8]Neither—I just don't like to drink, I answered patiently.

[9]Oh, I see. You're the type who proves himself different by playing the role of Mr. Nonconformist.

[10]That's partly it, I agreed. [11]I don't want to be an average Joe.

[12]But you can drink and still be yourself, an individual. Just be comfortable with yourself, she asserted.

[13]I responded, I do feel comfortable with myself. But I wouldn't if I drank just to be like everyone else here.

Sentences or sentence groups with missing quotation marks:

_____   _____   _____   _____   _____

_____   _____   _____   _____   _____

Passage B

[1]Once when I was walking down a lonely street, three boys came up to me. [2]Hey, Mister! one of them said. [3]Will you give us a nickel?

[4]I'm sorry, fellows, I replied. [5]I don't have any change to spare.

[6]All we want are three nickels, Mister, they said and suddenly surrounded me.

[7]Get out of my way, will you? I asked, trying to be polite. [8]I'm in a hurry.

[9]At this point the boy in front of me said, Stop trying to walk over me, Mister.

[10]As I raised my arm to move him aside, I felt a hand going into my back pocket. [11]I spun around and yelled, Give me that wallet! to the boy who had taken it. [12]I grabbed the wallet and the coin purse snapped open, with change spilling out over the sidewalk. [13]The boys scooped up the coins, chanting, Thanks for the change, Mister. [14]I wanted to belt one of them but decided it would be safer to walk quickly away.

Sentences or sentence groups with missing quotation marks:

_____   _____   _____   _____   _____

_____   _____   _____   _____   _____

NAME: _____

DATE: _____

TEST 11

Commas

Mistakes in each passage: 10

Passage A

¹Going to a big arena for a sporting event or musical performance means being bombarded by hard selling. ²The pitches begin on the road into the parking areas. ³As lines of cars wait to enter the lot salespeople will walk past the crawling cars. ⁴They will hawk programs souvenirs pennants and even droopy carnations. ⁵The ticketholder may pass up these items but they are only the first assault on his or her sales resistance. ⁶Near the arena's ticket gates are more vendors. ⁷In addition to the same programs and souvenir items they hawk T-shirts and different kinds of snacks. ⁸Inside the enormous building is a chain of concessionaires' booths with everything from hot dogs to cheap jewelry. ⁹People who continue to resist the hard sell have one last hurdle for there are still the hawkers who roam the aisles. ¹⁰Their voices can be heard crying out all across the rows of seats "Beer here!" or "Peanuts while they last!" ¹¹The last holdouts especially if they have children with them usually give in at this point. ¹²They fork over several dollars for a tiny bag of chips and a watery soda.

Sentences with missing commas (write down the number of a sentence as many times as it contains comma mistakes):

_____ _____ _____ _____ _____

_____ _____ _____ _____ _____

Passage B

[1]Studies have found that people have a psychological need for plants. [2]People who grew up in urban areas one survey revealed often mentioned the presence or absence of lawns in their neighborhood. [3]One person observed "I realized how much I missed lawns and trees after living in a city where concrete covered everything." [4]Unfortunately the city is a difficult environment for plants. [5]The soil of the city is covered mostly with buildings and pavements so there is little space for plants to grow. [6]Plants that are present are often hurt by haze smog and air pollution. [7]Some plants are more sensitive to pollution than others; snapdragons for example do poorly in polluted air. [8]When planners choose what kind of plants to place in urban areas they must consider the plants' chances for survival under the difficult growing conditions of city streets.

Sentences with missing commas (write down the number of a sentence as many times as it contains comma mistakes):

_____   _____   _____   _____   _____

_____   _____   _____   _____   _____

NAME: _____

DATE: _____

Commonly Confused Words

Mistakes in each passage: 10

Passage A

¹Recently, I was driving across town in heavy city traffic. ²Cars followed one another bumper-to-bumper, and their were bicyclists and pedestrians darting threw the streets. ³Beside the heavy traffic, it had begun to rain, making the traffic situation even worse. ⁴I was driving cautiously, keeping ten feet or so from the rear of the car in front of me. ⁵Than, in my rearview mirror, I noticed the woman behind me. ⁶Her car was so close our bumpers were almost locked. ⁷Her face was red and angry, and she tapped impatiently on her steering wheel. ⁸Suddenly, she saw a five-second brake in the traffic. ⁹She past me with a roar and squeezed in ahead of me. ¹⁰I though angrily, "Your a complete idiot!" and honked my horn. ¹¹She honked back at me and lifted her hand in an obscene gesture. ¹²I am a little ashamed at the affect this had on me—I was so enraged I wanted to drag her out of her car and punch her. ¹³It took me more than an hour to calm down completely and except the fact that the incident had been a very minor one.

Sentences with commonly confused words (write down the number of a sentence twice if it contains two commonly confused words):

_____   _____   _____   _____   _____

_____   _____   _____   _____   _____

Passage B

[1]If at all possible, try to take you're summer vacation any time accept during the summer. [2]First, by scheduling your vacation at another time of the year, you will avoid the crowds. [3]You will not have to fight the traffic around resort areas or drive passed dozens of motels with "No Vacancy" signs. [4]Beaches and campsites will be quite, to. [5]By vacationing out of season, you will also see many areas at there most beautiful, without the bother of summer's heat, thunderstorms, and insects. [6]Weather you go in spring or fall, you can travel by car without feeling stuck to your seat or to exhausted to explore the city or park. [7]Finally, an off-season trip can save you money. [8]Before and after the summer, prices at resorts drop, for fewer people are demanding reservations. [9]Its possible to stay too weeks for the price of one; or you might stay in a luxury hotel you might not otherwise be able to afford.

Sentences with commonly confused words (write down the number of a sentence twice if it contains two commonly confused words)*:*

_____ _____ _____ _____ _____

_____ _____ _____ _____ _____

Combined Editing Tests

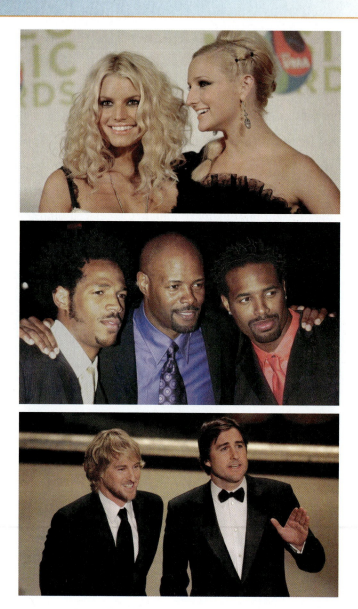

Psychologists have concluded that there are significant differences in being an only, oldest, middle, or youngest child. Which of these are you, and how did it influence the way you were brought up? Jot down the advantages and disadvantages that come to mind. Use the most important ideas on your list to develop a paragraph on how you think your position in your family affected you.

Editing for Sentence-Skills Mistakes

The fifteen editing tests in this section will give you practice in finding a variety of sentence-skills mistakes. People often find it hard to edit a paper carefully. They have put so much work, or so little work, into their writing, that it's almost painful for them to look at the paper one more time. You may simply have to *force* yourself to edit. Remember that eliminating sentence-skills mistakes will improve an average paper and help ensure a high grade on a good paper. Further, as you get into the habit of editing your papers, you will get into the habit of using the sentence skills consistently. They are a basic part of clear, effective writing.

NAME: _____

DATE: _____

COMBINED EDITING TEST 1

Identify the sentence-skills mistakes at the underlined spots in the selections that follow. From the box below, choose the letter that describes each mistake and write it in the space provided. (The same mistake may appear more than once.) Then, in the spaces provided between the lines, correct each mistake.

a. fragment	d. missing comma
b. run-on	e. faulty parallelism
c. missing apostrophe	f. misplaced modifier

Selection A

On the day when her divorce papers came. Roz tried to feel something. She
_____1_____

wanted to be very happy or feel sadness. However, she felt nothing a part of her life
_____2_____   _____3_____

had simply ended. She didnt care about Don anymore, and that disturbed her. She felt
_____4_____

guilty about not caring. Until she remembered that she had a right to happiness, too.
_____5_____

Selection B

When I was four years old I had the first traumatic experience of my life. My
_____6_____

family was staying at my aunts old house at the lake. I was chasing my cousin
_____7_____

Michelle toward the steps with untied shoelaces. Running too quickly I tripped and
_____8_____   _____9_____

fell. My mouth hit the bottom of the wooden steps. I thought I would die I must
_____10_____

have cried for hours. To this day, I still have a bump on my lower lip.

1. _____   3. _____   5. _____   7. _____   9. _____

2. _____   4. _____   6. _____   8. _____   10. _____

NAME: _____

DATE: _____

Identify the sentence-skills mistakes at the underlined spots in the selection that follows. From the box below, choose the letter that describes each mistake and write it in the space provided. (The same kind of mistake may appear more than once.) Then, in the spaces provided between the lines, correct each mistake. In one case, there is no mistake.

COMBINED EDITING TEST 2

a. fragment	d. missing capital letter
b. run-on	e. missing comma
c. dropped verb ending	f. no mistake

The worst thing that happen to me recently was that I decide to play a quick game
of touch football with some friends. I felt good physically when the game was over.
The next morning, however I learned that I was not in the shape I thought I was.
When I tried to get out of bed but couldn't. After my wife help me out of bed I felt
a little better. But all during the day I had to struggle whenever I got into or out of
my car. I thought the "monday soreness" was the end of it. Until the next morning,
when my wife had to help me put my shoes on. I could barely walk all day, I even
needed help getting out of my car. My body has delivered a loud and clear message
to me, forcing me to reconsider my imagined physical prowess.

1. _____   3. _____   5. _____   7. _____   9. _____

2. _____   4. _____   6. _____   8. _____   10. _____

NAME: _____

DATE: _____

Identify the sentence-skills mistakes at the underlined spots in the selection that follows. From the box below, choose the letter that describes each mistake and write it in the space provided. (The same mistake may appear more than once.) Then, in the spaces provided between the lines, correct each mistake. In one case, there is no mistake.

a. fragment	e. mistake in irregular verb
b. run-on	f. missing comma
c. dangling modifier	g. no mistake
d. mistake in subject-verb agreement	

When I was a child, my brother took advantage of my fear of ghosts. I would be taking a shower, and my brother would open the <u>door turn</u> out the lights, and
¹
start "wooing" until I began to cry. Then he would almost suffocate from laughing. Other times, he would make moaning sounds through the keyhole of my bedroom <u>door. Rattling the doorknob as well.</u> One night he did the worst thing of <u>all he took</u>
²   ³
out the main fuse in the fuse box, and all the lights in the house went out. Neither one of my parents <u>were</u> home at the <u>time, and I</u> was so petrified that at first I
⁴   ⁵
couldn't move. But I sure did move when my brother came running down the hall with a white sheet over his <u>head. Screaming</u> at the top of his lungs. He must have
⁶
chased me around the house for almost a half hour. I finally <u>stopped grabbed</u> an
⁷
apple out of the fruit basket, and <u>throwed</u> it at him as hard as I could. I missed him
⁸
but not the kitchen window. <u>Telling</u> my parents what happened later, they spanked
⁹
my brother. But thanks to him, I can't walk down a dark street <u>today. Without</u>
¹⁰
thinking there is someone behind me.

1. _____ 3. _____ 5. _____ 7. _____ 9. _____

2. _____ 4. _____ 6. _____ 8. _____ 10. _____

NAME: _____

DATE: _____

Identify the sentence-skills mistakes at the underlined spots in the selection that follows. From the box below, choose the letter that describes each mistake and write it in the space provided. (The same kind of mistake may appear more than once.) Then, in the spaces provided between the lines, correct each mistake.

a. fragment	e. missing capital letter
b. run-on	f. missing comma
c. mistake in irregular verb	g. faulty parallelism
d. mistake in apostrophe	

People often wonder why they have <u>spended</u> so much money at the <u>supermarket.</u>
₁
<u>On things they didn't intend to buy in the first place.</u> A recent survey indicates that
₂
75 percent of all grocery <u>shoppers'</u> make at least one impulse purchase. They might
₃
not have <u>ate</u> recently and reach for a package of <u>ritz</u> crackers to munch on while
₄ ₅
they go up and down the aisles. They may be lured by an eye-catching display or a
colorful <u>package over</u> one-third of all impulse purchases are made because the item
₆
is temptingly wrapped. When shoppers are waiting in the checkout <u>line a</u> final surge
₇
of buying fever often comes over them. They'll buy <u>magazines candy,</u> and other
₈
small items on the racks next to the checkout counter. There are ways of avoiding
impulse buying and <u>to save</u> money on groceries. Shoppers should make a list and
₉
stick to <u>it buy</u> no-frills brands, and eat well before going shopping.
₁₀

1. _____ 3. _____ 5. _____ 7. _____ 9. _____

2. _____ 4. _____ 6. _____ 8. _____ 10. _____

NAME: _____

DATE: _____

Identify the sentence-skills mistakes at the underlined spots in the selection that follows. From the box below, choose the letter that describes each mistake and write it in the space provided. (The same mistake may appear more than once.) Then, in the spaces provided between the lines, correct each mistake. In one case, there is no mistake.

a. fragment	e. missing quotation mark
b. run-on	f. missing comma
c. dangling modifier	g. no mistake
d. faulty parallelism	

I have never understood why my parents each felt so differently about me. They are both dead <u>now, I</u> guess I will never have the answer. I am convinced that my
₁
father did not love me. <u>Although never physically cruel,</u> there was little affection
₂
for me. He used <u>to say, I love all my children,</u> but I don't like them all." He once
₃
looked at me when he said this, adding, "You know what I mean, Karen." He never

seemed proud of me or <u>was there an interest in</u> what I was doing. <u>My report cards,</u>
₄   ₅
for example. He skipped the class plays I appeared in and rarely asked anything per-

sonal. He didn't say, "Do you have a boyfriend? What's he like?" Instead, he would

grunt, "Don't be late or you know what'll happen." On the other <u>hand my</u> mother
₆   ₇
seemed to care for me more than anyone else. Maybe she wanted to make up for my

father's behavior. She made clothes for me on her sewing machine and <u>decorating</u>
₈
<u>my room</u> the way I wanted it. <u>Also, driving me wherever I needed to go.</u> She asked
₉
me about school and about my friends. She would get my father out of the house so

that I could have a <u>party, she</u> would save her money to buy me special birthday and
₁₀
Christmas presents. Without my mother's special love, I think I would never have

survived my father's indifference.

1. _____   3. _____   5. _____   7. _____   9. _____

2. _____   4. _____   6. _____   8. _____   10. _____

NAME: _____

DATE: _____

Identify the sentence-skills mistakes at the underlined spots in the selections that follow. From the box below, choose the letter that describes each mistake and write it in the space provided. (The same kind of mistake may appear more than once.) Then, in the spaces provided between the lines, correct each mistake. In one case, there is no mistake.

a. fragment	e. dangling modifier
b. mistake in subject-verb agreement	f. missing capital letter
c. mistake in subject pronoun	g. no mistake
d. dropped -*ly* ending (adverb mistake)	

Selection A

Cindy had a weird but fascinating dream last night. Simply by turning the dial on

her magical television set. She could see what anyone in the world was doing at the
                              1

time. On one channel she could see her English instructor. He was sitting quiet by
                                                                              2

himself in a small room. Watching a late movie. On another channel, she could see
                          3

the president of the United States fast asleep with his wife in a White House bedroom.

Turning to another channel, the first boyfriend Cindy ever had were on screen. Him
                  4   5   6

and a young woman were having a conversation at a singles' bar.

Selection B

My brother and I was always different when we were little boys. Once my parents
              7   8

took us to see Santa Claus. Who was at the local department store instead of the North
                                    9

Pole. My brother asked Santa for a red wagon and world peace. I asked Santa, "how
                                                                                    10

much money do you make?"

1. _____   3. _____   5. _____   7. _____   9. _____

2. _____   4. _____   6. _____   8. _____   10. _____

NAME: _____

DATE: _____

Locate and correct the ten sentence-skills mistakes in the following passage. The mistakes are listed below. As you find each mistake, write the number of the word group containing it in the space provided. Then, in the spaces between the lines, correct each mistake.

3 fragments _____ _____ _____	1 missing set of quotation
3 run-ons _____ _____ _____	marks _____
1 dangling modifier _____	1 missing comma _____
1 mistake in pronoun point of	
view _____	

¹The main problem in my work as a substitute mail carrier is contending with dogs. ²Who are used to the regular carrier but not to me. ³The route I was assigned to last week featured a car-chasing German shepherd with a missing leg. ⁴As I walked up the lawn of the house where the dog stood guard I felt very uneasy. ⁵I could see the dog, who was sitting in the side yard. ⁶Giving me a hateful stare. ⁷As I deposited the mail at the front door, he let out several vicious snarls and barks. ⁸His owner appeared to get the mail, she yelled at him, You stay right where you are, Rex. ⁹I felt like asking her to stand there and watch Rex until I was back on the sidewalk; however, I didn't want to seem afraid. ¹⁰Walking slowly but eagerly away from the house, I heard the door click behind me, and you knew the owner had gone back inside. ¹¹When I almost reached the sidewalk, Rex began to bark again, but now the barking was louder and closer. ¹²I turned around and saw Rex coming at me in full, three-legged stride. ¹³With only three legs, I was sure that I could outrun him at least up to my truck. ¹⁴He was tearing at my pants as I reached the truck, I slid the door shut, using it to detach Rex from my trousers. ¹⁵Rex hurled himself at the door several times his owner called him back to the house. ¹⁶After catching my breath, I resolved not to return to the dog's place again ¹⁷At least not without a can of Mace.

NAME: _____

DATE: _____

Locate and correct the ten sentence-skills mistakes in the following passage. The mistakes are listed below. As you find each mistake, write the number of the word group containing it in the space provided. Then, in the spaces between the lines, correct each mistake.

3 fragments ____ ____ ____	1 missing apostrophe ____
1 mistake in subject-verb	1 missing capital letter ____
agreement ____	2 missing sets of quotation
1 mistake in verb tense ____	marks ____ ____
1 mistake in subject pronoun	
____	

[1]Kevin Miller is a stingy friend of mine. [2]When he comes to work, he never brings any money. [3]But always asks me if I have a dollar or two to lend him. [4]So that he can buy cookies or a small bag of potato chips. [5]He never offers to return the money. [6]When I remind him, he says, Oh, yeah, I'll get it to you soon, but he never does. [7]Another example of Kevins stinginess were the time he and me and two co-workers decided to go out during our lunch hour at the Red Rooster, a new restaurant. [8]Kevin suggested that we take his car, and as we were driving to the restaurant, he said his gas tank was empty. [9]He pulls into an exxon gas station and cheerfully said that five dollars for gas from each of us would be fine. [10]I was really fuming, especially because I could see that his gas tank was at least a quarter full. [11]Which was more than enough for the five-mile drive to the restaurant and back. [12]After we pulled into the restaurant parking lot, Kevin informed us that he would wait in the car while the rest of us ate. [13]I asked him in a hard voice, Don't you have any money? [14]Kevin's reply was, "Yeah, but I'm not going to spend it eating out when I can bring a sandwich from home and eat for nothing."

NAME: _____

DATE: _____

COMBINED EDITING TEST 9

Locate and correct the ten sentence-skills mistakes in the following passage. The mistakes are listed below. As you find each mistake, write the number of the word group containing it in the space provided. Then, in the spaces between the lines, correct each mistake.

2 fragments _____ _____	2 missing commas after intro-
2 run-ons _____ _____	ductory words _____ _____
1 mistake in irregular verb	2 missing commas in a series
_____	_____ _____
1 inconsistent pronoun point of	
view _____	

[1]While shopping one morning, I passed a weird-acting character on the street, he was sitting on a car fender, rocking violently up and down. [2]I was puzzled and, along with several other people, stopped and turned after I passed him. [3]In order to stare. [4]The man reached suddenly into his back pocket. [5]And took out a small packet containing miniature tools. [6]With a screwdriver in his right hand he leaned over and started to unscrew the license plate on the rear of the car. [7]Soon the license plate fell clattering to the ground. [8]The man then put his screwdriver away and just sat on the bumper for a minute. [9]Then he ran over to the open-air fruit stand nearby grabbed a banana and started eating it with the skin still on. [10]A woman working at the stand shouted, "Get out of here, you wild man." [11]However, she didn't try to take the banana away from him. [12]She shook her head, rolled her eyes, and turned her attention to a nearby customer. [13]The man suddenly seemed to become aware of the crowd watching him he heard someone laughing, and he begun to laugh also, but louder. [14]At the same time, his eyes filled with tears. [15]You suddenly felt ashamed and also guilty about watching him. [16]As I turned and walked away I heard the man's terrible laughing and sobbing echo behind me.

NAME: _____

DATE: _____

Locate and correct the ten sentence-skills mistakes in the following passage. The mistakes are listed below. As you find each mistake, write the number of the word group containing it in the space provided. Then, in the spaces between the lines, correct each mistake.

3 fragments _____ _____ _____	2 dropped verb endings _____ _____
2 run-ons _____ _____	1 missing capital letter _____
1 homonym mistake _____	1 missing apostrophe _____

¹When I met a girl named Barbara, my life started to change. ²Our relationship began one night last winter. ³A friend and I were having a couple of beers and shooting a game of darts at the Dewdrop Inn. ⁴The place was almost empty, there were about four people at the bar. ⁵Then Barbara and her friend walk in. ⁶Passing in front of us on there way to the bar. ⁷I nervously asked Barbara if she and her friend would like to play some darts. ⁸To my surprise, she said, "yes, we would." ⁹They beat us at darts, and then the four of us spent hours talking and laughing. ¹⁰Until Barbara and her friend said they had to go home. ¹¹I walked with her to her car and got up the courage to ask her out. ¹²Beaming, she said, "I was hoping you'd ask, or else I would have!"

¹³We started to see each other several nights a week. ¹⁴Becoming closer and closer to one another. ¹⁵We are now very happily married, and being with Barbara has truly change my life. ¹⁶When we met, I was often drinking from early in the morning to late at night. ¹⁷I didnt have a job, I felt as though I had nothing to work for. ¹⁸She changed me. ¹⁹I got a job and did well at it. ²⁰Then I applied to college, and I am now in school trying to learn and to succeed in life. ²¹I am proof that if a man has meaning in his life, he will be inspired to achieve.

NAME: _____

DATE: _____

Each numbered box in the application below contains a sentence-skills mistake. Identify each of the ten mistakes. As you find each, write the type of mistake you found in the space provided. Then correct it next to your answer. The first one has been done for you.

1. *missing comma: June 10, 2008*   6. _____

   _____   _____

2. _____   7. _____

   _____   _____

3. _____   8. _____

   _____   _____

4. _____   9. _____

   _____   _____

5. _____   10. _____

   _____   _____

Franklin Hospital • Employment Application

				Date of Application
				June 10 2008

Social Security # 123-45-6789	Last Name *Wiggins*	First Name *Troy*	Middle Initial *R.*

Address (Street number and name) *102 Penn Street*	City, State, and Zip Code *philadelphia, PA 19103*

Desired Position *"Evening Security Guard"*	Date Available to Start *Tomorow*	Home Phone	Business Phone

EDUCATION

Schools	Name and Location	Dates Attended (mo/yr) From: To:	Grad?	Major/Minor Course Work	Type of Degree
High School	*Central High school*	*9/02 to 6/06*	YES X NO		
College or University	*Bucks County College*	*9/06 to present*	YES NO X		
Other Training or Education	*Coarse in Web Design*		YES X NO		

WORK HISTORY (include volunteer experience. Use additional sheets if necessary.)

Current or Last Employer: *Home depot*	Address: *123 River Road Brooklawn NJ 08030*

Job Title: *Sales' Associate*	Supervisor's Name and Title *Sam Bosco, Manager*	Telephone Number

Dates Employed (mo/yr–mo/yr) *11/05 to present*	Starting Salary *$ 6.25/hour*	Ending or Current Salary *$ 7.00/hour*	Reason for Leaving *I want higher pay.*

List major duties in order of their importance in the job:

I stocked shelves, operated cash registers, and set up displays. Also trained new staff and assisted customers.

NAME: _____

DATE: _____

Each underlined area in the resume excerpt below contains a sentence-skills mistake. Identify the mistake and write its item number in the appropriate space in the box below. Then correct the mistake in the space above each error.

Missing capital letters: _____, _____   Inconsistent verb tense: _____

Dangling modifier: _____   Run-on: _____

Faulty parallelism: _____   Apostrophe mistake: _____

Fragment: _____, _____   Missing comma: _____

Andrea Barrett

530 South <u>cherry</u> Street
1

<u>Northridge CA</u> 91325
2

Phone: (805) 555-5555

OBJECTIVE: I wish to acquire a position as a teacher's assistant at a school that will offer me challenging work, <u>hours with flexibility,</u> and full benefits.
3

QUALIFICATIONS: <u>Organized, patient, and energetic, my experience with early childhood education is extensive.</u> <u>Having grown up with four little brothers.</u>
4 5
I know the challenges and responsibilities of caring for young children. <u>At the daycare center where I work.</u> I have taught lessons, <u>manage class trips,</u> and assisted
6 7
with classroom supervision for two years. My <u>co-workers'</u> give me their highest
8
recommendations. I know I will be an asset to your school. <u>I am a fast learner, I love children.</u>
9

continued

EDUCATION:

    2002–2006   Diploma, Glenview Heights High School

    2006–present   Bachelor's Degree (in progress), California State University

EMPLOYMENT:

Classroom Assistant, Happy hearts Daycare Center, (1/2005 to present)
₁₀

Helped teach a class of twenty-five preschoolers

Taught lessons, organized art projects, and supervised meals

NAME: _____

DATE: _____

Each underlined area in the cover letter below contains a sentence-skills mistake. Identify the mistake and write its item number in the appropriate space in the box below. Then correct the mistake in the space above each error.

Missing colon: _____	Homonym mistake: _____, _____
Missing apostrophe: _____	Dangling modifier: _____
Dropped verb ending: _____	Fragment: _____
Missing word: _____	Run-on: _____
Missing comma: _____	

Barbara Jenkins

Personnel Director

Buckeye Marketing Group

Cleveland, OH 44115

Dear Ms. Jenkins
        1

    I am responding to your ad in last Sundays newspaper that stated your com-
                                                    2
pany is searching for part-time phone receptionist. Friendly and hardworking, the
                                                                    3
job sounds like a perfect fit for me.

    I recently complete a business program wear I learned all the skills necessary
                            4   5
to be an effective receptionist. My training has prepared me to answer the phone
and deal with the public. I also learned to use the latest computer software. And
manage multiple tasks with speed and accuracy.
                        6

    In addition, I am comfortable working alone or as part of group. My schedule
                                                            7
is completely flexible. I can work days, evenings, and weekends, I hope to speak
                                                            8
with you about this position in the days ahead.

    Thank you for you're time and consideration.
                        9

Sincerely
    10
Maria Diaz

NAME: _____

DATE: _____

Each numbered line in the resume below contains a sentence-skills mistake. Identify the mistake and write its item number in the appropriate space in the box below. Then correct the mistake in the space above each error.

Missing capital letter: _____, _____	Homonym mistake: _____
Spelling error: _____	Missing –s ending: _____, _____
Missing comma: _____	Apostrophe error: _____, _____
Inconsistent verb tense: _____	

Zee Yang

[1]15 Peach street

[2]Atlanta GA 30303

Phone: (404) 330-6225

[3]**Objective:** I wish to obtain a full-time position with an oportunity for advancement and financial growth.

Work History:

Receptionist at Holiday Inn • Atlanta, GA • 2005 to present

Responsibilities:

4 • Used a computer system to register and bill guest

5 • Answered hotels main phone and assisted customers

6 • Processed payments and receipt

Server at P. F. Chang's China Bistro • Atlanta, GA 2002–2005

Responsibilities:

7 • Greeted and serve customers during lunch and dinner shifts

8 • Prepared appetizers and deserts for customers

9 • Assisted manager in training new server's

Education:

Atlanta Regional High School • Atlanta, GA

• Graduated June 2004

Special Skills:

• Skilled with Windows and Mac computers

10 • Fluent in chinese

NAME: _____

DATE: _____

COMBINED EDITING TEST 15

Each underlined area in the cover letter below contains a sentence-skills mistake. Identify the mistake and write its item number in the appropriate space in the box below. Then correct the mistake in the space above each error.

Missing period: _____   Spelling error: _____

Homonym mistake: _____   Slang: _____

Faulty parallelism: _____   Fragment: _____, _____

Run-on: _____   Apostrophe mistake: _____

Missing colon: _____

January 25, 2007

[1]Mr John Keenan

Furniture Warehouse

735 Industrial Drive

Denver, CO 80033

[2]Dear Mr. Keenan

I attended a job fair last week and discovered that [3]your currently searching for a shipping manager in your warehouse. [4]I was psyched to find out about the position. I think I am a great candidate for the job.

First of all, I am an experienced warehouse worker. I have worked as an assistant shipping manager at Sam's Club for two years. [5]And think I could fit nicely in your company. My current duties include driving a forklift, unloading delivery trucks, taking inventory, and [6]to supervise my coworkers.

[7]Beside having experience. I am also a reliable worker. [8]I always arrive to work on time, I never call out sick. [9]My supervisor's constantly praise my work, and I have [10] recieved many outstanding evaluations.

Please call me so we can talk in person about the position you're offering. I look forward to hearing from you.

Sincerely,

Wayne Thompson

Appendixes

Introduction

Six appendixes follow. Appendix A contains tips on how a computer can help in the writing process. Appendix B consists of further practice in using parts of speech, and Appendix C is a series of ESL pointers. Appendixes D and E consist of a diagnostic test and an achievement test that measure many of the skills in this book. The diagnostic test can be taken at the outset of your work; the achievement test can be used to measure your progress at the end of your work. Finally, Appendix F supplies answers to the introductory activities and the practice exercises in Part Two. The answers, which you should refer to only after you have worked carefully through each exercise, give you responsibility for testing yourself. (To ensure that the answer key is used as a learning tool only, answers are *not* given for the review and mastery tests in Part Two or for the reinforcement tests in Part Three. These answers appear only in the Instructor's Manual; they can be copied and handed out at the discretion of your instructor.)

Write a paragraph about a time you've experienced triumph in sports or some other area.

How a Computer Can Help

A computer is a powerful writing tool. Equipped with word-processing software, a computer can aid each phase of the writing process.

With a computer, for example, you can correct, move, or delete text with a mouse "click." You can also change fonts, set margins, space lines, or number pages with ease. A computer can even help you check spelling, grammar, and style in your writing.

Learning to use a computer is easy. Just as you don't need to know how a car works to drive one, you don't need to understand how a computer functions to use it. Once you have learned a few simple keystrokes, you can begin. You do not even need to own your own computer. Nearly every college has a computer center. There you will find computers with word-processing software and staff who can help you get started.

Tips on Using a Computer

- If you are using your school's computer center, allow enough time. You may have to wait for a computer or printer to be free. In addition, you may need several sessions at the computer and printer to complete your paper.

- Word-processing programs allow you to "save" your work with a mouse click. *Save your work frequently as you write your draft.* A saved file is stored safely on the computer or on an external disk, flash drive, or server. A file that is not saved will be lost if the program quits, the computer crashes, or the power is turned off.

- If you are using your own computer, keep your work in two places—the hard drive you are working on and a backup device such as a flash drive, disk, or recordable CD. Otherwise, save the file to a backup device and to your files on the school server or another server, or e-mail a copy to yourself (ask the staff in your computer center for help if needed). At the end of each session with the computer, copy your work onto the backup device. Then if the hard drive becomes damaged, you'll have the backup copy.

- Print out your work at the end of every session. Then you will have not only your most recent draft to work on away from the computer but also yet another backup in case something should happen to your disks.

- Work in single spacing so that you can see as much of your writing on the screen at one time as possible. Just before you print out your work, change to double spacing.

- Before making major changes in a paper, create a copy of your file. For example, if your file is titled "Worst Job," create a file called "Worst Job 2." Then make all your changes in that new file. If the changes don't work out, you can always go back to the original file.

Using a Computer at Each Stage of the Writing Process

Following are some ways to use a computer in your writing.

Prewriting

If you're a fast typist, many kinds of prewriting will go well on the computer. With freewriting in particular, you can get ideas onto the screen almost as quickly as they occur to you. A passing thought that could be productive is not likely to get lost. You may even find it helpful, when freewriting, to dim the screen of your monitor so that you can't see what you're typing. If you temporarily can't see the screen, you won't have to worry about grammar or spelling or typing errors (all of which do not matter in prewriting); instead, you can concentrate on getting down as many ideas and details as possible about your subject.

After any initial freewriting, questioning, and list making on a computer, it's often very helpful to print out a hard copy of what you've done. With a clean printout in front of you, you'll be able to see everything at once and revise and expand your work with handwritten comments in the margins of the paper.

Word processing also makes it easy for you to experiment with the wording of the point of your paper. You can try a number of versions in a short time. After you have decided on the version that works best, you can easily delete the other versions—or simply move them to a temporary "leftover" section at the end of the paper.

Preparing a Scratch Outline

If you have prepared a list of items during prewriting, you may be able to turn that list into an outline right on the screen. Delete the ideas you feel should not be in your paper (saving them at the end of the file in case you change your mind), and add any new ideas that occur to you. Then use the cut and paste functions to shuffle the supporting ideas around until you find the best order for your paper.

Writing Your First Draft

Like many writers, you may want to write out your first draft by hand and then type it into the computer for revision. Even as you type your handwritten draft, you may find yourself making some changes and improvements. And once you have a draft on the screen, or printed out, you will find it much easier to revise than a handwritten one.

If you feel comfortable composing directly on the screen, you can benefit from the computer's special features. For example, if you have written an anecdote in your freewriting that you plan to use in your paper, simply copy the story from your freewriting file and insert it where it fits in your paper. You can refine it then or later. Or if you discover while typing that a sentence is out of place, cut it out from where it is and paste it wherever you wish. And if while writing you realize that an earlier sentence can be expanded, just move your cursor back to that point and type in the added material.

Revising

It is during revision that the virtues of a computer really shine. All substituting, adding, deleting, and rearranging can be done easily within an existing file. All changes instantly take their proper places within the paper, not scribbled above the line or squeezed into the margin. You can concentrate on each change you want to make, because you never have to type from scratch or work on a messy draft. You can carefully go through your paper to check that all your supporting evidence is relevant and to add new support as needed here and there. Anything you decide to eliminate can be deleted in a keystroke. Anything you add can be inserted precisely where you choose. If you change your mind, all you have to do is delete or cut and paste. Then you can sweep through the paper, focusing on other changes, such as improving word choice, increasing sentence variety, eliminating wordiness, and so on.

If you are like many students, you will find it convenient to print out a hard copy of your file at various points throughout the revision. You can then revise in longhand—adding, crossing out, and indicating changes—and later quickly make these changes in the document.

Editing and Proofreading

A computer is a great tool for editing and proofreading. Instead of crossing out mistakes or using correction fluid or tape—or rewriting an entire paper to correct numerous errors—you can make all necessary changes directly to your work file. If you find editing or proofreading on the screen hard on your eyes, print out a copy. Mark any corrections on that copy, and then transfer them to your file.

If the word-processing software you're using includes spelling and grammar checks, by all means use them. The spell-check function tells you when a word is not in the computer's dictionary. Keep in mind, however, that the spell-checker cannot tell you how to spell a name correctly or when you have mistakenly used, for example, *their* instead of *there*. To a spell-checker, *Thank ewe four the compliment* is as correct as *Thank you for the compliment.* Also, use the grammar checker with caution. Any errors it doesn't uncover are still your responsibility, and it may signal possible errors that don't exist in your paper.

A freshly printed paper, with its clean appearance and handsome formatting, looks so good that you may feel it is in better shape than it really is. Do not be fooled by your paper's appearance. Take sufficient time to review your grammar, punctuation, and spelling carefully.

Even after you hand in your paper, save the computer file. Your instructor may ask you to do some revising, and then the file will save you from having to type the paper from scratch.

Parts of Speech

Words—the building blocks of sentences—can be divided into eight parts of speech. *Parts of speech* are classifications of words according to their meaning and use in a sentence.

This chapter will explain the eight parts of speech:

nouns	prepositions	conjunctions
pronouns	adjectives	interjections
verbs	adverbs	

Nouns

A *noun* is a word that is used to name something: a person, a place, an object, or an idea. Here are some examples of nouns:

Nouns			
woman	city	pancake	freedom
Alice Walker	street	diamond	possibility
Steve Martin	Chicago	Corvette	mystery

Most nouns begin with a lowercase letter and are known as *common nouns*. These nouns name general things. Some nouns, however, begin with a capital letter. They are called *proper nouns*. While a common noun refers to a person or thing in general, a proper noun names someone or something specific. For example, *woman* is a common noun—it doesn't name a particular woman. On the other hand, *Alice Walker* is a proper noun because it names a specific woman.

Insert any appropriate noun into each of the following blanks.

1. The shoplifter stole a(n) _____ from the department store.

2. _____ threw the football to me.

3. Tiny messages were scrawled on the _____.

4. A _____ crashed through the window.

5. Give the _____ to Keiko.

Singular and Plural Nouns

A *singular noun* names one person, place, object, or idea. A *plural noun* refers to two or more persons, places, objects, or ideas. Most singular nouns can be made plural with the addition of an *s*.

Some nouns, like *box*, have irregular plurals. You can check the plural of nouns you think may be irregular by looking up the singular form in a dictionary.

Singular and Plural Nouns

Singular	Plural
goat	goats
alley	alleys
friend	friends
truth	truths
box	boxes

For more information on nouns, see "Subjects and Verbs," pages 66–78.

Underline the three nouns in the following sentences. Some are singular, and some are plural.

1. Two bats swooped over the heads of the frightened children.

2. The artist has purple paint on her sleeve.

3. The lost dog has fleas and a broken leg.

4. Tiffany does her homework in green ink.

5. Some farmers plant seeds by moonlight.

Pronouns

A *pronoun* is a word that stands for a noun. Pronouns eliminate the need for constant repetition. Look at the following sentences:

> The phone rang, and Malik answered the phone.

> Lisa met Lisa's friends in the record store at the mall. Lisa meets Lisa's friends there every Saturday.

> The waiter rushed over to the new customers. The new customers asked the waiter for menus and coffee.

Notice how much clearer and smoother these sentences sound with pronouns.

> The phone rang, and Malik answered *it*. (The pronoun *it* is used to replace the word *phone*.)

> Lisa met *her* friends in the record store at the mall. *She* meets *them* there every Saturday. (The pronoun *her* is used to replace the word *Lisa's*. The pronoun *she* replaces *Lisa*. The pronoun *them* replaces the words *Lisa's friends*.)

> The waiter rushed over to the new customers. *They* asked *him* for menus and coffee. (The pronoun *they* is used to replace the words *the new customers*. The pronoun *him* replaces the words *the waiter*.)

Following is a list of commonly used pronouns known as *personal pronouns:*

Personal Pronouns						
I	you	he	she	it	we	they
me	your	him	her	its	us	them
my	yours	his	hers		our	their

Fill in each blank with the appropriate personal pronoun.

1. André feeds his pet lizard every day before school. _____ also

    gives _____ flies in the afternoon.

2. The reporter interviewed the striking workers. _____ told

    _____ about their demand for higher wages and longer breaks.

3. Students should save all returned tests. _____ should also keep

    _____ review sheets.

4. The pilot announced that we would fly through some air pockets. _____

    said that we should be past _____ soon.

5. Adolfo returned the calculator to Sheila last Friday. But Sheila insists that

    _____ never got _____ back.

There are several types of pronouns. For convenient reference, they are described briefly in the box below.

Types of Pronouns

Personal pronouns can act in a sentence as subjects, objects, or possessives.

> *Singular:* **I, me, my, mine, you, your, yours, he, him, his, she, her, hers, it, its**
>
> *Plural:* **we, us, our, ours, you, your, yours, they, them, their, theirs**

Relative pronouns refer to someone or something already mentioned in the sentence.

> **who, whose, whom, which, that**

Interrogative pronouns are used to ask questions.

> **who, whose, whom, which, what**

Demonstrative pronouns are used to point out particular persons or things.

> **this, that, these, those**

Note: Do not use *them* (as in *them* shoes), *this here, that there, these here,* or *those there* to point out.

continued

Reflexive pronouns are those that end in *-self* or *-selves*. A reflexive pronoun is used as the object of a verb (as in *Cary cut **herself***) or the object of a preposition (as in *Jack sent a birthday card to **himself***) when the subject of the verb is the same as the object.

Singular: **myself, yourself, himself, herself, itself**

Plural: **ourselves, yourselves, themselves**

Intensive pronouns have exactly the same forms as reflexive pronouns. The difference is in how they are used. Intensive pronouns are used to add emphasis. (*I **myself** will need to read the contract before I sign it.*)

Indefinite pronouns do not refer to a particular person or thing.

each, either, everyone, nothing, both, several, all, any, most, none

Reciprocal pronouns express shared actions or feelings.

each other, one another

For more information on pronouns, see "Pronoun Types," pages 216–230.

Verbs

Every complete sentence must contain at least one verb. There are two types of verbs: action verbs and linking verbs.

Action Verbs

An *action verb* tells what is being done in a sentence. For example, look at the following sentences:

Mr. Jensen *swatted* at the bee with his hand.

Rainwater *poured* into the storm sewer.

The children *chanted* the words to the song.

In these sentences, the verbs are *swatted, poured,* and *chanted.* These words are all action verbs; they tell what is happening in each sentence.

For more about action verbs, see "Subjects and Verbs," pages 68–70.

Insert an appropriate word in each blank. That word will be an action verb; it will tell what is happening in the sentence.

1. The surgeon _____ through the first layer of skin.

2. The animals in the cage _____ all day.

3. An elderly woman on the street _____ me for directions.

4. The boy next door _____ our lawn every other week.

5. Our instructor _____ our papers over the weekend.

Linking Verbs

Some verbs are *linking verbs*. These verbs link (or join) a noun to something that is said about it. For example, look at the following sentence:

The clouds *are* steel-gray.

In this sentence, *are* is a linking verb. It joins the noun *clouds* to words that describe it: *steel-gray.*

Other common linking verbs include *am, is, was, were, look, feel, sound, appear, seem,* and *become.* For more about linking verbs, see "Subjects and Verbs," pages 68–70.

In each blank, insert one of the following linking verbs: *am, feel, is, look, were.* Use each linking verb once.

1. The important papers _____ in a desk drawer.

2. I _____ anxious to get my test back.

3. The bananas _____ ripe.

4. The grocery store _____ open until 11 P.M.

5. Whenever I _____ angry, I go off by myself to calm down.

Helping Verbs

Sometimes the verb of a sentence consists of more than one word. In these cases, the main verb will be joined by one or more *helping verbs.* Look at the following sentence:

The basketball team *will be leaving* for the game at six o'clock.

In this sentence, the main verb is *leaving.* The helping verbs are *will* and *be.*

Other helping verbs include *do, has, have, may, would, can, must, could,* and *should.* For more information about helping verbs, see "Subjects and Verbs," pages 71–72, and "Irregular Verbs," pages 156–170.

Practice

6

In each blank, insert one of the following helping verbs: *does, must, should, could, has been.* Use each helping verb once.

1. You _____ start writing your paper this weekend.

2. The victim _____ describe her attacker in great detail.

3. You _____ rinse the dishes before putting them into the dishwasher.

4. My neighbor _____ arrested for drunk driving.

5. The bus driver _____ not make any extra stops.

Prepositions

A *preposition* is a word that connects a noun or a pronoun to another word in the sentence. For example, look at the following sentence:

A man *in* the bus was snoring loudly.

In is a preposition. It connects the noun *bus* to *man*. Here is a list of common prepositions:

Prepositions

about	before	down	like	to
above	behind	during	of	toward
across	below	except	off	under
after	beneath	for	on	up
among	beside	from	over	with
around	between	in	since	without
at	by	into	through	

The noun or pronoun that a preposition connects to another word in the sentence is called the *object* of the preposition. A group of words beginning with a preposition and ending with its object is called a *prepositional phrase*. The words *in the bus*, for example, are a prepositional phrase.

Now read the following sentences and explanations.

An ant was crawling *up the teacher's leg*.

The noun *leg* is the object of the preposition *up*. *Up* connects *leg* with the word *crawling*. The prepositional phrase *up the teacher's leg* describes *crawling*. It tells just where the ant was crawling.

The man *with the black mustache* left the restaurant quickly.

The noun *mustache* is the object of the preposition *with*. The prepositional phrase *with the black mustache* describes the word *man*. It tells us exactly which man left the restaurant quickly.

The plant *on the windowsill* was a present *from my mother*.

The noun *windowsill* is the object of the preposition *on*. The prepositional phrase *on the windowsill* describes the word *plant*. It describes exactly which plant was a present.

There is a second prepositional phrase in this sentence. The preposition is *from*, and its object is *mother*. The prepositional phrase *from my mother* explains *present*. It tells who gave the present. For more about prepositions, see "Subjects and Verbs," pages 70–71, and "Sentence Variety II," pages 267–283.

In each blank, insert one of the following prepositions: *of, by, with, in, without*. Use each preposition once.

Practice

7

1. The letter from his girlfriend had been sprayed _____ perfume.

2. The weed killer quickly killed the dandelions _____ our lawn.

3. _____ giving any notice, the tenant moved out of the apartment.

4. Donald hungrily ate three scoops _____ ice cream and an order of french fries.

5. The crates _____ the door contain glass bottles and newspapers.

Adjectives

An *adjective* is a word that describes a noun (the name of a person, place, or thing). Look at the following sentence.

The dog lay down on a mat in front of the fireplace.

Now look at this sentence when adjectives have been inserted.

The *shaggy* dog lay down on a *worn* mat in front of the fireplace.

The adjective *shaggy* describes the noun *dog;* the adjective *worn* describes the noun *mat.* Adjectives add spice to our writing. They also help us to identify particular people, places, or things.

Adjectives can be found in two places:

1. An adjective may come before the word it describes (a *damp* night, the *moldy* bread, a *striped* umbrella).

2. An adjective that describes the subject of a sentence may come after a linking verb. The linking verb may be a form of the verb *be* (he *is* **furious**, I *am* **exhausted**, they are **hungry**). Other linking verbs include *feel, look, sound, smell, taste, appear, seem,* and *become* (the soup *tastes* **salty**, your hands *feel* **dry**, the dog *seems* **lost**).

TIP The words *a*, *an*, and *the* (called *articles*) are generally classified as adjectives.

For more information on adjectives, see "Adjectives and Adverbs," pages 231–239.

Practice

8

Write any appropriate adjective in each blank.

1. The _____ pizza was eaten greedily by the _____ teenagers.

2. Melissa gave away the sofa because it was _____ and _____.

3. Although the alley is _____ and _____, Jian often takes it as a shortcut home.

4. The restaurant throws away lettuce that is _____ and tomatoes that are _____.

5. When I woke up in the morning, I had a(n) _____ fever and a(n) _____ throat.

Adverbs

An *adverb* is a word that describes a verb, an adjective, or another adverb. Many adverbs end in the letters *-ly*. Look at the following sentence:

> The canary sang in the pet store window as the shoppers greeted each other.

Now look at this sentence after adverbs have been inserted.

> The canary sang *softly* in the pet store window as the shoppers *loudly* greeted each other.

The adverbs add details to the sentence. They also allow the reader to contrast the singing of the canary and the noise the shoppers are making.

Look at the following sentences and the explanations of how adverbs are used in each case.

> The chef yelled **angrily** at the young waiter.
> (The adverb *angrily* describes the verb *yelled*.)

> My mother has an **extremely** busy schedule on Tuesdays.
> (The adverb *extremely* describes the adjective *busy*.)

> The sick man spoke **very** faintly to his loyal nurse.
> (The adverb *very* describes the adverb *faintly*.)

Some adverbs do not end in *-ly*. Examples include *very, often, never, always,* and *well.*

For more information on adverbs, see "Adjectives and Adverbs," pages 231–239.

Practice 9

Fill in each blank with any appropriate adverb.

1. The water in the pot boiled _____.

2. Carla _____ drove the car through _____ moving traffic.

3. The telephone operator spoke _____ to the young child.

4. The game show contestant waved _____ to his family in the audience.

5. Wes _____ studies, so it's no surprise that he did _____ poorly on his finals.

Conjunctions

A *conjunction* is a word that connects. There are two types of conjunctions: coordinating and subordinating.

Coordinating Conjunctions

Coordinating conjunctions join two equal ideas. Look at the following sentence:

Kevin *and* Steve interviewed for the job, *but* their friend Anne got it.

In this sentence, the coordinating conjunction *and* connects the proper nouns *Kevin* and *Steve*. The coordinating conjunction *but* connects the first part of the sentence, *Kevin and Steve interviewed for the job,* to the second part, *their friend Anne got it.*

Following is a list of all the coordinating conjunctions. In this book, they are simply called *joining words*.

Coordinating Conjunctions (Joining Words)

and	so	nor	yet
but	or	for	

For more on coordinating conjunctions, see information on joining words in "Run-Ons," pages 108–110, and "Sentence Variety I," pages 126–128.

Practice 10

Write a coordinating conjunction in each blank. Choose from the following: *and, but, so, or, nor.* Use each conjunction once.

1. Either Jerome _____ Alex scored the winning touchdown.

2. I expected roses for my birthday, _____ I received a vase of plastic tulips from the discount store.

3. The cafeteria was serving liver and onions for lunch, _____ I bought a sandwich at the corner deli.

4. Marian brought a pack of playing cards _____ a pan of brownies to the company picnic.

5. Neither my sofa _____ my armchair matches the rug in my living room.

Subordinating Conjunctions

When a *subordinating conjunction* is added to a word group, the words can no longer stand alone as an independent sentence. They are no longer a complete thought. For example, look at the following sentence:

Karen fainted in class.

The word group *Karen fainted in class* is a complete thought. It can stand alone as a sentence. See what happens when a subordinating conjunction is added to a complete thought:

When Karen fainted in class

Now the words cannot stand alone as a sentence. They are dependent on other words to complete the thought:

When Karen fainted in class, we put her feet up on some books.

In this book, a word that begins a dependent word group is called a *dependent word*. Subordinating conjunctions are common dependent words. Below are some subordinating conjunctions.

Subordinating Conjunctions				
after	before	since	when	wherever
although	even if	though	whenever	whether
as	even though	unless	where	while
because	if	until		

Following are some more sentences with subordinating conjunctions:

After she finished her last exam, Irina said, "Now I can relax."
(*After she finished her last exam* is not a complete thought. It is dependent on the rest of the words to make up a complete sentence.)

Lamont listens to books on tape **while** he drives to work.
(*While he drives to work* cannot stand by itself as a sentence. It depends on the rest of the sentence to make up a complete thought.)

Since apples were on sale, we decided to make an apple pie for dessert.
(*Since apples were on sale* is not a complete sentence. It depends on *we* **decided** *to make an apple pie for dessert* to complete the thought.)

For more information on subordinating conjunctions, see information on dependent words in "Fragments," pages 80–84; "Run-Ons," pages 113–114; "Sentence Variety I," pages 128–130; and "Sentence Variety II," pages 273–274.

Practice

11

Write a logical subordinating conjunction in each blank. Choose from the following: *even though, because, until, when, before.* Use each conjunction once.

1. The bank was closed by federal regulators _____ it lost more money than it earned.

2. _____ Paula wants to look mysterious, she wears dark sunglasses and a scarf.

3. _____ the restaurant was closing in fifteen minutes, customers sipped their coffee slowly and continued to talk.

4. _____ anyone else could answer it, Leon rushed to the phone and whispered, "Is that you?"

5. The waiter was instructed not to serve any food _____ the guest of honor arrived.

Interjections

An *interjection* is a word that can stand independently and is used to express emotion. Examples are *oh, wow, ouch,* and *oops.* These words are usually not found in formal writing.

"*Hey!*" yelled Maggie. "That's my bike."

Oh, we're late for class.

A Final Note

A word may function as more than one part of speech. For example, the word *dust* can be a verb or a noun, depending on its role in the sentence.

I *dust* my bedroom once a month, whether it needs dusting or not. (verb)

The top of my refrigerator is covered with an inch of *dust.* (noun)

APPENDIX C
ESL Pointers

This section covers rules that most native speakers of English take for granted but that are useful for speakers of English as a second language (ESL).

Articles

Types of Articles

An *article* is a noun marker—it signals that a noun will follow. There are two kinds of articles: indefinite and definite. The indefinite articles are *a* and *an*. Use *a* before a word that begins with a consonant sound:

> **a d**esk, **a p**hotograph, **a u**nicycle

> (*A* is used before *unicycle* because the *u* in that word sounds like the consonant *y* plus *u,* not a vowel sound.)

Use *an* before a word beginning with a vowel sound:

> **an e**rror, **an o**bject, **an h**onest woman

> (*Honest* begins with a vowel sound because the *h* is silent.)

The definite article is *the:*

> **the** sofa, **the** cup

An article may come right before a noun:

> **a** magazine, **the** candle

Or an article may be separated from the noun by words that describe the noun:

> **a** popular magazine, **the** fat red candle

TIP There are various other noun markers, including quantity words (*a few, many, a lot of*), numerals (*one, thirteen, 710*), demonstrative adjectives (*this, these*), adjectives (*my, your, our*), and possessive nouns (*Raoul's, the school's*).

533

Articles with Count and Noncount Nouns

To know whether to use an article with a noun and which article to use, you must recognize count and noncount nouns. (A *noun* is a word used to name something—a person, place, thing, or idea.)

Count nouns name people, places, things, or ideas that can be counted and made into plurals, such as *pillow, heater,* and *mail carrier (one pillow, two heaters, three mail carriers).*

Noncount nouns refer to things or ideas that cannot be counted and therefore cannot be made into plurals, such as *sunshine, gold,* and *rust.* The box below lists and illustrates common types of noncount nouns.

Common Noncount Nouns

Abstractions and emotions: **justice, tenderness, courage, knowledge, embarrassment**

Activities: **jogging, thinking, wondering, golf, hoping, sleep**

Foods: **oil, rice, pie, butter, spaghetti, broccoli**

Gases and vapors: **carbon dioxide, oxygen, smoke, steam, air**

Languages and areas of study: **Korean, Italian, geology, arithmetic, history**

Liquids: **coffee, kerosene, lemonade, tea, water, bleach**

Materials that come in bulk or mass form: **straw, firewood, sawdust, cat litter, cement**

Natural occurrences: **gravity, sleet, rain, lightning**

Other things that cannot be counted: **clothing, experience, trash, luggage, room, furniture, homework, machinery, cash, news, transportation, work**

The quantity of a noncount noun can be expressed with a word or words called a *qualifier,* such as *some, more, a unit of,* and so on. In the following two examples, the qualifiers are shown in *italic* type, and the noncount nouns are shown in **boldface** type.

How *much* **experience** have you had as a salesclerk?

Our tiny kitchen doesn't have *enough* **room** for a table and chairs.

Some words can be either count or noncount nouns depending on whether they refer to one or more individual items or to something in general:

Three **chickens** are running around our neighbor's yard.

(This sentence refers to particular chickens; *chicken* in this case is a count noun.)

Would you like some more **chicken**?

(This sentence refers to chicken in general; in this case, *chicken* is a noncount noun.)

Using *a* or *an* with Nonspecific Singular Count Nouns

Use *a* or *an* with singular nouns that are nonspecific. A noun is nonspecific when the reader doesn't know its specific identity.

A photograph can be almost magical. It saves a moment's image for many years.

(The sentence refers to any photograph, not a specific one.)

An article in the newspaper today made me laugh.

(The reader isn't familiar with the article. This is the first time it is mentioned.)

Using *the* with Specific Nouns

In general, use *the* with all specific nouns—specific singular, plural, and noncount nouns. A noun is specific—and therefore requires the article *the*—in the following cases:

- When it has already been mentioned once:

  An article in the newspaper today made me laugh. **The** article was about a talking parrot who frightened away a thief.

  (*The* is used with the second mention of *article*.)

- When it is identified by a word or phrase in the sentence:

  The CD that is playing now is a favorite of mine.

  (*CD* is identified by the words *that is playing now*.)

- When its identity is suggested by the general context:

  The service at Joe's Bar and Grill is never fast.

  (*Service* is identified by the words *at Joe's Bar and Grill*.)

- When it is unique:

  Some people see a man's face in **the** moon, while others see a rabbit.

  (Earth has only one moon.)

- When it comes after a superlative adjective (for example, *best*, *biggest*, or *wisest*):

  The funniest movie I've seen is *Young Frankenstein*.

Omitting Articles

Omit articles with nonspecific plurals and nonspecific noncount nouns. Plurals and noncount nouns are nonspecific when they refer to something in general.

Stories are popular with most children.

Service is almost as important as food in successful restaurants.

Movies can be rented from many supermarkets as well as video stores.

Using the with Proper Nouns

Proper nouns name particular people, places, things, or ideas and are always capitalized. Most proper nouns do not require articles; those that do, however, require *the*. Following are general guidelines about when not to use *the* and when to use *the*.

Do not use *the* for most singular proper nouns, including names of the following:

- *People and animals* (Katie Couric, Fluffy)
- *Continents, states, cities, streets, and parks* (South America, Utah, Boston, Baker Street, People's Park)
- *Most countries* (Cuba, Indonesia, Ireland)
- *Individual bodies of water, islands, and mountains* (Lake Michigan, Captiva Island, Mount McKinley)

Use *the* for the following types of proper nouns:

- *Plural proper nouns* (the Harlem Globetrotters, the Marshall Islands, the Netherlands, the Atlas Mountains)
- *Names of large geographic areas, deserts, oceans, seas, and rivers* (the Midwest, the Kalahari Desert, the Pacific Ocean, the Sargasso Sea, the Nile River)
- *Names with the format* "the _____ of _____" (the Strait of Gibraltar, the University of Illinois)

Practice 1

Underline the correct word or words in parentheses.

1. (Wallpaper, The wallpaper) in my room is white with yellow stripes.

2. (Robots, The robots) are being developed to help disabled people.

3. My mother bought (a new jacket, the new jacket).

4. (A new jacket, The new jacket) is made of soft brown wool.

5. (Happiest day, The happiest day) of my life was when my first child was born.

6. (The Hawaiian Islands, Hawaiian Islands) are among the world's most popular vacation sites.

7. This morning, the swimming pool felt as cold as (Arctic Ocean, the Arctic Ocean).

8. (Mars, The Mars) is named after the Roman god of war.

9. Brownsville, Texas, is a city on (Gulf of Mexico, the Gulf of Mexico).

10. (Happiness, The happiness) shone all over Maria's face when she saw her good grades.

Subjects and Verbs

Avoiding Repeated Subjects

In English, a particular subject can be used only once in a word group with a subject and a verb (that is, a clause). Don't repeat a subject in the same word group by following a noun with a pronoun.

> Incorrect: My *parents they* live in Miami.
>
> Correct: My **parents** live in Miami.
>
> Correct: **They** live in Miami.

Even when the subject and verb are separated by several words, the subject cannot be repeated in the same word group.

> Incorrect: The *windstorm* that happened last night *it* damaged our roof.
>
> Correct: The **windstorm** that happened last night **damaged** our roof.

Including Pronoun Subjects and Linking Verbs

Some languages omit a subject that is a pronoun, but in English, every sentence other than a command must have a subject. In a command, the subject *you* is understood: (You) Hand in your papers now.

> Incorrect: The soup tastes terrible. *Is* much too salty.
>
> Correct: The soup tastes terrible. **It is** much too salty.

Every English sentence must also have a verb, even when the meaning of the sentence is clear without the verb.

> Incorrect: The table covered with old newspapers.
>
> Correct: The table **is** covered with old newspapers.

Including *There* and *Here* at the Beginning of Sentences

Some English sentences begin with *there* or *here* plus a linking verb (usually a form of *to be: is, are,* and so on). In such sentences, the verb comes before the subject.

There are ants all over the kitchen counter.

(The subject is the plural noun *ants,* so the plural verb *are* is used.)

Here is the bug spray.

(The subject is the singular noun *spray,* so the singular verb *is* is used.)

In sentences like those above, remember not to omit *there* or *here.*

Incorrect: *Are* several tests scheduled for Friday.

Correct: **There are** several tests scheduled for Friday.

Not Using the Progressive Tense of Certain Verbs

The progressive tenses are made up of forms of *be* plus the *-ing* form of the main verb. They express actions or conditions still in progress at a particular time.

The garden **will be blooming** when you visit me in June.

However, verbs for mental states, the senses, possession, and inclusion are normally not used in the progressive tense.

Incorrect: I *am knowing* a lot about auto mechanics.

Correct: I **know** a lot about auto mechanics.

Incorrect: Gerald *is having* a job as a supermarket cashier.

Correct: Gerald **has** a job as a supermarket cashier.

Common verbs not generally used in the progressive tense are listed in the following box.

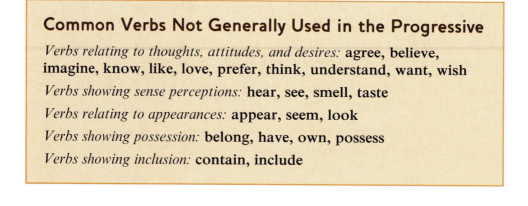

Common Verbs Not Generally Used in the Progressive

Verbs relating to thoughts, attitudes, and desires: **agree, believe, imagine, know, like, love, prefer, think, understand, want, wish**

Verbs showing sense perceptions: **hear, see, smell, taste**

Verbs relating to appearances: **appear, seem, look**

Verbs showing possession: **belong, have, own, possess**

Verbs showing inclusion: **contain, include**

Using Gerunds and Infinitives after Verbs

Before learning the rules about gerunds and infinitives, you must understand what they are. A *gerund* is the *-ing* form of a verb that is used as a noun:

Reading is a good way to improve one's vocabulary.

(*Reading* is the subject of the sentence.)

An *infinitive* is *to* plus the basic form of the verb (the form in which the verb is listed in the dictionary), as in **to eat**. The infinitive can function as an adverb, an adjective, or a noun.

On weekends, Betsy works at a convenience store **to make** some extra money.

(*To make some extra money* functions as an adverb that describes the verb *works*.)

I need a pencil **to write down** your telephone number.

(*To write down your telephone number* functions as an adjective describing the noun *pencil*.)

To forgive can be a relief.

(*To forgive* functions as a noun—it is the subject of the verb *can be*.)

Some verbs can be followed by only a gerund or only an infinitive; other verbs can be followed by either. Examples are given in the following lists. There are many others; watch for them in your reading.

Verb + gerund (*enjoy + skiing*)
Verb + preposition + gerund
(*think + about + coming*)

Some verbs can be followed by a gerund but not by an infinitive. In many cases, there is a preposition (such as *for, in,* or *of*) between the verb and the gerund. Following are some verbs and verb-preposition combinations that can be followed by gerunds but not by infinitives:

admit	be used to	feel like	suspect of
apologize for	believe in	finish	talk about
appreciate	deny	insist on	thank for
approve of	discuss	look forward to	think about
avoid	dislike	postpone	
	enjoy	practice	

Incorrect: The governor *avoids to make* enemies.

Correct: The governor **avoids making** enemies.

Incorrect: I *enjoy to go* to movies alone.

Correct: I **enjoy going** to movies alone.

Verb + infinitive (*agree* + *to leave*)

Following are common verbs that can be followed by an infinitive but not by a gerund:

agree	decide	manage
arrange	expect	refuse
claim	have	wait

Incorrect: I *arranged paying* my uncle's bills while he was ill.

Correct: I **arranged to pay** my uncle's bills while he was ill.

Verb + noun or pronoun + infinitive (*cause* + *them* + *to flee*)

Below are common verbs that are first followed by a noun or pronoun and then by an infinitive, not a gerund.

cause	force	remind
command	persuade	warn

Incorrect: The flood *forced them leaving their home.*

Correct: The flood **forced them to leave their home.**

Following are common verbs that can be followed either by an infinitive alone or by a noun or pronoun and an infinitive:

ask	need	want
expect	promise	would like

Rita **expects to go** to college.

Rita's parents **expect her to go** to college.

Verb + gerund or infinitive
(*begin + packing* or *begin + to pack*)

Following are verbs that can be followed by either a gerund or an infinitive:

begin	**hate**	**prefer**
continue	**love**	**start**

The meaning of each of the above verbs remains the same or almost the same whether a gerund or an infinitive is used.

> I love **to sleep** late.
>
> I love **sleeping** late.

With the verbs below, the gerunds and the infinitives have very different meanings.

forget	**remember**	**stop**

> Yuri **forgot putting money** in the parking meter.
>
> (He put money in the parking meter, but then he forgot that he had done so.)
>
> Yuri **forgot to put money** in the parking meter.
>
> (He neglected to put money in the parking meter.)

Underline the correct word or words in parentheses.

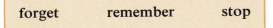

1. The parakeet (likes, it likes) to have its neck scratched.

2. My daughter is in the first grade. (Is learning, She is learning) to read.

3. (Is a letter, There is a letter) waiting on your desk.

4. I cannot sleep because a streetlamp (is shining, shining) in my bedroom window.

5. My plans for today (are including, include) shopping for groceries and studying for a test.

6. Is there something wrong? You (seem upset, are seeming upset).

Practice

2

7. You really should (apologize for to insult, apologize for insulting) your friend.

8. My grandfather (believes in saving, believes in to save) his money.

9. Mark (waited applying, waited to apply) for college until the last moment.

10. We (decided to hav*e*, decided having) pizza for lunch.

Adjectives

Following the Order of Adjectives in English

Adjectives describe nouns and pronouns. In English, an adjective usually comes directly before the word it describes or after a linking verb (a form of *be* or a "sense" verb such as *look*, *seem*, or *taste*), in which case it modifies the subject of the sentence. In each of the following two sentences, the adjective is **boldfaced** and the noun it describes is *italicized*.

> Marta has **beautiful** *eyes*.

> Marta's *eyes* are **beautiful**.

When more than one adjective modifies the same noun, the adjectives are usually stated in a certain order, though there are often exceptions. Following is the typical order of English adjectives:

Typical Order of Adjectives in a Series

1. Article or other noun marker: a, an, the, Helen's, this, seven, your

2. Opinion adjective: rude, enjoyable, surprising, easy

3. Size: tall, huge, small, compact

4. Shape: triangular, oval, round, square

5. Age: ancient, new, old, young

6. Color: gray, blue, pink, green

7. Nationality: Greek, Thai, Korean, Ethiopian

8. Religion: Hindu, Methodist, Jewish, Muslim

9. Material: fur, copper, stone, velvet

10. Noun used as an adjective: book (as in *book report*), picture (as in *picture frame*), tea (as in *tea bag*)

Here are some examples of the order of adjectives:

an exciting new movie

the petite young Irish woman

my favorite Chinese restaurant

Greta's long brown leather coat

In general, use no more than two or three adjectives after the article or other noun marker. Numerous adjectives in a series can be awkward: *that comfortable big old green velvet* couch.

Using the Present and Past Participles as Adjectives

The present participle ends in *-ing*. Past participles of regular verbs end in *-ed* or *-d;* a list of the past participles of many common irregular verbs appears on pages 165–166. Both types of participles may be used as adjectives. A participle used as an adjective may come before the word it describes:

There was a **frowning** *security guard.*

A participle used as an adjective may also follow a linking verb and describe the subject of the sentence:

The *security guard* was **frowning**.

While both present and past participles of a particular verb may be used as adjectives, their meanings differ. Use the present participle to describe whoever or whatever causes a feeling:

a **disappointing** *date*

(The date *caused* the disappointment.)

Use the past participle to describe whoever or whatever experiences the feeling:

the **disappointed** *neighbor*

(The neighbor *is* disappointed.)

Here are two more sentences that illustrate the differing meanings of present and past participles.

The waiter was **irritating**.

The diners were **irritated**.

(The waiter caused the irritation; the diners experienced the irritation.)

Following are pairs of present and past participles with similar distinctions.

annoying / annoyed	exhausting / exhausted
boring / bored	fascinating / fascinated
confusing / confused	tiring / tired
depressing / depressed	surprising / surprised
exciting / excited	

Practice

3

Underline the correct word or wording in parentheses.

1. Under my desk at work I keep a (black square little, little square black) heater.

2. The thieves took a (beautiful antique sapphire, beautiful sapphire antique) necklace.

3. The birthday party was held in a (terrific new Mexican, Mexican new terrific) restaurant.

4. Children who are (bored, boring) can get into all kinds of mischief.

5. Larry enjoys life in the country, but his wife finds it too quiet and (bored, boring).

Prepositions Used for Time and Place

The use of a preposition in English is often not based on the preposition's common meaning, and there are many exceptions to general rules. As a result, the correct use of prepositions must be learned gradually through experience. Following is a chart showing how three of the most common prepositions are used in some customary references to time and place:

Use of *On*, *In*, and *At* to Refer to Time and Place

Time

On *a specific day:* on Wednesday, on January 11, on Halloween

In *a part of a day:* in the morning, in the daytime (but *at* night)

> ***In*** *a month or a year:* in October, in 1776
>
> ***In*** *a period of time:* in a second, in a few days, in a little while
>
> ***At*** *a specific time:* at 11 P.M., at midnight, at sunset, at lunchtime
>
> **Place**
>
> ***On*** *a surface:* on the shelf, on the sidewalk, on the roof
>
> ***In*** *a place that is enclosed:* in the bathroom, in the closet, in the drawer
>
> ***At*** *a specific location:* at the restaurant, at the zoo, at the school

Underline the correct preposition in parentheses.

Practice

4

1. I drink coffee only (in, at) the morning.

2. The class will begin (on, at) 8 A.M.

3. Kate needs a baby-sitter (on, at) Tuesday night.

4. There is some fruit (in, at) the refrigerator.

5. (At, In) just one hour, my cousin will be here.

Review Test

Underline the correct word or words in parentheses.

1. We have (room, rooms) for one more passenger in the car.

2. (Is, There is) no need for you to be so angry.

3. Nancy was (embarrassing, embarrassed) when she suddenly forgot her teacher's name.

4. Giving a wrong answer in front of the whole class is (embarrassing, embarrassed).

5. The old dog spends most of its time sleeping on an (old brown ugly, ugly old brown) chair.

6. I feel like (to stay home, staying home) tonight.

7. My girlfriend (understands, is understanding) me very well.

8. We'll look forward to seeing you (on, at) Friday night.

9. The loud (thunder, thunders) made it difficult to talk.

10. I promise (calling, to call) when I get back in town.

Sentence-Skills Diagnostic Test

Part 1

This diagnostic test will help check your knowledge of a number of sentence skills. In each item below, certain words are underlined. Write *X* in the answer space if you think a mistake appears at the underlined part. Write *C* in the answer space if you think the underlined part is correct.

The headings within the text ("Fragments," "Run-Ons," and so on) will give you clues to the mistakes to look for. However, you do not have to understand the heading to find a mistake. What you are checking is your own sense of effective written English.

Fragments

_____ 1. After I had done fifty push-ups. I felt like a worn-out rubber band. I wasn't planning to move until the middle of next week.

_____ 2. My little brother loves to go out at night, especially when the moon is full. My sister is convinced he's a werewolf.

_____ 3. Shelly stood on tiptoe and craned her neck. Trying to see over the heads of the people in front of her. Finally she decided to go home and watch the parade on television.

_____ 4. Janet was excited about the job interview. She decided to have her hair done. And bought a new briefcase so she would look like an executive.

Run-Ons

_____ 5. The instructor assigned two chapters of the book, he also handed out a library research project.

_____ 6. Something was obviously bothering Martha a small muscle in her temple was throbbing.

_____ 7. The tires on my Chevy are <u>worn, but</u> the car itself is in good condition.

_____ 8. I could afford the monthly car <u>payments, I</u> did not have enough money to pay for insurance as well.

Standard English Verbs

_____ 9. Aunt Agatha <u>sees</u> much better when she puts on her bifocals.

_____ 10. The game was lost when the other team <u>score</u> a fourth-quarter touchdown.

_____ 11. At the end of the hike, we <u>was</u> covered with mosquito bites.

_____ 12. Martina <u>have</u> only three more courses to take to earn her degree.

Irregular Verbs

_____ 13. That show must be a rerun; I <u>seen</u> it at least twice.

_____ 14. If I had <u>taken</u> more notes in that class, I would have done better on the exam.

_____ 15. I accidentally <u>throwed</u> away the parking ticket when I cleaned out the glove compartment <u>of</u> my car.

_____ 16. At the end of the practice session, all the players <u>drank</u> Gatorade.

Subject-Verb Agreement

_____ 17. The major story on all the news programs <u>concerns</u> the proposed tax hike.

_____ 18. There <u>was</u> only two handkerchiefs left in the drawer.

_____ 19. My sister and her husband <u>take</u> my father bowling every Thursday night.

_____ 20. Each of my little boys <u>need</u> a warmer jacket for the winter.

Consistent Verb Tense

_____ 21. After I checked my bank balance, <u>I realized I</u> did not have enough money for a new car stereo.

_____ 22. Upon finding a seat on the bus, Ralph unfolded his newspaper, <u>turns</u> to the sports section, and began to read.

Pronoun Reference, Agreement, and Point of View

_____ 23. All students should try their best to get good grades.

_____ 24. My first year in college I stayed in a dorm, where they chose a roommate for me.

_____ 25. Our company never gives bonuses to its employees, no matter how hard you work.

Pronoun Types

_____ 26. Paula writes much better than me.

_____ 27. My sister and I have both gotten part-time jobs.

Adjectives and Adverbs

_____ 28. The children smiled so sweet that I knew they were up to something.

_____ 29. The professor spoke honestly to me about my writing strengths and problems.

_____ 30. Weighing 350 pounds, Max the Mauler was the most heaviest of the four wrestlers in the ring.

_____ 31. Soap operas are more enjoyable to Martha than game shows.

Misplaced Modifiers

_____ 32. At the electronics store, we bought a DVD Player that has a stop-action feature.

_____ 33. I returned the toy to the store that was broken.

Dangling Modifiers

_____ 34. While playing cards, two pizzas were eaten.

_____ 35. Glancing out the window, Felipe saw a strange car pull into the driveway.

Faulty Parallelism

_____ 36. Before I can settle down to studying, I must take out the garbage, dry the dishes, and the leftovers have to be put away.

_____ 37. Three ways of treating a cold are bed rest, chicken soup, and taking vitamin C.

Capital Letters

_____ 38. Daylight saving time usually ends on the last <u>sunday</u> in October.

_____ 39. Last summer I worked as a stock boy at <u>Target</u>.

_____ 40. Most of the people who live in that neighborhood are <u>doctors</u>.

_____ 41. Vince yelled, "<u>hurry</u> up, the show's starting in ten minutes."

Numbers and Abbreviations

_____ 42. So far <u>7</u> students have dropped out of my math course.

_____ 43. The assignment starts on page <u>132</u> of the math book.

_____ 44. Norm's insurance <u>co.</u> increased his rates after he was involved in a car accident.

End Marks

_____ 45. Are you going to the church service tomorrow<u>.</u>

_____ 46. I wondered if I should give Terry a call<u>.</u>

Apostrophe

_____ 47. <u>Lucys</u> goal is to become the head nurse at the same hospital where her <u>mother</u> once worked.

_____ 48. I <u>wasnt</u> able to sleep at all the night after my wisdom <u>teeth</u> were pulled.

_____ 49. I did some careful thinking before I rejected my <u>lawyer's</u> advice in the matter.

_____ 50. Several storm <u>windows'</u> in the house are badly cracked.

Quotation Marks

_____ 51. Benjamin Franklin once wrote, "<u>Fish and visitors begin to smell after three days."</u>

_____ 52. I'll be with you in just a moment, the harried <u>salesperson said."</u>

_____ 53. If <u>that's your opinion," said Fran, "you're more narrow-minded than I thought."</u>

_____ 54. <u>Time is money, the manager said, and I don't have much."</u>

Comma

_____ 55. The dessert consisted of homemade ice cream and a choice of fresh straw-berries blueberries or peaches.

_____ 56. My brother, who lifts weights, rarely loses an argument.

_____ 57. When I opened the door to my apartment I quickly sensed that something was wrong.

_____ 58. It was supposed to rain heavily all day, but we only got a light drizzle in the morning.

Spelling

_____ 59. If I had controlled my time better this semester, I would have been a successful student.

_____ 60. Maureen has alot of definitions to study for her biology test.

_____ 61. My roommate wants to hold partys in our apartment every weekend.

_____ 62. The house we just bought has two baths and a sunken liveing room.

Omitted Words and Letters

_____ 63. As a child, I always cut the crusts my bread.

_____ 64. All three record stores in the mall have sales on select new releases.

_____ 65. All the outside doors in our house have dead-bolt lock.

Commonly Confused Words

_____ 66. I'm very sorry to hear that your not feeling well.

_____ 67. You can't judge a book by it's cover.

_____ 68. The car was going much to fast to stop at the light.

_____ 69. The tenants decided to take their landlord to court.

Effective Word Choice

_____ 70. Our car was totaled in the accident; we're lucky to be alive.

_____ 71. Without financial aid, my children are going to have a lot of trouble trying to make ends meet.

_____   72. Ernest <u>was promoted</u> more quickly than other employees in the company.

_____   73. My <u>expectancy</u> is to become a doctor someday.

_____   74. <u>In my personal opinion,</u> I think that a tax hike is ridiculous.

_____   75. <u>Because of the fact that</u> Jennifer missed the final exam, she failed the course.

Part 2 (Optional)

Do the following at your instructor's request. This second part of the test will provide more detailed information about skills you need to know. On separate paper, number and correct all the items you have marked with an *X*. For example, suppose you had marked the word groups below with an *X*. (Note that these examples were not taken from the actual test.)

4. <u>When I picked up the tire.</u> Something in my back snapped. I could not stand up straight as a result.

7. The phone started <u>ringing, then</u> the doorbell sounded as well.

15. <u>Marks</u> goal is to save enough money to get married next year.

29. Without checking the rearview <u>mirror the</u> driver pulled out into the passing lane.

Here is how you should write your corrections on a separate sheet of paper:

4. When I picked up the tire, something in my back snapped.

7. The phone started ringing, and then the doorbell sounded as well.

15. Mark's

29. mirror, the driver

There are more than forty corrections to make in all.

Sentence-Skills Achievement Test

Part I

This achievement test will help you check your mastery of a number of sentence skills. In each item below, certain words are underlined. Write *X* in the answer space if you think a mistake appears at the underlined part. Write *C* in the answer space if you think the underlined part is correct.

The headings within the test ("Fragments," "Run-Ons," and so on) will give you clues to the mistakes to look for.

Fragments

_____ 1. After I finished my morning classes. I had a quick lunch in the cafeteria. Then I hurried off to my job as a supermarket cashier.

_____ 2. My family loves outdoor sports, especially touch football. We often play outside until it's dark.

_____ 3. Simone waved her hand back and forth. Trying to catch the instructor's attention. She wanted to ask a question and make a comment about the lecture.

_____ 4. The instructor handed back my term paper. She told me to rewrite the conclusion. And retype the footnotes so that the form was correct.

Run-Ons

_____ 5. Myrna was angry at herself, she had forgotten to pick up some potatoes on the way home.

_____ 6. My husband often sings in the morning our cat hides under the bed.

_____ 7. Ed is an absentminded person, so he writes notes to help himself remember things.

_____ 8. I kept drinking cups of coffee, I had a lot of studying to do that night.

Standard English Verbs

_____   9. My husband <u>thinks</u> more clearly in the morning than at night.

_____   10. When the pile of rags caught on fire, Theo <u>reach</u> for the hose.

_____   11. At Saturday's football game, we <u>was</u> the only couple that brought an umbrella.

_____   12. I don't think that Ray <u>have</u> thought enough about his future.

Irregular Verbs

_____   13. My boyfriend and I <u>seen</u> the new Tom Cruise movie last night.

_____   14. We should not have <u>taken</u> the children shopping with us today.

_____   15. The second baseman fielded the grounder, stepped on the bag, and then <u>throwed</u> to first for a double play.

_____   16. My cotton sweater <u>shrank</u> so much in the wash that I gave it to my daughter.

Subject-Verb Agreement

_____   17. The price of the theater tickets <u>seems</u> much too high.

_____   18. There <u>was</u> only three pieces of wood left in the pile.

_____   19. The new tenant and her little boy <u>make</u> a lot of noise.

_____   20. Each of the office secretaries <u>work</u> from 9 to 5.

Consistent Verb Tense

_____   21. My father interrupted me as I studied my accounting and <u>asked</u> me to balance his checkbook.

_____   22. When they got back from the party, Ann lost her temper, <u>screams</u> at her husband, and then refused to talk about the cause.

Pronoun Reference, Agreement, and Point of View

_____   23. All registered voters should do <u>their</u> civic duty at the polls.

_____   24. Carol joined the sorority because <u>they</u> have the same interests that she has.

_____   25. I'm going to move out of the city because <u>you</u> never feel safe there.

Pronoun Types

_____ 26. Larry had a lot more to eat than <u>me</u>.

_____ 27. My brother and <u>I</u> are getting married in the same month.

Adjectives and Adverbs

_____ 28. The dress was made <u>beautiful</u>, with a full silk lining and covered buttons.

_____ 29. The boy walked <u>timidly</u> up to the baseball player and asked for his autograph.

_____ 30. Which would you say is the <u>more harder</u> exercise—swimming or jogging?

_____ 31. General Psychology is the <u>most interesting</u> course I am taking this semester.

Misplaced Modifiers

_____ 32. At the campus bookstore, I just bought a diary <u>that has a genuine leather cover.</u>

_____ 33. Most people do not go on summer vacations <u>that are poor.</u>

Dangling Modifiers

_____ 34. <u>While carrying the packages out of the store,</u> my ankle was sprained.

_____ 35. <u>Jogging down the street,</u> Phil was almost hit by a car.

Faulty Parallelism

_____ 36. This weekend, Steve has to mow the lawn, take the dog to the vet, <u>and the family station wagon needs to be washed.</u>

_____ 37. Barbara was frightened, upset, and <u>a nervous wreck;</u> she had three exams in the next two days.

Capital Letters

_____ 38. The sale ends this coming <u>tuesday</u>.

_____ 39. I just got a call from <u>allstate</u> that my insurance is being dropped.

_____ 40. Frank's goal is to become a successful <u>accountant</u> someday.

_____ 41. Linda asked, "<u>who</u> wants to go out and get some more ice?"

Numbers and Abbreviations

_____ 42. Before the game was over, <u>four</u> players had been ejected.

_____ 43. Your doctor's appointment has been scheduled for <u>8:15</u> tomorrow morning.

_____ 44. I spent almost ten <u>hrs.</u> studying for the exam.

End Marks

_____ 45. Do you know where Bob is tonight<u>?</u>

_____ 46. Tisha wondered how long the sprain would take to heal<u>.</u>

Apostrophe

_____ 47. <u>Sams</u> proudest moment came when he got his first A on a paper.

_____ 48. <u>Doesnt</u> your bank stay open late on Fridays?

_____ 49. The <u>doctor's</u> advice contradicted that of the other doctor I had seen.

_____ 50. The little girl at the front door explained that she had some <u>puppies'</u> for sale.

Quotation Marks

_____ 51. <u>Benjamin Franklin once wrote, "There never was a good war or a bad peace."</u>

_____ 52. <u>"I'd rather make a fast nickel than a slow dollar, the store owner said."</u>

_____ 53. <u>"Don't come back after lunch," the boss said, "because you're fired."</u>

_____ 54. <u>"After you finish writing the essay," said the instructor, be sure to proofread it carefully."</u>

Comma

_____ 55. Stella has just learned that she is allergic to <u>shrimp crabmeat and salmon.</u>

_____ 56. My Uncle <u>Al, who is very forgetful, always</u> asks me my name.

_____ 57. As the vampire was about to bite his <u>victim he</u> saw that the sun was shining.

_____ 58. Last summer I worked in a <u>factory, but</u> this summer I'll have a job in a resort hotel.

Spelling

_____ 59. Through someone's mistake, my name was <u>dropped</u> from the list of graduating seniors.

_____ 60. It's <u>alright</u> with me if you skip breakfast.

_____ 61. There are three unidentified <u>bodys</u> in the police morgue.

_____ 62. The counselor asked how many courses I planned on <u>takeing</u> next semester.

Omitted Words and Letters

_____ 63. <u>The kids in street played ball with cutoff broom handles.</u>

_____ 64. <u>Sharp splinters jutted out of the wooden pilings on the pier.</u>

_____ 65. <u>I need at least a thousand dollar to pay off my debts.</u>

Commonly Confused Words

_____ 66. If <u>your</u> in the mood for some shopping, so am I.

_____ 67. The supplement helps my body get <u>it's</u> daily dose of potassium.

_____ 68. Caroline is <u>to</u> self-centered to be a good friend.

_____ 69. The players will forfeit <u>their</u> salaries if they go on strike.

Effective Word Choice

_____ 70. Someone broke into my car and <u>ripped off</u> my radio.

_____ 71. I need a new coat; my old corduroy one has <u>seen better days.</u>

_____ 72. The employee layoff was <u>handled in a sensitive way</u> by the company.

_____ 73. My parents are <u>desirous of my earning</u> a college degree.

_____ 74. <u>Owing to the fact that</u> we don't play cards, we weren't invited to the party.

_____ 75. <u>Personally, my own belief</u> is that every home will have a computer someday.

Part 2 (Optional)

Do the following at your instructor's request. This second part of the test will provide more detailed information about skills you need to know. On separate paper, number and correct all the items you have marked with an *X*. For example, suppose you had marked the word groups below with an *X*. (Note that these examples were not taken from the actual test.)

4. When I picked up the tire. Something in my back snapped. I could not stand up straight as a result.

7. The phone started ringing, then the doorbell sounded as well.

15. Marks goal is to save enough money to get married next year.

29. Without checking the rearview mirror the driver pulled out into the passing lane.

Here is how you should write your corrections on a separate sheet of paper:

4. When I picked up the tire, something in my back snapped.

7. The phone started ringing, and then the doorbell sounded as well.

15. Mark's

29. mirror, the driver

There are more than forty corrections to make in all.

Answers to Introductory Activities and Practice Exercises in Part Two

This answer key can help you teach yourself. Use it to find out why you got some answers wrong—you want to uncover a weak spot in your understanding of a given skill. By using the answer key in an honest and thoughtful way, you will master each skill and prepare yourself for many tests in this book that have no answer key.

SUBJECTS AND VERBS

Introductory Activity (page 66)

Answers will vary.

Practice 1 (68)

1. I ate
2. Alligators swim
3. April failed
4. movie ended
5. Keiko borrowed
6. children stared
7. newspaper tumbled
8. Lola starts
9. job limits
10. windstorm blew

Practice 2 (69)

1. sister is
2. chips are
3. defendant appeared
4. Art became
5. ride . . . seems
6. building was
7. weeks . . . were
8. banana split . . . cake . . . look
9. Jane . . . feels
10. rooms . . . seem

Practice 3 (69)

1. clock runs
2. player . . . is
3. shoppers filled
4. trucks rumbled
5. children drew
6. picture fell
7. Chipmunks live
8. uncle monopolized
9. tomatoes were
10. company canceled

Practice 4 (70)

1. For that course, you need three different books.
2. The key to the front door slipped from my hand into a puddle.
3. The checkout lines at the supermarket moved very slowly.
4. With his son, Jamal walked to the playground.
5. No quarrel between good friends lasts for a very long time.
6. In one weekend, Martha planted a large vegetable garden in her backyard.
7. Either of my brothers is a reliable worker.
8. The drawer of the bureau sticks on rainy days.
9. During the movie, several people walked out in protest.
10. At a single sitting, my brother reads five or more comic books.

Practice 5 (72)

1. He has been sleeping
2. foundations . . . were attacked
3. I have not washed
4. instructor had not warned
5. bus will be leaving
6. You should not try
7. They have just been married
8. He could make
9. Kim has decided
10. employees should have warned

Practice 6 (73)

1. hypnotist locked . . . and sawed
2. Trina began . . . and finished
3. Nissans, Toyotas, and Hondas glittered
4. Tony added . . . and got
5. car sputtered, stalled, and . . . started
6. Whiteflies, mites, and aphids infected
7. Ruth disconnected . . . and carried
8. We walked . . . and bought
9. Tony and Lola looked . . . and . . . bought
10. aunt and uncle married, . . . divorced, . . . and . . . remarried

FRAGMENTS

Introductory Activity (79)

1. verb
2. subject
3. subject . . . verb
4. thought

Practice 1 (83)

Answers will vary.

Practice 2 (83)

NOTE: The underlined part shows the fragment (or that part of the original fragment not changed during correction).

1. Although the air conditioner was working, I still felt warm in the room.
2. When Tony got into his car this morning, he discovered that he had left the car windows open. The seats and rug were soaked, since it had rained overnight.
3. After cutting fish at the restaurant all day, Jenny smelled like a cat food factory.

4. Franco raked out the soggy leaves that were at the bottom of the cement fishpond. When two bullfrogs jumped out at him, he dropped the rake and ran.
5. Because he had eaten and drunk too much, he had to leave the party early. His stomach was like a volcano that was ready to erupt.

Practice 3 (86)

1. Eli lay in bed after the alarm rang, wishing that he had $100,000.
2. Investigating the strange, mournful cries in his neighbor's yard, George found a puppy tangled in its leash.
3. As a result, being late for class. *Correction:* As a result, I was late for class.

Practice 4 (86)

Rewritten versions may vary.

1. Glistening with dew, the gigantic web hung between the branches of the tree.
2. Kevin loves his new puppy, claiming that the little dog is his best friend. *Or:* Kevin loves his new puppy. He claims that the little dog is his best friend.
3. Noah picked through the box of chocolates, removing the kinds he didn't like. *Or:* He removed the kinds he didn't like.
4. The grass I was walking on suddenly became squishy because I had hiked into a marsh of some kind. *Or:* The reason was that I had hiked into a marsh of some kind.
5. Steve drove quickly to the bank to cash his paycheck. *Or:* He had to cash his paycheck.

Practice 5 (88)

1. For example, managing to cut his hand while crumbling a bar of shredded wheat. *Correction:* For example, he managed . . .
2. All day, people complained about missing parts, rude salespeople, and errors on bills.
3. For example, using club soda on stains. *Correction:* For example, she suggests using . . .

Practice 6 (89)

Rewritten versions may vary.

1. My little boy is constantly into mischief, such as tearing the labels off all the cans in the cupboard.
2. For example, a hand-carved mantel and a mahogany banister. *Correction:* For example, it had . . .
3. For instance, chewing with his mouth open. *Correction:* For instance, he chewed . . .

4. A half hour later, there were several explosions, with potatoes splattering all over the walls of the oven. *Or:* Potatoes splattered all over the walls of the oven.

5. Janet looked forward to seeing former classmates at the high school reunion, including the football player she had a wild crush on.

Practice 7 *(90)*

Rewritten answers may vary.

1. Fred went to the refrigerator to get milk for his breakfast cereal and discovered about one tablespoon of milk left in the carton. *Or:* He discovered about one tablespoon of milk left in the carton.

2. Then noticed the "out of order" sign taped over the coin slot. *Correction:* Then I noticed . . .

3. Our neighborhood's most eligible bachelor got married this weekend but did not invite us to the wedding. *Or:* But he did not invite us to the wedding.

4. Also, was constantly criticizing Larry's choice of friends. *Correction:* Also, he was constantly . . .

5. Wanda stared at the blank page in desperation and decided that the first sentence of a paper is always the hardest to write. *Or:* And she decided that the first sentence of a paper is always the hardest to write.

RUN-ONS

Introductory Activity *(103)*

1. period
2. but
3. semicolon
4. Although

Practice 1 *(106)*

1. down. He
2. station. A
3. panicked. The
4. exam. The
5. wood. One
6. hand. Guests
7. earth. Earthworms
8. party. A
9. time. Her
10. stacks. The

Practice 2 *(107)*

1. class. His
2. increasing. Every
3. properly. We
4. it. Half
5. places. Our
6. water. This
7. speeding. He
8. times. Nobody
9. names. For
10. victory. His

Practice 3 *(107)*

Answers will vary.

Practice 4 *(109)*

1. , and
2. , for
3. , but
4. , for
5. , for
6. , but
7. , and
8. , so
9. , but
10. , so

Practice 5 *(110)*

Answers will vary.

Practice 6 *(111)*

1. service; the
2. game; the
3. cool; everyone
4. year; an
5. stop; he

Practice 7 *(112)*

Answers may vary.

1. insecticide; otherwise, the
2. props; also, I (*or* in addition *or* moreover *or* furthermore)
3. basement; instead, he
4. week; consequently, I (*or* as a result *or* thus *or* therefore)
5. semester; in addition, she (*or* also *or* moreover *or* furthermore)

Practice 8 *(112)*

1. seat; however,
2. match; as a result,
3. headache; furthermore,
4. razors; consequently
5. hair; nevertheless,

Practice 9 *(113)*

Answers may vary.

1. because
2. When
3. While *or* When
4. After *or* When
5. before

Practice 10 *(114)*

1. Because (*or* Since) Sharon didn't understand the instructor's point, she asked him to repeat it.
2. Although (*or* Even though) Marco remembered to get the hamburger, he forgot to get the hamburger rolls.

3. After Michael gulped two cups of strong coffee, his heart started to flutter.
4. When a car sped around the corner, it sprayed slush all over the pedestrians.
5. Although (*or* Even though) Lola loved the rose cashmere sweater, she had nothing to wear with it.

SENTENCE VARIETY I

The Simple Sentence
Practice 1 *(126)*

Answers will vary.

The Compound Sentence
Practice 2 *(127)*

Answers may vary; possible answers are given.

1. My cold grew worse, so I decided to see a doctor.
2. My uncle always ignores me, but my aunt gives me kisses and presents.
3. We played softball in the afternoon, and we went to a movie in the evening.
4. I invited Rico to sleep overnight, but he wanted to go home.
5. Police raided the club, for they had gotten a tip about illegal drugs for sale.

Practice 3 *(128)*

Answers will vary.

The Complex Sentence
Practice 4 *(129)*

Answers may vary; possible answers are given.

1. When the instructor announced the quiz, the class groaned.
2. Because Gene could not fit any more groceries into his cart, he decided to go to the checkout counter.
3. If your car is out of commission, you should take it to Otto's Transmission.
4. After I received a raise at work, I called my boss to say thank you.
5. Since we owned four cats and a dog, no one would rent us an apartment.

Practice 5 *(130)*

Answers may vary; possible answers are given.

1. Although Ruth turned on the large window fan, the room remained hot.

2. Since the plumber repaired the water heater, we can take showers again.
3. After I washed the sheets and towels, I scrubbed the bathroom floor.
4. You should go to a doctor because your chest cold may get worse.
5. When the fish tank broke, guppies were flopping all over the carpet.

Practice 6 *(131)*

Answers may vary; possible answers are given.

1. The magazine article that made me very angry was about abortion.
2. The woodshed, which I built myself, has collapsed.
3. The power drill that I bought at half price is missing.
4. Rita Haber, who is our mayor, was indicted for bribery.
5. The chicken pies that we ate contained dangerous preservatives.

Practice 7 *(132)*

Answers will vary.

The Compound-Complex Sentence
Practice 8 *(132)*

1. Because . . . and
2. When . . . so
3. Although . . . and
4. Since . . . for
5. If . . . or

Practice 9 *(133)*

Answers will vary.

Review of Coordination and Subordination
Practice 10 *(133)*

Answers will vary. Many other combinations are possible.

1. After Louise used a dandruff shampoo, she still had dandruff, so she decided to see a dermatologist.
2. Omar's parents want him to be a doctor, but Omar wants to be a salesman. He impresses people with his charm.
3. While the instructor conducted a discussion period, Jack sat at his desk with his head down. He did not want the instructor to call on him, for he had not read the assignment.
4. When Lola wanted to get a quick lunch at the cafeteria, all the sandwiches were gone, so she had to settle for a cup of yogurt.

5. As I was leaving to do some shopping in town, I asked my son to water the back lawn. He seemed agreeable, but when I returned three hours later, the lawn had not been watered.

6. Because I had eaten too quickly, my stomach became upset. It felt like a war combat zone, so I took two Alka-Seltzer tablets.

7. Midge, who enjoys growing things, is always buying plants and flower seeds, but not many things grow well for her. She doesn't know why.

8. My car was struck from behind yesterday when I slowed suddenly for a red light. The driver of the truck behind me slammed on his brakes, but he didn't quite stop in time.

9. Ed, who desperately needed a job, skimmed through the help-wanted ads, but nothing was there for him. He would have to sell his car, for he could no longer keep up the payments.

10. Since the meat loaf didn't taste right and the mashed potatoes had too much salt in them, we sent out for a pizza. It was delivered late, and it was cold.

STANDARD ENGLISH VERBS

Introductory Activity (143)

played . . . plays
hoped . . . hopes
juggled . . . juggles

1. past time . . . -ed or –d
2. present time . . . -s

Practice 1 (145)

1. hates	6. C
2. messes	7. blurs
3. feels	8. thinks
4. covers	9. pretends
5. smells	10. seems

Practice 2 (146)

Charlotte behaves rudely whenever she speaks on her cell phone. First of all, she answers the phone anytime it rings, even at a restaurant or the movies. Then she raises her voice and acts as if the caller is sitting right next to her. Sometimes she waves her hands or laughs loudly. She never notices how people roll their eyes at her. She even asks others near her to be quiet while she talks. If she keeps this up, no one will go anywhere with her–unless she leaves the phone at home.

Practice 3 (147)

1. raced	6. decided
2. glowed	7. C
3. walked	8. needed
4. sighted	9. scattered
5. stared	10. Decided

Practice 4 (147)

Bill's boss shouted at Bill. Feeling bad, Bill went home and cursed his wife. Then his wife screamed at their son. Angry himself, the son went out and cruelly teased a little girl who lived next door until she wailed. Bad feelings were passed on as one person wounded the next with ugly words. No one managed to break the vicious circle.

Practice 5 (149)

1. has	6. was
2. does	7. did . . . was
3. is	8. were
4. are	9. had
5. was . . . had	10. am

Practice 6 (150)

1. ~~be~~ is	6. ~~have~~ had
2. ~~is~~ are	7. ~~done~~ did
3. ~~has~~ have	8. ~~have~~ had
4. ~~don't~~ doesn't	9. ~~has~~ had
5. ~~is~~ are	10. ~~was~~ were

Practice 7 (150)

My mother sings alto in our church choir. She has to go to choir practice every Friday night and is expected to know all the music. If she does not know her part, the other choir members do things like glare at her and are likely to make nasty comments, she says. Last weekend, my mother had houseguests and did not have time to learn all the notes. The music was very difficult, and she thought the other people were going to make fun of her. But they were very understanding when she told them she had laryngitis and couldn't make a sound.

IRREGULAR VERBS

Introductory Activity (156)

1. R . . . screamed . . . screamed
2. I . . . wrote . . . written
3. I . . . stole . . . stolen
4. R . . . asked . . . asked

5. R . . . kissed . . . kissed
6. I . . . chose . . . chosen
7. I . . . rode . . . ridden
8. R . . . chewed . . . chewed
9. I . . . thought . . . thought
10. R . . . danced . . . danced

Practice 1 (160)

1. ~~ate~~ eaten
2. ~~done~~ did (*or* had done)
3. ~~wore~~ worn
4. ~~wrote~~ written
5. ~~gived~~ gave
6. ~~be~~ was
7. ~~broke~~ broken
8. ~~lended~~ lent
9. ~~seen~~ saw
10. ~~knewed~~ knew

Practice 2 (160)

1. (a) sees
   (b) saw
   (c) seen
2. (a) chooses
   (b) chose
   (c) chosen
3. (a) takes
   (b) took
   (c) taken
4. (a) speaks
   (b) spoke
   (c) spoken
5. (a) swims
   (b) swam
   (c) swum
6. (a) drives
   (b) drove
   (c) driven
7. (a) wears
   (b) wore
   (c) worn
8. (a) blows
   (b) blew
   (c) blown
9. (a) begins
   (b) began
   (c) begun
10. (a) goes
    (b) went
    (c) gone

Practice 3 (163)

1. lays
2. lay
3. Lying
4. laid
5. lay

Practice 4 (164)

1. sit
2. setting
3. set
4. sat
5. set

Practice 5 (165)

1. rise
2. raise
3. risen
4. raised
5. rises

SUBJECT-VERB AGREEMENT

Introductory Activity (171)

Correct: The results of the election are very surprising

Correct: There were many complaints about the violent TV show.

Correct: Everybody usually gathers at the waterfront on the Fourth of July.

1. results . . . complaints
2. singular . . . singular

Practice 1 (173)

1. stain ~~on the sheets~~ comes
2. coat, ~~along with two pairs of pants~~, sells
3. roots ~~of the apple tree~~ are
4. sisters, ~~who wanted to be at his surprise party~~, were
5. albums ~~in the attic~~ belong
6. cost ~~of personal calls made on office telephones~~ is
7. cups ~~of coffee in the morning~~ do
8. moon ~~as well as some stars~~ is
9. wiring ~~in the apartment~~ is
10. Chapter 4 ~~of the psychology book, along with six weeks of class notes~~, is

Practice 2 (174)

1. are lines
2. were dogs
3. were dozens
4. are pretzels
5. were Janet and Maureen
6. are rats
7. were boys
8. is house
9. were fans
10. lies pastry

Practice 3 (175)

1. hopes
2. dances
3. deserves
4. were
5. appears
6. offers

7. owns
8. has

9. thinks
10. has

Practice 4 (175)

1. match
2. have
3. are

4. plan
5. are

Practice 5 (176)

1. were
2. stumble
3. blares

4. give
5. appears

CONSISTENT VERB TENSE

Introductory Activity (186)

Mistakes in verb tense: Alex <u>discovers</u> . . . <u>calls</u> a . . .
<u>present</u> . . . <u>past</u>

Practice 1 (187)

1. causes
2. decided
3. picked
4. hopes
5. informs

6. sprinkled
7. discovered
8. asked
9. overcharges
10. swallowed

ADDITIONAL INFORMATION ABOUT VERBS

Practice 1 (Verb Tense; 194)

1. had walked
2. was feeling
3. had placed
4. was trying
5. is growing

6. had looked
7. has studied
8. has seen
9. was watching
10. had thrown

Practice 2 (Verbals; 196)

1. P
2. G
3. G
4. I
5. I

6. P
7. P
8. I
9. P
10. G

Practice 3 (Active and Passive Verbs; 197)

1. Eliza organized the surprise party.
2. The comedian offended many people.
3. The neighbors pay for the old woman's groceries.

4. The boys knocked the horse chestnuts off the trees.
5. The exorcist drove the devil out of Regan.
6. Four perspiring men loaded the huge moving van.
7. The inexperienced waiter dropped a tray of glasses.
8. My forgetful Aunt Agatha is always losing umbrellas.
9. Barry Bonds finally broke Babe Ruth's home run record.
10. The airport security staff found a bomb in the suitcase.

PRONOUN REFERENCE, AGREEMENT, AND POINT OF VIEW

Introductory Activity (201)

1. b
2. b
3. b

Practice 1 (203)

NOTE: The practice sentences could be rewritten to have meanings other than the ones indicated below.

1. Mario insisted that it was Harry's turn to drive.
   Or: Mario insisted to Harry, "It's my turn to drive."
2. I failed two of my courses last semester because the instructors graded unfairly.
3. Don's parents were very much pleased with the accounting job Don was offered.
   Or: The accounting job Don was offered pleased his parents very much.
4. Tony became very upset when he questioned the mechanic.
   Or: The mechanic became very upset when Tony questioned him.
5. I was very nervous about the unexpected biology exam.
6. Paul told his younger brother, "The dog chewed your new running shoes."
7. My cousin is an astrologer, but I don't believe in astrology.
8. When Liz was promoted, she told Elaine.
   Or: Liz told Elaine, "You have been promoted."
9. Whenever I start enjoying a new television show, the network takes it off the air.
10. When the center fielder heard the crack of the bat, he raced toward the fence but was unable to catch the ball.

Practice 2 *(204)*

1. they . . . their
2. it
3. them
4. it
5. they

Practice 3 *(207)*

1. his
2. her
3. his
4. his
5. her
6. his
7. her
8. she
9. its
10. his

Practice 4 *(208)*

1. I always feel hungry
2. they have finished
3. they work
4. we can never be sure
5. she should register
6. he or she should check
   Or: If people plan . . . they should check
7. I do not get paid for all the holidays I should
   Or: One does not get paid . . . one should
8. you should take action
9. we had
10. we want it

PRONOUN TYPES

Introductory Activity *(216)*

Correct sentences:

Ali and I enrolled in a computer course.

The police officer pointed to my sister and me.

Lola prefers men who take pride in their bodies.

The players are confident that the league championship is theirs.

Those concert tickets are too expensive.

Our parents should spend some money on themselves for a change.

Practice 1 *(219)*

1. her *(O)*
2. I *(S)*
3. they *(arrived* is understood) *(S)*
4. her *(O)*
5. she *(S)*
6. he *(S)*
7. She *(S)*

8. We *(S)*
9. I *(am* is understood) *(S)*
10. She and I *(S)*

Practice 2 *(220)*

Answers will vary. Below are some possibilities.

1. me
2. me *or* him
3. me *or* her *or* him *or* them
4. me *or* her *or* him *or* them
5. me *or* her *or* him
6. I *or* he *or* she
7. I *or* he *or* she
8. them
9. him *or* her *or* them
10. us

Practice 3 *(222)*

1. who
2. that
3. who
4. whom
5. who

Practice 4 *(222)*

Answers will vary.

Practice 5 *(223)*

1. its
2. his
3. mine
4. their
5. ours

Practice 6 *(224)*

1. That dog
2. This fingernail
3. Those girls
4. those shopping bags
5. that corner house

Practice 7 *(225)*

Answers will vary.

Practice 8 *(226)*

1. himself
2. themselves
3. yourself (or yourselves)
4. themselves
5. ourselves

ADJECTIVES AND ADVERBS

Introductory Activity (231)

Answers will vary for 1–4.

adjective . . . adverb . . . *ly* . . . *er* . . . *est*

Practice 1 (234)

1. kinder . . . kindest
2. more ambitious . . . most ambitious
3. more generous . . . most generous
4. finer . . . finest
5. more likable . . . most likable

Practice 2 (234)

1. most comfortable
2. most difficult
3. easiest
4. less
5. best
6. longest
7. most memorable
8. more experienced . . . most experienced
9. worse . . . worst
10. better

Practice 3 (235)

1. violently
2. quickly
3. angrily
4. considerable
5. gently
6. really
7. regularly . . . regular
8. quietly . . . angrily
9. carefully . . . exact
10. Slowly . . . surely

Practice 4 (236)

1. well
2. good
3. well
4. well
5. well

MISPLACED MODIFIERS

Introductory Activity (240)

1. Intended: The farmers were wearing masks.
   Unintended: The apple trees were wearing masks.
2. Intended: The woman had a terminal disease.
   Unintended: The faith healer had a terminal disease.

Practice 1 (241)

NOTE: In each of the corrections below, the underlined part shows what was a misplaced modifier.

1. Driving around in their car, they finally found a Laundromat.
2. In the library, I read that Chuck Yeager was a pilot who broke the sound barrier.
   Or: I read in the library that Chuck Yeager was a pilot who broke the sound barrier.
3. Taking the elevator, Evelyn was thinking about her lost chemistry book.
4. Lola selected a donut filled with banana cream from the bakery.
   Or: From the bakery, Lola selected a donut filled with banana cream.
5. Howard worked almost twenty hours overtime to pay some overdue bills.
6. Tickets have gone on sale in the college bookstore for next week's championship game.
   Or: In the college bookstore, tickets have gone on sale for next week's championship game.
7. I returned the orange socks that my uncle gave me to the department store.
8. Looking through the binoculars, the camper saw the black bear.
9. I earned nearly two hundred dollars last week.
10. In the refrigerator, mushrooms should be stored enclosed in a paper bag.

Practice 2 (243)

1. In our science class, we agreed to go out to dinner tonight.
   Or: We agreed in our science class to go out to dinner tonight.
2. On a rainy day in June, Bob and I decided to get married.
   Or: Bob and I, on a rainy day in June, decided to get married.
3. Weighed down with heavy packages, Suki decided to hail a taxi.
   Or: Suki, weighed down with heavy packages, decided to hail a taxi.
4. Without success, I've looked everywhere for an instruction book on how to play the guitar.
   Or: I've looked everywhere without success for an instruction book on how to play the guitar.
5. Over the phone, Mother told me to wash the car.
   Or: Mother told me over the phone to wash the car.

DANGLING MODIFIERS

Introductory Activity (248)

1. Intended: The giraffe was munching leaves.
   Unintended: The children were munching leaves.
2. Intended: Michael was arriving home after ten months in the army.
   Unintended: The neighbors were arriving home after ten months in the army.

Practice 1 (250)

1. Since it was folded into a tiny square, I could not read the message.
   Or: I could not read the message, which was folded into a tiny square.
2. As I waded into the lake, tadpoles swirled around my ankles.
3. C
4. Hanging on the wall was a photograph of my mother.
   Or: I saw a photograph of my mother hanging on the wall.
5. Settling comfortably into the chair, I let the television capture my attention for the next hour.
   Or: After I settled comfortably into the chair, the television captured my attention for the next hour.
6. As I was driving home after a tiring day at work, I saw the white line become blurry.
   Or: Driving home after a tiring day at work, I saw the white line become blurry.
7. The batter hit his first home run, which soared high over the left-field fence.
8. Since the rug was threadbare and dirty, Myrna knew the time had come to replace it.
   Or: Myrna knew the time had come to replace the rug, which was threadbare and dirty.
9. After we spent most of the night outdoors in a tent, the sun rose and we went into the house.
   Or: After spending most of the night outdoors in a tent, we went into the house when the sun rose.
10. While they were hot and sizzling, we bit into the apple tarts.
    Or: We bit into the apple tarts, which were hot and sizzling.

Practice 2 (251)

Answers will vary.

FAULTY PARALLELISM

Introductory Activity (256)

Correct sentences:

I use my computer to write papers, to search the Internet, and to play video games.

One option Sonja has was to stay in the Air Force; the other was to return to college.

Dad's favorite chair has a torn cushion, a stained armrest, and a musty odor.

Practice 1 (258)

1. aching arms
2. freshly made soups
3. bad-tempered
4. replacing weather stripping
5. her green eyes
6. read her magazine
7. praying
8. attended
9. complaining about her strict parents
10. chased by bill collectors

Practice 2 (259)

Answers will vary.

SENTENCE VARIETY II

-ing Word Groups
Practice 1 (267)

Suggested combinations are shown below. Other combinations are possible.

1. Refusing to get out of bed, Ginger pulled the blue blanket over her head.
2. Puttering around in his basement workshop, Dad is able to forget the troubles of the day.
3. Swaying to the music, the crowd of dancers moved as one.
4. Trying to protect himself from the dampness of the room, George wrapped a scarf around his neck.
5. Caressing her hair, the woman listened intently to the earnest young man.

Practice 2 (268)

Answers will vary.

-ed Word Groups
Practice 3 (269)

Suggested combinations are shown below. Other combinations are possible.

1. Bothered by roaches, I called an exterminator.
2. Baffled by what had happened, Sam grew silent.
3. Stunned by the last-minute touchdown, the crowd began to file slowly out of the stadium.
4. Amused but reluctant to show how I felt, I tried to stifle my grin.
5. Exhausted from working all day, Cindy lay on the couch.

Practice 4 (269)
Answers may vary.

-ly Openers
Practice 5 (270)

Suggested combinations are shown below. Other combinations are possible.

1. Quietly, the burglars carried the television set out of the house.
2. Nervously, Janelle squirmed in her seat as she waited for her turn to speak.
3. Patiently, I reinforced all the coat buttons with strong thread.
4. Quickly, he finished answering the last question on the test.
5. Excitedly, I tore the wrapping off the present.

Practice 6 (271)
Answers will vary.

To Openers
Practice 7 (272)

1. To prepare for the track season, Doug ran five miles a day all summer.
2. To help you understand Al better, you should meet his parents.
3. To get the stain off her hand, she will have to use an abrasive soap.
4. To get to the church on time, I left the house early.
5. To make the automatic banking machine work, I punched in my code number.

Practice 8 (272)
Answers will vary.

Prepositional Phrase Openers
Practice 9 (273)

Suggested combinations are shown below. Other combinations are possible.

1. During my work break, I sat napping in the lunchroom corner with my head on my arm.
2. On many evenings during the winter, we played basketball in the church gym.
3. Before going to bed, Fred Grencher studies his bald spot with grave concern in his bathroom mirror.
4. On a sharp curve during the race, the car skidded on an oil slick.
5. Without slowing down, the teenage driver raced his car to the busy intersection in the heart of town.

Practice 10 (274)
Answers will vary.

Series of Items: Adjectives
Practice 11 (275)

1. The angry little boy stomped on the tiny red bug.
2. The tall thin man slowly wiped his sweaty forehead with a dirty blue bandanna.
3. My sister is intelligent, good-natured, and humorous.
4. The shy, timid boy looked at the grinning curly-haired girl.
5. A short, muscular bald man wearing wrinkled green work clothes strode into the noisy, smoke-filled tavern.

Practice 12 (276)
Answers will vary.

Series of Items: Verbs
Practice 13 (276)

1. When the popular comedian walked from behind the curtain, the crowd applauded, stomped their feet, and shouted, "Hi . . . oh!"
2. Everywhere in the cafeteria students were pulling on their coats, scooping up their books, and hurrying off to class.
3. By 6 A.M., I had read the textbook chapter, taken notes on it, studied the notes, and drunk eight cups of coffee.
4. I pressed the Rice Krispies into the bowl, poured milk on them, and waited for the milk to soak the cereal.
5. I am afraid the dentist's drill will slip off my tooth, bite into my gum, and make me jump with pain.

Practice 14 *(277)*

Answers will vary.

PAPER FORMAT

Introductory Activity *(284)*

In "A," the title is capitalized and centered and has no quotation marks around it; there is a blank line between the title and the body of the paragraph; there are left and right margins around the body of the paper; no words are incorrectly hyphenated.

Practice 1 *(286)*

1. Hyphenate only between syllables (al-ways).
2. Don't put quotation marks around the title.
3. Capitalize the major words in the title (The Generation Gap in Our House).
4. Skip a line between the title and first line of the paper.
5. Indent the first line of the paper.
6. Keep margins on both sides of the paper.

Practice 2 *(286)*

Answers may vary slightly.

1. Selfishness in Young Children
2. The Benefits of Daily Exercise
3. My Stubborn Son *or* My Stubborn Teenage Son
4. Essential College Study Skills
5. Drawbacks and Values of Single Life

Practice 3 *(287)*

Answers may vary slightly.

1. The worst day of my life began when my supervisor at work gave me a message to call home.
2. Catholic church services have undergone many changes in the last few decades.
3. An embarrassing incident happened to me when I was working as a waitress at the Stanton Hotel.
4. Correct
5. Many television commercials that I watch are degrading to human dignity.

CAPITAL LETTERS

Introductory Activity *(291)*

1–13: Answers will vary, but all should be capitalized.
14–16: On . . . "Let's . . . I

Practice 1 *(294)*

1. Halloween . . . Thanksgiving
2. If . . . I'm
3. Ford . . . Connecticut . . . Florida . . . Goodyear
4. *Newsweek . . . Time . . . People*
5. Northside Improvement Association . . . Third
6. Soundworks . . . Washington Boulevard . . . Panasonic
7. Fort Gordon . . . Germany
8. Thursday . . . Weight Watchers'
9. February . . . *Return . . . Dracula . . . Alien*
10. Old Navy . . . Taco Bell

Practice 2 *(298)*

1. Aunt Esther
2. Spanish . . . Aerobic Exercise
3. Dr. Purdy's
4. Latino . . . Southwest
5. Intermediate Math

Practice 3 *(298)*

1. summer . . . sunbathe . . . magazines
2. week . . . tune . . . melody
3. high school . . . states . . . college
4. title . . . paper . . . instructor . . . grade
5. friend . . . college . . . degree . . . life

NUMBERS AND ABBREVIATIONS

Introductory Activity *(307)*

Correct choices:
First sentence: 8:55 . . . 65 percent
Second sentence: Nine . . . forty-five
Second sentence: brothers . . . mountain
Second sentence: hours . . . English

Practice 1 *(309)*

1. five . . . three	6. 23
2. Two	7. May 31, 1976
3. 8:30	8. 2 . . . 5
4. nine o'clock	9. 50 percent
5. $282	10. five . . . twelve

Practice 2 *(310)*

1. cousin . . . apartment
2. Wednesday
3. account . . . month
4. moving . . . president . . . company

5. pounds . . . weeks
6. favorite . . . especially
7. secretary . . . temporary . . . minute
8. brother . . . high school
9. gallon . . . streets
10. hospital . . . room

END MARKS

Introductory Activity *(314)*

1. depressed.
2. paper?
3. parked.
4. control!

Practice 1 *(316)*

1. continue?
2. road!
3. arthritis.
4. visit?
5. wallet.
6. cars.
7. sunglasses!
8. *Rings.*
9. cried.
10. wig?"

APOSTROPHE

Introductory Activity *(320)*

1. To indicate missing letters and shortened spellings
2. To show ownership or possession
3. Because "families" signals a plural noun, while "family's" indicates ownership or possession.

Apostrophe in Contractions
Practice 1 *(322)*

he's	we're
aren't	hasn't
you're	who's
they've	doesn't
wouldn't	where's

Practice 2 *(322)*

1. I'll . . . you'll
2. It's . . . wouldn't
3. shouldn't . . . you're
4. isn't . . . weren't
5. I'd . . . who's . . . it's

Practice 3 *(322)*

Answers will vary.

Practice 4 *(323)*

1. They're . . . their
2. You're . . . your
3. Who's . . . whose
4. It's . . . it's
5. you're . . . their . . . it's

Apostrophe to Show Ownership or Possession
Practice 5 *(324)*

1. Lola's sneakers
2. Veronica's lipstick
3. His brother's house
4. The car's tires
5. Joe's bicycle
6. the blue jay's nest
7. my paper's title
8. My mother's arthritis
9. My sister's boyfriend
10. anybody's game

Practice 6 *(325)*

2. Georgia's
3. friend's
6. Albert's
7. daughter's
8. boss's
4. teacher's
5. girlfriend's
9. night's
10. son's

Practice 7 *(326)*

Answers to the sentence feature of this exercise will vary.

1. Cary's
2. neighbor's
3. car's
4. sister's
5. doctor's

Apostrophe versus Simple Plurals
Practice 8 *(327)*

1. onions: simple plural meaning more than one onion
   Rons: Ron's, meaning "eyes of Ron"
   eyes: simple plural meaning more than one eye
2. mothers: mother's, meaning "recipe of my mother"
   relatives: simple plural meaning more than one relative
   friends: simple plural meaning more than one friend
3. Sailors: simple plural meaning more than one sailor
   stations: simple plural meaning more than one station
   ships: ship's, meaning "alarm of the ship"
4. kites: kite's, meaning "string of the kite"
   branches: simple plural meaning more than one branch
5. guys: simple plural meaning more than one guy
   colleges: college's, meaning "football game of our college"
   movies: simple plural meaning more than one movie
6. daughters: daughter's, meaning "belonging to my daughter"
   prayers: simple plural meaning more than one prayer
   schools: simple plural meaning more than one school

7. tubes: simple plural meaning more than one inner tube

rivers: river's, meaning "rushing currents of the river"

currents: simple plural meaning more than one current

8. directors: director's, meaning "specialty of the director"

films: simple plural meaning more than one film

vampires: simple plural meaning more than one vampire

9. copies: simple plural meaning more than one copy

company's: company's, meaning "tax returns of the company"

returns: simple plural meaning more than one return

years: simple plural meaning more than one year

10. Scientists: simple plural meaning more than one scientist

Africa's: Africa's, meaning "Congo region of Africa"

relatives: simple plural meaning more than one relative

dinosaurs: simple plural meaning more than one dinosaur

Apostrophe with Plural Words Ending in -s
Practice 9 (329)

1. firefighters'
2. drivers'
3. friends'
4. grandparents'
5. soldiers'

QUOTATION MARKS

Introductory Activity (338)

1. Quotation marks set off the exact words of a speaker.
2. Commas and periods following quotations go inside quotation marks.

Practice 1 (340)

1. "Have more trust in me," Lola said to her mother.
2. The instructor asked Sharon, "Why are your eyes closed?"
3. Christ said, "I come that you may have life, and have it more abundantly."
4. "I refuse to wear those itchy wool pants!" Ralph shouted at his parents.
5. His father replied, "We should give all the clothes you never wear to the Salvation Army."

6. The nervous boy whispered hoarsely over the telephone, "Is Linda home?"
7. "When I was ten," Lola said, "I spent my entire summer playing Monopoly."
8. Tony said, "When I was ten, I spent my whole summer playing basketball."
9. The critic wrote about the play, "It runs the gamut of emotions from A to B."
10. "The best way to tell if a mushroom is poisonous," the doctor solemnly explained, "is if you find it in the stomach of a dead person."

Practice 2 (341)

1. Greg said, "I'm going with you."
2. "Everyone passed the test," the instructor informed the class.
3. My parents asked, "Where were you?"
4. "I hate that commercial," he muttered.
5. "If you don't leave soon," he warned, "you'll be late for work."

Practice 3 (341)

Answers will vary.

Indirect Quotations
Practice 4 (342)

2. Lynn replied, "I thought you were going to write them this year."
3. Eric said, "Writing invitations is a woman's job."
4. Lynn exclaimed, "You're crazy!"
5. Eric replied, "You have much better handwriting than I do."

Practice 5 (343)

1. He said that as the plane went higher, his heart sank lower.
2. The designer said that shag rugs are back in style.
3. The foreman asked Jake if he had ever operated a lift truck.
4. My nosy neighbor asked if Ed and Ellen were fighting.
5. Mei Lin complained that she married a man who eats Tweeties cereal for breakfast.

Practice 6 (344)

1. The young couple opened their brand-new copy of Cooking Made Easy to the chapter titled "Meat Loaf Magic."

2. Annabelle borrowed Hawthorne's novel The Scarlet Letter from the library because she thought it was about a varsity athlete.

3. Did you know that the musical West Side Story is actually a modern version of Shakespeare's tragedy Romeo and Juliet?

4. I used to think that Richard Connell's short story "The Most Dangerous Game" was the scariest piece of suspense fiction in existence–until I began reading Bram Stoker's classic novel Dracula.

5. Every year at Easter, we watch a movie such as The Robe on television.

6. During the past year, Time featured an article on DNA titled "Building Blocks of the Future."

7. My father still remembers the way that Sarah Brightman sang "Think of Me" in the original Broadway production of The Phantom of the Opera.

8. As I stood in the supermarket checkout line, I read a feature story in the National Enquirer titled "Mother Gives Birth to Alien Baby."

9. My favorite song by Aretha Franklin is the classic "Respect," which has been included on the CD Aretha's Best.

10. Absentmindedly munching a Dorito, Hana opened the latest issue of Newsweek to its cover story, "The Junk Food Explosion."

COMMA

Introductory Activity (354)

1. a
2. b
3. c
4. d
5. e
6. f

Practice 1 (356)

1. red, white, and blue
2. laundry, helped clean the apartment, waxed the car, and watched
3. patties, special sauce, lettuce, cheese, pickles, and onions

Practice 2 (356)

1. Cold eggs, burnt bacon, and watery orange juice are the reasons I've never returned to that diner for breakfast.
2. Andy relaxes by reading Donald Duck, Archie, and Bugs Bunny comic books.
3. Tonight I've got to work at the restaurant for three hours, finish writing a paper, and study for an exam.

Practice 3 (357)

1. When I didn't get my paycheck at work, . . . According to the office computer,
2. After seeing the accident, . . . Even so,
3. To get her hair done, . . . Once there, . . . Also,

Practice 4 (357)

1. Even though Tina had an upset stomach, she went bowling with her husband.
2. Looking back over the last ten years, I can see several decisions I made that really changed my life.
3. Instead of going with my family to the mall, I decided to relax at home and to call up some friends.

Practice 5 (359)

1. deadline, the absolute final deadline,
2. cow, a weird creature, . . . dish, who must also have been strange,
3. Tod, voted the most likely to succeed in our high school graduating class, . . . King Kongs, a local motorcycle gang,

Practice 6 (359)

1. My sister's cat, which she got from the animal shelter, woke her when her apartment caught fire.
2. A bulging biology textbook, its pages stuffed with notes and handouts, lay on the path to the college parking lot.
3. A baked potato, with its crispy skin and soft inside, rates as one of my all-time favorite foods.

Practice 7 (360)

1. C
2. mountain, and
3. eating, but
4. speech, and
5. C
6. car, but
7. C
8. shops, but
9. C
10. math, for

Practice 8 (361)

1. fries," said Lola. . . . She asked, "What
2. Coke," responded Tony.
3. grief," said Lola. . . . "In fact," she continued, "how much

Practice 9 (361)

1. "You better hurry," Thelma's mother warned, "or you're going to miss the last bus of the morning."

2. "It really worries me," said Marty, "that you haven't seen a doctor about that strange swelling under your arm."

3. The student sighed in frustration and then raised his hand. "My computer has crashed again," he called out to the instructor.

Practice 10 (362)

1. sorry, sir,
2. 6, 1954,
3. June 30, 2010,
4. Seas, P.O. Box 760, El Paso, TX 79972
5. Leo, turn

Practice 11 (363)

1. When I arrived to help with the moving, Jerome said to me that the work was already done.
2. After the flour and milk have been mixed, eggs must be added to the recipe.
3. Because my sister is allergic to cat fur and dust, our family does not own a cat or have any dust-catching drapes or rugs.
4. The guys on the corner asked, "Have you ever taken karate lessons?"
5. As the heavy Caterpillar tractor rumbled up the street, our house windows rattled.
6. Las Vegas, Miami Beach, San Diego, and Atlantic City are the four places she has worked as a bartender.
7. Thomas Farley, the handsome young man who just took off his trousers, is an escaped mental patient.
8. Hal wanted to go to medical school, but he does not have the money and was not offered a scholarship.
9. Joyce reads a lot of fiction, but I prefer stories that really happened.
10. Because Mary is single, her married friends do not invite her to their parties.

OTHER PUNCTUATION MARKS

Introductory Activity (373)

1. list: eggs
2. life-size
3. (1856–1939)
4. track;
5. breathing—but alive.

Practice 1 (374)

1. work:
2. Sears:
3. Hazlitt:

Practice 2 (375)

1. death; in . . . death; and
2. ridiculous; for example,
3. National Bank; Jay . . . State Bank; and

Practice 3 (376)

1. condition—except
2. minutes—in fact,
3. work—these

Practice 4 (377)

1. sixty-five dollars . . . sixty-five cents
2. ten-year-old . . . self-confident
3. split-level

Practice 5 (377)

1. charts (pages 16–20) in
2. prepare (1) a daily list of things to do and (2) a weekly study schedule.
3. drinkers (five or more cups a day) suffer

DICTIONARY USE

Introductory Activity (381)

1. fortutious (fortuitous)
2. hi/er/o/glyph/ics
3. be
4. oc/to/ge/nar'/i/an
5. (1) Identifying mark on the ear of a domestic animal
   (2) Identifying feature or characteristic

Answers to the activities are in your dictionary. Check with your instructor if you have any problems.

SPELLING IMPROVEMENT

Introductory Activity (393)

Misspellings:
akward . . . exercize . . . buisness . . . worryed . . . shamful . . . begining . . . partys . . . sandwichs . . . heros

Practice 1 (396)

1. studied
2. advising
3. carries
4. stopping
5. terrified
6. compelled
7. retiring
8. hungrily
9. expelling
10. judges

Practice 2 *(397)*

1. groceries
2. towns
3. policies
4. bodies
5. lotteries
6. passes
7. tragedies
8. watches
9. suits
10. bosses

OMITTED WORDS AND LETTERS

Introductory Activity *(404)*

bottles . . . in the supermarket . . . like a windup toy . . . his arms . . . an alert shopper . . . with the crying

Practice 1 *(405)*

1. When I began eating the box of chicken I bought at the fast-food restaurant, I found several pieces that consisted of a lot of crust covering nothing but chicken bones.
2. Gwen had an instructor who tried to light a piece of chalk, thinking it was a cigarette.
3. In his dream, Ray committed the perfect crime: he killed his enemy with an icicle, so the murder weapon was never found.
4. Dr. Yutzer told me not to worry about the sore on my foot, but I decided to get a second opinion.
5. As the little girl ate the vanilla sugar cone, ice cream dripped out of a hole at the bottom onto her pants.
6. When thick black clouds began to form and we felt several drops of rain, we knew the picnic would be canceled.
7. After spending most of her salary on new clothes, Susan looks like something out of a fashion magazine.
8. As wasps buzzed around the room, I ran for a can of Raid.
9. Keith put the pair of wet socks in the oven, for he wanted to dry them out quickly.
10. Because the weather got hot and stayed hot for weeks, my flower garden started to look like a dried flower arrangement.

Practice 2 *(406)*

1. boyfriends . . . blows
2. curses
3. paragraphs . . . events
4. windshields . . . cars
5. houses . . . highways
6. days . . . times
7. billboards
8. chairs . . . pillows
9. watchtowers . . . states
10. motorists . . . trucks

Practice 3 *(407)*

Answers will vary.

COMMONLY CONFUSED WORDS

Introductory Activity *(411)*

1. Incorrect: your
   Correct: you're
2. Incorrect: who's
   Correct: whose
3. Incorrect: there
   Correct: their
4. Incorrect: to
   Correct: too
5. Incorrect: Its
   Correct: It's

Homonyms *(412–422)*

Sentences will vary.

all ready . . . already
brake . . . break
coarse . . . course
here . . . hear
hole . . . whole
it's . . . its
knew . . . new
no . . . know
pear . . . pair
past . . . passed
piece . . . peace
plain . . . plane
principal . . . principle
write . . . right
then . . . than
there . . . their . . . they're
through . . . threw
to . . . two . . . too . . . too
wear . . . where
weather . . . whether
whose . . . who's
you're . . . your

Other Words Frequently Confused (422–430)

Sentences will vary.

an . . . a
except . . . accept
advise . . . advice
affect . . . effect
among . . . between
besides . . . beside
can . . . may
cloths . . . clothes
dessert . . . desert
does . . . dose
fewer . . . less
former . . . latter
learn . . . teach
loose . . . lose
quite . . . quiet
though . . . thought

Incorrect Word Forms (430–431)
being that

1. Since (or Because) she's a year older
2. because (or since) the bus drivers
3. Since (or Because) I didn't

can't hardly, couldn't hardly

1. I can hardly
2. You can hardly
3. You could hardly

could of, must of, should of, would of

1. Anita must have
2. I should have
3. they would have
4. she could have

irregardless

1. regardless of the price
2. regardless of their age
3. Regardless of the risk

EFFECTIVE WORD CHOICE

Introductory Activity (438)

Correct sentences:
1. After a disappointing movie, we devoured a pizza.
2. Mourning the death of his best friend, Tennyson wrote the poem "In Memoriam."

3. Psychological tests will be given on Wednesday.
4. I think the referee made the right decision.

1 . . . 2 . . . 3 . . . 4

NOTE: The answers may vary for all of the following word-choice practices.

Practice 1 (440)

1. If you don't start working regularly in this course, you're going to fail the midterm exam.
2. Last year, Tarah was excited about her new job, but now she is so annoyed at her boss that she wants to quit.
3. We were badly beaten in the football game.
4. If people keep saying bad things about Gene, soon no one will be friends with him.
5. I got so anxious when the instructor called on me that my mind went blank.

Practice 2 (441)

Answers will vary for written versions.
1. Underline shed any light on; substitute *reveal the reason.*
2. Underline heaved a sign of relief; substitute *was relieved.*
3. Underline began selling like hotcakes; substitute *became a best seller.*
4. Underline could not have cared less; substitute *did not care.*
5. Underline feeling under the weather; substitute *sick.*

Practice 3 (442)

Answers will vary.

Practice 4 (443)

1. My television is broken.
2. We went to the mall to see the new fall clothes.
3. José said he didn't like fish.
4. The fans booed when the pitcher made a bad throw.
5. How long have you lived in that city?

Practice 5 (445)

1. Because it was raining, I didn't go shopping.
2. I do not feel that prostitution should be legalized.
3. Please call me to arrange an interview.
4. While I was sick, I missed three math tests.
5. Only well-trained people get high-paying jobs.

Credits

PHOTO CREDITS

page 3, © BananaStock/SuperStock; page 13, © Purestock/SuperStock; page 43, © Edward Bock/ Corbis; page 65, © Kwame Zikomo/SuperStock; page 93, © Kayte M. Deioma/PhotoEdit; page 128, © Digital Vision/PunchStock; page 177, © Kord.com/age fotostock/SuperStock; page 225, U.S. Department of Defense; page 232, © Alan Oddie/PhotoEdit; page 294, © age fotostock/ SuperStock; page 316, © Alan Schein Photography/Corbis; page 365, Photo by Karen Neal/© ABC/ courtesy Everett Collection; page 400, © Barbara Stitzer/PhotoEdit; page 453 (top), © photo by John Chapple/Rex USA, courtesy Everett Collection; page 453 (bottom), © AP Photo/Eric Gay; page 454 (top), © Bill Aron/PhotoEdit; page 454 (bottom), © Michael Newman/PhotoEdit; page 467 (top), © New Regency Pictures/Twentieth Century Fox Film Corp/Photofest; page 467 (bottom), © CBS/Photofest; page 494 (top), © Mario Anzuoni/Reuters/Corbis; page 494 (middle), © Frank Trapper/Corbis; page 494 (bottom), © AP Photo/Mark J. Terrill; page 515, © David Cannon/Getty Images; Collaborative Activity icon: © Odilon Dimier/PhotoAlto/Getty Images; Online Learning Center icon: © DAJ/Getty Images

Index

A

A, an, 423
Abbreviations, 309–310
Accent marks, 385
Accept, except, 423
Achievement tests, 552–557
Action verbs, 524–525
Added-detail fragments, 87–89, 91
Adjectives, 232–239, 527–528, 542–544
   defined, 232
   in series, 274–276
   using for comparison, 233
Adverbs, 235–239, 529
   defined, 235
Advice, advise, 424
Affect, effect, 424
All ready, already, 412
American Heritage Dictionary, 382, 384, 388
Among, between, 425
An, a, 423
Antecedent, 204
Apostrophe, 320–337
   in contractions, 321–323
   to show ownership or possession, 323–329
Articles, 533–537

B

Beside, besides, 425
between, among, 425
Brainstorming; *See* List making
Brake, break, 413

C

Can, may, 425
Capital letters, 291–306
   main uses of, 292–295
   other uses of, 296–298
   and run-ons, 106–108
   unnecessary use of, 298–299
Clichés, 440–442

Clothes, cloths, 426
Clustering, 41, 44–45, 55
Coarse, course, 413
Colon, 374
Combined editing tests, 494–513
Combined mastery tests, 454–466
Commas, 354–372
   and dependent statements, 131
   main uses of, 355–363
   and run-ons, 108–110
   unnecessary use of, 363–364
   with everyday material, 361–362
Comma splice, 104–105, 107, 117
Commonly confused words, 394, 411–437
   homonyms 412–422
   incorrect word forms, 430–431
Communication, 4–6
Complex sentence, 125, 128–132
Compound-complex sentence, 125, 132–133
Compound sentence, 125–128
Compound subjects, 73–78, 175
Compound verbs, 73–78
Computers and the writing process, 514–519
Conjunctions, 530–531
   coordinating, 108, 530
   subordinating, 531–532
Consistent verb tense, 186–191
Coordination, 126, 133
Course, coarse, 413

D

Dangling modifiers, 248–255
   defined, 249
Dash, 375-376
Demonstrative pronouns, 224–225
Dependent word fragments, 80–84, 91
Dependent words, 80, 113–114, 128, 133
Desert, dessert, 426
Details
   organizing, 33, 38–40
   providing, 27–28, 31–33

   recognizing, 23–27
   selecting, 29–30
   supporting, 17–18
Diagnostic tests, 546–551
Dictionary use, 381–392
   etymology, 388
   irregular nouns, 387
   irregular verbs, 386
   meanings, 387
   parts of speech, 386
   pronunciation, 384–386
   spelling, 383
   syllabication, 383
   synonyms, 389
   titles of good desk dictionaries, 388
   usage labels in, 388
Does, dose, 427
Draft, 49–50

E

Editing, 41, 52–54, 56–57
   and the computer, 518–519
Editing and proofreading tests, 467–493
Editing tests, combined, 494–513
-ed word groups, 268–269
effect, affect, 424
Effective word choice, 438–451
Effective writing, 11–40
End marks, 314–319
   exclamation point, 316
   period, 314–315
   question mark, 315
English as a second language; *See* ESL pointers
ESL pointers, 533–545
   adjectives, 542–544
   articles, 533–537
   prepositions, 544–545
   subjects and verbs, 537–542
Except, accept, 423
Exclamation point, 316